The Path to Immortality

CLIMB THE HIGHEST MOUNTAIN SERIES

The Path to Immortality

Mark L. Prophet · Elizabeth Clare Prophet

The Everlasting Gospel

SUMMIT UNIVERSITY ⚈ PRESS

Gardiner, Montana

Library of Congress Control Number: 200593610
ISBN: 1-932890-09-2

SUMMIT UNIVERSITY 🌙 PRESS®

Printed in the United States of America

Cover: *Zoroaster,* a painting by Nicholas Roerich.

Note: Our understanding of life and the universe is that all things are in
polarity: plus/minus, Alpha/Omega, yang/yin, masculine/feminine. The
worlds of Spirit and Matter are in polarity as two manifestations of God's
universal presence. In this relationship, Spirit assumes the positive-yang-
masculine polarity, and Matter assumes the negative-yin-feminine
polarity. Thus, we have used masculine pronouns to refer to God and
feminine pronouns to refer to the soul, the part of ourselves that is
evolving in the planes of Matter. Also, in order to avoid the sometimes
cumbersome or confusing expressions of gender-neutral language, we
have occasionally used masculine pronouns to refer to the individual.
These usages are not intended to exclude women.

10 09 08 07 06   5 4 3 2 1

And I saw another angel fly in the midst of heaven, having the everlasting gospel to preach unto them that dwell on the earth, and to every nation, and kindred, and tongue, and people,

Saying with a loud voice, Fear God, and give glory to him; for the hour of his judgment is come: and worship him that made heaven, and earth, and the sea, and the fountains of waters.

REVELATION

Contents

2 · Planes of Consciousness   115

4 · Entities   305

5 · The Messengers   415

Figures

Preface

THE *PATH TO IMMORTALITY* IS THE seventh book in the Climb the Highest Mountain series. In this volume we will explore some of the mysteries of creation and their application in the Macrocosm of the universe and in the microcosm of man.

This study penetrates beyond the veils of mortal existence to reveal man as a spiritual being—spanning the planes of Spirit and Matter. Through this understanding, we can come to know what immortality *really* means, and also the path by which we may reach that goal.

For immortality is not simply a magical formula (though such a formula may exist), nor is it something that automatically happens in the rapture of the end times. In fact, immortality is a spiritual-material science—one that has been discovered by mystics through the ages. A door to that science is opened in these chapters. Not everything can be written, but the keys are given that will unlock new dimensions of being for those who apply them.

Chapter 4 of this volume moves on to an exposé of entities, the unseen forces that so often divert us from our spiritual path and divine plan. This is a subject that is often overlooked by the spiritual seeker, but with the knowledge provided here and with determined use of the tools that are given, the student of the Masters can find a new freedom of soul and Spirit.

This volume concludes with "The Messengers." In this chapter, Mark and Elizabeth Prophet speak of their own calling as Messengers and place this in the context of the ongoing cycles of God's revelations to man.

The Climb the Highest Mountain series has been outlined by the Ascended Master El Morya in thirty-three chapters; this book contains chapters 20 through 24 of the complete work. The concepts presented here build upon the foundational material in the six books that precede it. This volume in turn provides a foundation for what will follow in the remaining two books.

If this is your first exploration of the Climb the Highest Mountain series, we welcome you to your study of these teachings from the Ascended Masters, which have been called the Everlasting Gospel, the scripture for the age of Aquarius. For those who are taking up this book after reading previous volumes, we wish you God-speed in your continuing journey to climb the highest mountain.

THE EDITORS

Introduction

"AND I WILL PRAY THE FATHER, and he shall give you another Comforter, that he may abide with you for ever; even the Spirit of truth; whom the world cannot receive, because it seeth him not, neither knoweth him: but ye know him; for he dwelleth with you, and shall be in you."[1]

The Comforter who comes to teach us all things is the very Presence of the Holy Spirit. In the Person of that Holy Spirit we always find the Person of the Christed One.

The promise of the comfort of the Lord Jesus Christ to us has never failed you or me. We may not always have been aware of the presence of that Person or of the great teaching imparted to the inner soul. But the teaching is there, and we are not left comfortless. We find comfort through many avenues that are the enlightenment of the Holy Spirit.

One of the great sources of comfort that has come to me in this life and in previous lifetimes has been an understanding and a perception of the Law of Cycles. The Law of Cycles is magnificent to behold. But if we are not aware of its presence, we are just as bereft of it as we are bereft of the Holy Spirit.

Finding not that Spirit in the sacred fire breath or the beating of our hearts, we know not that we have had the visitation of the Lord. Not perceiving the Law of Cycles all around us, within us, without us, in the microcosm and the Macrocosm, we therefore do not sense the shadow of the Almighty that is ever upon us.

It has long been known that history repeats itself, and that we should learn its lessons well. Not only does history unfold in cycles, but the corruption and concealment of history's highest wisdom signals cyclic death of nations. Indeed, the ship of modern historians is lost in its own sea of academic encrustation. On board its decks archaeologists squint to see the horizon. And lost with them all, theologians—too blinded by twisted dogma to navigate by heaven's stars.

Will this ship of blind leaders of the blind crack and sink once more, to take our civilization to the bottom of the sea? The Masters man the Lighthouse beacon, searching for the ship. But time after time, man has failed to recognize the Brotherhood's source of Truth, driving the benevolent adepts behind closed doors and secret glyphs.

The cycles of man on earth tell the story of our beings. Records hid in mountain chambers hold the history of our planet. Once again the Masters choose to dare the scorn of science. "If any man have ears to hear, let him hear.... Take heed what ye hear: with what measure ye mete, it shall be measured to you: and unto you that hear shall more be given."[2]

The race consciousness is compartmentalized in man but unified in the universal sense that all consciousness merges into one. Its streams and tributaries flow into one ocean of consciousness, and individual expansion of consciousness is brought about through mastering the art of flow beyond the personal level.

One of the factors that creates a veil between the micro-cosm and the Macrocosm is that each individual must work from his own level of consciousness, and his consciousness is limited by his own residual concepts. While he may aspire to a higher state of consciousness, his entire understanding concerning his physical environment, natural science, law and the humanities, as well as his search for spiritual mastery, must evolve from his present state of experience and consciousness.

There are, however, means whereby the individual can be lifted temporarily from a lesser state of consciousness to a much higher one. It is possible for man to bypass whole flights of cosmic achievement in order that there might be engendered within him upliftment, inspiration and a subsequent storing in the memory body of fragments of heaven that will be found useful in the attainment of higher planes of consciousness.

Vital consciousness possesses the quality of *flow*. Like a majestic river, it moves along the shores of identity where recognized markings provide a delineation of experience, even as a clock marks the hours. Poets, writers and composers of music tell of moments of intense inspiration when they are attuned to Nature and are able to experience a release of intelligence far beyond their ordinary mind. These states cannot always be invoked at will, and times seem to manifest whimsically.

In Truth, the markings along the shores of Identity and its manifestation are arbitrary, and planes of consciousness are of wide and mingling latitudes. Nevertheless, "as Above, so be-low": the consciousness of mankind below, when attuned with higher octaves, may experience simultaneously a taste of the bliss experienced by the soul in her own higher perceptions, of which in normal consciousness the outer self is unaware.

While many people, for example, may use the facilities of a research library, such aids in the hands of a scientist can be

employed more effectively than they would be by the layman. In a similar way, the Ascended Masters wield greater power from their plane of consciousness than do unascended mankind, and their power can and does affect the billions of lifestreams upon earth when it is called into action. The Law states that the call compels the answer. Without the call, heaven has no right to interfere in mortal free will.

When we study planes of consciousness, we find that whereas an animal possesses awareness of others and of his own environment, man is Self-conscious, possessing not only awareness of the outer self and of circumstances, but also of his internal world. Directly behind his inner world is the plane of consciousness where an individual moves from self-centered goals and selfish love to a relatively selfless love, offering himself to the cause of bringing happiness and enlightenment to his fellowmen. Needless to say, he will ultimately share in all the good that he sows.

Humanitarians fall into two classes: those who seek to benefit society and future generations through material means —education, social, political and economic—and those who seek to influence the course of human events spiritually and in a manner calculated to bring in a Golden Age of enlightenment. The spiritual values that human life may hold stem from the inheritance of one's spiritual achievement and from current environmental influences of a spiritual nature. These factors culminate in service both to God and to man's real progress.

Above the environmental level, we see shining through the belt of cosmic consciousness and higher awareness the first designations of the adept—an individual versed in the alchemy of purity, service and love that denotes one holding a degree of proficiency in the spiritual arts. The adept is able to magnetize (to draw forth) great benefits to himself, his contemporaries, society in general and the work of the spiritual Hierarchy.

Without spiritual values, humanitarians fall short of the mark, and at best can only perpetuate a materialistic civilization.

Beyond the plane of what we term the "neophyte adept" are several grades. One is that of the unconscious adept. Even though the inner attunement of such an individual is not perceived by his outer self, he serves the cosmic plan upon earth, standing as a bulwark against destructive and manipulative forces that would rob mankind of their spiritual inheritance. In this group are individuals of many professions, including ministers and priests whose dogma would not permit total acceptance of the Truths of this work and the Ascended Masters, yet who do uphold the high moral standards and social responsibilities that heaven advocates.

Beyond this degree is that of the master adept—one who possesses conscious knowledge of his own position and attunement with the spiritual Hierarchy upon the planet. The adept on this level also enters into karmic and cosmic councils, helping to decide what is the best course for the Hierarchy to take in order to assist the evolutions of the human family and to move all of life toward the highest spiritual goals.

In addition, the master adept is often able to intercede for another person, either on the basis of his friendship with God or on the basis of personal petition for the needy by direct apprehension of divine grace (as Abraham found favor with God). The master adept maintains a high plane of consciousness at all times.

Above this level in the Hierarchical scheme are the unascended masters, those blessed individuals who, while having attained great strides in spiritual and natural evolution, are still limited by the veil of flesh as to that which they can accomplish. Possessing great spiritual insight and a desire to serve, these also are planetary links between the humanity of earth and the Hierarchy. Without them, communication would be very difficult for many.

These blessed souls act as mediators at the level of the Holy Christ Self and serve in the same capacity between the Divine Presence and the unascended, relatively imperfect patterns of the human. The unascended master functions as mediator between an emerging humanity and the mighty Hierarchies of Light known as the Great White Brotherhood*—the spiritual legions, the cosmic league of affinities, comprising Cosmic Beings, Elementals, Angels and Ascended Masters. Those working in this group hold a very high responsibility and opportunity for service. Theirs is a specific plane of consciousness.

When dealing with the ladder of Light (a metaphor symbolizing the stages of initiation), which scales the many planes of consciousness, a specific number of steps is possible of attainment to the consciousness from that of the common man to and including the grade of the Ascended Masters. Beyond the level of the Ascended Master consciousness is what is known as the Buddhic consciousness, and beyond the level of the Buddha there are other planes. In fact, the steps, or planes of consciousness, attainable by man are infinite: we have received definite proof of this from the great spiritual heights of Life within the so-called Royal Family of the Central Sun.

Once an individual has entered into the victory of his ascension in the Light, he is free to go on and pass through initiation after initiation, being changed, as Saint Paul said, "from glory unto glory, even as by the Spirit of the Lord."[3] In

---

* The Ascended Masters of the Great White Brotherhood, united for the highest purposes of the brotherhood of man under the Fatherhood of God, have risen in every age from every culture and religion to inspire creative achievement in education, the arts and sciences, God-government and the abundant Life through the economies of the nations. The word "white" refers not to race but to the aura (halo) of white light surrounding their forms. The Brotherhood also includes in its ranks certain unascended chelas of the Ascended Masters. Jesus Christ revealed this heavenly order of saints "robed in white" to his servant John in Revelation.

the realm where time and space are compressed as marks of revelation, achievement and service, the godly, dwelling in a paradise of immortal perfection, are constantly invited to move forward into the transcendence of the Godhead. There is no ultimate anywhere in the universe, and the higher planes of consciousness are all a part of the great Tree of Life, seen in one form in the ancient legend of the tree Yggdrasil.* It is the Tree of Heaven in whose branches the birds of the air come and nest.[4]

The Tree of Life that is in the midst of the Paradise of God bears cosmic fruit, and those counted worthy to eat of the fruit of the Tree of Life do indeed live forever.[5] How this can be attained and how man can expand in consciousness and its planes—from the subterranean levels of the flesh and blood that can never inherit the Kingdom of God[6] to a spiritual state where veil after veil drop from before the eyes of consciousness in the blessedness of Divine Oneness—is the wonderful story of the living Christ unfolded for the students of the Ascended Masters.

The first Adam truly is of the earth, earthy, but the second man (the Christ) is the Lord from heaven.[7] This teaching from Saint Paul in itself shows the evolution of the universal man, Adam Kadmon, and the evolution of the individual man, you and me. It shows that as we have borne the image of the earth, so we shall bear the image of the heavenly.

Down through the years, it has been the pleasure of the Masters to present planes of consciousness, ladders of Light, and other dramatizations calculated to hold before the con-

---

* In Norse legend, the universe is supported by a great ash or yew tree, known as Yggdrasil. The tree extends through all the nine worlds (through every plane of consciousness). It is watered by a sacred well, a winged dragon gnaws at its roots, and an eagle sits in its branches. The image of the world tree is also found in ancient Slavic mythology, which holds that the universe is held by a giant oak tree, and in the Hindu image of the banyan tree.

sciousness some markings of record in order that men might establish a reckoning as to where they are in their search for God. In this work, under the auspices of the great Masters, it has been our determination to illustrate, in part, a principle of flow that was brought to our attention some time ago by the God and Goddess Meru, whose retreat is near Lake Titicaca in South America. According to the principle of flow, consciousness advances quite naturally to assimilate new and transmutative concepts that enable individuals to win their victory over outer circumstances.

However, as long as the weight of mankind's concern is for mere academic knowledge, as long as men seek to "measure their progress with a micrometer," as one of the great Masters has commented, so long will they be caught up in the mechanics of attainment, rather than the fruits thereof.

Through our remarks on the planes of consciousness, we hope to make it possible for individuals to lose the sense of littleness that often plagues the children of earth. Men ought to enter instead into that largesse of heart that rejoices in the accomplishments of another, in the accomplishments of the Masters of Wisdom and those of the blessed Creator himself.

Through the concept of flow, it will be seen with the inner eye that God is ever releasing great bursts of Cosmic Light into manifestation all over the universe, and through the Eternal Fount right within men's hearts, Life knocks at the door as cosmic opportunity. If one can but develop the technique of flow, progress will come automatically and systematically. It is not so important, then, to judge one's progress by the attainment of a specific plane of consciousness as it is to search out how one can eliminate negative karma-making devices from the human psyche.

The practice of tolerance, forgiveness and pure love, the amplification of Ascended Master qualities of service to the

Hierarchy and to one's fellowmen, and the recognition by men that the greatest progress is often made by the greatest service will eliminate certain impediments from the disciple's path. Thereby, the way is smoothed and planes of consciousness unfold as a rolling terrain whose course is ever upward toward the summit of each individual's existence.

That which lies behind in the plowed furrow will then not be so important as the open field ahead. By the grace of forgiveness of oneself and others, the love of God will be accepted. Man will stand face to face with the Creator. The only begotten Son will stretch forth his hands to God, who will open the gates or, if necessary, break the dams of human emotion that have barred man from God, and he will let flow, buoyantly and joyously, all of the Good that God is. With the childlike sense that all is right with God and thus all must come right with the world, man receives vestments of renewed opportunity to prove by deeds the actuality of the Logos.

This act sweeps the personal self and all humanity along in the great love tide of the consciousness of the Eternal Father and brings more complete awareness of the nearness of the Mother of the World. Thus, concern for planes of consciousness vanishes in the great onrush that is progress, and Life is seen as opportunity's manger opening an endless way, wholly engrossed in the miracle of just being.

MARK AND ELIZABETH PROPHET
Messengers of the Masters

Chapter 1

The Law
of Cycles

*And I looked, and, behold,
a whirlwind came out of the
north, a great cloud, and a fire
infolding itself, and a brightness
was about it, and out of the
midst thereof as the colour of
amber, out of the midst of the
fire.*

*Also out of the midst
thereof came the likeness of
four living creatures. And this
was their appearance; they had
the likeness of a man.*

EZIKIEL

The galaxy is spinning out its spiral arms in space.
The cosmic magnet drives the heart of worlds—
    fluids of life pulsating in a rhythmic ebb and flow.
Chromosomes align in precise array.
Behold the miracle of creation!

Gaze into the deep night sky
    and see the pulsar beating in perfect time.
Drink the words of the poet
    as he sings in perfect rhyme.
The electron in cyclic rhythm with the proton.
The planets in rhythm with the sun.
The solar system in rhythm with the galaxy.
Reverberations of the spheres in space
    echo in the silence of our meditation.

There is harmony in God's creation!
There is rhythm.
There is flow.
And cycles turn the wheels of time
    as the Great Mother nurtures the procession of life.

ELIZABETH CLARE PROPHET

 # The Law of Cycles

Discipline for a Purpose

"**I** HEARD THE DISCIPLINE OF GOD, AND I perceived it as the manifestation of his order. Out of the chaos and dimension of mortal mind and confusion, I perceived the luminous orb of Christed intelligence strike as from the star Alpha Draconis deep onto the pyramidal line.

"And I saw the chamber of the King; and I saw the chamber of the Queen; and I saw the pyramid of lives; and I saw the Master Mason draw his line; and I saw the security of the divine geometry.

"I saw the cubit stone, and I saw the measure of a man; and I saw that every man must strive to fit the master plan. And knowledge was needed and a torch, and the chamber must be traversed; and initiation must come; and man must pass from death unto Life. For the sun and the stars and the luminous orbs of creation are concentric focuses, orbs of Light—masses of Light, masses of energy, of density, of outpicturization. And man is so and knows it not, for the whirling galaxy within is also under dominion.

"As ships without rudder or compass or captain, so do compassless lives cross uncharted seas, and individuals are lost, hearing not the voice of the Ancient Mariner, the voice of Truth that parts the veil of mortal lies and leads men to pass from the bondage of Egypt across the Red Sea beyond the Desert of Sinai and into the Land of Promise.

"In an age when the world is marked by a lack of discipline, and rebellion against order is everywhere manifest, right while the secular society continues to exhibit a certain stability to which men look, I think it is essential that order be examined by mankind as heaven's first Law.

"If order is heaven's first Law, how can we, then, permit men to contemplate chaos or disorder as giving rise to something of virtue. The very power of the Mind of God that framed the world was to draw energy into a cohesive whole so that design, by Universal Law, could manifest through a cosmic geometry in the myriad forces of nature with all of their many patterns: helices, cones, squares, circles, ellipsoids, triangles, polygons and other geometric forms. The use to which nature has put all of these figures ought to show mankind that the Mind of God has, indeed, drawn upon the laws of cosmic geometry to produce in the world of form a perfection of order that is very beautiful in structure.

"The contemplation of universal order by mankind ought to show that no happenstance was involved in the mysteries of creation, but only a magnificent pattern of delight, of order, of intent and of purpose.

"The Great Pyramid of Life rises from the giant square of the Divine Architect's Mind, a Mind that contains all right angles and produces out of the four corners of substance the beauty of perfection, rising from the spheres of mortal dimension.

"Let men understand the meaning of this; for the base of life is in form, but it rises out of form. The social order, the order of nations and even the order of Hierarchy—all are constructed geometrically; and the cubit stones that compose these divisions are held together by the power of love that deems no sacrifice too great.

"You, then, to whom the Word is given, you who aspire to the disciplines of the Spirit, should understand that a tightly knit order of things is essential, because without the closeness of the cubit stones, the pyramid would not adhere; without it, even the pressures of roots and grass would separate stone from stone. Therefore, you will understand that the closely knit construction that smoothes the way for each stone to fit against another is the compassion of God. It is the design of the Grand Architect that smoothes the way and enables harmony to exist in the consciousness of mankind. And one day mankind will become 'Divine-kind,' for this is the purpose of all creation."[1]

Penetrating the Secrets of Creation

We approach the Law of Cycles with reverence for the Creator whose Self-expression it contains. All evidences of its outworking in man, the earth, the elements and the stars are but the tracings of his Being, footprints in the sands, tracks in the upper snows. Wherever we behold his markings as cyclings of infinity tumbling through the finite coils of time and space, there he has been. There his awful, wonderful Presence is—just beyond the veiled spirals of his creation.

Attempting to penetrate the Law of Cycles, we find secrets

sublime and all-encompassing—the being of man the microcosm, in man the Macrocosm. These secrets have remained closely guarded by the adepts of the mystery schools for thousands of years, for an understanding of these laws provides a predictable platform of evolution—and the power to initiate cycles of our own.

Kuthumi's Work on Cycles

The Ascended Master Kuthumi has influenced science and world thought for thousands of years. And it is he who has taught the Law of Cycles as fundamental to a comprehensive world view.

Embodied as the great master Pythagoras, Kuthumi expounded the law of the harmony of opposing forces. He taught how all of manifestation is composed of vibration in various states of interaction and equilibrium. We will see how this profound understanding is inherent in the cyclic law.

Kuthumi

During the 1800s, Kuthumi—known to his Western students as Koot Hoomi Lal Singh, or K.H.—was an advanced adept. He had conquered the usual ravages of time on the physical form, and it is said that for decades he continued to have the same youthful appearance. He was able to control the elements and to project a double of his physical body anywhere on the planet to perform his duties or to teach his disciples.

Much of his life remains a mystery, but we know he directed the course of the Theosophical Society from an esoteric school of adepts in a remote Himalayan valley inaccessible to anyone uninvited. Below him were advanced chelas (students). Above him were several Chohans (Lords, or Masters) and the Maha Chohan. The strictest codes of esoteric discipline were kept.

Kuthumi taught with profound scholarship, and he had a mind able to penetrate the veils of time and read the akashic records of earth's history. The knowledge of his Chohans was of intergalactic dimensions, and they guided him closely in all of his dealings with his chelas. Much to the wonder of his fellow adepts and to the consternation of his Chohans, Kuthumi attempted to bring to Western man some of the long forbidden mysteries of the occult Brotherhood.

In a letter sent to the English philosopher A. O. Hume in 1882, published in the book *The Mahatma Letters,* Kuthumi wrote, "I would not refuse what I have a right to teach. Only I had to study for fifteen years before I came to the doctrines of cycles and had to learn simpler things at first.... Let me tell you that the means we avail ourselves of are all laid down for us in a code as old as humanity to the minutest detail, but everyone of us has to begin from the beginning, not from the end. Our laws are as immutable as those of Nature, and they were known to man and eternity before this strutting game cock, modern science, was hatched."[2]

More than a hundred years have passed since that letter, and indeed the cycle has turned. Science is beginning to prove with her instruments and detectors many laws and facts previously considered to be occult meanderings. It is by dispensation of the Lords of Mind that we may now penetrate some of these teachings, along with the revelations brought forth by the Ascended Masters.

Where shall we start our excursion through the vast ocean of God's creation? The wonder of it all is that no matter where we start, by following any cycle of life to its origin, there we stand gazing face-to-face with God. For he is the originator of all cycles. He is the driving force spinning at the pivot point of all form.

The Cycle Defined

A cycle is "an interval of time during which a sequence of a recurring succession of events or phenomena is completed."[3] It is also defined as a "recurrent sequence of events which occur in such order that the last event of one sequence immediately precedes the recurrence of the first event in a new series."

Place your hand on your heart and feel the cycles of your heart's pulsation, the beat of your physical life sustaining the vehicles of your soul's evolution in Matter. Look up at a light-bulb and know that it shines because electricity is pulsating at a cycle of sixty times per second through its filament. Listen to a piece of music and hear the cyclic vibration of the violin strings resonating through the eardrum as sound.

All of cosmos can be comprehended in terms of cycles. The warp and woof of creation is manifest in currents of spiritual sound vibrating according to cyclic law. The very atoms and electrons of this world of form bow to the cyclic interchange of Spirit into Matter, Matter into Spirit—all-encompassed in the one element from which all of Life issues forth.

The marriage of science and true religion brings forth the progeny of wisdom and higher understanding. Some of the elements of the Law of Cycles we will discuss clash with what is regarded as current scientific fact or archaeological proofs.

The Cosmic Magnet

To understand one of the basic tenets of the Law of Cycles, we must delve into the deepest mysteries of our Spirit/

Matter universe. Here we contact the simplest and grandest of all cycles: the dual pulsation that is the heartbeat of cosmos. Here we find the one element, forever in equilibrium, forever pulsating in the rhythmic cycles that reverberate down to the inner core of every atom.

The entire religious philosophy of the yin/yang of Taoism is built upon the existence and importance of the cyclic interchange between an infinite hierarchy of opposing, or complementary, forces. It is the grand cycle of Alpha-to-Omega.

We hear it singing the song of the atom within our very own cosmos. It is the inhalation and exhalation of the Godhead. It is the interdimensional pattern of flow between Spirit and Matter—in Sanskrit, *Purusha* and *Prakriti*—the two poles of the cosmic magnet that sustains all of life. Truly, our study of the Law of Cycles is a meditation on our own inner Being.

The Truth all mankind seek is based on the irrefutable Law that Spirit and Matter are not opposites: they are the twofold nature of God's Being that remain forever as the Divine Polarity. This primary cycle we are considering is the simplest relationship of two forces—and the most all-encompassing action. If we clearly embrace the cyclic flow and unity between the Spirit/Matter or Father/Mother principles of motion, it is as if we are given a library card to God's storehouse of universal knowledge.

As Kuthumi said, let us begin at the beginning, and all of the vast complexities of God's infinite cycles will become clear upon the illuminated background of the original cycle.

All form is the result of motion. To have motion implies a point toward which the motion occurs and away from which it proceeds. This, in its grandest conception, is the cosmic magnet, the Father/Mother flow.

A magnet attracts and a magnet repels. If you hold a

horseshoe magnet in your hand, you can discover that there is a point of perfect equilibrium in the space exactly between the two opposite poles. At the heart of the polarity is unity and harmony.

All of cosmos is a magnet in the Macrocosmic sense. Sanat Kumara—known throughout religious literary history as "the Ancient of Days"—teaches about this cycle of universal flow:

"Those who would explore the far reaches of space, both inner and outer, should understand that the Divine Feminine is the womb of creation that is impregnated with Life by the Spirit of God. The material universe is the negative polarity whereas the spiritual universe is the positive polarity of the Godhead. Matter, meaning *Mater* [Latin for Mother], is the chalice that receives the invigorating, life-giving essence of the sacred fire. Thus the Father principle completes the cycle of manifestation in the world of form through the Mother aspect, and child-man is nourished by the balancing, sustaining action of Life whose twofold nature [Spirit/Matter, masculine/feminine] is epitomized in the Christ."[4]

This divine polarity exists throughout cosmos—from the balanced pulsation of the Great Central Sun to the systemic equilibrium of the hydrogen atom.

We learn from the science of sound and from the archives of the Brotherhood that all manifested cosmos is the interplay of vibrations—a vast web of electromagnetic waves oscillating at different numbers of cycles per second. And what is a vibration if not a cyclic motion related to a framework of time and space orientation?

The range of cycles is infinite—from one cycle in billions of years to billions of cycles each second (see figure 1). All are derivatives of the one pulsation we observe pivoting around the point of infinite equilibrium of the cosmic magnet.

FIGURE 1: Cycles of the Cosmos

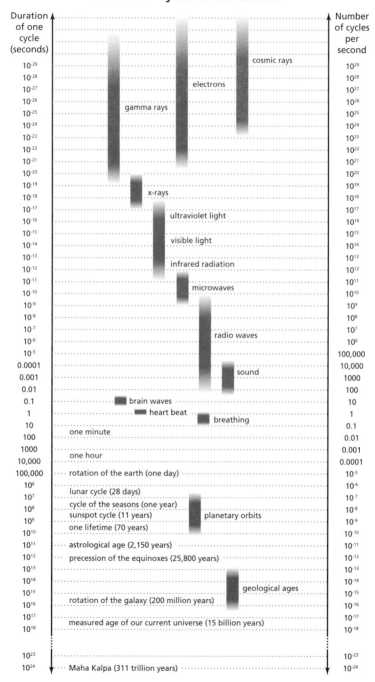

The Grand Cycle

Before we become immersed in this web of creation, let us take a step up our mountain of observation and consider the grandest, longest, most mysterious cycle in the world of form. The length of this cycle is calculated in terms of trillions of years, and we find ourselves reaching for a volume that might be called the life of Brahma.

Writing from the home of Kuthumi at Shigatse* in the Himalayas, gazing at an iceberg before him, Morya, one of the adepts who guided the Theosophical Society, wrote to A. P. Sinnett in January of 1882: "Nothing in nature springs into existence suddenly, all being subjected to the same law of gradual evolution. Realize but once the process of the *maha* cycle, of one sphere, and you have realized them all. One man is born like another man, one race evolves, develops, and declines like another and all other races. Nature follows the same groove from the 'creation' of a universe down to that of a mosquito. In studying esoteric cosmogony, keep a spiritual eye upon the physiological process of human birth; proceed from cause to effect.... Cosmology is the physiology of the universe spiritualized, for there is but one law."[5]

We will do just that. First we will learn of the cycles of Brahma, of God, as he unfolds the myriad systems of worlds. Then we will learn of man the microcosm. Eventually, the cycles of becoming will spread before us.

Considering the nature of atoms, Morya continues, they "polarize themselves during the process of motion and [are] propelled by the irresistible Force at work. In Cosmogony and the work of nature the positive and the negative or the active and passive forces correspond to the male and female

---

* Xigaze, a town in southeast Tibet

principles. Your spiritual efflux comes not from 'behind the veil' but is the male seed falling *into* the veil of matter. The active is attracted by the passive principle and the Great Nag, the serpent emblem of the eternity, attracts its tail to its mouth forming thereby a circle (cycles in the eternity) in that incessant pursuit of the negative by the positive.... The one and chief attribute of the universal spiritual principle—the unconscious but ever active life-giver—is to expand and shed; that of the universal material principle to gather in and fecundate [to make fruitful]. Unconscious and non-existing when separated, they become consciousness and life when brought together. Hence again—Brahma, from the root 'brih' the Sanskrit for 'to expand, grow or to fructify.' "[6]

The Law of Cycles is infinite in duration and infinite in form. Look back into the recesses of time and perceive the shadowed reality of beginningless cycles of the life of Brahma.

Man has always pondered the mysteries of creation. Scientists through the ages—astronomers, cosmologists, physicists—have developed various scenarios of the beginning of the universe.

The big bang theory states that around fifteen billion years ago, all of space and matter was compressed into an infinitely small point. All of a sudden, the big bang—and the physical universe was born. The explosion occurred and Life began to evolve from the subatomic particle to our present universe.

Those who believe in this theory quietly hide their eyes from the question, "What came before the big bang? What was the cause behind the effect?"

Though the theory may explain one aspect of one cycle of cosmic evolution, it doesn't provide the framework for an integrated and all-embracing cosmo-conception.

Let us reach for the deeper perspective held in the retreats of the Brotherhood in the heart of the Himalayas. Not material scientists but great scientists of the Spirit, the Ascended Masters and Cosmic Beings can provide infant mankind with a perspective that spans endless eternities of creation.

In their view, the Law of Cycles is the key to the alternating cycles of the explosion and implosion of the Matter universes as they proceed in and out of Spirit.

Exploring the Puranas

From the ancient epochs of India, history has preserved a series of writings called the Puranas. These are the teachings of great Masters originally recorded in an extremely remote period in earth's history.

The word *Purana* means "that which lives from ancient times," or "the records of ancient events." There are generally five subjects covered in these most ancient writings: (1) the creation of the universe; (2) re-creation after destruction or deluge; (3) the genealogy of the gods and teachers; (4) the *manvantaras,* or *Manu-antaras,* the great periods of time with the Manu as the primal ancestor; and, finally, (5) the histories of the Solar and Lunar dynasties.

One of the great Puranas is called the Bhagavata Purana. In section III, the revered teacher Maitreya sets forth the revelation of the cycles of cosmic creation. He teaches about the days and nights of Brahma and the infinite cycles of beginnings and endings and new beginnings. We now shake the dust from this ancient text, totally neglected by Western historians, as we read these ancient records from Lord Maitreya to his pupil Vidura.

"O Vidura, beyond the three worlds ... a day consists of one thousand cycles of four yugas. The night is also of the same duration when the creator of the universe goes to sleep. At the end of the night, the creation of the world starts and proceeds so long as it is God Brahma's day which covers the period of fourteen Manus. Every Manu rules during his own period which is somewhat longer than seventy-one cycles [each consisting] of four yugas."[7]

Yuga is the Sanskrit word for a "world-period." The Sanskrit names for the four yugas are *Satya Yuga, Treta Yuga, Dvapara Yuga* and *Kali Yuga.* Each successive age brings with it a different stage of civilization and a different mode of man's consciousness. In each of the yugas, man is given the spiritual tools that most effectively assist him to succeed in the cycles of evolution.

Just as the Great Cycle of Brahma's life is the archetype of man's personal cycles, so it is true with the yugas. The four yugas span millions of years in spheres of cosmic evolution, but we are taught that man himself goes through innumerable cycles of his own four yugas—as he walks the rounds toward reunion with God. We can compare the cycles of the evolution of the soul in the mastery of the four lower bodies, the four quadrants of being, with the cyclings of the four yugas. Thus the mastery of time and space is built upon this Law of Cycles.

The four yugas recur in cycles. The duration of the cycle of four is said to be 4,320,000 years. The reign of each of the fourteen Manus according to Maitreya is calculated as 306,720,000 years (71 x 4,320,000), and one day of Brahma is 4,320,000,000 years.

Although these figures are exoteric in nature, it is said that they closely follow the numbers in the "Secret Works." These durations have remained closely guarded by the Brotherhood, because as Pythagoras said, "All is number." There is great power resident within a true knowledge of the hidden laws of numerical cycles, and only certain keys can be given. It is true though, that the above figures relate to calculations of the great astronomers Narada and Asuramaya, regarded in India as having lived on Atlantis and possessing intimate knowledge of these matters.

Continuing with Maitreya's discourse: "In the eras of Manus, Kings in the lineage of Manu are born in succession. Hermits, Gods, King of Gods and his attendants are born simultaneously. This is Brahma's daily creation, whereby the three worlds are made to function and in which the birds, beasts, men, pitrs* and Gods are born according to their karmas. In the Manu-eras, the Supreme Lord retains ... and protects the universe by incarnating as Manus and manifesting himself in other human forms. At the end of Brahma's day ... he restrains his prowess, and with everything else withdrawn in him due to the force of Kala,† he keeps quiet. When it is nightfall without any moon or the sun in existence, the three worlds ... lie concealed in him.... In due course of time, with such days and nights as described above, even the long span of life of hundred years of this (God Brahma) comes to an end."[8]

The word *year* refers to a cosmic cycle of Brahma's life, spanning billions of years. The Hindu chronologers have based their temporal calculations on astronomical configurations—the positions of the stars in the zodiac in relation to our earth. One hundred cosmic years is regarded as a whole period of Brahma's age, called the *Maha Kalpa,* or "Great Cycle." It is the longest single cycle we can detect. We are told that its duration is 311,040,000,000,000 years in length.

Maitreya continues in the Bhagavata Purana, "Half of the life [of God Brahma] is called parardha. The first parardha [of his life] has passed. Now the other half is running."[9] In our great cycle, our Maha Kalpa, we have turned past the axial

---

* *Pitrs:* usually interpreted as the spirits of the departed ancestors of men. However, H. P. Blavatsky explains that they are more accurately described as the "ancestors, or creators of mankind" (*Theosophical Glossary* [Los Angeles: The Theosophy Company, 1930]).

† *Kala:* the unfolding principle of time.

point of the course of cosmos. God has once again exhaled his breath of Life as fohat and the long inbreath has begun to return all to the spiritual source once again. The beginningless, endless cycle—as all things emanate from and return to the One.

When outer man becomes congruent with the spiritual essence of his own Divine Monad, he then becomes the drop merging into the ocean of God. Our individualized personalities had a beginning in the warp and woof of manifestation, but the core of the atom of our being, our spiritual Monad, began when God himself began.

The Law of Karma

The Law of Karma, of perfect retribution, is intimately related to the Law of Cycles.

We can know with absolute surety that if we send out hatred or negative vibrations, sooner or later they will cycle back to ourselves—and we will have to expend energy to revibrate our murky creation.

We can also know that the Self-generated impulse toward God, toward Good, toward service of our fellowman will, with infinite precision, cycle back also and add to our momentum of Light and our return to Wholeness. This is the Law of Karma. It is the mathematically predictable Law of Cycles. It is the most simple yet profound manifestation of justice.

By willingly coming into congruence with the cycle of involution, evolution and ascension, we know that at the end of this round, we will indeed see the face of God.

Can we imagine what it would be like if the Law of Cycles didn't exist, if we had no way of knowing where to direct our striving to return to a state of wholeness?

Spirit and Matter

We find described in these scriptures the endless rhythmic pulsation of cosmic creation called in the East the *Maha Kalpa,* or "Great Cycle." Though there are infinite cycles within cycles, the overall flow consists of an outbreath and an inbreath, an Alpha thrust of creation followed by the Omega return to the heart of Brahma. At the end of each creative cycle is the *pralaya.** At best, then, the big bang theory becomes a crude statement of the sublime cosmic moment of the birth of worlds when the sine wave passes from imperceptible to perceptible reality—that is, from what we call Spirit to what we call Matter.

Delving deeper into the mysteries of creation, we come to the awareness that all is Spirit. All forms of Matter—even the densest physical substance—are the crystallized fire mist of spiritual essence. The successive lives of Brahma can be conceived of by our limited minds as immense cyclic arcs of pure Spirit involuting into the veils of denser Matter, and then evoluting back to the ethereal, spiritual origin.

Our relative position in the grand cycle of our personal or planetary cycle can be understood as the ratio of Spirit to Matter. As Brahma outbreathes the web of creation, there is a densification as the universe puts on its seven coats of skins.

An axial point is reached in the cycle where the outbreath is expended and inbreath begins. It is the point of the lowest descent of the arc of Spirit into Matter. It is the state of equilibrium of the positive and negative poles of the cosmic magnet. It is the halfway point in the cycle that Maitreya mentioned we have passed.

Then there is the period of return to Spirit. All that has

---

* *Pralaya:* Sanskrit, "period of rest."

become involved in material form begins its process of etherealization and return to the one Source—and to the period of pralayic rest—once again to begin a new cycle of becoming.

This is the night of Brahma, when all is drawn back into the Godhead. During this period of rest, all the patterns of creation—the whole divine DNA chain, if you will, the patterns by which stars will be born, spiral nebulae, whole systems and galaxies—are being gathered within, like a seed. There is a manifestation of divine intelligence, the stirring, the shaking of divine intelligence in the sea, the drawing by the fingers of God of the various graphs and patterns and hieroglyphs that are going to manifest in the various systems of worlds. And when the whole is complete, then once again comes the dawn of creation and the exhalation of the breath of God.

The path of the ascension is the means whereby sons of God preserve an identity as a single cell in the being of Brahma throughout the pralayas and throughout the inhalation and the exhalation of God. To endure as a cell in the consciousness of God when that God is at perfect rest is to enter with him into the cosmic cycle of nirvana. To do this, one must pass through the nexus of the cycle, which nexus we term the Word.

We read in the Vedas: "In the beginning was Brahman with whom was the Word, and the Word is Brahman."[10] In order to be in Brahman, we must be in the Word. "No man cometh unto the Father, but by me."[11] That *me* is the supreme I AM THAT I AM manifest as the Word. By the Law of Cycles, then, we are set upon our courses spiraling once again through the nexus of being, the nexus being the Word itself, the Law of Cycles being the emanation of the Word.

The Law of Transcendence

As we ponder the immense odyssey of God's Being through eternal rounds of beginnings and endings, we can ask the fateful question: Why? What is the purpose of it all if the universe is just an endless cycle of rounds with man floating on a speck of dust in space cast loose on a shoreless ocean? What is the nature of the Godhead as he exists through endless cycles in infinite space?

The answer, we are told, is that the Law of Cycles implements the Law of Transcendence. God is a transcendent being, and with each new outbreath he evolves to a greater state of cosmic perfection and beauty.

The cycles are not really circles or sine waves but they are spirals—spirals of infinite expansion according to the geometry of the golden ratio (1:1.618...). Each cycle of evolution takes in more of God. Each round sends us into wider spheres of the body of God's cosmos.

The individualities enmeshed in the fabric of the Godhead eventually reach a point in evolution where they span the cyclic lifetimes of Brahma. With each new pulsation, after each successive pralaya, the imprint of higher planes of perfection impregnates the gestating Cosmic Egg.

The endless cyclic patterns of cosmic evolution would be an abominable injustice if not for the fact that each new cycle begins at a higher point of perfection. This universe is not an infernal merry-go-round that spins in space.

What meaningless boredom, what hellish drudgery it would be to have to return forever to the same place in the cycle like a broken record. God and all of his creation is continually transcending itself, with the leading edge of consciousness always able to contact new vistas of infinity and to create greater manifestations of divine purpose.

How does man the individual fit into this vast cosmic plan of transcendent cycles? How can we apply the Law of Cycles for the purpose of greater acceleration around the rings of initiation?

The Law of Correspondences

In the far-distant past, Hermes, Messenger of the Gods, delivered to us the nucleus of the Law of Cycles—"as Above, so below."

We still retain what is called "The Emerald Tablet" of Hermes. This short but concise teaching formed the core of the most ancient Masonic orders and schools of the Brotherhood. It begins with these words:

> True, without any error;
> certain, very true;
> That which is Above,
> is as that which is below;
> and that which is below,
> is as That which is Above;
> for achieving the Wonders
> of the Universe.[12]

This is the Law of Analogy, the Law of Correspondences, and it provides us with the sense of divine order that is indeed the sense of justice.

The Law of Correspondence states that the creation corresponds to the Creator, that man corresponds to God. Therefore, the Real Image of man is congruent with his God Source by design, by intent, by Law. The design is one of transcendent cycles, mirrored all the way through the veils of Matter into the coil of the densest atom.

The intent is for man, the individual, to become a beneficent co-creator with the Godhead, to span cosmic cycles, to be the one who breathes out galactic systems and provides the impulse of coherent love that binds the particulate atoms into a meaningful platform of evolution. The Law is the law of recurrent cycles ever transcending the previous round. The Law of Transcendence offers us the comfort of the highest hope.

As the cycles of cosmos spiral upward into greater and greater dimensions, so man can forever transcend the veils of Matter that form the schoolrooms for his soul's evolution. The transcendent teaching of the Christ reveals infinite possibilities for God and man. It destroys the lie of eternal damnation. It opens the door of opportunity for repentance and healing. It is absolute justice in manifestation.

It is not easy for mortal man to stretch his mind beyond the boundaries of infinity. Maitreya has taught that a lifetime of Brahma, a universe lasting trillions of years, appears as a single atom when merged in the body of the great Puruśa. The planets spinning around our sun are like one atom in the body of the Milky Way galaxy—the galaxy having over a hundred billion sun centers, each with its own system of worlds. The Being ensouling the galaxy is aware of our world as an atom in his body, teeming with sentient life evolving.

And then there is man—the oversoul and God to a vast universe of his inner identity. We are cells in the Body of God, and we have fifty trillion cells that compose our body. Each one of those cells has intelligence, has a spark of divinity. Think of it. Each one of our cells considers us as the Godhead of its universe, the originator of its life impulses. Paul said, "Know ye not that ye are the temple of God, and that the Spirit of God dwelleth in you?"[13]

How far along the vibratory spectrum of cosmic Life can we go in each direction?

Who is to say that there isn't a complex system of life-forms resident on the surface of each electron as it spins in polar equilibrium to its nuclear sun center—just as our earthy sphere of cosmic dust spins around its sun, teeming with Life? The mortal mind cannot tell. But Beings with vast awareness have told us that the cycles of God are infinite in all directions.

Let us consider man the microcosm, who is also the Macrocosm, and behold the workings of cyclic law as we trace the course of man's evolution in the hierarchical ladder of being.

Let us first consider man and his indivisible parts and define thereby which portion of man travels along the endless cycles of evolution.

Man—the Microcosm

Man is a sevenfold creation. The Great White Brotherhood has always taught that the number seven is the primary harmonic quantity. Man is composed of seven sheaths, or bodies, bestowed upon him by the Lords of Form who, in turn, are sevenfold in their own nature.

Pythagoras explained the theory of the eternal Monad to his inner disciples. According to the adept Kuthumi, the reincarnation of Pythagoras, the Monad can be considered as the upper two principles of man's sevenfold being.

It is this reflective spark of divinity that sends forth our soul to cycle through the veils of maya. And through the threefold flame (the spiritual flame within the heart), this soul constructs around herself* the temporary lower vehicles used to draw in experience of God's nature. It is the sacred fire infolding more and more of itself.

---

* Whether housed in a male or female body, the soul is the feminine principle and Spirit is the masculine principle of the Godhead. The soul, then, is addressed by the pronouns *she* and *her*.

Each of the seven bodies of man has a different frequency and therefore provides a unique opportunity to focus the individuality of God's consciousness. These seven forcefields of awareness are: (1) the I AM Presence, also known as the Electronic Presence of God, which holds the pattern of the Real Self; (2) the Causal Body of man, which surrounds the I AM Presence as the chalice for all Good that the individual has elected to qualify in word, thought and deed since the moment of creation when the blueprint of his identity was sealed in the fiery core of the God Self; (3) the Christ Self, focal point for the manifestation of the Universal Christ within the individual through the action of the Holy Spirit; (4) the etheric, or memory, body, vehicle for the soul, holding the blueprint of the perfect image to be outpictured in the world of form; (5) the mental body, vehicle for the Mind of God through Christ; (6) the emotional body, vehicle for God's feelings and energy in motion; and (7) the physical body, vehicle for God's power and focal point for the crystallization of the energies of the other six bodies in form.

The four lower bodies are man's opportunity to manifest the Christ in the dimensions of time and space. These bodies are reference points for man's mastery of himself and his environment through the mastery of the Four Cosmic Forces known as earth, air, fire and water. These Cosmic Forces form the square at the base of the Pyramid of Life; and unless they are in balanced manifestation within the four lower bodies, neither man nor his creations can be perfected or made permanent.

The etheric, or memory, body corresponds to the side of the north in the City Foursquare and at the base of the pyramid. It is the fire body and, as such, has the highest vibration of the four lower bodies. The etheric body, or etheric envelope, is the only one of the four lower vehicles that is permanent. It is carried over from one embodiment to the next, whereas the mental, emotional and physical bodies go through the process of disintegration according to the cyclic laws of their substance. Like all of substance in Matter, they are subject to the Law of Cycles governing integration and disintegration, or the manifestation of form and the return to formlessness. (Nevertheless, all virtue and righteousness that man qualifies through these bodies is stored in the Causal Body so that nothing of value or enduring worth is ever lost.)

The soul is the as-yet-nonpermanent atom in God's body. She is infused with the germinal seed to become ruler of a cosmos. This she must do by the exercise of free will.

It is the soul as the extension of the I AM Presence and Causal Body that is given opportunity to spin the "Deathless Solar Body" out of the fibers of akasha.

FIGURE 2: The Seven Bodies of Man

1	I AM Presence	The Divine Monad	SPIRIT
2	Causal Body		
3	Higher Mental Body / Christ Self		
4	Etheric / Memory	Permanent	MATTER
5	Mental	Non-permanent	
6	Emotional / Astral		
7	Physical		

The seven bodies of man are seven forcefields of awareness, each one having a different frequency and therefore providing a unique opportunity to focus the individuality of God's consciousness. These bodies are shown pictorially in the Chart of Your Divine Self (facing page 88).

The Circle

The riddle of eternity and evolution is contained within the symbol of the circle. The circle is a cross section of a spiral that begins in the square of the base of the Pyramid and rises to the apex of realization in the Capstone of Life. And there in the center of the Capstone, the Law of Transcendence functions through the Eye of God. For when the spiral passes through the All-Seeing Eye, it transcends the dimensions of form and passes from Matter to Spirit. This is the fulfillment of the Law of Cycles that begins in the heart of God and culminates in every perfect creation.

The eternal Logos is the dot in the center of the circle, the beginning and the ending of cycles that are composed of circles, layer upon layer. Energy that begins as a spiral in Spirit descends into Matter, there to coalesce around the Flame and then, in the twinkling of an eye—the Eye of God—to return to Spirit over the descending and ascending spirals of God's consciousness.

Beholding the circle of God's love, Justinius, Captain of Seraphic Hosts, was wont to exclaim:

"I beheld the predication of God, the First Cause, un-sullied, magnificent in brightness, qualifying each monadic release with the intensely glowing similitude of the Divine. What a delight of sameness, defrauding none; jealousy was unborn. But the Fire remained not tiny and not finite. It was a growing spiral of concept. From the dot the circles emerged and, as the hands of a clock, spun a cone in space that, like a golden ladder, scaled the heights, probed the depths and unified the diverse.

"Where is division, then, among us? It is not. All that divides is not among us. All that seeks to conquer is not among us, for we are enamored by his love; and the blush of a flower petal is translucent unto us; for his Light streams through the substance as a window lattice of exquisitry."[14]

The heavenly bodies are undergoing cyclic evolution within the larger infinite spiral of God's Being in Spirit—passing through material manifestation and returning to Spirit. In the Macrocosm as well as in the microcosm, circling spirals trigger the flow of energy into and out of form.

Throughout the universe the pattern of cyclic return is reproduced again and again with infinite precision, traversing eternity, expanding according to the golden ratio. The circle is a cross section of a spiral that has neither beginning nor ending, but appears to be finite as it passes through the physical universe in the form of planets, stars, suns and galaxies.

Although the circle itself is without beginning or ending, at any point on the circumference of the circle, the hand of God may draw an intersecting line, thereby creating a beginning and an ending. Thus are cycles initiated and worlds (whirls) born.

FIGURE 3: Time Is a Cycle within an Eternal Spiral

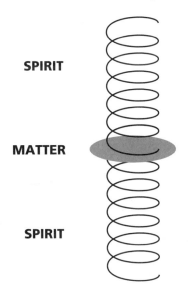

SPIRIT

MATTER

SPIRIT

The finite universe is a slice of an infinite spiral. The circle in this diagram could be a galaxy, a sun system, a star, a planet or you. Where the spiral passes from Spirit to Matter, the cycle is arrested. The evolution of the spiral that passes from Spirit through Matter and back to Spirit is according to the golden ratio (1.618...).

The whirl of fohatic release, directed by the guiding will of a God-free being, can send reverberating vibrations careening through space. Drop a stone into a still pond and watch the cyclic wave patterns continue to flow and flow in smooth rhythm. Drop a stone into an agitated pond, and there results a complex of wave-pattern interchange, but the cycle initiated by the stone continues to affect the water. Thus it is by the hand of God and by his emissaries.

Once man has passed through the cycles of the initiatic process—the spirals of destiny that unlock the total pattern of his identity—he earns the right to be congruent with the dot in the center of the Great Circle of Life. That dot in the center of the circle is the point of dynamic equilibrium resident in all of creation.

There is always that central point of balance, called the *laya center* in Hindu esoteric science. To become one with this power center, this dot of equilibrium in the center of God's circle, is to be able to direct the power of *fohat* as it courses along the vibratory pathways we create.

Visualize a simple sine wave. This represents a rhythmic cycle of a particular frequency. There is a rising curve, then a falling curve, and then a rising curve, and so forth. According to the Law of Cycles, there must be a force that pulls the current of God's undifferenti- 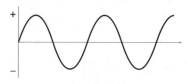 ated energy into the rising curve. And there must be an opposite force that attracts this stream of energy (represented by the line) into the falling curve. These are the positive and negative poles active at the core of all cycles.

To be the dot in the center of the circle is to become the harmony of the polar forces—to be the axis in the spinning sphere of creative force. It is the pivot point of cyclic flow. It is reached in samadhi. It is utilized by adepts to control the fire of space.

All of manifested cosmos is the interplay of cyclic vibrations, initiated somewhere, somehow, by someone. As we ascend the scales of evolution, we are entrusted with the divine power and authority to initiate cycles that may last forever.

If you find the point of balance anywhere in cosmos, you can travel unperturbed through the successive neutral centers all the way to the center of the Great Central Sun. All the centers of all the cycles are congruent in the highest dimension of cosmos. Find one center and you have found them all. Find your first love and you have found all loves. Remain at the point of balance, of perfect love, and you reside in the heart of God.

This great secret pathway through the tunnels of cyclic equilibrium, designed into the fabric of Life, is God's great gift to man. Become the dot in the center of his circle, correspond to the pulsation of his heart, and look forward to infinite horizons of beauty and perfectionment.

The Molding of Substance

The ancient wisdom teaches us that there is one element, one cosmic substance—*akasha*—from which all form is made. It is fluidic in motion, ethereal, and interpenetrates all substance. Without weight, without color of its own, it takes on the properties of vibratory patterns imposed upon it—patterns that can be impressed on it by sound and by thought.

Even Spirit has form. As we recede into the eternal depths of creation and rise into infinitely higher planes of consciousness, still there is form—and all conforms to the Law of Cycles.

FIGURE 4: The Laya Center

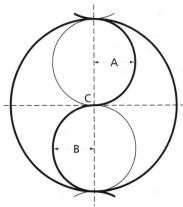

This diagram helps us to understand this great secret of the Law of Cycles. The point in the center of the circle is the *laya center*, the etheric neutral point. We can describe this center as the nirvanic disassociation of all form merging all into primordial akasha. The cycle flows from top to bottom in a regular cycle forming the pattern known as the T'ai Chi. The central point of the cycle is the point of latency during all periods of *pralaya*, or rest. It is the point of transition between the Alpha thrust and the Omega return. It is said in *The Secret Doctrine* that "whatsoever quits the laya state becomes active life; it is drawn into the vortex of motion; Spirit and Matter are the two equilibrized states." All atoms issue forth from the center point of the creative pulsation of the Godhead, and every one of those atoms has its own neutral center. As Above, so below.

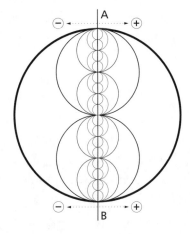

In this diagram, we symbolize cycles within cycles ad infinitum. The vertical line in the middle (A–B) represents the neutral center common to all cycles in cosmos. It is the axial point in the secret chamber of God's creative heart.

All cycles, all vibrations, and therefore all Matter varies according to the frequency and angle of deviation from the neutral, balanced, undifferentiated laya center.

The most common form of electricity is a cyclic flow of a form of akasha vibrating sixty times each second. The magnitude of potential energy, called voltage, is a function of how far away from the neutral center of the cycle the energy has been made to flow. The greater the distance, the more energy available because there is a greater polarity built between the plus and minus crests of the cycle. The same is true in the world of man and Spirit. Man can send out greater or lesser vibrations of energy from the power center in his heart.

All substance, all form, all life is the result of force causing Matter to move. Force can be generated voluntarily, consciously, by an intelligent being. The infinite Hierarchy of Ascended Beings turns the wheels and cycles of worlds by the force of their will. Brahma uses force to mold galaxies. The Masters use force to mold ideas and create the various pockets of life in the universe.

Force can also be the impulse of the unconscious, meticulously accurate mechanism that drives the substratum of the material planes. Matter cannot be divorced from Spirit.

In order to have motion, there must be a medium through which vibrations can occur. The fluid nature of akasha responds to vibrational force in a wavelike, cyclic flow—just like the pebble thrown into the fluid pond. Motion is the alteration of akasha that is inherently in a state of harmony, of rest, of equilibrium. Apply any force into the ocean of akasha and cycles of motion result.

The myriad forms we see in the universe are the conglomerate wave patterns resulting from simple or complex combinations of sine waves moving in cycles. The days and nights of Brahma, if symbolized in two dimensions, would be an even, rhythmic flow between the two poles of the cosmic magnet. The allness of the one element is driven into motion by the will of God.

FIGURE 5: Cycles and Spirals

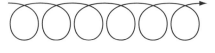

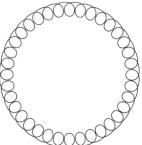

A cycle is a spiral of energy that moves in a linear or circular pattern for the purpose of transforming frequencies between planes of consciousness. Each circle or revolution within the spiral conducts energy through the planes of fire, air, water and earth.

The Return to the Center

Within the circle, the mystery of the beginning and the ending of God is solved. God himself is the circle that has neither beginning nor ending of cycles. Until man becomes one with God, he is but a dot on the circumference, following the patterns of the Infinite and fulfilling in the finite the cycles of Life. But once he has passed through the cycles of initiation— the spirals of destiny that unlock the total pattern of his identity—he earns the right to be congruent with the dot in the center of the Great Circle of Life. His being has become a spiral; therefore, according to the Law of Correspondences, it must merge with the Spiral that is without beginning or ending, the Spiral that is God. To this end has he engaged his energies in the recurrent cycles: to fulfill the mantra of his being and to return to the center of the circle.

God has neither beginning nor ending because his Being takes in the universe of cycles and all that precedes and follows them in the formed and unformed dimensions of Spirit. But for a brief interim, man seems to have a beginning and an ending because he identifies with a slice of the spiral that initiates in Spirit, evolves through Matter, and returns to Spirit. When man's beginnings and his endings are seen as part of the never-ending cycles of God's Self-awareness, he will realize that although the spirals of his own life travel in a linear pattern through the limited spheres of outer manifestation, there is, in reality, no end to the involution and evolution of his consciousness.

When man returns to God, aligning the energies he has gathered in spirals with the Great Spiral that is God's Being, both God and man transcend their former state, and the Law of Cycles implements the Law of Transcendence. God transcends himself as man transcends himself, for God is in man and man is in God. Through the merging of cycles, man becomes more of God and God becomes more in man; hence new creations are continually being born into spirals that expand the circle of the Infinite One.

Saint Germain propounded the great mystery of the Law of Cycles in this wise:

"God is, and because he is, man is. This has been said before; let it be said again. If God is—and we know that he is—and if he is Law—and we know that he is—then that Law is not only the Law of Life but it is also the Law by which Life can be exercised.

"Man should first of all develop the habit of infiring himself with determination, becoming thereby a literal spark plug of cosmic identification. Man should be happy to identify with God in the present, for in the future he is destined to become a God in manifestation. He will be one with God; his consciousness will merge with God's; therefore he will no longer be found as man. This is why it was said of old, 'No man can see God and live as man.'[15] For, having come face to face with the Reality of God's Being, man must either become that Reality through total identification with it—or be consumed.

"Why, then, should he while away the hours and gamble away his life? True commitment is the safest offering and the best example. True commitment does not permit the individual to accept the spheres of limitation; on the contrary, it enables him to realize his unlimited potential, to be a way-shower and to triumph over all outer conditions.

"This triumph is to be found in the consciousness of cosmic adornment, in the putting-on of the vestments of immortality. Is God able? Then man is able. Is God wise? Then man is wise. Is God free? Then man is free. It is in the acceptance of these immaculate concepts of each one's divinity and in their implementation that the fabric of the Inner Being becomes the seamless garment of the Christ."[16]

Linear Patterns of the Finite Whirl

Whereas the circle is the symbol of the Infinite Mind, it is ever the finite mind that perceives the world in terms of linear patterns, having a point of origin and a finalized ending. The descent of the energies of the Infinite World (whirl) into the finite world (whirl) takes place by way of the spiral that appears as a straight line or a ray. From the Sun Center of Being, the ray descends to the point of precipitation, and there at the place where Spirit becomes Matter, a flame is born as the focus of creation.[17]

The pyramid is the symbol of the descent of Spirit into Matter and of the ascent of Matter into Spirit. Having the square as its base in Matter, which rises to a point in Spirit, the pyramid is the key to precipitation in the planes of Spirit and Matter. The square is to the finite as the circle is to the Infinite, and thus the squaring of the Circle of Cosmic Identity within the pyramid is achieved whenever Spirit becomes Matter; whereas the circling of the square of microcosmic identity within the pyramid occurs whenever Matter becomes Spirit.

The circle always contains the complete identity, the blueprint for manifestation. Therefore, the square of physical creation is suspended within the circle of its metaphysical or etheric counterpart, making contact therewith at four equidistant points on the circumference. Without that contact, without the fusion of the square of Matter and the circle of Spirit, creation is unborn.

The four sides of the square that form the base of the pyramid represent the four planes of God's consciousness—

FIGURE 6: The Squaring of the Circle

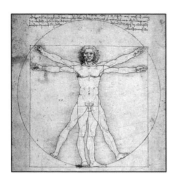 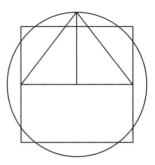

The principle of the squaring of the circle is illustrated in Leonardo da Vinci's famous illustration of the proportions of man and also in the Great Pyramid. A circle with radius equal to the height of the Great Pyramid would have the same circumference as the base of the pyramid itself.

earth, air, fire and water. These Cosmic Forces correspond to the four lower bodies of man and are necessary for the precipitation of form in the spiritual as well as the material universe. The four equilateral triangles that compose the sides of the pyramid symbolize the four lower bodies that rise from these four planes. The equal sides of the triangles represent the balanced action of the threefold flame destined to be outpictured within each of the four lower bodies through man's attainment of self-mastery under the Four Cosmic Forces.

Using the face of a clock, let us now diagram a cross section of the spiral of materialization, which will reveal the Law of Cycles governing the precipitation of form. Superimposing the square upon the circle, we see that the four corners touch the circumference at four equidistant points, which we will designate as the 12, 3, 6 and 9 o'clock lines.

Each of the four quadrants thus formed represents a plane of consciousness through which the descending clockwise spiral—which we shall call the monad—must pass in order for

FIGURE 7: The Four Quadrants Defined

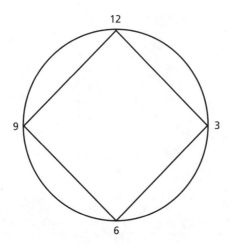

The square intersects the circle at four
equidistant points, defining quadrants.

Spirit to become Matter. Within each of the four planes, ruled
by the Four Cosmic Forces, are three subplanes, making a
total of twelve planes, or frequencies, which are sustained by
the Twelve Hierarchies of the Sun.

The cycles of precipitation begin and end at the 12 o'clock
line, and each revolution of the energy spiral around the clock
is one complete cycle whereby Spirit descends through the
planes of fire, air, water and earth before it achieves total
integration in Matter. The Twelve Hierarchies of the Sun
govern the deceleration process that occurs as the Monad
passes through each of the twelve houses or lines of the clock.
Precipitation occurs as the twelve frequencies and their
corresponding godly virtues are absorbed in succession by the
Monad beginning in the twelfth house and returning to it over
the clockwise spiral.

Between 12 and 3, the spiral passes through the etheric
plane where the action of the fire element predominates;

FIGURE 8: Twelve Planes of Consciousness

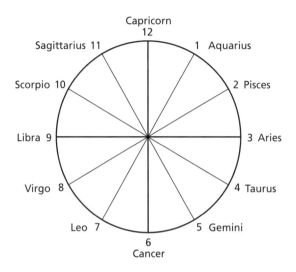

Within each quadrant of the circle are three subplanes. These define twelve planes, or frequencies of consciousness. These are sustained by the Twelve Hierarchies of the Sun, which are known by the names of the twelve signs of the zodiac.

between 3 and 6 it passes through the mental plane where the action of the air element predominates; between 6 and 9 it passes through the emotional plane where the action of the water element predominates; and between 9 and 12 it passes through the physical plane where the action of the earth element predominates.

As the Monad passes through the 12, 3, 6 and 9 o'clock intersections, there is a step-down in the velocity of the spiral—a "shifting of gears," so to speak—for the descent, with an accompanying release of Christ-power. Thus, the potential for precipitation is greatest: (a) where earth becomes fire (at the 12 o'clock line), (b) where fire becomes air (at the 3 o'clock line), (c) where air becomes water (at the 6 o'clock line) and (d) where water becomes earth (at the 9 o'clock line).

FIGURE 9: The Initiation of Cycles through the Squaring of the Circle

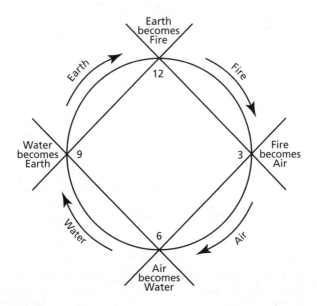

At the four cardinal points of transmutation, there is a release of Christ-power through divine alchemy. This power gives the impetus for rotation, or the creation of spirals, in the heart of the universe and in the heart of the atom.

Thus the pattern of the circle is the basis for what is known as the "crystallization of the mist"—the mist being defined as the "unformed" and the crystal being defined as the "formed." Although there is a tendency to equate Matter with "form" and Spirit with the "formless," we must realize that Spirit is not without form, but that its patterns, being infinite, cannot be contained within the dimensions of Matter unless the cycles that begin in Spirit are arrested by or take on the linear patterns—that is, unless the circle becomes the square. This, then, is what happens when "the patterns made in the heavens," or spiritual bodies, descend via the clockwise spiral through the four quadrants to become "the patterns made in the earth," or material bodies.[18]

FIGURE 10: The Squaring of the Circle and the Circling of the Square

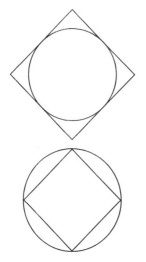

In the squaring of the circle, Spirit becomes Matter: when the circle becomes the square, Spirit Unformed is suspended in Matter Formed.

In the circling of the square, Matter becomes Spirit: when the square becomes the circle, Matter Formed is suspended in Spirit Formed.

The Four Sacred Rituals

"In the beginning God created the heaven and the earth. And the earth was without form, and void; and darkness was upon the face of the deep. And the Spirit of God moved upon the face of the waters. And God said, Let there be light: and there was light."[19]

The Spirit of God flows throughout his creation according to the Law of Cycles. The action of the sacred fire in man and in nature fulfills the fiat of the Light through four alchemical rituals: (1) The Ritual of Creation (+), (2) the Ritual of Preservation (+), (3) the Ritual of Disintegration (–), and (4) the Ritual of Sublimation (–). Let us now examine the patterns of these rituals:

I. The Ritual of Creation is accomplished as the energies of God descend from Spirit to Matter over the clockwise or positive spiral passing through the planes of fire, air, water and earth. This is the Alpha cycle of materialization, or precipitation; it is the going-out or evolutionary process that is a masculine activity of the sacred fire.

II. The Ritual of Preservation, the sustaining of form in Matter and in Spirit, is accomplished via the clockwise figure-eight pattern (moving in a clockwise direction from the point of origin on the 12 o'clock line) as energy flows through the planes of fire, water, air and earth. This is a masculine activity of the sacred fire, used to seal energy in a given matrix.

III. The Ritual of Disintegration is accomplished as the energies of God return from Matter to Spirit over the counter-clockwise spiral for the purposes of canceling unworthy creations through the planes of earth, water, air and fire. This is the Omega cycle of disintegration or dematerialization. It is the involutionary or negative spiral, used to free energy of the imperfect patterns of the human consciousness. This pattern is also used in the "going-within" cycle that is the feminine activity of the sacred fire.

IV. The Ritual of Sublimation, the spiritualization, or ascension, of form and consciousness, is accomplished via the counterclockwise figure-eight pattern (moving in a counter-clockwise direction from the point of origin on the 12 o'clock line) as energy flows through the planes of earth, air, water and fire. This action of sublimation (to make sublime, to refine) is used to immortalize or make permanent the works of God and man.

These are the cycles of the Word which in the Beginning was with God—was God—and without which was not anything made that was made.[20] The creation of the hills, the earth, the stars and man—in fact the evolution of Life everywhere—follows these same patterns, which are governed by the universal Law of Cycles.

FIGURE 11: The Four Alchemical Rituals

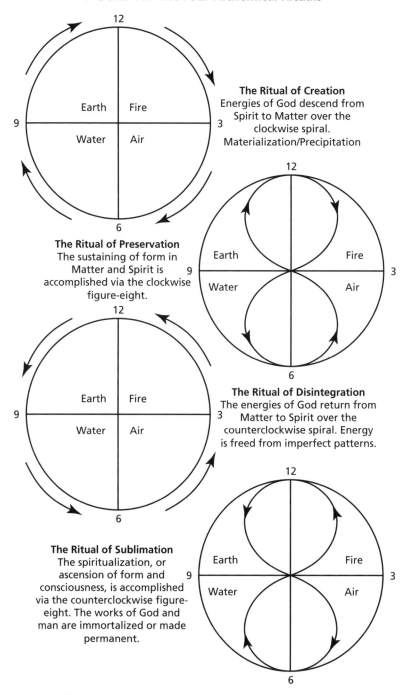

The Ritual of Creation
Energies of God descend from
Spirit to Matter over the
clockwise spiral.
Materialization/Precipitation

The Ritual of Preservation
The sustaining of form in
Matter and Spirit is
accomplished via the clockwise
figure-eight.

The Ritual of Disintegration
The energies of God return from
Matter to Spirit over the
counterclockwise spiral. Energy
is freed from imperfect patterns.

The Ritual of Sublimation
The spiritualization, or
ascension of form and
consciousness, is accomplished
via the counterclockwise figure-
eight. The works of God and
man are immortalized or made
permanent.

FIGURE 12: The Flow of Cycles

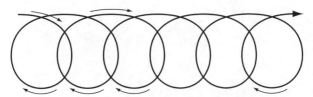

Ritual of Creation – Clockwise Spiral

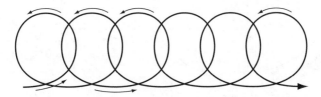

Ritual of Disintegration – Counterclockwise Spiral

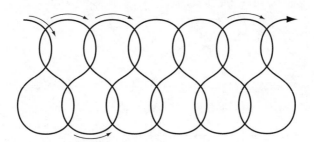

Ritual of Preservation – Clockwise Figure Eight

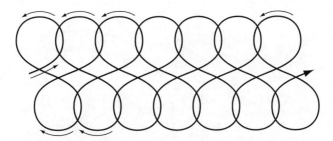

Ritual of Sublimation – Counterclockwise Figure Eight

Spirit's Pillar

In the Book of Exodus, the involuting and evoluting spirals are described as "the pillar of fire by night" and "the pillar of cloud by day" that guided the children of Israel across the desert and into the Land of Promise.[21] The inner meaning of the word "spiral" is "Spirit's pillar." The pillar of fire is the involuting spiral "infolding itself"—the focalization of the white-fire core in the night side of Life. It is the indrawing of the spirit of man into the center of Being to absorb the energies of the Godhead in preparation for the expansion that begins with the dawn.

The "pillar of fire" becomes the "pillar of cloud" when the concentrated energies of the Christ are diffused, creating the cloud effect; and within the cloud is the Spirit of God bearing witness unto itself in the planes of Matter. Thus the evolutionary spiral governs the day, or yang, cycle when man's energies are actively engaged, and the involutionary spiral governs the night, or yin, cycle when man's energies are passively engaged. (See the Chart of the Hours, chapter 1, book 9 of the Climb the Highest Mountain series.)

The action of concentration, the Spirit, or Yang, expression of the Godhead, is always balanced by the action of diffusion, the Mater, or Yin, expression of the Godhead. The Lord of the Third Ray, Paul the Venetian, beautifully described the Yang and Yin of life in this way:

"Both concentration and diffusion are necessary in order to create at will, yet each requires its own perspective. Through diffusion, consciousness is able to expand in infinite degrees and to assimilate vast panoramas of the universe. Through concentration, consciousness magnifies a part of the Whole in order to produce in the microcosm a true rendering of the eternal beauty of the Macrocosm. In the process of focalization, we learn to discern the myriad facets of creation. Then, taking in the wonder of it all, we expand (diffuse) our consciousness from one glory to another, until at last we are able to move in the direction God intended."[22]

Man's progress in Spirit and in Matter can be plotted on a graph as a sine wave, a series of rising and falling curves. The upward sweep is the ascending (involuting) spiral, which man uses to gather the energies of the Spirit, and the downward sweep is the descending (evoluting) spiral, which he uses to anchor in Matter through the Law of Correspondences the potential of his gathering.

People say that there are ups and downs to Life. In reality, Life *is* a series of cycles, each one composed of an ascending and a descending spiral. These cycles govern every facet of man's life as well as his soul development. When man masters the Law of Cycles, he becomes the master of himself and of his world. Through the Law of Cycles, man is ever transcending

FIGURE 13: Graph of Man's Ascending Consciousness

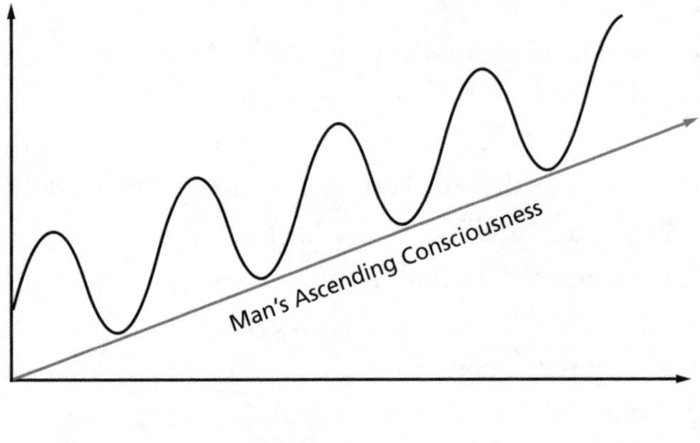

The peaks represent contact with Spirit for the purpose of anchoring form in Spirit. The valleys represent involvement in Matter for the purpose of anchoring Spirit in form. The ups and downs are actually the ins and outs of man's consciousness, the giving and the receiving, the active and the passive.

his former state, for each spiral is the bending of the bow for a greater mark of attainment.

Patterns in the Heavens and Patterns in the Earth

By the Law of Correspondences implemented through the Law of Cycles, the patterns made in the heavens are fulfilled in the patterns made in the earth. Both man and the universe were created by correspondence to the archetypal pattern of the Logos—and the Word was sent forth and the Word became flesh. The very act of creation fulfills the Law of Correspondences, for neither God nor man can create without first having an idea in mind to which their creation must correspond.

When the LORD desires to extend a portion of his consciousness into individual manifestation, he seals the pattern of individualization within an electronic circle of his identity called the I AM Presence. This pattern becomes the focal point for the magnetization of the Causal Body around the Divine Monad as it journeys through the spheres of the Great Central Sun. * Subsequently, the same pattern is stamped upon the soul and the etheric body as these pass through the spheres of individualization in the Causal Body. As this process takes place, the life pattern is anchored in the 144 chakras. (This process will be explained in more detail in the next chapter.) The pattern of the Image Most Holy locked within his being enables man to relate to his divinity; without it he would have nothing in common with his Maker.

By cosmic decree all planes manifesting below the level of the I AM Presence must correspond to the archetypal pattern

---

* This process is described in chapter 4, "Hierarchy," of book 3 in the Climb the Highest Mountain series, *The Masters and the Spiritual Path.*

held in the forcefield of the Christ Self. This Mediator for the interaction of the Law of Correspondences between the Divine Self and the human self focuses the immaculate concept of the life pattern at the nexus of the figure eight, which is assimilated by the soul and the four lower bodies as the regeneration of positive and negative spirals through the chakras takes place.

The qualification of the sacred fire through the chakras according to the Law of Cycles is the key to the implementation of the Law of Correspondences. As Saint Germain has explained to students of alchemy:

"Like crystal beads descending upon a crystal thread, the energies of the creative essence of Life descend into the chalice of consciousness. Neither halting nor delaying in their appointed course, they continue to fall into the repository of man's being. Here they create a buildup for good or for ill as each iota of universal energy passes through the recording nexus and is imprinted with the fiat of creation.

"The fiat reflects the intent of the will of the individual monad. When the fiat is withheld, there is an idling of the great cosmic furnace as the talent of the descending chaliced moment is rejected by the consciousness and becomes an opportunity lost. Where there is no qualification, no fiat of intent, the energy retains only the God-identification of the talent without the stamp of individualization; and thus it falls into the coffers of the lifestream's record without having received so much as an erg of qualification.

"The creative process, then, is of little significance to the individual who does not recognize the mandate to create; for by his nonrecognition, he forfeits his God-given prerogative. As a result of man's neglect of his responsibility, the fiat of God was given that is recorded in the Book of Revelation, 'Thou art neither cold nor hot: I would thou wert cold or hot.

So then because thou art lukewarm, and neither cold nor hot,
I will spew thee out of my mouth.'[23]

"The fiat to create must be heeded, but let us pray God
that men heed well the sovereign responsibility that Life has
given them, to create after the pattern of the divine seed! Well
might they emulate the Elder Gods of the race and the Royal
Priesthood of the Order of Melchizedek in their creative
endeavors, that they might convey upon the energy-chain of
Life that peculiar and fascinating aspect of cosmic genius that
is the nature of the eternal God."[24]

When man superimposes the human consciousness of
imperfection upon the positive and negative spirals of energy
flowing through his chakras, he is forcing the sacred fire into
patterns that are unnatural. While his energy is thus imprisoned in imperfect forms, it is impossible for man to fulfill
the Law of Correspondences in his being. He can outpicture
only disintegration and death, because his energy flows in the
patterns of negation that he himself has created. By this
unfortunate misuse of free will, man subverts the natural
tendency of the Light to follow the patterns of the Alpha and
Omega spirals released from his own Causal Body.

Through the misqualification of positive Alpha spirals, man
sustains evil in form. Through the misqualification of negative
Omega spirals, man is consumed by his own evil momentums.
Thus, until the patterns of the human consciousness are
broken and the Alpha and Omega energies are freed to flow in
the natural spirals of the Christ, man himself is not free.

The "Negative" Spiral

Some question has arisen concerning the fact that we refer
to a downhill trend or a momentum of decay as a *negative*
spiral. We shall clarify. Both God and man are required to use

the clockwise spiral in order to create. Whether man chooses to create Good or Evil, he must use this pattern; for unless the energy-monad passes through the planes of fire, air, water and earth, and unless it receives in succession the frequencies of the twelve houses, creation cannot come forth.

Man has been given free will within the limitations of time, space and energy allotment. Within the bounds of these cycles, God does not interfere with man's creations. When man therefore chooses to create Evil, he is practicing black magic; when he chooses to create Good, he is practicing white magic. Both practices require the use of the clockwise spiral to create form and the clockwise figure eight to preserve form. Once the Rituals of Creation and Preservation have been completed, the dividing of the way takes place: the form is either sublimated (spiritualized) via the counterclockwise figure eight (if it is made in the image of the Christ and sealed in the perfect polarity of the Alpha and Omega spirals) or it is voided via the counterclockwise spiral (if it is made after the images of the Antichrist and sealed in the imperfect polarity of duality).

The cycles of man's creations are limited by his own time-space-energy opportunity. Whatever man creates can be preserved only so long before the Law requires that it be either immortalized or voided; for the Almighty will not suffer his energies to be crucified in unholy concepts, nor will he allow them to be used to sustain imperfect forms. Such abuse of the sacred fire is the abomination of desolation standing in the holy place where it ought not.[25]

Those who have used the positive spirals and figure-eight patterns to realize the beauty and perfection of higher spheres will find at the end of their cycle of opportunity that their creations will be immortalized via the counterclockwise figure-eight pattern. Those who have not will find at the end of their cycle that their creations will be voided via the counterclockwise spiral.

It is the nature of the white-fire core to polarize to perfection—and to reject the imperfect patterns superimposed upon it by man. The violent reactions in the nature kingdom are examples of the *expulsion* of mankind's discord and impurity by the electrons and the elementals themselves. The unwinding of human habit patterns in man and in nature, then, is accomplished by means of the negative spiral. Nature abhors a vacuum of evil. Therefore, when the so-called half-life of evil is spent, the positive spiral and figure eight used to create and sustain it collapse into a negative spiral and the disintegration ritual ensues. This is the unwinding of the coils of mortification—as the grave clothes were unwound from the body of Lazarus.[26]

When speaking of "negative" or evil conditions within man's consciousness, we refer to them as negative spirals. The reader should understand the two uses of the word *negative:* (1) In its purest sense, *negative* refers to the feminine, yin or Omega aspect of the creation. In the strictest use of the word, the term *negative spiral* refers to (a) a counterclockwise spiral through which disintegration takes place or (b) a counterclockwise figure eight through which sublimation takes place. (2) The term *negative spiral* has also come to mean misqualified energy or evil in a state of decay, because the feminine spiral is the last stage of the manifestation of evil once the positive spiral and the clockwise figure eight have collapsed into a negative spiral for the purpose of disintegration.

When man allows his energies to flow into the creation and preservation of discordant thoughts, feelings and acts, he can expect that disease, old age and death will follow when the cycle of the negative spiral takes over; for all that is aligned with evil momentums will follow the disintegration ritual prescribed by cosmic law.

The only way in which man can avoid the disintegration cycle is to invoke the sacred fire to spiritualize the energies of his entire consciousness, being and world. When the violet fire is passed through his imperfect creations, the patterns are transmuted, the Image of the Christ is restored, and the pure forms ascend into his Causal Body via the counterclockwise figure-eight pattern. The Ritual of Sublimation is the practical alternative to the disintegration cycle provided by God as a way out for unascended man, bound by his own misqualified energies and their negative spirals.

When man invokes the sacred fire according to the Law of Cycles, the sedimentation of centuries of his own misqualified substance is removed and the crystal etching of his cosmic blueprint is uncovered. As a mandala of perfection, the archetypal pattern then acts as a magnet to draw the energies of the Presence into the four lower bodies, where the Image of the Christ is destined to be born in man. Through the application of the Law of Cycles, man can break down his human momentums and build up his divine momentums, thereby becoming all that God intended him to be.

Those who are emerging from bad habits of living may at first take the new wine—the pure Alpha and Omega energies —and put it into the old bottles of their human momentums. However, beginning students on the Path should not allow themselves to be discouraged if the tremendous influx of Light from on high—released as the result of their newfound devotion to the Christ—activates momentums of carnal desire through the misqualification of energy in the lower chakras. Rest assured that in the soul who has surrendered totally, the Light *will* consume the "mist-qualifications" as well as those human momentums that impede the natural flow of the Alpha and Omega spirals. If the student is dauntless in his determination, "holding fast to the good,"[27] the enduring and the true, the momentums of these patterns will be broken, and the energy will be reversed as the descending and ascending spirals fulfill in him their preordained destiny according to the Law of Correspondences. Then he will know a freedom and a joy never dreamed possible in his former state.

The Fiat of Perfection

Through centuries of binding habit, man has come to believe that he corresponds to imperfection; alas, he has made imperfection the law of his being and he has thereby become a law unto himself. But Alpha, the Great Beginning, has spoken from the Great Central Sun:

"It is my will to exalt in you a sense of the perfectionment of your mission.

"There are those in all walks of life on this planetary body who know not of my existence, and it troubles me not, in one sense of the word, but it is of concern solely because of my love. For were they to know of my existence, I could give them greater peace. Were they to attune with me, I could bestow upon them more blessedness, more of the treasures of heaven.

"I am gazing upon the records of thy lifestreams, O blessed ones. I witness the miracle of thy being. By fingers of living fire, I am probing thy destiny. That which has been lacks much. That which thou shalt be is thy hope. I manifest no scorn for thee, for thou art children of my own longing. Thy misfortune is my own. I am identified in the bond of our love. Though it has escaped the senses of men, it has never escaped me. I roll back the very substance of the universe. I push through akasha. I part the veil. I enfold thee in my radiance.

"The sentinels of Light that guard the pathway of my words and energy take each release and step it down. These sentinels of Light are straining, beloved ones, to hold back the

flood tide. I tell you this that you may realize the expansion
that is to be.

"I cannot deceive you, O my children. I cannot say unto
you, 'Ye are the fullness of God'—save it manifest in you.
Your Presence is my Presence. Your externals are your own
creation. These are becoming. These are being burnished.
These are being tried by the sacred fire. These are being tried
by the fire that trieth every man's work of what sort it is.[28] The
molding power of the God flame within thee is not puny; it is
mighty."

Speaking to Omega, his consort, Alpha then said: "They
[the inhabitants of this planet] are the children of our heart,
wanderers on the periphery of Life's experience; but I perceive
in the radiant akashic record before me their immergence into
the Sun of Even Pressure at the center of the planetary body*
and their emergence and progression in the planetary chain
through the cycles of beloved Helios and Vesta, the shattering
of the bonds that have bound them to Terra and their release
in the ritual of the ascension. I perceive for them the climbing
of the ladder that leads toward service in our kingdom without
end.

"Here stand, in the heart of their individualized God
Presence, future Solar Logoi. Here stand those who shall ensoul systems of worlds. How can they fear! How can their
destiny keep from them itself! What manner of truth is this?
What false expression has captivated their minds and hearts?
Then let it cease to be in the outer octaves of expression, and
let the governing authorities of all the Hierarchies issue the
necessary fiats. Let it be done!"[29]

With God all things are possible.[30] Man can form new
habits to make his life correspond to perfection, and he can

---

* the white-fire core, the central sun of the earth

rejoice as each spiral of imperfection is unwound and replaced with a spiral of perfection. The habits of the human self have no real tie to his true nature; but the habits of the Christ Self are natural to his consciousness, for they correspond to the original design of his lifestream as envisioned by his Creator and deposited within his innermost being through the 144 chakras.

In the next chapter, we shall see how the Law of Correspondences exacts the purification of the planes of Spirit and Matter through the chakras, for they are seeds of Light, energy cycles, frequency spirals that correspond to the patterns of the Causal Body. By the Law of Attraction, the chakras magnetize the energy from the Presence, which descends into the four lower bodies to outpicture the Image of the Christ according to the Law of Correspondences. As the energies flowing through the chakras are qualified by the seven rays according to the Law of Cycles, the balance of the Christ consciousness appears within the heart and regulates the release of Light as Above in the Presence, so below in the planes of Spirit and Matter focused in the being of man. The lower self becomes congruent with the Christ, and the Christ becomes congruent with the I AM Presence. At this point, man transcends himself in God, and God transcends himself in man.

The Law of Transcendence

Prior to his ascension, Confucius pointed out to his students the operation of the Law of Cycles, which implements the Law of Transcendence. Standing on the bank of a river, he said, "Everything flows on and on like this river, without pause, day and night."[31]

Our knowledge of the laws governing cycles should teach us to regard the transitory as a section of a spiral, the necessary function of the cycle as it passes through time and space. The world in which we live is seen, then, as a point of reference for the Law of Transcendence—not as an end in itself, but as part of the moving stream that, when properly directed, carries the soul to the fulfillment of her eternal destiny.

Our spirits should be tethered, then, not to that which is in a state of flux, but to the laws that enable us to control the flux. For by the application of these laws, we can transcend the finite slice of the spiral and fashion within this changing whirl an immortal identity that shall become fixed as the Northern Star, even as it, too, moves on in the ever-transcending cycles of universal progression.

The Taoist circle, the T'ai Chi Tu (as it was known by neo-Confucian cosmologists), symbolizes the Law of Transcendence, also referred to as the Law of Positive Change. This circle of life is divided by an "S" figure, called the ridgepole, into two equal parts, one white and the other black. The whalelike forms thus created each have an "eye" in the center of the "head" and appear to be pursuing one another. This "Diagram of the Supreme Ultimate" illustrates how through movement the yang principle of the Deity is produced. When the cycle of movement is complete, quiescence, the yin principle of the Deity, is born (out of the "tail" of the white "whale"). Again, when the cycle of quiescence is complete, movement is reborn (out of the "tail" of the black "whale"). Thus movement and quiescence, the active and the passive aspects of nature, eternally give rise to one another.

The white "eye" within the black "whale" symbolizes the soul who has descended into Matter, who is pursuing the Light; whereas the black "eye" in the center of the white "whale" symbolizes the soul who has won her permanent identity in Spirit. Eventually, the Light (Spirit) will swallow up

FIGURE 14: The T'ai Chi Tu:
Diagram of the Supreme Ultimate

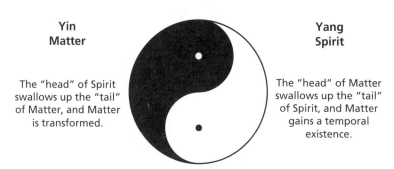

Yin
Matter

The "head" of Spirit
swallows up the "tail"
of Matter, and Matter
is transformed.

Yang
Spirit

The "head" of Matter
swallows up the "tail"
of Spirit, and Matter
gains a temporal
existence.

The ridgepole represents the oneness from
which the male and female principles, the
positive and negative, the yang and yin of
creation emerge.

the darkness (Matter) as the serpent swallows its tail; even so, the darkness (Matter) gains a temporary existence by swallowing up the Light (Spirit).

The ridgepole represents the oneness from which the male and female principles, the positive and negative, the yang and yin of creation emerge. These have also been called the firm and the yielding.

By the interaction of the Alpha (yang) and Omega (yin) energies of Life, creation comes forth and cycles are initiated. Being found in the likeness of the Father-Mother God, the creation produces after its kind: cycles of energy produce other cycles of energy, and all things continue in a state of flow. Thus, transformation and transcendence are the fulfillment of the Law of Cycles—whirls without end, which Confucius observed in the flow of a river.

The balanced interchange of the energies of the descending and ascending spirals in man—of the crystal cord and the caduceus—whereby Spirit becomes Matter and Matter becomes Spirit, simultaneously produces the manifestation of the

divine polarity of the Father-Mother God; and then the ritual
of the fullness of Christ-wisdom, Christ-love and Christ-power
is born. When the Law of Cycles is fulfilled in man, he is
found wearing the wedding garment and he is bidden to the
marriage feast—the union of the lower self with the Higher
Self is performed by the Christ.

Transcendence, then, is the Law of Life. It is the progression of cosmos, of suns, stars and galaxies, embracing
greater and greater measures of Divinity as being flows with
the patterns of the descending and ascending[32] spirals, the
outbreathing and the inbreathing of God's consciousness. The
opportunity for man to transcend his current level of
achievement originates in the transcendent nature of his
Creator. Even the Supreme Monad, the Almighty One, is
continually transcending himself according to the Law of
Cycles; and if it were not so, transcendence would not exist as
an opportunity for the creation.

Vesta gives us a glimpse of the opportunity for transcendence that the Solar Lords periodically release to step up
the spirals in the microcosm that they may become congruent
with the spirals in the Macrocosm:

"The solar rings are being activated to beam forth to the
earth, even through the physical sun, a new outpouring of
infinite grace. The effect of the step-up in the radiation
patterns of our Sun to the planets of this system will be to
shorten the days of man's travail, if he will but accept the
proffered gift. When limitation is cast aside and the limitless
Light of God is perceived, then intelligence is no longer
tethered to the old matrices of human reason, but creates
instead new patterns of expansion that lead to the abundant
Life."[33]

The "solar rings" of which the Sun Mother speaks are
spirals of God's consciousness that infire the universe with

love, wisdom and power and draw the creation higher and higher into an expanding spiral of perfection that is without end.

Thus, the Law of Cycles governs cosmos. God himself involutes: drawing his energies within the center of Macrocosmic manifestation, like "a fire infolding itself," the full potential of his Being is concentrated within the white-fire core of the Great Central Sun. All of the cycles that are to be outpictured throughout universes unborn are there, compressed, spiral within spiral, wheel within wheel, atomic energies imploding Light, which explode at the moment of the Great Command to give birth to a star, a sun or a universe. And so God evolutes, and that which was once the dot within the center of the circle becomes the circumference of the Macrocosm.

No one can achieve in the Macrocosmic sphere of Being that which he has not first attained within the microcosmic core of his identity. In moments of meditation, man must return to the white-fire core that is his spiritual potential—his Life and his only hope for immortality. Withdrawing from all sense consciousness, he must recede into the nucleus of his being as an involuting sun. Moving within in a counterclockwise spiral,* he feels himself before the white-fire ball within the flaming center of his heart. Here all is stillness, a sea of flame, a kernel of Light within the center of the Center. Here in the Holy of Holies man gathers strength for the new day.

To this end you may use the following meditation technique to prepare your consciousness for the inflow of purity, which must be invoked daily if it is to be sustained.

---

* He uses the ritual of disintegration not for the purpose of self-annihilation but for self-realization through "de-integrating" himself from the world.

White-Fire Ball Meditation

Begin by placing your attention upon the Chart of Your Divine Self (facing page 88). When you are at peace and in harmony with all life, center your consciousness in the white-fire core of Being, which you may visualize as a small white ball at the base of the threefold flame within your heart. Withdraw your senses from their perceptions of the world— your ties to other persons, your thoughts of outer things—for only by so doing can you draw your total being into the white-fire ball.

Become first the ball and then the flame within the center of the ball. Picture yourself within the ball, rising up the shaft of the crystal cord to the center of your Christ Self-awareness. Tarry here and absorb the radiance of the pure love, pure wisdom and pure power focused in the threefold flame of your Christ Self. Retaining the vision of yourself within the white-fire ball, continue up the shaft of the crystal cord to the center of the Divine Monad, the threefold flame in the heart of your own I AM Presence.

Feel yourself becoming one with God until you are no longer consciously defined apart from his Being but are aware only of your Self in God, as God. Bask in the bliss of reunion and realize that here in the Holy of Holies you are experiencing a fragment of that which will one day come to you through the ritual of the ascension.

After some moments, feel yourself returning slowly down the shaft of the crystal cord. Concentrating both your God Self-awareness and your Christ Self-awareness within the white-fire ball, descend to the point of contact in form, the threefold flame within your heart. Realize that here in the chalice of the four lower bodies you are anchoring the potential of the Father, the Son and the Holy Spirit.

As long as you remain in the consciousness of the Flame of Life, you have the authority to command—and life will obey. God will speak through you, the Word (the Christ) will go forth and the Spirit will fulfill your decree. Therefore, conscious of the dominion of the Trinity, in humble reverence for the Presence of the Three-in-One, give this prayer for purity:

In the name of my own beloved mighty I AM Presence and Holy Christ Self, beloved Jesus the Christ and the Holy Spirit, I humbly invoke the flame of God's purity:

Open the door to purity!
Open the door to purity!
Let the breezes blow and trumpet purity
Over the sea and over the land:
Let men understand
The voice of Cosmic Christ command!

I come to open wide the way
That men without fear may ever say:
I AM the purity of God
I AM the purity of love
I AM the purity of joy
I AM the purity of grace
I AM the purity of hope
I AM the purity of faith
And all that God can make of joy
    and grace combined!

Lord, I AM worthy of thy purity! I would have thy purity surge through me in a great cosmic burst to remove from the screen of my mind, my thoughts and my feelings every appearance of human vibratory action and all that is impure in substance, thought or feeling.

Replace all that right now with the fullness of the Mind of Christ and the Mind of God, the manifest power of the resurrection spirit and the ascension flame, that I may enter into the Holy of Holies of my being and find the power of transmutation taking place to free me forever from all discord that has ever manifested in my world.

I AM purity in action here, I AM God's purity established forever, and the stream of Light from the very heart of God that embodies all of his purity is flowing through me and establishing round about me the power of invincible cosmic purity which can never be requalified by the human.

Here I AM; take me, O God of Purity. Assimilate me and use me in the matrices of release for the mankind of earth. Let me not only invoke purity for myself, but also let me invoke purity for every part of Life. Let me not only invoke purity for my family, but also for all the family of God neath the canopy of heaven.

I thank thee and I accept this manifest right here and now with full power as the purity and authority of thy words spoken through me to produce the instantaneous manifestation of thy cosmic purity in my four lower bodies, intensifying hourly and accelerating those bodies until they attain the frequency of the ascension flame!

The Transcendent Nature of God

Because man's being is patterned after the infinite cycles, it must follow the Law of Cycles. Until he experiences the white-fire core and knows himself as Spirit's essence—as the mist—he cannot fulfill the evolutionary process that takes place on the periphery of the sphere in the crystallization of the mist.

The Masters have shown us that although linear patterns correspond with life in a form sense, eternity is made up of recurrent, never-ending cycles. These cycles, or energy-patterns, of which man and the universe are comprised ultimately, become spirals without beginning or ending, wholly constructive and continually ascending. Given these facts, we can draw only one conclusion: Transcendence is the Law of Life, and, in reality, there can be no other.

Imbued with the knowledge of this law, we are no longer startled by the great Truth that even the Divine One, the Almighty Father of us all, is continually transcending himself, spiraling higher and higher into ascending octaves of perfection. This perfection he first involutes within his consciousness and then evolutes into manifestation. And if the Creator himself follows the Law of Cycles, then man must realize that like Father, like son; it is impossible for him to achieve outside of himself that which he has not first attained within. This is the Law of Cycles that Archangel Gabriel has explained to us:

"Blessed ones, do you see that in the radiant plan of God it is necessary for there to be a progressive expansion from the cosmic origin of things back to the very radiant heart of God? This is in order that the pralayas may manifest, that it may come to pass that in the manvantaras, we may send forth the Cosmic Flame to expand and breathe out the universe in accordance with the ancient vedas. Then, after the grand exhalation has been accomplished, we draw all of that which has been created into a cosmic period of nirvanic rest, in order that a more noble and grand breathing-forth may occur as the expanding universe moveth forth in accordance with the holy will of God."[34]

We may not grasp this principle in its entirety with our finite minds, and this is not necessary, but that which we have gleaned helps us to realize that the nature of God is transcendent. And if this be true, then it follows that the nature of man made in his image is also transcendent.

The transcendent teaching of the Christ reveals infinite possibilities for God and man. It destroys the lie of eternal damnation and opens the door of opportunity for repentance and healing. Truly, man can transcend his former state of consciousness. Forsaking the ways of the flesh, he can embrace the way of the Spirit. Verily, by the Law of Transcendence, the promise is fulfilled, "Though your sins be as scarlet, I will make them as white as wool."[35]

"Thy sins be forgiven thee!" is a practical manifestation of the Law of Transcendence as it applies to those evolving from a state of imperfection to one of perfection. Forgiveness is diagrammed as an ascending spiral (having a counterclockwise figure-eight pattern) whereby man transcends his former state and realizes the fiat of the LORD, "Behold, I make all things new."[36]

Since God is ever transcending himself, the patterns in the heavens are without limit, and all can therefore draw upon the Spirit of Universal Creativity to build the kingdom of God on earth. This is Life as it was meant to be; and this is how man can become a co-creator with God even as the promise was made of old to Abraham, "I will multiply thy seed as the stars of the heaven, and as the sand which is upon the sea shore."[37]

Man must never fear progressive change nor should he spurn the opportunity to transcend himself; for when the Spirit of the LORD bids him rise, he may know that by immutable law the spiral of the God flame has gone before him to carve out the very stones of his own fiery destiny: no lonely path that He Himself has not walked, no seas that He has not charted, no rugged cliff that He has not scaled. Everywhere He has left engrams in the crystals of the elements by which man can decipher and unlock the full potential of his transcendent being.

The Revelation of Ezekiel

The prophet Ezekiel, whom the LORD sent to Judah during the Babylonian exile, is considered the father of Judaism and the architect of the new order. Regarding Babylonia as Jehovah's agent for the chastisement of the rebellious children of Israel,[38] Ezekiel accepted the LORD's commission to be "a watchman unto the house of Israel,"[39] to warn both the wicked and the righteous.

Before going forth to proclaim the law of individual responsibility and the practical faith that implements religious zeal through works as well as worship, Ezekiel was prepared and commissioned by the LORD. As he stood on the banks of the Chebar Canal in the land of the ancient Chaldees, c. 592 B.C., "the heavens were opened," and he "saw visions of God ... and the hand of the LORD was there upon him."[40]

And so the prophet wrote, "And I looked, and, behold, a whirlwind came out of the north, a great cloud, and a fire infolding itself, and a brightness was about it, and out of the midst thereof as the colour of amber, out of the midst of the fire."[41]

The whirlwind was the descending spiral that comes out of the north, out of the Presence of the I AM. The "great cloud" and the "fire infolding itself" were the evoluting and involuting spirals of being that came forth from the white-fire core to coalesce form in Spirit and in Matter. The "brightness" was the manifestation of the imploding/exploding Christ consciousness. In the midst thereof was the seed, not of the serpent's egg, but of the Divine Manchild, which he describes as having the color of amber. This brilliant focus was the golden-pink glow ray, the love-wisdom of the Father-Mother God sent by the Solar Logoi, Helios and Vesta, to fulfill the mandate of creation.

Having thus appeared, the LORD of Hosts proceeded to bless Ezekiel with one of the most sublime visions ever to be witnessed by unascended man. Through it he unfolded the mystery of Life—the individualization of the God flame—and he answered the question of the Psalmist, "What is man that Thou art mindful of him?"[42] He showed him the Law of Cycles in operation in the microcosm of his being; and by this larger view of life, he gave Ezekiel, his chosen one, the courage to fulfill his mission as the watchman of the LORD. The interpretation of the account that follows (from Ezekiel 1) will make plain the glory that he described:

> *Also out of the midst thereof came the likeness of four living creatures. And this was their appearance; they had the likeness of a man.*

Ezekiel witnessed the descent into form of the Alpha and Omega spirals and their individualization in the square of the Four Cosmic Forces that forms the base of the Pyramid of Christed Being. The "living creatures," as we shall see, provide the archetypal pattern for the four lower bodies of man.

The prophet took care to note:

> *And their feet were straight feet; and the sole of their feet was like the sole of a calf's foot: and they sparkled like the colour of burnished brass.*

The "straight feet" symbolize the descent of the Alpha and Omega stars, the positive and negative polarities of Spirit's energies, descending into Matter and their distribution through the four lower bodies. The calf's foot has a cloven hoof, which indicates that within each of the positive and negative spirals there is a plus and a minus spin. The feet "sparkled like the colour of burnished brass" because in the perfect balance of the divine polarity, the brilliance of the Christ appears.

Ezekiel's description of the four lower bodies and the meshing of their frequencies is superb:

> *And every one had four faces, and every one had four wings.*
>
> *And they had the hands of a man under their wings on their four sides; and they four had their faces and their wings ... and their wings were stretched upward; two wings of every one were joined one to another, and two covered their bodies.*

The wings symbolize the connecting spirals, each wing having its own unique electronic charge (see chart of "Frequencies of Individualization" through Hierarchy, figure 15), that join the four lower bodies through the planes of earth, air, fire and water at the four cardinal points on the circumference of the circle.

The "hands of a man under their wings on their four sides" symbolize the precipitation into form of the will of God, the activating principle of Life. The hand of God extends to the hand of man the means to make the manifestation of the Four Cosmic Forces in Matter congruent with their manifestation in Spirit. Thus, the two wings that join the creatures together are on the cardinal points of the clock (i.e., 12, 3, 6 and 9); and the two that cover their bodies are on the lines between the cardinal points (i.e., 1, 2, 4, 5, 7, 8, 10 and 11). The frequency of these "covering" spirals establishes the forcefields of transition between the cardinal points, preceding the stepping-down action that occurs on the 12, 3, 6 and 9 o'clock lines.

The symbology of the faces reflects the depth of the ancient wisdom made known to the prophet:

FIGURE 15: Frequencies of Individualization through Hierarchy

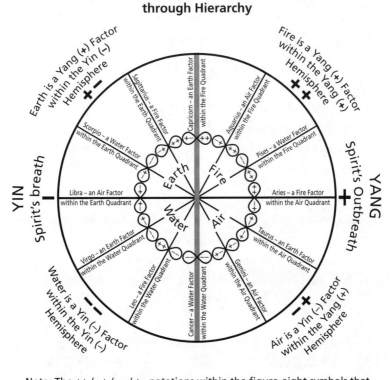

Note: The ++ / —+ / — / +— notations within the figure-eight symbols that form the central ring are to be read from the center of the circle. As indicated around the outer circle, ++ stands for fire, —+ for air, — for water, and +— for earth. These notations are a visual representation of the information recorded on the line of the clock that bisects the figure eight. For example, "Libra, an air factor…" shows —+ in the corresponding half of the figure eight, and "… within the earth quadrant" shows +—.

As for the likeness of their faces, they four had the face of a man, and the face of a lion, on the right side: and they four had the face of an ox on the left side; they four also had the face of an eagle.

The four faces on the living creatures symbolize the four elements anchored within each of the four lower bodies. The face of the man relates to the fire element, anchoring the image of the Christ Self in the etheric body. The face of the lion relates to the water element, focusing the potential of God-control within the emotional body. The face of the ox relates to the earth element, tying into the physical body the devotion and strength of the Higher Self. The face of the eagle relates to the air element, drawing the intelligence of the Mind of God through the mental body.

And they went every one straight forward: whither the Spirit was to go, they went; and they turned not when they went.

The symmetry of the four lower bodies, designed after the archetypal pattern of the Divine Manchild, responds to the Spirit, the I AM Presence, and turns neither to the right nor to the left of the pure crystal stream of the water of the River of Life. The geometric square upon which the City Foursquare is builded seals the energies of the four lower bodies in the frequencies of the Four Cosmic Forces. The perfect pattern of the square is man's great defense against misqualification from within and without.

As for the likeness of the living creatures, their appearance was like burning coals of fire, and like the appearance of lamps: it went up and down among the living creatures; and the fire was bright, and out of the fire went forth lightning.

In this manner the LORD revealed to Ezekiel the action of the sacred fire in man, the ascending energies of the caduceus and the descending Light from the I AM Presence over the crystal cord distributed through the heart chalice and released to the 144 points of Light in the being of man through the seven major chakras and the seven major subchakras.*

---

* The chakras and the subchakras are described in the next chapter.

And the living creatures ran and returned as the appearance of a flash of lightning.

The relationship of the four lower bodies to the Divine Monad is comparable to that of the whirling electrons to the nucleus. In a perfected being, the electrons are in a state of flow, (i.e., the energies that sustain form are continually descending and ascending from the heart of the Presence to the creation in Matter). Ezekiel actually saw the electrons as they "ran and returned" from God to man, producing the Song of the Atom, the perfect balance of God in man and man in God.

Now as I beheld the living creatures, behold one wheel upon the earth by the living creatures, with his four faces.

The appearance of the wheels and their work was like unto the colour of a beryl: and they four had one likeness: and their appearance and their work was as it were a wheel in the middle of a wheel.

The "one wheel upon the earth by the living creatures" is the symbol that prior to man's ascension appears in the base of the Pyramid in place of the negative spiral that formed his electronic belt. During the initiation of the transfiguration, man is actually standing in the center of the wheel that focuses the pattern of the cone of fire that rises from the base of the Pyramid midst the swirling pillars of the threefold flame that now envelop his form.

This symbol of man's victory is a cross section of the action of the masculine and feminine rays of the sacred fire in man. The inner wheel shows the masculine action, the energies of God descending from the Presence over the crystal cord, and the outer wheel shows the feminine action, the energies of the Holy Spirit rising from the base of the spine via the caduceus. Jesus referred to these dual functions when he said,

FIGURE 16: Yang and Yin Phases of Cycles

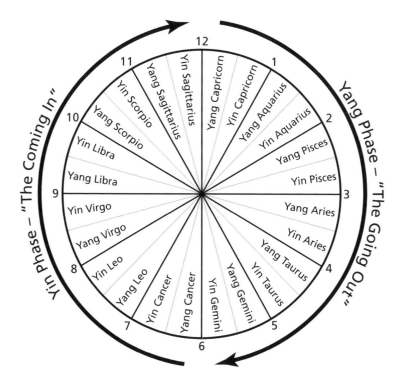

The first half of any cycle is the Alpha / Yang / + phase,
the second half the Omega / Yin / – phase.
Twelve to six on the clock is therefore the Alpha phase, and each
subdivision of the clock in turn has its own Alpha and Omega phases.

"I AM the vine, ye are the branches."[43] We shall first examine
the inner wheel—the vine; then we shall examine the outer
wheel—the branches.

When the Spirit of Life comes forth from the I AM
Presence, it appears as a ray of Light descending from the
Heart of the Sun to the heart of the son, entering the physical
body through the soft spot in the cranium. This ray is composed of two six-pointed stars, the Alpha and Omega spirals
of Spirit's thrust into Matter. The two stars of this inner
wheel, one having the plus (or clockwise) spin and the other

FIGURE 17: The Alpha and Omega Stars in the Inner Wheel

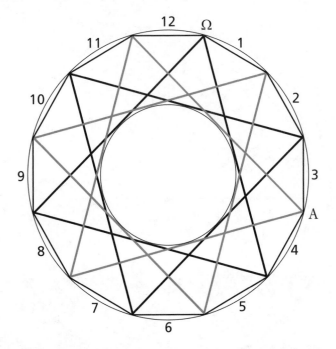

The Alpha star, having its northern point at the 3:30 line (in the Aries-Yin cycle) contains the fire (plus) and the air (minus) triangles. The Omega star, having its northern point at the 12:30 line (in the Capricorn-Yin cycle) contains the earth (plus) and the water (minus) triangles.
There are thirty-six intersection points of the lines of these two stars.

the minus (or counterclockwise) spin, rotate in opposite directions to form the evoluting and involuting spirals that spring up as the threefold flame of the Christ within the heart flame.

The Alpha star, having its northern point at the 3:30 line (in the Aries-Yin cycle) contains the fire (plus) and the air (minus) triangles. The Omega star, having its northern point at the 12:30 line (in the Capricorn-Yin cycle) contains the earth (plus) and the water (minus) triangles. Although balanced within itself in the positive and negative polarity of Alpha and Omega, this descending action of the sacred fire imparts a positive (masculine) charge to the seven major chakras as the

FIGURE 18: The Alpha and Omega Stars in the Outer Wheel

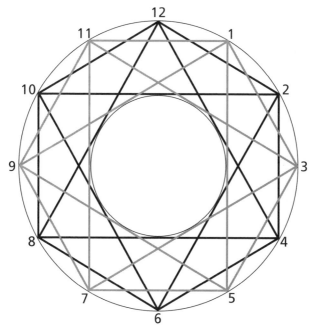

The Alpha and Omega stars within the negative spiral are each
framed by a hexagon. There are eighty-four intersection points
of the lines of these two stars.

energies are distributed through the threefold flame within
the heart.

*The appearance of the wheels and their work was
like unto the colour of a beryl: and they four had one
likeness: and their appearance and their work was as it
were a wheel in the middle of a wheel.*

When we examine the outer wheel, which diagrams the
feminine action of the sacred fire in man, the "branches" of
the rising caduceus, we see that the Alpha and Omega stars
within this negative spiral are each framed by a hexagon.
Whereas the dodecagon holds the pattern for the masculine
impetus of the crystal cord in the inner wheel, the hexagons

frame the feminine impetus of the Holy Spirit magnetized by the Seed Atom. As we consider the mystery of the heavenly and earthly patterns, we remember that the 12 o'clock line marks the beginning of the yang, or going out phase of each cycle, whereas the yin, or return, phase commences at the 6 o'clock line as the monad revolves around the Hub of Being. These numbers are not only positions on the clock, but they are also keys to the precipitation of the Christ consciousness through the union of the masculine and feminine action that occurs each time one revolution or cycle is completed.

Ezekiel's comment that "their work was like unto the colour of a beryl" gives us another clue to the hexagon mystery. The beryl molecule ($Be_3Al_2Si_6O_{18}$) occurs in yellow, pink, white, green and blue-green *hexagonal* prisms.* During the vision, the Prophet's faculties were raised to levels beyond the ordinary; the akashic record shows that his ability to perceive macrocosmic patterns and energies within a microcosmic forcefield included an awareness of atomic structures. Ezekiel's simile was scientific beyond his time; it was intended to serve as a vital key for those who would later interpret the vision, the account of which was written in code in order that it might be preserved intact for centuries, even while it remained hidden from the profane.

The reference to the *colour* of beryl provides us with another key. On the outer wheel, the Omega star, which contains the earth (plus) and the water (minus) triangles, intersects the circle on the 12, 4, 8 and 2, 6, 10 lines. The Alpha star, which contains the fire (plus) and air (minus) triangles, intersects the circle on the 11, 3, 7 and 1, 5, 9 lines. The rays that hold the focus for the caduceus pattern and the precipitation of the Christ consciousness within the chakras coalesce

---

* Yellow beryl is known as heliodor, pink as morganite, white as goshenite, green as emerald, and blue-green as aquamarine.

FIGURE 19: The Threefold Flame

When the descending masculine ray and the ascending feminine ray
unite in the heart chalice, the mist of both rays becomes crystallized in
the threefold flame. This flame has three "plumes" that embody the
three primary attributes of God and that correspond to the Trinity.
The blue plume (on your left) embodies God's power and corresponds
to the Father. The yellow plume (in the center) embodies God's wisdom
and corresponds to the Son. The pink plume (on your right)
embodies God's love and corresponds to the Holy Spirit.

on the *six* points of each hexagon (which are the *twelve* lines
of the clock) and in the center of the circle in the following
order: the blue (or blue-green) beryl ray at the 12 and 3
o'clock lines; the green beryl ray at the 6 and 9 o'clock lines;
the pink beryl ray at the 10, 4, 7 and 1 o'clock lines; and the
white beryl ray as the dot in the center focusing the potential
of the Seed Atom in the outer wheel and that of the white-fire
core in the inner wheel. The "Chart of the Crystallization of
the Mist" (figure 20) gives the plus and minus spins of the
triangles that form the plus and minus stars of the positive
action in the inner wheel and the negative action in the outer
wheel.

FIGURE 20: The Crystallization of the Mist

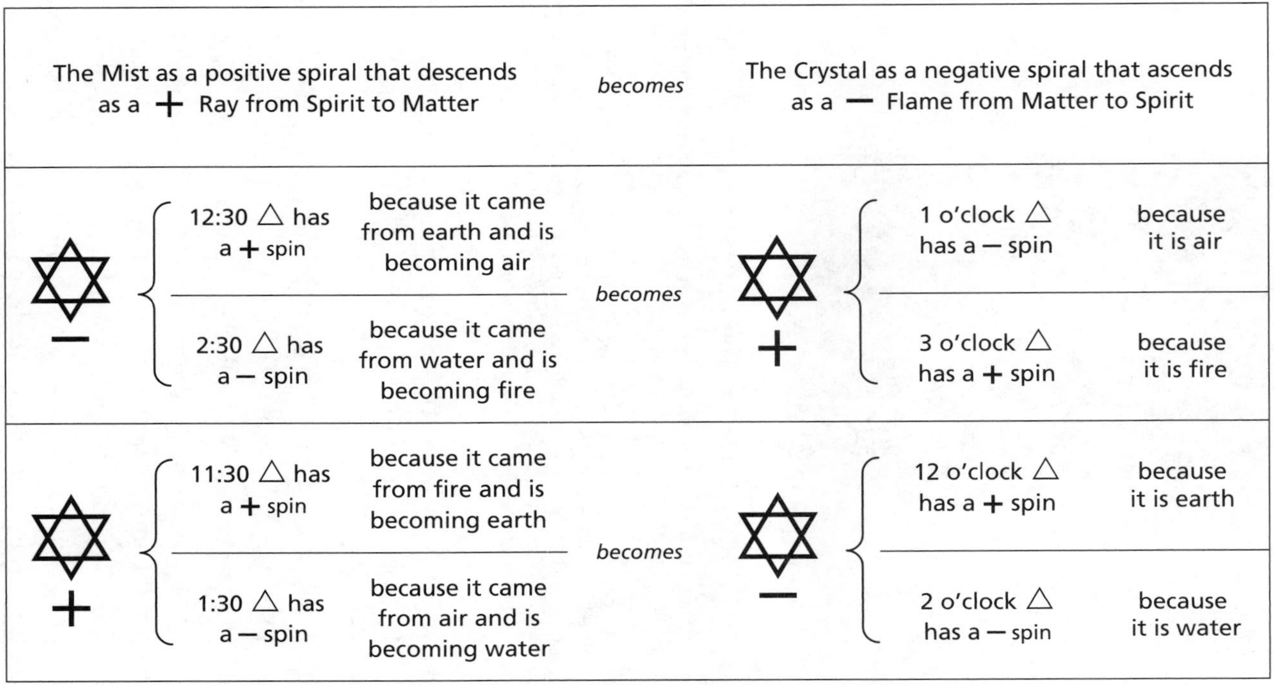

The Mist as a positive spiral that descends as a **+** Ray from Spirit to Matter

becomes

The Crystal as a negative spiral that ascends as a **—** Flame from Matter to Spirit

12:30 △ has a + spin — because it came from earth and is becoming air

2:30 △ has a — spin — because it came from water and is becoming fire

becomes

1 o'clock △ has a — spin — because it is air

3 o'clock △ has a + spin — because it is fire

11:30 △ has a + spin — because it came from fire and is becoming earth

1:30 △ has a — spin — because it came from air and is becoming water

becomes

12 o'clock △ has a + spin — because it is earth

2 o'clock △ has a — spin — because it is water

The positioning of the triangles of the inner-wheel stars on the midpoint between the lines of the clock (11:30, 12:30, 1:30, etc.) signifies that the energies of the inner spiral are not yet crystallized, for crystallization always occurs on the *twelve* lines of the clock. When the descending masculine ray and the ascending feminine ray unite in the heart chalice, the mist of both rays becomes crystallized in the threefold flame. Although the energies of the crystal cord and the caduceus unite in all the chakras, the flame "ignites" only within the plane of Spirit-Fire and Matter-Fire (or the heart). (A diagram of the planes of Spirit and Matter is included in chapter 3.)

It is essential that we pause to realize that the mist also came forth from the crystal, the crystal that is manifesting in the plane of Matter in the heart of the Great Central Sun referred to as the City Foursquare. Here the crystallization of the mist is at a much higher frequency, a more refined plane of consciousness than the crystallization of the mist in the plane of Matter in which mankind is presently evolving. Nevertheless, we must understand Life as a series of spirals in which the crystal becomes the mist, the mist becomes the crystal, and the crystal becomes the mist ad infinitum. With each transformation, there is a greater expansion of Light and a corresponding release of the Christ consciousness. It is through this process that man becomes more of God and God becomes more of man.

Therefore, we can understand that the triangle intersecting the 12:30 line represents the mist that is emerging from crystallization in the higher plane of air (Aquarius) on the 1:00 o'clock line, and is moving toward crystallization in the lower plane of earth (Capricorn) on the 12 o'clock line. The triangle intersecting the 11:30 line represents the mist that is emerging from crystallization in the higher plane of fire (Sagittarius) on the 11 o'clock line and is moving toward crystallization in the

FIGURE 21: The Rotation of the Alpha and Omega Stars in the Inner Wheel

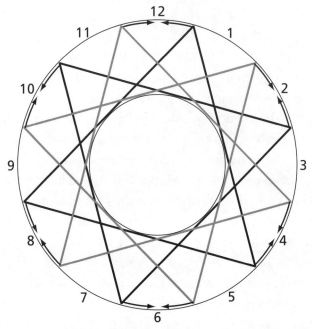

As the Alpha and Omega stars spin in opposite directions in both the inner and outer wheels, the points of their triangles converge on the twelve points of the clock.

lower plane of earth (Capricorn) on the 12 o'clock line.

As the Alpha and Omega stars spin in opposite directions in both the inner and outer wheels, the points of their triangles converge on the twelve points of the clock. The fusion of the energies of the Father-Mother God that occurs when the stars are thus congruent both within and without results in the crystallization of the threefold flame within the heart. Although both the masculine and feminine rays are required for crystallization, symbolically the descending ray (Spirit) represents the mist and the ascending ray (Matter) represents the crystal.

The stars within the inner circle, then, are shown in a state of transition; they are the mist that must pass through the white-fire core to become the crystal. Because they are between rays or houses (the houses of the Twelve Solar Hierarchies), they are white. The stars within the outer circle are shown in a state of crystallization; they, therefore, assume the colors of the beryl ray.

The threefold flame within the heart is the fire that activates the 144 chakras that focus the 144 planes of the Divine Consciousness in the being of man. The thirty-six (thirty-three plus three) plus intersections within the central mandala (in the inner wheel), which occur wherever two lines cross, represent the thirty-three initiations that the soul must pass by the balanced action of the threefold flame before his ascension.

These initiations are marked by the thirty-three vertebrae in the spinal ladder,* each vertebra representing a plane of attainment as well as a note in the cosmic scale. The number thirty-six indicates that the initiations of the Twelve Hierarchies of the Sun must be passed through the attainment of self-mastery under the rays of power, wisdom and love, the plumes of the threefold flame.

The additional twelve intersections occurring at the twelve points of the dodecagon make a total of forty-eight initiations in the inner wheel, signifying that under the aegis of the masculine ray, each of the four lower bodies must also focus the mastery of the Christ consciousness through the Twelve Hierarchies of the Sun.

On the outer wheel there are eighty-four intersections focusing the initiations administered by the Solar Hierarchies in conjunction with the Elohim, the Archangels and the Chohans of the Rays, who teach the mastery of the twelve

---

* Seven in the cervical region; twelve in the dorsal region; five in the lumbar region; five in the sacral region; and four in the coccygeal region, making a total of thirty-three.

planes of solar consciousness through the qualification of the Christly virtues of the seven rays through the seven chakras (7 x 12 = 84).

The rituals of initiation are also wheels within wheels, spirals within spirals, triangles within stars, which build the positive and negative momentums of attainment that frame the antahkarana of the soul's ascending consciousness. Upon the loom of victory, the delicate filigree of the Deathless Solar Body is woven.

Our investigations concerning the chakras, the caduceus, the Kundalini and the flow patterns of the masculine and feminine rays are fully discussed and diagrammed in the next chapter. In this chapter the interpretation of the vision must suffice that the modern student of mysticism might find in the revelation given to Ezekiel the foundation of the Ascended Masters' teachings on cosmic law.

> *As for their rings, they were so high that they were dreadful; and their rings were full of eyes round about them four.*
> *And when the living creatures went, the wheels went by them: and when the living creatures were lifted up from the earth, the wheels were lifted up.*

The "rings" of the creatures are the solar rings, the aura that surrounds the manifestation of the Christ, in both the microcosm and the Macrocosm. The solar fires were so immense that Ezekiel describes them as "dreadful." Once he became accustomed to their brilliance, he saw that they were "full of eyes."

The rings seal each of the four lower bodies within their respective planes; likewise each of the bodies has its own auric forcefield and emanation. Each solar ring contains the focuses of the seven chakras and is a unique mandala governed by the release of Light through each chakra. The intersecting lines in the designs of the mandalas are points for the expansion of the Christ consciousness, for whenever two or more rays or spirals converge, there is a burst of energy. In such wise, flames are born and cycles are initiated. (These heavenly fireworks may take place in the aura of the Divine Manchild as well as in the stars and suns and spiral nebulae within a galaxy.) These focuses of imploding/exploding Light appeared to Ezekiel as "eyes," and indeed the 144 chakras are orbs whereby God perceives and holds contact with His body in the microcosm, and man perceives and holds contact with the Body of God in the Macrocosm. They are wheels of the Deity focusing his divinity in man.

> *Whithersoever the spirit was to go, they went, thither was their spirit to go; and the wheels were lifted up over against them: for the spirit of the living creature was in the wheels.*

"The Spirit [the I AM Presence] of the living creature was in the wheels." The image of the Christ, the divine blueprint of the lifestream, is stamped upon the chakras. Thus, by the Law of Attraction, the four lower bodies follow the Spirit, for they are made after the likeness of the Spirit: they are tethered to one another through the mandalas of the chakras and through the "wheels" or solar rings.

> *And the likeness of the firmament upon the heads of the living creature was as the colour of the terrible crystal, stretched forth over their heads above.*

The "terrible crystal" over the heads of the creatures signifies that the mandala for the crown chakra, the thousand-petaled lotus, is congruent with the chakra through the Lodestone of the Presence. The caduceus action completed and

**FIGURE 22: The Vision of Ezekiel,
as Interpreted in the Bear Bible, 1569**

{ the Seed Atom raised, the fire of the sun rests upon the heads
   of the four lower bodies.

> *And when they went, I heard the noise of their
> wings, like the noise of great waters, as the voice of the
> Almighty, the voice of speech, as the noise of an host:
> when they stood, they let down their wings.*

And there was a voice from the firmament that was over their heads, when they stood, and had let down their wings.

The descending and ascending currents within the wings (pinions of Light or spirals of frequency connecting the links between the planes of consciousness) creates a friction in the atmosphere that is like the noise of great waters, the voice of the Almighty. Standing indicates a rising action, an integration into the Christ consciousness, whereby there is no longer any need for the "creatures" to be connected by their wings, for they are one in the center of the white-fire core. The voice from the firmament is the voice of the Real Self, the Christed Being of man.

And above the firmament that was over their heads was the likeness of a throne, as the appearance of a sapphire stone: and upon the likeness of the throne was the likeness as the appearance of a man above upon it.

The sapphire-blue throne is the seat of the Almighty, the I AM Presence. The blue symbolizes the Fatherhood of God that is individualized in the God Presence.

And I saw as the colour of amber, as the appearance of fire round about within it, from the appearance of his loins even upward, and from the appearance of his loins even downward, I saw as it were the appearance of fire, and it had brightness round about.

As the appearance of the bow that is in the cloud in the day of rain, so was the appearance of the brightness round about. This was the appearance of the likeness of the glory of the LORD. And when I saw it, I fell upon my face, and I heard a voice of one that spake.

In this the most sublime moment of his vision, Ezekiel saw the Causal Body of man as a rainbow surrounding the I AM Presence, whose brilliance was blazing in all directions. The color of amber suggests the likeness of the Presence to the sun. Thus, over twenty-five centuries ago Ezekiel perceived through the Law of Cycles the vision of the I AM Presence, the Christ Self and the four lower bodies of man, much as these are represented in the Chart of Your Divine Self (facing page 88).

Having reached the plane of the Most High God, his consciousness congruent with his Presence ("the Spirit entered into me when he spake unto me"), Ezekiel heard the voice of the Almighty speak to him saying, "Son of man, I send thee to the children of Israel ..."

The Prophet received his vital commission from the LORD, who has never given unto man a commandment without also providing him with the wisdom and strength to obey it. Ezekiel went forth with many signs and visions following this initial revelation of his own Divine Selfhood.

The individualization of the God flame in the Presence appears in the likeness of a man because it is this aspect of the Creator's identity that he maintains in Spirit as a focus for the manifestation of himself in Matter. The I AM Presence provides the electronic pattern for the Christ Self and the four lower bodies. This does not mean that God maintains the appearance of a man in all planes of his Self Conscious–awareness, for God is universal love—omnipresent, omniscient and omnipotent. He manifests with and without form or correlation to finite patterns.

Those who worship him as the *Impersonal Impersonality* (+ +) describe Him as a powerful all-pervading Spirit proscribed by neither form nor dimension. They affirm that "God is a Spirit: and they that worship him must worship him in spirit and in truth."[44]

FIGURE 23: Four Personalities of God

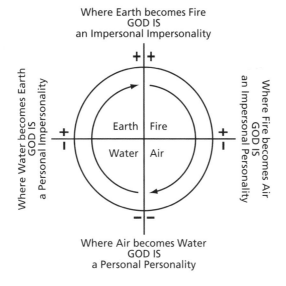

Where Earth becomes Fire
GOD IS
an Impersonal Impersonality

Where Earth becomes Earth
GOD IS
a Personal Impersonality

Where Fire becomes Air
GOD IS
an Impersonal Personality

Earth | Fire

Water | Air

Where Air becomes Water
GOD IS
a Personal Personality

Those who worship him as the *Personal Personality* (– –) see His face smiling down upon them, reflected in the pool of their being even as Adam "... heard the voice of the LORD God walking in the garden in the cool of the day."[45]

Those who worship him as the *Impersonal Personality* (+ –) recognize God as both the mist and the crystal. They see him first as the essence of Universal Spirit and then as Spirit merging with its individualization. They proclaim with Job, "I have heard of thee by the hearing of the ear: but now mine eye seeth thee."[46]

Those who see him as the *Personal Impersonality* (– +) wait upon the LORD in the supreme hope that "yet in my flesh shall I see God."[47] They know that the body is the temple of the living God and that if he is indeed the God of the universe, the waters of his mind must ultimately become the Word made flesh. They know that even as the earth is the LORD's and the fullness thereof, so the LORD *is* the fullness of the earth made manifest.*

* The reader may find it valuable to further study this section on Ezekiel's revelation after reading the section on the chakras and the caduceus in chapter 2.

Man Is a Spiral

It must be understood that man himself is a spiral, a spiral of such magnificent wonder and complexity as to defy over-simplification, a spiral of symmetry so pure as to challenge the complexities imagined by mortals.

Man is a spiral that begins as a dot in the center of God's Being, evolves to the periphery, and returns once again to the center. Man is an hourglass. In the nexus of his consciousness, eternity becomes time and space, cycles cross, the finite meets the Infinite, and the triangles of God ▽ (descending into mani-festation) and man △ (ascending into deification) converge in the star of destiny ✡. Here the fires of Spirit and Matter unite in the brilliance of the Christ—as Above, so below!

Man is a figure eight of macrocosmic-microcosmic won-der, spiraling within and without. He is the coordinate of the Hub of Creation. In him whirls are born, through him whirls transcending whirls pursue the receding Sun. Escaping the finite, he merges with the Infinite. Man is the never-ending spiral through which God himself evolves. He is the focal point for the configurations of cosmic law in Matter and in Spirit.

The four lower bodies of man are actually four descending spirals that merge as one great spiral. His etheric and mental bodies are the positive and negative spirals (triangles) of the Alpha Star, or the masculine ray; his physical and emotional bodies are the positive and negative spirals (triangles) of the Omega Star, or the feminine ray.

The four spirals are necessary for all alchemical precipi-tation in man and nature. Without these building blocks, the Ritual of Creation cannot take place. The spirals are actually transformers for the converting of energy from the planes of Spirit to the planes of Matter. The velocity of the spirals is governed by the Four Cosmic Forces to which they corre-spond, and it is through the integration of these forcefields that the transition between Spirit and Matter is made.

The four lower bodies of man are the spirals that brace the four sides of the Pyramid of his being. Not to be confused with the soul consciousness evolving through them or with the Real Identity of man, these wheels within wheels provide the vehicles for the Flame that burns within the four quadrants of the Cosmic Cube, forming the base of the Pyramid where heaven and earth converge to transcend each other through the Law of Cycles.

The Law of Cycles governs the release of energy from God to man, from the very Hub of His Self Conscious–awareness to the farthest outpost of His Self-realization in form. The cycles of man's incarnations, his opportunities for self-mastery, the journey of the soul through the spheres of the Causal Body— all are governed by cosmic law—the Law of Cycles. Life is a series of spirals intended to advance the soul progressively higher in the evolutionary chain. Within the giant spiral that constitutes man's total being and life plan there are many lesser cycles, the velocity and the rhythm of each being governed by its relation to the whole.

A day is the cycle of a flame as it spirals through the twelve houses of the sun in the yin and yang phases. A week, a month or a year is a cycle of the rays of the Causal Body governed by the interaction of the energies of the white-fire core of the earth and the sun as these in turn relate to other heavenly bodies. These cycles are going on simultaneously within man, and they order his world both within and without. Even modern scientists are beginning to recognize the circadian rhythm of man's biological clock.

Just as there are cycles governing the existence of atoms and cells whose duration is measured in microseconds, so there are cycles that are fulfilled annually or within a decade or a century. The movement of cosmic cycles through man is governed by the electronic pattern of his I AM Presence, by the ranges of his solar consciousness, and by his personal karma invoked by his free will—all of which determine the frequency of his spirals and their correspondence with the spirals of the Macrocosm.

There is room for an expansion of solar faculties (the potential of the soul born of the Sun) in every individualized focus of the God flame. And this expansion, implemented through the ascending spiral, is a most wonderful part of the divine plan. As a child in kindergarten often looks upon sixth-grade pupils with envy and admiration, as a senior in high school gazes upon college freshmen with longing eyes, so unascended disciples may view their Ascended Masters with awe and with the holy expectancy that they, too, might walk in the footsteps of the Elect of God. It is altogether natural that man should aspire beyond his present level, for as Saint Germain once said:

"In a very real sense, the Mind of God is in the mind of man; and the mind of man is in the Mind of God. The Mind of God provides the link between the mind of man and Himself; and, as a smaller computer is able to exercise itself by tying into a larger computer, so man takes on the skeins of destiny and finds that in time, by the exercise of God-ideas, he becomes a godly man."[48]

The possibilities for progress are always stimulating to the individual; for the keen, fresh, youthful desire to learn, to serve and to "come up higher" is ingrained within the soul fashioned after the nature of God, who is eternally expanding his Spirit. The being and person of man, in reality, is a fragment of the God flame, a delightful spark that may continually gather in the spiral of self more of the divine fire and thus expand the diameter of being as he becomes more and more charged with the limitless Light of the Great Source.

Shortening the Days for the Elect

Jesus prophesied that "the days would be shortened for the elect."[49] Some will ask, "How can this be? Who can alter the universal cycles? (in man?)" With God all things are possible. Using the plumb line of Truth, the Great Geometer can bisect the cycles of man's travail when man himself elects to accelerate the spirals of his being by intensifying the action of the sacred fire within them. Since time and space are spirals of energy in motion, the greater the motion of energy man can control within his forcefield, qualified with Christly virtue, the greater the quotient of time and space he will have in his command—compressed within a given cycle of opportunity.

Man should first learn to magnetize the violet fire within the center of his spirals, for it is necessary to remove the dross that impedes the flow of Light around the coils of his consciousness. Then he is free to invoke the seven rays in order to step up the action of the Light in his four lower bodies. The cycles of his initiations, of the balancing of his karma, of his divine plan, and even of his ascension, can be accelerated as he hallows the space within his spirals with the Presence of the Holy Spirit, whose power enables him to accomplish in a few years that which would otherwise take several embodiments to fulfill. Witness the ministry of Jesus and Paul. The days were indeed shortened for these elect men of God.

What happens to those who fail to invoke the sacred fire and, in addition, fail to pass the tests of life that come to rich and poor alike with cyclic regularity? The answer is obvious— the days of working out their karma are lengthened. Instead of rising when their spiral comes full circle, they either stay on the same old treadmill, repeating the round over and over again, or they go down in a negative spiral of disintegration without ever having fulfilled the cycles of creation, preservation and sublimation.

The following decree may be used to invoke the violet
flame for the clearing of the chakras and the four lower bodies:

> Radiant spiral violet flame,
>> Descend, now blaze through me;
> Radiant spiral violet flame,
>> Set free, set free, set free!
>
> Radiant violet flame, O come,
>> Drive and blaze thy Light through me;
> Radiant violet flame, O come,
>> Reveal God's power for all to see;
> Radiant violet flame, O come,
>> Awake the earth and set it free.
>
> Radiance of the violet flame,
>> Explode and boil through me;
> Radiance of the violet flame,
>> Expand for all to see;
> Radiance of the violet flame,
>> Establish Mercy's outpost here;
> Radiance of the violet flame,
>> Come, transmute now all fear.

Tests come to all daily. Saint Paul said, "I die daily,"[50]
signifying that the ego must be surrendered for the sake of the
Christ Self. Each successive spiral is an initiation, an opportunity to choose between the ego and the Christ. There are
tests that come once in a lifetime, and upon one man's
decision the lives of millions may depend, most especially his
own. The right decision made at the right moment can be the
key to victory. Saint Germain said he won his ascension by
making two million right decisions! And how well we know
that the wrong decision of a single lifestream has caused continents to fall and worlds to crumble.

Such tests cannot be taken over the next day or even in the

next embodiment, for the Law requires that history come full cycle—perhaps an energy spiral of ten thousand years will be spent ere the moment of opportunity come again. Had the Master Jesus failed his supreme test, the cycles of the planet and of the entire solar system would have been interrupted, and the cosmic timetable for the manifest action of the Christ consciousness would have been set back indefinitely. We all have our cosmic moments—moments in eternity when the stage is set, the lights are lowered, the curtain rises, and there we stand alone—the whole world waiting for a star to be born.

One never knows when one's failure, seemingly insignificant, will affect the progress of a planet or a star; and in the final analysis, is not the value of one life ruined by a bad example or a wrong decision as great as that of a sun or a galaxy? Wherever we walk, we leave the momentum of our spiral as footprints in the sand, footprints that millions will follow, their spirals conforming to our own. Although our life may at times seem useless and not even worth living, we must count the value of the many souls who will follow after us. For them we keep on keeping on; for if we break the cycle, there will be no spiral for them to follow—and they will surely lose their way. This is the meaning of Hierarchy.

As man intensifies the velocity of his spirals, he intensifies his awareness of eternity, for all that stands between man, who is fixed at a point in time and space, and his Real Identity, which is posited in eternity, is the momentum flowing through his spirals, the whirlwind action of the sacred fire that is governed by the Law of Cycles.

The greater man's attainment of cosmic consciousness, the greater will be the diameter of his spirals, for his spirals are a function of his aura. The auric emanations of a lifestream are measured by the quality and intensity of the spirals he releases through his chakras. The spirals of a Buddha easily envelop a planet; the spirals of the Elohim contain galaxies; and those of the Solar Logoi form the antahkarana of the universe. By contrast, undeveloped lifestreams may not even retain their daily allotment of Light, employing God's energy in a common way, a provincial way simply to dominate others on the planet with their often foggy mundane consciousness.

And so, the world is submerged in a sea of energy in motion. Here are spirals of Light within spirals of Darkness, forcefields of Good interpenetrating forcefields of Evil, linear concepts reinforcing grids of mediocrity. These are the wheat and the tares that can only be separated at the time of harvest. While men sleep, the enemy plants the bad seed in their subconscious minds; and when they awaken, their thoughts and feelings are no longer their own because their energies follow the pattern of the serpent's egg. These seeds are multiplied to produce the lowest common denominator of the mass consciousness. But only when they come full cycle can they be gathered into bundles and burned in the sacred fire.

The negative spiral that forms man's electronic belt is bound to countermand the fiats of Light cycling from his heart chakra. Like coils wrapped around a magnet, the spirals of negation lodged within the electronic belt must be methodically unwound until the force of wrong habit is broken. Using the Ritual of Sublimation to reverse the trends of one's negative spirals can be an altogether joyous experience if one can impersonalize the impressions of evil stamped upon his consciousness at the same time that he personalizes the Image of the Christ by making it his own.

According to the Law of Correspondences, the lower is intended to conform to the higher manifestation of God; but often mankind's momentums of evil are so great that the children of God, having failed to invoke the cycles of their own divinity, conform instead to the negative spirals of the world.

Alas, the magnet of their Light is not sufficient to counter-balance the vortices of Darkness, and when they are confronted by the tests of life, they are found wanting. These may invoke the Electronic Presence of any Ascended or Cosmic Being to be anchored within their forcefield twenty-four hours a day until they attain their victory over all outer conditions.

When an Ascended Master superimposes his Electronic Presence upon the aura of an unascended devotee, his auric coils are expanded by the principle of cosmic magnetization. By the Law of Correspondences, the threefold flame and the spirals of the Ascended Master's consciousness impel all lesser expressions within the devotee to conform to the perfection of the Master's Presence. This dispensation is one among many opportunities available to those who know the Law and are following the Path in the order of Hierarchy.[51]

Those who answer the call to come apart and be separate from worldly spirals must be prepared to overcome the dragon of worldly desire. And once its back is broken, the children of God dance around the Divine Magnet—the Lodestone of the Presence—and their spirals are magnetized to the pillar of the Christ.

Let all understand that the laws governing the flow of energy and the alchemical process are unerring in both the spiritual and the physical universe. As we have seen, these same laws govern the cycles of man's ascension. This is the science of salvation that is essential to man's overcoming. Not the doctrine that he believes, but the laws that he practices determine man's salvation. Man's predestination to immortality, then, is conditional upon his application of cosmic laws; and his sovereign will allows him to choose to embrace his destiny, which was preordained in the beginning by the mathematics of the Master Logician.

The Dark Cycle

The Great Divine Director once said, "The recalcitrance of human nature has been building over centuries of neglect of spiritual opportunity by embodied mankind. Their gaze has been focused outwardly; and whereas all life around them moves on in cyclic fashion, as falling leaves descend to the ground and die, they do not seem to reach out readily, eagerly and hopefully to discover the inner purposes of Life.... In the main, man is moving forward and spiraling upward; but some, by reason of karmic violations, move upward only to fall backward into careless decay."[52]

The world and its spirals of discord have invoked the pied piper who is luring young and old alike down the highway of spiritual oblivion. We who recognize the destructive trends of our time must stand up and be counted with the stalwart men and women of the past who resisted even to the death the negative correspondences of their times and thereby secured the foundations of an age to come.

It is unthinkable that the torch that has been passed to this generation should be trampled underfoot by the hordes of night, that the fires of the heart should be snuffed out in a superstate where God is denied and where man becomes the instrument to wage wars for material conquest and the slaughter of the innocents. It is unthinkable that the churches of the world should turn against the prophets and the saints, challenging the Laws of God in the name of reform—social, moral or political. But all of this and more, foretold by Mary at Fátima, will surely come to pass if man fails to cry halt to the perversions of cyclic law that are rampant on a world scale. It will come to pass if mankind continues to distort the Image of the Christ and to invert the Light of the Presence.

As in the last days of the cities of the plain when the LORD said, "Because the cry of Sodom and Gomorrah is great, and because their sin is very grievous, I will go down now, and see whether they have done altogether according to the cry of it, which is come unto me; and if not, I will know,"[53] so in 1969 the Brotherhood sent seven cosmic investigators to observe the problems of the times, to make a systematic inquiry, and then to report their findings and recommendations to the Lords of Karma and to the Solar Hierarchies.

These Great Beings of Light simulated physical bodies; they dressed according to the fashions of the times and moved in the large cities and places of the greatest concentration of karma and human effluvia. In a like manner the LORD sent his angels to investigate Sodom before the final decree was given for its destruction. These "angels" sojourned at the house of Lot, and they were taken for ordinary men by the mob that thronged without. On the basis of their report—they did not find ten righteous men in Sodom—the city was destroyed.[54]

Thus it has always been prior to cataclysm, and so it is today. The coming of the cosmic investigators is an indication of the advancing cycle. By this we know that time is short; their appearance marks the end of an age. Even now the planetary body is passing through what is known as a dark cycle, brought about as the result of mankind's collective failure to challenge the negative spirals that have been mounting for centuries.

We had been warned of an impending dark cycle in a number of dictations, one given as early as October 1967, by the God Meru who said that unless mankind turned from their violations, the sign of the dark cycle would begin on January 18, 1969. A number of Cosmic Beings, including the Great Divine Director, voiced their approval of the recommendations of the Solar Lords, for they declared that it was no longer an act of mercy to allow mankind to think that they could flaunt the Law and escape the consequences of their acts. These

Great Beings pointed out that (due to the great mercy of the Law) many were unable to see in the cycle of a given embodiment the return of their karma. Therefore, instead of loving God more for his great love and patience toward them, some grew to despise him, while others became convinced that he did not exist.

As a result of their deliberations, the decree went forth that mankind must bear their karmic burden if they did not reverse their negative momentums and turn to serve the Light by January 18, 1969. The return of their karma had long been held in abeyance by those Intelligences who sought to lead the race into ascending spirals of self-mastery before requiring the balancing of the energies misqualified in ignorance. Now the individual and the race as a whole would be required to stand, face and conquer those abuses of the Law recorded in their electronic belts. This would be a time of great travail, "of weeping and gnashing of teeth"[55] as Jesus said. Hence the term "dark cycle."

On December 31, 1968, in the New Year's message of the Lord of the World, Gautama Buddha petitioned the Lords of Karma for a "half-a-time," another six-month cycle, a final opportunity for mankind "to mend their fences, to prepare their defenses, to turn from materialism to the pathway of peace." The Karmic Board granted the petition of the Lord of the World, postponing the date of reckoning to July 18, 1969, but only on the condition that Israel and the Arab states cease their aggressions. In announcing this action Gautama said, "The warlike manifestations currently being exercised in the Holy Land represent to us the most dangerous single factor that is calculated to plunge mankind headlong into a holocaust of planetary destructivity."[56]

By the month of April in that year, the crisis in the Middle East was still in a deadlock, neither side willing to compromise for the sake of world peace. With global warfare posing a mounting threat, it was the consensus of the Lords of Karma to use mankind's own karma as a means of averting world calamity. They saw that by accelerating the return of karma, they could accelerate the lessons of karma, hoping thereby to bring some measure of sanity to the world community and to forestall mankind's self-annihilation. The karmic hammer fell therefore, and on April 23, 1969, the Dark Cycle began.

Whereas the people of the world had not come to the knowledge of the Truth out of love and gratitude for the Creator, they would now be forced to witness a more rapid return of their own misqualified energies. The impact of these energies was intended to bring about a chastening in the hope that mankind would realize God's infinite power, wisdom and love, together with their own ultimate destiny. Although this would be a time of great hardship for many people, it was hoped by the entire Spirit of the Great White Brotherhood that many would turn from their lethargy to serve the Light; that many would be drawn into the teachings of the Ascended Masters and find their way back to God.

The Masters also know this will be a period of threshing for organized Christianity, where the old churches will enter an era of greater apostasy and deviation from the Reality of the living Christ. Sensitivity training, social reforms, protests and much darkness will in this era become a substitute for Light and the real Christ. The Church will often be used by the Evil One himself as a tool to further divert humanity into the ashes of Sodom and the cults of darkness.

As Vesta said, "Heaven does not wish to convey the doomsday concept to mankind. But again and again the Law of Cycles has proclaimed the end of an era, when the firmness of the Karmic Lords rang clear: 'Stop the actions that spread pain and hurt among men, that fail to reverence Life and opportunity, that are the result of old encrusted concepts based on vicious human greed! Replace all that is darkness by the vibrant Light of Cosmic Omnipresence!' "[57]

On August 17, 1969, the Ascended Master El Morya announced the decree issued by the Karmic Lords pertaining to impending cataclysm, which mankind themselves have invoked by their disobedience:

"The beauty of Reality knocks at the door; the breath of Reality is inbreathed by the hungry soul, and the strength of ten thousand arms is injected into the consciousness. Millions of hearts beat; they are sustained by one breath of His love. Yea, He sustaineth all things; and nothing is sustained without Him. His mercy endureth forever; but the world, in its pallor of ignorance, continues to drink the dregs of the cup of wrath.

"Hence, I come to you to forewarn you this night that the Lords of Karma have also tussled mightily over the fate of the present generation. And now comes forth the decree that signifies to mankind an unknown quantity. But we who have read the record warn that the decree could well signify a minor cataclysm or a series of minor cataclysmic actions—both that which we may term social cataclysm and that which we may term a rebellion of nature—as the elements themselves seek to shrug off the imposition of injustice that men have continually fostered upon nature.

"We say, then, that the world might well tremble; for this decree is an attempt of the hand of God in karmic interaction to bring about the realization, to a world maddened and reeling, that life cannot always continue in a state of degradation or of fraudulent calm. Rather, I say, the Lords of Karma have arisen; the cup of wrath is trembling in their hands, and the world should well take heed.

"Therefore, I, El Morya, borne from the heart of love for the will of God, bring to you the understanding of the Divine

Nature that seeks to purge the earth by the purifying power of the Light, that seeks to produce the fruit of the Divine Image in all, that yearns to wipe away the tears from the eyes of men, but that understands that the karmic juggernaut will roll if mankind will do nothing to stop its onward rush, and in its roll, it will crush many beneath its wheels of piercing Reality.

"They have created it. They have sown it. They shall reap it. We have long sought to stay these actions; but now the Karmic Board has said, 'No longer!' Only a valiant action on the part of mankind or the interference of those who stand above the Karmic Lords can withhold it. Only they can stop the action. And we say this to you that you may be forewarned, that you may understand that the dire disasters that may well occur in the world will be of mankind's own making; they will be of mankind's own doing, a proof of their senseless activity.

"When it comes, as come it must, ere they change not, I say to you, when it comes, pray God that it shall produce good fruit; for we are well aware that chastisement, as well as love, has quickened mankind's perception. We are aware that divine firmness and divine grace, which manifest as a yielding to mankind of the banner of freedom for the individual, also produce after their kind. But the latter is the gift, often, of the former; for many times, out of sternness comes a realization of the Reality of God. And when this comes about, the individual is able to reap the sweet fruit of universal reason.

"And so tonight, to you whom we love, to those who have extended so much hope to the earth, we say to you, fear not for yourselves, 'weep not for yourselves or for your children,'[58] but weep, rather, for the children of the earth who have sown in darkness and who will now reap in darkness. We shall act to spread the Light everywhere, to continue the waving of the banner of the Lord of the East Wind. And this Wind will dry

up the evil oils that men have poured upon the earth that they
might set fire to the earth and burn it.

"We say, let us stay the hand wherever we can, even of
karma. But we understand that all cannot be stayed; and this,
too, is the mercy of God. This, too, is his grace! This, too, is
for the interaction of lives in order that the molding power of
the Spirit may produce such fruit of wholeness and beauty in
the Golden Age, now forming amidst the ashes of confusion,
that the world shall once again hopefully be restored to the
former place, to the excellence of the Divine Image, which we
hold inviolate in the Flame."[59]

Concerning planetary travail Gautama wisely counseled:
"Times of struggle and of darkness are not real, but to those
enmeshed in them they seem so; and the same godly recognition that man can penetrate the veils of illusion and find the
inner way of peace in the most disturbing conditions should
help him to understand that this is obtained not by struggle so
much as by faith. For, if men would cease the struggle for
peace and would simply manifest it, the problems of the world
would vanish.

"We do not seek by platitudes to bind up the wounds of
the world, but we send forth the thrust of our Spirit, envelop-
ing the earth in the Cosmic Christ efforts of our octaves of
Light. You can valiantly assist us in that which we are doing
by maintaining harmony in your feeling world, by refusing to
give acceptance to any condition less than perfection, and by
realizing that the thinking that makes conditions so can always
be directed or even diverted into channels of Wholeness.

"You must never give up or cease from your loving of
humanity, for thus you learn to love your Creator. But greater
wisdom from on high always reveals that there are interacting
responsibilities that are charged to the individual's record. So
many seek to be divested of responsibility. They want to let

someone else act for them. We, as Ascended Beings, act for millions of lifestreams. But we, too, feel that individuals can learn to think and act for themselves. They must, of course, exercise care, study the approved Way, and summon the fire of the soul to produce automatically its perfection in their worlds."[60]

On another occasion the Lord of the First Ray commented on a dictation given by the Ancient of Days concerning the Law of Recurring Cycles and the parable of the talents:

"Sanat Kumara emphasized that those who are not making use of spiritual graces and gifts extended to them will find that which they have being taken from them; and that those who are multiplying their God-given talents will find more given unto them; and that those who pursue selfishness will be thrown into the outer darkness of their own human creation where 'there shall be weeping and gnashing of teeth.'[61]

"The casting of man into outer darkness where his own unhappiness shall cause many to cry 'Let the mountains fall upon us, and let the hills cover us'[62] shall bring about—in the terror of the outer darkness—a greater yearning and more diligent seeking for the Light. The ministering legions of heaven have sometimes felt that the mercy of God has almost seemed to pamper the indignities man has inflicted against His holiness. It has seemed almost as though the universal and infinite love of God in his outpouring of grace has been too indulgent of man and his inharmonies. Actually the time allotted to the span of infinite mercy and grace has not been so long as some might think. For the Law functions according to the accurate Law of Recurring Cycles.

"In past ages these same events occurred; therefore, that which is now happening is but a recurrence of the eternal Law, the wheel having now returned to this mark. I am hopeful, therefore, that those who have understanding will seek to

expand it still further; that those who are not yet skilled in the cosmic laws will with patience and diligence both study and wait for the unfolding of greater Light from on high, as God dispenses his bounties through many hands. As has been said, those whom God loves he chastens.[63] Therefore the chastisement of the outer darkness and the gnashing of teeth is designed to awaken men to the hidden hungers of their souls and the dangers that beset their continual disobedience and defiance of the Law."[64]

Through the inept handling of the Law of Cycles, an age can be lost; whereas through the wise exercise of its precepts, a Golden Age can be forged. Through excellence in the Law and Christly poise, man can save himself and the planet and then move on to higher worlds and conquests. What, indeed, shall it profit a man if he shall gain control of the material world and then shall lose his soul or be cast away?[65]

Let us gird up our total consciousness for the Armageddon that must be fought and won by every man.* Let us determine as never before that we will put all of our energies into the salvation of this planet and its peoples. This noble cause was not given by the mind of man, but by the Mind of the Creator. For it is the only means whereby man can earn the right to come up higher. Victory is a prerequisite to salvation, for victory fulfills the Law of Transcendence.

The downward spirals of life need not continue; they can be challenged; they must be challenged. Let us raise man, and nature will follow. Let us accelerate the soaring cycles of man's consciousness, and the regeneration of true happiness will fill his whirling spirals with the hum of cosmic joy. The night of lost opportunities is far spent and the day of understanding is at hand. The torch has been passed. Let us never let

---

* For an analysis of the inner and outer battle of Armageddon, see chapter 3 of *Paths of Light and Darkness*, book 6 of the Climb the Highest Mountain series.

it go. Let us hold it high that the cycles may produce in our time a valiant victory for us and all time to come. E Pluribus Unum! One giant spiral of victory out of many hearts united in the law of love.

Worlds Ascended

When the dark cycles are reversed in man and the universe, worlds ascend. The laws that govern the ascension of the sons and daughters of God apply to planets, solar systems and galaxies alike. When a sphere has completed its cycle and its evolutions have all ascended, it will have fulfilled its function as a cosmic laboratory for gods in embryo now moved on to other worlds and seeking to conquer there.

This idea may seem devastating to those who call the planet home; but if the Earth is considered in the context of the purpose for which it was manufactured in the great solar laboratories of nature, its duration can be estimated at billions of years. The lifespan of a planet encompasses a scheme so vast as to defy the equations of the mind of man. Thus, to unascended man whose cycles of spiritual evolution provide ample opportunity for his progressive freedom, the earth may well "abide forever."

The immortalizing of a sphere such as our earth or of a cluster of worlds such as our solar system occurs through the gradual etherealization of the planes of earth, air, water and fire via the counterclockwise figure-eight spiral. This takes place as all of the misqualified energies that had ever been sent forth by the evolutions of the planet are transmuted through mankind's invocation of the fires of God's heart by prayer, decree and service. As the lifestreams assigned to the sphere fulfill their individual cycles through the ascension, the energy whirl in which they abide is also accelerated toward that goal.

When 51 percent of the world's karma—the misqualified energy that is the collective responsibility of all who have ever embodied on the planet—is balanced, a golden ball is precipitated around the sphere. This ball is a manifestation of the Christ consciousness of all who have ever attained self-mastery on that world. It is suspended within the Cosmic Cube precipitated by the representatives of the Four Cosmic Forces. Those who hold the balance of the City Foursquare in the four lower bodies of the earth are Oromasis and Diana, Aries and Thor, Neptune and Luara, Virgo and Pelleur. It is their consciousness of the Christ that maintains the flow of the Four Cosmic Forces in nature and that focuses within the Cube the planetary pattern of the ascension.

This ritual of whirls ascending is going on throughout the universe, fulfilling the Law of Transcendence. Beloved Vesta, the Sun Goddess of our solar system, recently spoke on the fiery destiny of the sons and daughters of God as well as of planets:

"Precious hearts of Light, I kneel before the divinity within you. I am humble before the Light and the potential expansion of the Light that God has ordained within you—that you, beloved ones, and your twin flames are destined to become solar hierarchies, gods and goddesses of suns and systems of worlds, for one day you shall stand where we stand in the heart of the Sun. You shall look out upon the universe and see how the radiance of the Light that you have released has been directly responsible for the ascension not only of individuals but also of planetary bodies. For planets do ascend, beloved ones, after they have fulfilled their cosmic destiny: after the four lower bodies of a planet have been purified and its evolutions have all ascended, then the planet, too, ascends into the consciousness of the Christ that preordained it in the beginning.

"And so there are entire solar systems in the ascended state and whose components are expanding together as a mighty chord in this universe. These hold a pattern of perfection that you can invoke to raise your own solar system. You may call for the momentum of the Electronic Forcefield of worlds ascended to be charged into your world unascended and to bring this entire solar system into its God-destiny that was ordained in the Beginning.*

"Do you see, precious hearts of Light, as you contemplate the vast distances of your universe, as you study the stars and think upon the wide reaches of space, can you not adjust your consciousness and feel youself becoming one with the entire galaxy and universe, as planets and stars and spiral nebulae whirl within your forcefield? Do you not understand, then, that this truly is taking place in the microcosm and you are already gods and goddesses of your own systems of worlds?"[66]

Each of the seven root races destined to fulfill their life plan on the planet Earth make a unique contribution to the solar mandala of the planet. This mandala, composed of the multifaceted aspects of the Christ Selves of these lifewaves, is actually the focus of the soul, or the solar consciousness, of the earth. This mandala magnetizes the energies of the Great Central Sun for the precipitation of the divine plan of the earth. The individual Causal Bodies of the evolutions of the earth act as a single giant electrode for the raising of the planetary body.

Appropriately, the thoughtform for 1971, released by the Lord of the World on New Year's Eve, was a large golden ring surrounding the earth while the upper figure in the Chart of Your Divine Self, the I AM Presence and Causal Body, is superimposed over the whole planet.

---

* The combined momentums of the first three root races, who completed their round victoriously on earth, may also be invoked on behalf of those of the 4th, 5th, 6th and 7th root races who have yet to emerge triumphant.

Moving with the Cycles of Life

The Great Divine Director speaks of the importance of moving with the cycles of Life: "There is a cycle to every life and to every life a cycle. There is a coil of energy into which you are born—a coil of energy that, like a flaming fountain of Light, is given by God to buoy up the soul into the arms of the All-Father. This is the coil of Light that is like the wave which when taken at its crest leads on to victory.[67] It is a tide of the Great Central Sun, a tide that is greater than the affairs of men. It is a tide of fiery destiny.

"As you diagram the course of your ascension, you must then take into consideration that all things in heaven and in earth must follow the Law of Cycles. As it is written, 'There is a time to sow and a time to reap, a time to live and a time to die, a time to laugh and a time to weep.'[68] And so the great learned ones have counseled their disciples concerning the cycles of Life.

"The undulating currents of Alpha and Omega represent the positive thrust and the negative return along the line of individual destiny. Many do not succeed in Life because when they ought to be riding at the crest of the wave, they are in the ebb of the tide, and when they ought to be in the gentle enfolding waters, they are farther out to sea.

"It is a question of timing, of rhythm and of moving according to the rhythm of the heartbeat of God. As the yogi times the inbreathing and the outbreathing according to his own pulse, so the devotee of the Brotherhood ought to measure his comings and his goings according to the great cycles of the Great Central Sun....

"And so, then, the key to planning your ascension—and I wish that you would plan your ascension and plan it carefully and look at your calendars on the decades that are coming—[is that] you must see that every high communion, every exalted experience is for the thrust into Matter so that you can transmute karma at these levels of existence, so that you can anchor the fire and thereby earn by initiation the thrust of a new high in the Holy of Holies.

"I trust that I have made this diagram clear and I trust that you will sit down and give consideration to the great highs that you have had in your life. Remember those moments when you have touched the hem of the garment of God's emissaries in your meditation and then tried to remember. What did you do in the succeeding hours? What did you do on the following day or in the following week? Did you not find yourself totally surrounded by circumstances of weight and entanglement and confusion? And perhaps you did not retain your attunement because you did not know the Law of Cycles....

"Now this is a technique that you must use. Knowing full well that you are preparing to plummet into the lower ranges of human consciousness, you do what a bird does when he must do the same. You pull your wings together, you tuck your head in, you garner that energy in a spiral of involution within your heart and you dive.

"You do not leave your wings or your head or your feet out. You do not allow your energy to be dispersed in a large aura, for it is more difficult to control. The more you attenuate Light, the more responsibility you have to be aware of every particle of that Light. This is the difference between being yang and yin, masculine or feminine, concentrated or attenuated.

"Therefore, when you are going in for the test, you take all of that energy, you lock it within the heart, and then no man can take the crown of Life, no man can steal that energy of your life. And so you keep yourself closely knit together, you

go into the fray, you go in for the dip, you make your contact, you release the necessary Light to those evolutions who are waiting to be fed, waiting to be nourished by you, and you ascend again.

"And when you come into the great exalted heights, then you unfold your garments, you open your arms wide. For you are in the presence of the Ascended Hosts once again, and you place your trust in them, you open your chakras, you receive the Light, you garner the Light, and you are ready for the next cycle of the going within....

"Well, now that you know the Law of Cycles, I expect that you shall become experts on the toboggan of life and learn how to go up and down the hills and how to wax those sleds for greater performance, for greater dexterity and speed. For you know a moving target is the most difficult to seize. And therefore, if you will have inertia, let it be the inertia of perpetual motion rather than the inertia of rest unless, of course, that rest be your rest in motion....

"Now precious ones, if you will take these keys, each and every one and use them, I know that you will be more victorious, more alert and therefore more victorious. You will pass greater and greater initiations and therefore earn the opportunity for greater and greater initiations.

"Take, then, your calendar, take note of the upswing and the downswing. Make use of the cosmic tide and you will reach the shore of your divinity."[69]

The Return to the Center

We have seen that it is impossible for man to gain self-mastery while his perspective is confined within patterns of linear thinking; for the human consciousness, failing to see the beginning and the ending of the spiral, becomes caught in the arrested cycle of its own finite sense of existence. East of Eden, where the God consciousness has been dethroned, the cult of material success compensates for the frustrations and fears that plague the carnal mind. Lacking the vision of the total plan, the human competes for recognition in the things of the world, making personal aggrandizement its method of achievement.

Whereas the Christ consciousness was lost with the divine inheritance, the human proceeds to enlarge the ego to develop greater security. Thus it is found to be farther and farther out of phase with the spiral of its own true identity; it is only "as below," not "as Above."

In order to become "as Above," man must learn to shed the snakeskin of the linear consciousness that crawls upon its belly. He must learn to replace it with the spherical consciousness of those who have returned to the center of the Divine Monad—the Ascended Masters and Cosmic Beings who are the embodiment of universal love. Only then will he find his rightful place in the Cosmic Sun; only then will he find relief from the stresses and strains of the outer struggle, the turmoil that always manifests when the four "creatures" (the four lower bodies) are out of alignment with the square within the circle and are thus incapable of functioning as chalices for the Christ consciousness, for the trinity of the threefold flame of Life.

The return to the center of spherical Being through the Law of Cycles reveals Golden-Rule living as the natural order of the universe, for it accomplishes the reciprocal exchange of Light between those who share the burden of Light released at the intersecting lines of the mandala. The interchange of spirals between the Macrocosm and the microcosm is based upon the indispensable scientific principle of doing unto others as you would have them do unto you. Upon this golden law is based the ebb and flow of Light within man's being. As we shall see in our study of the chakras, it is only by reaping and sowing according to love's design that one can permanently survive in a universe that is a cross section of the relentless, ongoing spiral of God's Being.

When man has fulfilled his cosmic destiny according to the Law of Cycles, he is able to realize in the center of the Golden Sun of Illumination that which is Real and that which is unreal. Involuting into the white-fire core, the star that was once man becomes a sphere. Evoluting as a miniature sun of being, his consciousness merges with cosmos.

When the patterns of finite man become congruent with the Infinite Man, the microcosm becomes the Macrocosm. And traveling upon the great cycles of Life, rising on spirals of infinite wisdom, love and power, he experiences unforeseen bursts of comprehension, new ideas of loveliness, and the implementation of his total being in an ecstasy that defies description.

The Point of Peace

As man evolves through the folds of time and space, the key to safe passage through the initiatic tests is harmony and balance. The vicissitudes of life can all be viewed objectively from the balance point in the center of our heart, which is congruent with the center of God's heart. We can move through all cycles and not be removed from this stable point if we but apply this science of cycles.

To illustrate this, visualize an ordinary seesaw in a playground. It is a flat board resting on a central pivot point. As a child mounts on each end of the board, they create a cyclic movement that would look like a sine wave if represented in a graph. But notice that the center of the board, the center of the

FIGURE 24: The Seven Chakras

Scientists and spiritual healers have proven that the body of man is a magnet. All magnets create cycles of positive and negative flow, yet there is always a point of perfect equilibrium between the two polarities. As prana flows through our system, the heart is the point of balance. But the point of perfect harmony is beyond the physical heart—in the secret chamber of the heart. It is from this point of peace and power that we can send forth the auric emanations to heal our personal microcosm and the world outside the boundary of our skin.

cycle, is absolutely stationary. The children can be moving wildly, frantically on the ends, and the center is always balanced and stable.

Thus it is with all cycles, and thus it can be through all of life. This cyclic center in man is the heart chakra, as we see in figure 24.

The body of man is a magnet. This has been proven by scientists and spiritual healers alike. We recall that all magnets create cycles of positive and negative flow. The heart is that point of equilibrium of the flow of prana through our system. There is a place of perfect harmony in the secret chamber of the heart, which is beyond the physical heart, pulsating in cyclic rhythm seventy-two times a minute every day of our lives.

This is why the Masters tell us to go there, to go to this point of balance in our hearts—because there is the point of peace. But it is also the point of power.

Return through the Word

The path of the ascension is the means whereby sons of God preserve an identity as a single cell in the being of Brahma throughout the pralayas and throughout the inhalation and the exhalation of God.

As we noted earlier, in each yuga, man is given specific spiritual tools to assist him in his evolution. It is said that we are presently in a Kali Yuga—a cycle of returning karma, the darkest of all four of the cycles. Sanat Kumara, the Great Guru, assigns forms of communion with God that are befitting the evolutions of man within the yugas.

Sanat Kumara has told us that in this yuga, the key to contacting God is the Science of the Spoken Word. Using this science, practiced by adepts East and West for thousands of years, we can send forth auric emanations from the point of power within the center of our heart to heal our personal microcosm and the world outside the boundary of our skin.

To endure as a cell in the consciousness of God when that God is at perfect rest is to enter with him into the cosmic cycle of nirvana. To do this, one must pass through the nexus of the cycle—the Word.

The eternal Logos is the dot in the center of the circle, the beginning and ending of cycles that are composed of circles, layer upon layer.

In the beginning was Brahman, and the Word was with Brahman, and the Word was with Brahman in the beginning. Therefore, in order to be in Brahman, we must be in the Word. "No man cometh to the Father, but by me."[70] That "me" is the supreme I AM THAT I AM manifest as the Word.

It is a swaddling garment wound around about the earth. The very currents of the earth's surface, the very emanations from its sun center, the Law of Cycles, the comfort flame, the hum just below the level of our own hearing transfer to us this comfort of the cyclic law of the sounding of God's Word.

Life is ongoing, and the Law of Cycles promises us that Life will go on. God's heart will beat on. The wheel of cyclic return will rotate on the spokes of our karmic creations.

By the Law of Cycles, then, we are set upon our courses spiraling through once again the nexus of being, the nexus being the Word itself, the Law of Cycles being the emanation of the Word. As we become congruent with the dot in the center of God's circle, the power is bestowed upon us to imprint the cyclic energies of God with the pattern of our God-oriented idea or desire.

This is the way to return to God as a permanent atom in his Being—through this Word that has incarnated in the Avatars with the cyclic Law of Manifestation. The great Manus, the lawgivers of the ages and of their races, upheld the cycle of the Word whereby all seed going forth from the great Tree of Life might return through the Word as the Law of Cycles.

There is joy in this Law of Cycles. And the joy of this marriage of science and religion is *you* at the nexus of infinity, *you* converging with that living Word.

"A Circle of Spiral"
by Gautama Buddha

Spiral may undulate,
　　　spiral may rise,
　　　　　　or spiral may fall,

But ultimately
　　　the Light within you
　　　　　　must answer the call.

Identity echoes
　　　far over the sea,
　　　　　　It calls unto you
　　　　　　　　and it calls unto me:

Be your own Self,
　　　the God of all Truth—
　　　　　　Live your own life
　　　　　　　　in the youth of real proof.

I AM is Identity
　　　the world to enflame,
　　　　　　the Spirit of God,
　　　　　　　　the gift of his name—

The Wonderful Counselor,
　　　the Prince of all Peace,
　　　　　　by God-registration,
　　　　　　　　Let vanity cease!

Reveal then the hidden
　　　and uphold the right
　　　　　　We view now ahead
　　　　　　　　a release of God's might.

For union must live
in the deeds men will do
That shall stand as real proof
in the hearts of the few—

Who become then the many
as the kingdom reborn
In that day of Christ hope
that blest golden morn.

Sweet Sons of the Father
God's banner uphold—
By thought, word and deed
this Great Law unfold.

To *every thing there is a season,*
        and a time to every purpose under the heaven:
A *time to be born, and a time to die;*
    a time to plant,
    and a time to pluck up that which is planted;
A *time to kill, and a time to heal;*
    a time to break down, and a time to build up;
A *time to weep, and a time to laugh;*
    a time to mourn, and a time to dance;
A *time to cast away stones,*
    and a time to gather stones together;
    a time to embrace,
    and a time to refrain from embracing;
A *time to get, and a time to lose;*
    a time to keep, and a time to cast away;
A *time to rend, and a time to sew;*
    a time to keep silence, and a time to speak;
A *time to love, and a time to hate;*
    a time of war, and a time of peace.
What *profit hath he that worketh*
    in that wherein he laboureth?
I *have seen the travail, which God hath given*
    to the sons of men to be exercised in it.
He *hath made every thing beautiful in his time:*
    also he hath set the world in their heart,
    so that no man can find out the work
    that God maketh from the beginning to the end.

ECCLESIASTES 3

Chapter 2

Planes of Consciousness

If thine eye be single, thy whole body shall be full of light.

MATTHEW

Planes of Consciousness

The Crystal Chalices

COSMIC ENERGY-SPIRALS OF GOD'S consciousness, cascading from the Great Central Sun over the crystal cord, pass through the individualized I AM Presence and the Christ Self, and spring up as a threefold flame fountain within the heart chalice, whence they flow to myriad pools of Light in the being of man. These pools, or radiating centers, called "chakras," are the focus for the distribution of the cosmic energy-spirals to the four lower bodies of man.

We shall also refer to the chakras as crystal chalices, for although they have a whirling action (*chakra* is a Sanskrit word meaning "wheel"), they also function as receptacles for the crystal waters of the River of Life that flows from God to man and from man to God.

The terms "chakra" and "chalice" are used interchangeably because it is important that students develop the "grail consciousness" when meditating upon the centers, even while they visualize the whirling action of the sacred-fire wheels. The centers should, therefore, be thought of first as cups consecrated to contain the pure essence of the Holy Spirit, then as wheels within wheels focusing the power of the Great Central Sun Magnet in the microcosmic world of man.

A "Chart of the Crystal Chalices" (figure 25) is included in this chapter. The first column of this chart gives the English and Sanskrit names for the seven major chalices, which are anchored in the etheric body in a straight line parallel to the spine. The chakras "flower" on the surface of the physical body opposite the organs named in the second column; these organs serve as the focal point in the physical body for the specialized function of each of the chakras. The third column shows the seven rays intended to be released through the chalices and the number of their petals or waves, a factor determined by the ray, the frequency, and the plane in which the chalice is found.

The fourth column shows the perversions of the color rays through the chalices produced by the accumulation of astral substance over the centers; these colors may vary according to the misqualifications released through them. Some clairvoyants have seen these astral colors emanating from the chakras of unascended lifestreams and have erroneously thought them to be the natural emanations of the chalices. Those who wish to verify the colors of the chakras should call for the Electronic Presence of Jesus the Christ to display the cosmic radiance of the chalices as they appear in his Ascended Light Body.

The fifth column lists the seven bodies of man, whose patterns are fulfilled in the planes of Spirit and Matter through the seven chalices. The sixth column lists the seven main subchakras and their colors.

There are 144 chakras in the body of man. We shall not attempt to list the remaining 130 centers; suffice it to say that

FIGURE 25: Crystal Chalices (Chakras) in the Being of Man

Seven Major Chalices	Focus in the Physical Body	Corresponding Color Rays and Number of Petals	Perversions of the Color Rays	Seven Bodies of Man		Seven Main Subchakras and Their Color Rays
Crown *Sahasrara*	Pineal	2nd Ray Yellow 972 Petals	Chartreuse or Orange	I AM Presence	Plane of Spirit	*Lalna* Between the *Ajna* and the Crown Pale Yellow
Third Eye *Ajna*	Pituitary	5th Ray Green 96 Petals	Off-white	Causal Body	Plane of Spirit	
Throat *Vishuddha*	Thyroid	1st Ray Blue 16 Petals	Silver	Etheric		Thymus Left of the Heart Yellow
Heart *Anahata*	Heart	3rd Ray Pink 12 Petals	Dark Gray or Light Orange	Christed Self	Mediator between Spirit and Matter	Spleen Golden Pink
Solar Plexus *Manipura*	Pancreas	6th Ray Purple and Gold 10 Petals	Gray, Maroon	Emotional	Plane of Matter	Hands (2) Yellow with Pink Aura
Seat of the Soul *Svadhishthana*	Ovaries or Testes	7th Ray Violet 6 Petals	Dark Red	Mental	Plane of Matter	
Base of the Spine *Muladhara*	Perineum	4th Ray White 4 Petals	Red and Orange	Physical		Feet (2) Yellow

they are scattered throughout the etheric body as anchoring points for the release of the 144,000 virtues that radiate from the Great Central Sun. Let us turn our attention instead to the vital functions of the seven major crystal chalices.

The chakras serve first as transformers for the stepping down of the frequencies of God's energy and for the release of the Four Cosmic Forces—earth, air, fire and water—in the planes of Spirit and Matter. The seven major chakras are conductors for the flow of energy to the seven subcenters and the remaining 130 chakras, which anchor the Light of God as stars in the firmament of man's being.

In addition, the crystal chalices were designed by God as the open doors through which the seven rays are intended to flow from man's being—lighting his world, weaving the seamless garment and forming the antahkarana between man and man and between man and God.

As crystals, the seven major chalices focus in the etheric body the intricate soul patterns that are to be woven in the mental, emotional and physical vehicles. As cups, they retain the pure white Light that sustains the life pattern in man. Thus, through these various functions that we shall now discuss and diagram, the chakras serve as focal points for the interaction of the cosmic energy-spirals between the Macrocosm and the microcosm.

The Law of Giving and Receiving

Through the chalices, the Law of Giving and Receiving is fulfilled in man. It is the divine intent that man qualify the white Light released from his heart flame through the seven chakras with Christly virtues colored by the seven rays and vibrating in consonance with the eternal Logos.

Simultaneously, man is intended to draw in through the

The Chart of Your Divine Self

chalices the essence of the Holy Spirit (prana), which occurs universally as electronically charged Light particles. Thus the balancing activities of Alpha and Omega (of giving and receiving) are intended to be fulfilled in the outbreathing and the inbreathing of Light through the chalices.

Energy is released from the chalices in positive (clockwise) evolutionary spirals. Energy drawn into the chalices enters in negative (counterclockwise) involutionary spirals. The centrifugal (positive) and centripetal (negative) action that is produced when these dual processes function at maximum efficiency causes the chalices to open like flowers unfolding their petals and to spin like miniature dazzling suns. Sparkling like diamonds as they whirl, the crystals give off an electrical charge that quickens the whole being of man, making him a veritable polestar in the transitory world.

The number of petals (or waves) in each chakra is determined by the ray, the plane and the frequency of the centrifugal and centripetal action of the intertwining plus and minus energies. These factors also produce the basket-weave effect that has been noted in the chalices.

When thus fulfilling their God-intended purposes in illumined man, the chalices are convex. In unillumined man, who still functions as part of the mass consciousness, the chalices are submerged in a sea of astral substance that prevents them from either radiating the Light of the I AM Presence or drawing in the essence of the Holy Spirit for the nourishment of the four lower bodies.

In this state of nonfulfillment, the centers cannot even be called chalices: they are dull and sluggish, silvery instead of crystal, and appear as moons under the sea instead of stars in the firmament. They are concave and their petals are not fully opened.

Subject to the ebb and flow of the tides of human emotion,

and not knowing how to "breathe out" the Light of the Presence nor how to "breathe in" the essence of the Holy Spirit, unillumined man turns to the stimuli of the world to keep his centers and his four lower bodies energized. Misusing the negative spiral in the chakras, he substitutes the sucking in of astral energies for the drawing in of the essence of the Holy Spirit. Misusing the positive spiral, he spews out from his chakras the perversions of the seven rays and the Christly virtues, discoloring his aura and contaminating his planetary home.

Secrets of the Causal Body

Lines of force are sustained as highways of Light between man and his God Presence when man allows the seven rays and their Christly virtues to flow through the crystal chalices.

For example, tracing the golden ray of illumination after it is released through the crown chalice, we see that it circles the earth in a clockwise spiral following the Ritual of Creation. As man qualifies the stream of energy flowing through his crown chakra with the purity of wisdom's ray, it is amplified according to the intensity of his devotion to the flame.

As it circles the earth, this energy-spiral makes a complete cycle through the four lower bodies of the planet, passing through the planes of fire (etheric), air (mental), water (emotional) and earth (physical), gathering through the Law of Attraction energies of like vibration. Then it ascends via the counterclockwise figure-eight pattern according to the Ritual of Sublimation to the second band in the Causal Body—the gold or yellow band, to which it corresponds in color and virtue.

The energies released from the six remaining chakras follow the same rituals of creation and sublimation, circling the earth—cycling through the four planes and then ascending to the Causal Body.

The brilliant emerald-green ray of precipitation is released through the third eye as the vision and vitality of man's abundant creations. The sapphire-blue ray of the will of God is released through the throat chakra as the power of the spoken Word to coalesce in form the blueprint of the life pattern held in the etheric body. The pink ray of divine love is released through the heart chalice as the fire of love that binds the creation through the consciousness of the Christ Self.

The purple-and-gold ray of ministration and service is released through the solar plexus as the flow of peace that weaves the etheric patterns into the emotional body. The violet ray of freedom, transmutation and forgiveness is released through the seat of the soul, anchoring the image of the Christ Mind in the mental body. And the white flame of purity and discipline is released through the base chalice as the creative power of the I AM Presence anchored in the physical body.

The Hub of Life

There is a very special reason why the seven rainbow rays released through the prism of each man's Christ consciousness are distributed through the seven crystal chalices. There is a reason why the color, the frequency and the Christly virtues of these emanations correspond to the seven bands in the Causal Body. In order to understand the laws governing the activities of the seven rays in the seven bodies of man, we must go back to the creation of man in the very center of God's androgynous consciousness, the white-fire core of the Great Central Sun.

This Spiritual Sun behind the physical sun in the center of the universe is not, as it would seem, in back of the physical sun; it is congruent with or superimposed upon it, but in another dimension. Man's own Causal Body is a miniature replica of the Great Central Sun. Moreover, every atom in manifestation is built upon this same pattern of energy spirals evolving spheres within spheres.

The color bands of the Great Central Sun as well as of the atom are planes of God's consciousness differentiated only by their frequency, or vibration; and the white-fire core is the focus of Spirit becoming Matter and Matter becoming Spirit. Thus in the Hub (the center of the Spirit-Matter cosmos) and in the heart of every atom, the Spiritual Sun and the physical sun coexist. Here in the white-fire core, the simultaneous manifestation of Spirit and Matter provides the necessary components for creation. Here and only here can creation be born.

Eleven concentric rings surround the core of God's Being. These, together with the center, make up the twelve planes of consciousness found in the Atom of God—seven outer rays and five "secret" rays.

The rings of the five secret rays are found between the white-fire core and the yellow band. These planes do not pertain to existence as we know it upon this earth, but rather to man's latent divinity, which remains unrealized except by the few Avatars who have risen even beyond the levels of initiation required for the attainment of Christhood.

The full knowledge and use of the secret rays by the evolutions of this world has not been authorized by the Solar Lords, who require the planetary mastery of the seven planes of the Christ consciousness through the seven color rays before the powers of the secret rays are conferred upon evolving humanity.* Therefore, the white-fire core and the six spheres

---

* We can, however, invoke the Ascended Master who is known as Mighty Cosmos to release the action of the secret rays in our behalf that they will spiritualize consciousness in the planes of Matter.

FIGURE 26: The Twelve Spheres of the Causal Body

The five secret rays, between the white and yellow bands of the Causal Body, are perpendicular (orthogonal) to the seven rays.

beyond the five secret rays are the planes that relate to the evolution of God's consciousness as humanity in their present evolution are able to experience and express it.

The planes of the secret rays are actually perpendicular to the planes of the seven rays. For this reason they are not shown on the Causal Body in the Chart of your Divine Self, although they exist as potential in the Causal Body of every son and daughter of God made in the divine likeness.

The Individualization of the God Flame

The great miracle of Life is that the Universal God can individualize himself within the white-fire core of Being at any point in space he so desires. The creation of the Divine Monad, the individualized I AM Presence, takes place when the Spirit of God projects the Light seed of his image into the ovoid of Matter* in the Hub of the Great Central Sun. Through the resulting union of the essence of Spirit and Matter, of Yang and Yin, in the plane of Matter-Earth, a miniature white-fire core is formed in the heart of the Sun.

This is the moment of the individualization of the God Flame. This is the birth of the androgynous sphere of Being out of which proceed twin flames representing the Father-Mother God. Each of these twin flames forms the nucleus of an individualized I AM Presence. Then, within the heart of each I AM Presence (which retains the balance of the yin and yang aspects of the Godhead) the seed of the Christ Self is sealed, born out of the union of the Alpha and Omega spirals in the white-fire core.

In order to evolve as a replica of the Being of God, each Divine Monad—"whose seed is within itself"—must pass through the twelve planes of God's solar consciousness, which comprise the twelve spheres of the Great Central Sun. That which the Monad absorbs from the Sun is preordained by its fiery destiny—the blueprint of its evolution that is impressed upon the white-fire core of the I AM Presence. The uniqueness of twin flames is in the pattern of their fiery destiny, which is never duplicated. Although at the moment of birth the Causal Bodies of twin flames are identical (but in polarity), the subsequent evolution of the twin flames in the world of form determines what momentums are gathered in their individual Causal Bodies. Although they may pursue divergent paths of creativity, their electronic pattern remains the same.

---

* The term "Matter," when referring to the planes of God's consciousness, does not imply the density of the "earth, earthy" but a level or frequency that manifests as the coordinate of Spirit in the white-fire core and in the purple, violet and pink spheres of the Great Central Sun.

FIGURE 27: The Creation of Twin Flames

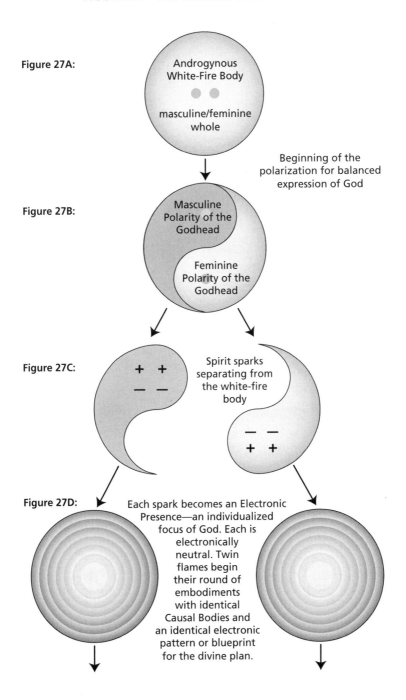

Figure 27A:

Androgynous
White-Fire Body

masculine/feminine
whole

Beginning of the
polarization for balanced
expression of God

Figure 27B:

Masculine
Polarity of the
Godhead

Feminine
Polarity of the
Godhead

Figure 27C:

+ +

− −

Spirit sparks
separating from
the white-fire
body

− −

+ +

Figure 27D:

Each spark becomes an Electronic
Presence—an individualized
focus of God. Each is
electronically
neutral. Twin
flames begin
their round of
embodiments
with identical
Causal Bodies and
an identical electronic
pattern or blueprint
for the divine plan.

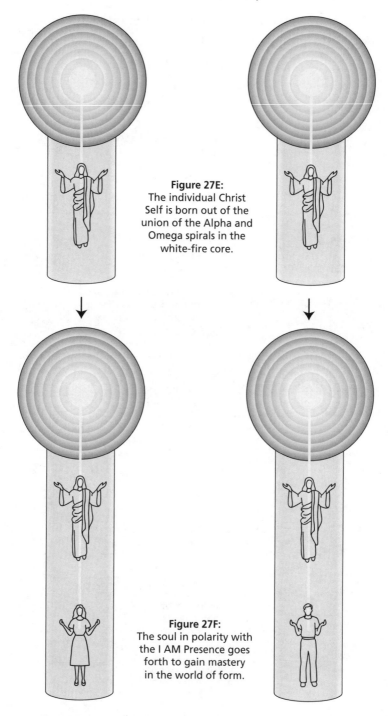

Figure 27E:
The individual Christ Self is born out of the union of the Alpha and Omega spirals in the white-fire core.

Figure 27F:
The soul in polarity with the I AM Presence goes forth to gain mastery in the world of form.

On the "Chart of the Chalices in the Causal Body" (figure 28) we have labeled the planes of God's Consciousness, showing how the four cosmic forces correspond to the seven color rays in the planes of Matter and Spirit. In every Monad, whether a sun, a star or an atom, the white-fire core is the plane of Matter-Earth. The second sphere, the yellow band, is the plane of Spirit-Earth. The third sphere, the pink band, is the plane of Spirit-Fire and Matter-Fire. The fourth sphere, the violet band, is the plane of Matter-Air. The fifth sphere, the purple band, is the plane of Matter-Water. The sixth sphere, the green band, is the plane of Spirit-Air. And the seventh sphere, the blue band, is the plane of Spirit-Water.

Between the planes of Matter-Earth (the white-fire core) and Spirit-Earth (the yellow band) are located the spheres of the five secret rays. The order of the planes of God's consciousness focused within these five secret rays is the same as that of the five outer spheres of the Causal Body; i.e., the first secret ray is the plane of Matter-Fire and Spirit-Fire, the second secret ray is the plane of Matter-Air, the third secret ray is the plane of Matter-Water, the fourth secret ray is the plane of Spirit-Air, and the fifth secret ray is the plane of Spirit-Water.

The relationship of the five secret rays to the seven color rays is similar to that of the black notes to the white notes on the piano. The cosmic tone, color, frequency and dimension of the secret rays is, so to speak, halfway between that of the color rays; but in position they are perpendicular to the planes of Matter-Earth and Spirit-Earth. Because the planes of Matter-Earth and Spirit-Earth are necessary for the creation of form in both Spirit and Matter, the five secret rays are incomplete without the seven color rays—just as the five black notes on the piano are incomplete without the seven white notes.

FIGURE 28: Chart of the Chalices in the Causal Body

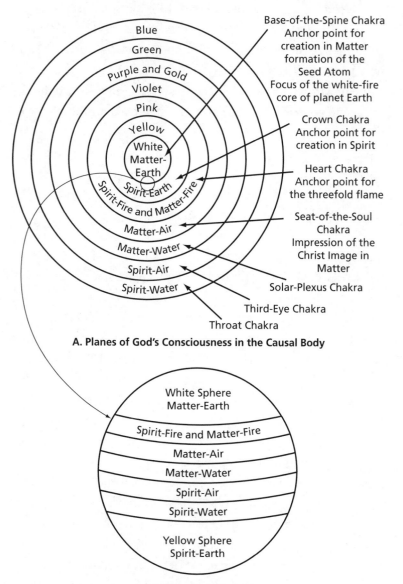

A. Planes of God's Consciousness in the Causal Body

B. Planes of God's Consciousness in the Secret Rays

This diagram shows how the chakras are developed in the etheric body
as the soul cycles through each of the twelve spheres of
the Causal Body before taking physical embodiment.

FIGURE 29: The Four Cosmic Forces Distributed in Polarity through the Upper and Lower Chakras

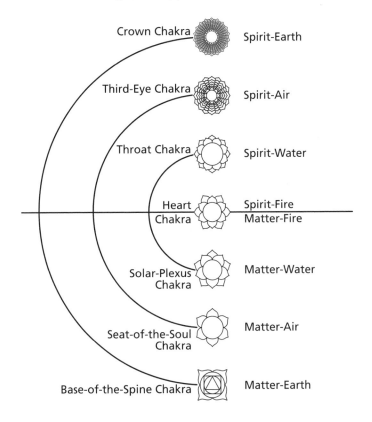

Crown Chakra — Spirit-Earth

Third-Eye Chakra — Spirit-Air

Throat Chakra — Spirit-Water

Heart Chakra — Spirit-Fire / Matter-Fire

Solar-Plexus Chakra — Matter-Water

Seat-of-the-Soul Chakra — Matter-Air

Base-of-the-Spine Chakra — Matter-Earth

You will note in the chart of the planes of God's consciousness anchored in the chakras (figure 29) that the being of man is suspended between Spirit-Earth (the crown chakra) and Matter-Earth (the base-of-the-spine chakra). It is through the polarity of the Father-Mother God, anchored in these chakras as the Lodestone of the Presence (crown +) and the Seed Atom (base –) that the being of man is sustained in form both in Spirit and in Matter.

It is precisely because the Earth planes are not represented in the five secret rays that these rays represent the formless aspect of God's consciousness. This fact also explains their location between the white and yellow spheres, causing the rays to be braced between the planes of Matter-Earth and Spirit-Earth in the Causal Body, and enabling them to be integrated with the energy spirals of the form creation when necessary.

The Creation of the Causal Body

The individual Causal Bodies of twin flames are formed as each individualized I AM Presence, sealed within its own White Fire Body, revolves through the twelve spheres of the Great Central Sun, gathering unto itself the solar momentum of each sphere according to the pattern of its fiery destiny. Thus, layer upon layer, as the Divine Monad spirals through the twelve rings of God's Causal Body according to pre-ordained cycles, the microcosmic world of the Divine Monad is born within the Macrocosm.

In figure 30, "The Journey of the Soul through the Twelve Houses in the Causal Body," we have shown how the Monad, as it cycles through the twelve spheres of the Sun, passes through and comes under the influence of the Twelve Solar Hierarchies, adding to its Causal Body one sphere with each revolution. The twelve flames of the Twelve Hierarchies, together with the seeds of the Godly virtues, are magnetized within each sphere to serve as focuses for future initiations through which the soul must pass in the world of form under their respective houses. Each of these twelve focuses also holds the pattern for one of the 144 chakras.

After making one complete rotation around the clock within the first sphere, the plane of Matter-Earth, (the origin and fulfillment of cycles being in the twelfth house), the Monad passes through the twelve o'clock line to the next

FIGURE 30: The Journey of the Soul through the Twelve Houses in the Causal Body

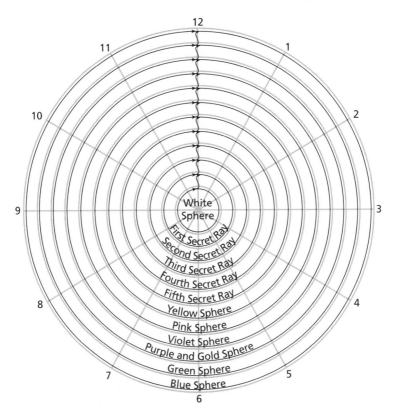

sphere, which is the plane of the first secret ray. After spiraling through the spheres of the five secret rays, one cycle within each sphere, systematically gathering unto itself the rays of the spheres and the flames of the houses, the Monad proceeds through the spheres of the six remaining color rays. Having completed its journey at the twelve o'clock line in the blue sphere, its twelve cycles fulfilled, the creation of the Causal Body is complete and the Divine Monad is projected out from the Sun to expand the glory of Life as a star in the Macrocosmic Body of God.

The Journey of the Soul and the Creation of the Crystal Chalices

Simultaneously, as the individualized I AM Presence spirals through the spheres of the Great Central Sun, the soul consciousness—that is, the image of the I AM Presence that is impressed upon the substance of Matter-Earth*—spirals through the spheres of the individualized Causal Body that are being formed. During the journey of the soul through the world of the Divine Monad, the etheric body is woven and the 144 crystal chalices are anchored within it.

Through the seven major chakras and seven subchakras and the 130 minor chakras that come under their influence, the twelve planes of God's consciousness are anchored within the soul and its etheric envelope. This anchoring of God's consciousness in man is necessary in order for him to function as an integrated being in the planes of both Spirit and Matter, and in order for him to become a co-creator with God, lowering into the plane of Matter the fiery destiny locked within his Causal Body. The goal of Life is for man to become "as Above, so below": man must precipitate "below" in his four lower bodies all that God has placed as potential "Above" in the three higher bodies (in the I AM Presence, the Causal Body and the Christ Self). By tracing the journey of the soul through the individualized Causal Body we shall see how the 144 chakras are positioned in the etheric body, the soul receiving one chakra as it enters each of the Twelve Houses in each of the twelve spheres.

Beginning in the white sphere of Matter-Earth, the soul

---

* Even as Spirit is yang and Matter is yin, so the soul that descends into Matter is referred to as "she" and the I AM Presence that holds the focus of the God-identity in Spirit is referred to as "he." Malleable and evolving, the soul is that "feminine" part of God that must go through experience in the transitory world in order to return to the unchanging yet transcendent "masculine" Spirit of the I AM Presence.

receives the base-of-the-spine chakra plus the eleven minor chakras that come under its influence. The Seed Atom, containing the image of the Christ, the electronic pattern of the Monad that will be stamped upon the lower vehicles, is suspended within the base-of-the-spine chakra. The Seed Atom is in turn the white-fire core of a miniature Causal Body that is formed around it focusing the twelve planes of God's consciousness in the plane of Matter. The Seed Atom is the focus of the Divine Mother, of the Feminine Ray of the Godhead, which anchors in Matter the energies of Spirit.

Passing through the spheres of the five secret rays, the soul and its etheric envelope receive the focuses of the seven major subchakras and the fifty-three minor chakras under the influence of the secret rays.* Proceeding on to the second sphere, the yellow band, the soul and the etheric envelope receive the crown chakra, the focus of Spirit-Earth and the eleven minor chakras that come under its influence. Here in the plane of Spirit the Lodestone of the Presence is anchored. A miniature replica of the white-fire core of the I AM Presence, this is the focus of the Divine Father. And so the divine polarity of the Father-Mother God focused at the top of the head and the base of the spine assures man that he, too, has the opportunity of becoming androgynous.

The power-wisdom of the Father infusing the love-purity of the Mother produces the Christ consciousness in the heart chalice, which is anchored in the etheric body together with the corresponding eleven minor chakras during the soul's journey through the third sphere, the pink band of the Causal

---

* The hands focus the plus and minus spirals of one secret ray; the feet focus the plus and minus spirals of another. In this way the five secret rays are anchored in the seven major subchakras. Ten minor chakras come under the influences of the hands, ten under the feet and eleven under each of the other three subchakras, making fifty-three minor chakras under the seven major subchakras—a total of sixty focuses of the secret rays in the body of man. The remaining eighty-four chakras are focuses of the seven color rays.

Body. Here Spirit-Fire and Matter-Fire function as coefficients of Spirit-Earth and Matter-Earth. These sacred fires produce the threefold flame, the balanced action of love, wisdom and power, the coordinates of Father, Son and Holy Spirit. Here in the center of being, the mandala of the lifestream, the flaming crystal of the Christ Self, is placed over the heart chakra to magnify the energies of the Flame of Life.

Next, the soul and its etheric body pass through the fourth sphere, the violet band, where it receives the seat-of-the-soul chakra, the focus of Matter-Air, together with the eleven minor chakras under its influence. Through this chalice the image of the Christ Mind is anchored in the mental body in order that it might be stamped upon the seed of both male and female (the sperm and the ovum) to carry the life pattern for incoming souls. Here the solar radiance is anchored in order that the divine blueprint may be manifest in Matter—"as Above, so below." Here the flame of freedom gives the soul the choice of deciding between the human will and the Divine Will. If it chooses the Divine, then that Mind which was in Christ Jesus will indeed be manifest in the creations of every son and daughter of God.

In the fifth sphere, the purple band tinged with gold, the soul and the etheric body receive the sun chalice, or solar plexus, the focal point for the release of the solar radiance in the plane of Matter, together with the eleven minor chakras under its influence. Through this chakra the emotional body develops the fiery destiny of the soul in the plane of Matter-Water. Great opportunity for the expansion of the fires of the soul occurs in this plane; for when properly governed, man's emotions (his energies in *motion*) can release a tremendous impetus for good in the form world. Needless to say, when ungoverned, they are the cause of man's undoing.

In the sixth sphere, the green band, the soul and the etheric body receive the third-eye chalice, the focus of Spirit-Air. Through the vision of the All-Seeing Eye of God anchored in this chakra, man is able to lower into the planes of Spirit and Matter the patterns of his Causal Body. Whereas these patterns are released into the plane of Matter through the seat-of-the-soul chakra and the lower mental body, they come forth in the plane of Spirit through the third eye when the consciousness has returned to the single-eyed vision of the Edenic state.

During their journey through the seventh sphere, the blue band, the soul and the etheric body receive the throat chakra, the focus of Spirit-Water. When the power of the spoken Word is released through this chakra, the patterns of the etheric body become the Word made flesh. When the soul has completed her cycles through the twelve bands of the individual Causal Body and accepts the divine mandate to descend into form, it is the power of the spoken Word that causes the essence of liquid fire (Spirit-Water) to coalesce the form of the three lower vehicles according to the electronic pattern of the lifestream—and the Word becomes flesh.

Figure 29 (page 131) gives an eye-picture of how the Four Cosmic Forces are distributed in polarity through the upper and lower chakras. The Christ Self, acting as the Mediator between Spirit and Matter, focuses the planes of both Spirit-Fire and Matter-Fire in the heart chakra. Born within the white-fire core of God's Being, the Christ becomes the Hub of the microcosm. Keeping the flame between the Higher Self and the lower self, the Christ is the integrator of Life where Spirit is becoming Matter and Matter is becoming Spirit.

The Soul Takes Form

The descent of the soul into embodiment follows the cycle of the clock as surely as the suns and stars and atoms. In the

Ritual of Creation, the formation of the etheric body is accomplished in the fire quadrant under the direction of the Hierarchies of the twelve, one and two o'clock lines. This ritual, an activity of the planes of Spirit-Fire and Matter-Fire, is begun in the heart chalice of the individualized I AM Presence and the Christ Self when the soul is formed; it is completed when the soul fulfills its twelfth round through the Causal Body.

The immaculate conception of the soul—the divine mandate for her descent into form—and the conception of the physical body take place under the direction of the Hierarchy of the three o'clock line. The formation of the mental body occurs in the air quadrant under the direction of the Hierarchies of the three, four and five o'clock lines. This ritual, an activity of the planes of Spirit-Air and Matter-Air, is fulfilled through the third-eye and seat-of-the-soul chalices during the first three months of gestation of a child in the womb.

The focusing of the solar radiance for the precipitation of the emotional body occurs in the water quadrant under the direction of the Hierarchies of the six, seven and eight o'clock lines. This ritual, an activity of the planes of Spirit-Water and Matter-Water, is fulfilled through the throat and solar-plexus chakras during the second three months of gestation.

The completion of the physical body occurs in the earth quadrant under the direction of the Hierarchies of the nine, ten and eleven o'clock lines. This ritual, an activity of the planes of Spirit-Earth and Matter-Earth, is fulfilled through the crown and base chakras during the final three months of gestation.

Although the patterns of the three lower bodies are fulfilled in the manner described, they develop simultaneously during the nine-month period of gestation. One need only observe the positions of the Twelve Hierarchies and the cosmic forces they represent on each line of the clock to see how the four planes of God's consciousness are woven into the fabric of the soul for the intermeshing of the four lower bodies. For example, during the first month of gestation the Hierarchy of Aries on the three o'clock line focuses the fire element in the mental body. During the second month of gestation the Hierarchy of Taurus on the four o'clock line focuses the earth element in the mental body. During the third month the Hierarchy of Gemini focuses the air element in the mental body, and so on around the clock until the moment of birth, when the soul begins a new cycle of opportunity in form. All of the Twelve Hierarchies of the Sun focus their particular momentum of service to the incoming soul to the Hierarchy in charge of the cycle and ritual of the month.

From the moment of conception, the child's soul is an active participant in forming the body she is to inhabit to fulfill her mission in life. Throughout the entire nine months of gestation, the soul may go back and forth from her body in the womb to higher planes of existence in the heaven-world. Each time the soul enters her body, she anchors more of her soul substance in that body. As gestation progresses, the spirit, or the essence, of the soul becomes a part of the blood and the cells—a part of the brain, the heart and all of the organs.

At the moment of birth (the timing of which is integral to the soul's mission), under the direction of the Hierarchy of the twelve o'clock line, the soul comes down the spiritual birth canal, which is like a large funnel, and the threefold flame is anchored in the heart chalice. Prior to birth the heart and necessary functions of the fetus are sustained by the threefold flame of the mother through the placenta and the umbilical cord, which bear a striking resemblance to the Causal Body and the crystal cord.

The soul is fully integrated with the body at the moment of birth, and a curtain of forgetfulness is drawn over the memory body of the soul at that time. The soul then no longer has full memory of her preexistence in the heaven-world or in past lives.

As the sheath, or mantle, of the soul, the etheric body remains intact from one embodiment to the next, retaining the impressions stamped upon it by the qualification of energy occurring in the three lower vehicles. Each time the soul takes form, the mental, emotional and physical bodies are formed anew, according to the patterns stored in the etheric body.

The Meshing of the Four Lower Bodies

The four quadrants of the circle represent phases of Matter, levels of energy through which the God flame is progressively coalesced, beginning with fire and culminating in physical precipitation. These phases of Matter constitute the substance of the four lower bodies.

The trines (figure 31) are the triangles formed by connecting the lines of this clock corresponding to the same element. Thus there are four trines, corresponding to fire, air, water and earth. These represent the activity of the threefold flame qualifying the levels of Matter. They mesh to anchor the elements of man's consciousness as memory, thoughts, feelings and physical form.*

Through this activity, the fire body is directly linked to each of the other three lower bodies. So is the physical body. For all of man's lower bodies must partake of God's fire, and they all exist in the realm of Matter—therefore they all take on a level of physical form.

The mental, emotional and physical bodies anchor the fire body to provide man with memory and a chalice for the divine plan, the fiery essence of his God-identity. The etheric, mental

---

* For further information about the Twelve Hierarchies of the Sun and the twelve lines of the clock, see Elizabeth Clare Prophet, *Predict Your Future: Understand the Cycles of the Cosmic Clock.*

FIGURE 31: The Meshing of the Four Lower Bodies

The etheric and physical bodies register the four elements.
The mental and emotional bodies register in only three planes.

The etheric body is anchored in
the mental (3), emotional (7)
and physical (11) bodies
through the fire trine.

The mental body is anchored in
the etheric (1), mental (5)
and physical (9) bodies
through the air trine.

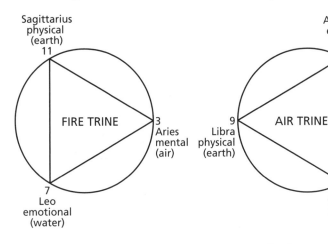

The emotional body is anchored
in the etheric (2), emotional (6)
and physical (10) bodies
through the water trine.

The physical body is anchored
in the etheric (12), mental (4)
and emotional (8) bodies
through the earth trine.

and emotional bodies anchor the physical body to provide man with physical form through which he can crystallize unique fire-blossoms of love.

But thoughts and feelings can act independently. Thus the mental and emotional bodies do not directly mesh with each other, although often they outwardly influence each other. The etheric, mental and physical bodies (but not the emotional body) anchor the mental body, thoughtforms that are living chalices, agents for the fiery Mind of God. The etheric, emotional and physical bodies (but not the mental body) anchor the emotional body to provide man with feeling and to break down the barriers of duality. Inasmuch as the mental body lacks the emotional tie and the emotional lacks the mental tie, their contact with each other is achieved through the etheric (mental contact with the emotional) or through the physical (emotional contact with the mental).

Patterns for the Distribution of Energy in Man

With the anchoring of the threefold flame in the heart chalice, the distribution of energy through the chakras begins. The sending forth of energy from God to man is an activity of the masculine ray—of Spirit projecting the sacred fire into the planes of Matter for the purpose of the evolution of the soul in form. The return of energy from man to God is an activity of the feminine ray—of Matter returning to Spirit in the involutionary spiral. Figure 32 illustrates the masculine action of the sacred fire in man. Figure 33, showing the caduceus or return cycle of energy from the base to the crown chakra, illustrates the feminine action of the sacred fire in man. Let us first consider the activity of the masculine ray.

**FIGURE 32: The Pattern of Distribution of the Energy
through the Heart for the Purpose of Creation
in the Upper and Lower Chakras
Masculine Action of the Sacred Fire in Man**

Divine Father
Lodestone of the Presence

Crown Chakra
Spirit-Earth

Third-Eye Chakra
Spirit-Air

Throat Chakra
Spirit-Water

Heart Chakra
Spirit-Fire / Matter-Fire

The white fire that
descends to the heart
is distributed to the
upper and lower
chakras according to
the ritual of creation
(clockwise spiral),
passing through the
planes of fire, air,
water and earth.

Solar-Plexus Chakra
Matter-Water

Seat-of-the-Soul Chakra
Matter-Air

Base-of-the-Spine Chakra
Matter-Earth

Divine Mother
Seed Atom
(Kundalini)

FIGURE 33: The Caduceus Pattern
Feminine Action of the Sacred Fire in Man

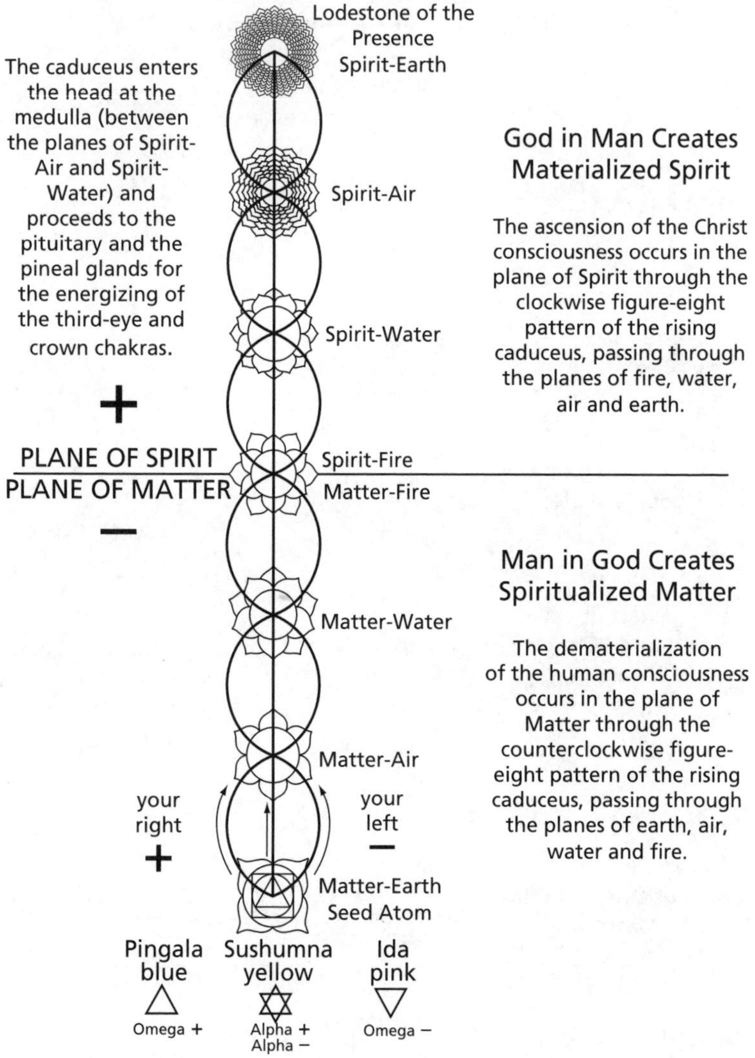

Lodestone of the
Presence
Spirit-Earth

The caduceus enters the head at the medulla (between the planes of Spirit-Air and Spirit-Water) and proceeds to the pituitary and the pineal glands for the energizing of the third-eye and crown chakras.

Spirit-Air

Spirit-Water

+

PLANE OF SPIRIT
PLANE OF MATTER

Spirit-Fire

Matter-Fire

−

God in Man Creates Materialized Spirit

The ascension of the Christ consciousness occurs in the plane of Spirit through the clockwise figure-eight pattern of the rising caduceus, passing through the planes of fire, water, air and earth.

Man in God Creates Spiritualized Matter

The dematerialization of the human consciousness occurs in the plane of Matter through the counterclockwise figure-eight pattern of the rising caduceus, passing through the planes of earth, air, water and fire.

Matter-Water

Matter-Air

your right

your left

+

−

Matter-Earth
Seed Atom

Pingala blue	Sushumna yellow	Ida pink
△	✡	▽
Omega +	Alpha + Alpha −	Omega −

The raising of the pingala indicates degrees of mastery over the physical body and the earth element.

The raising of the sushumna indicates degrees of mastery over the etheric and mental bodies and the fire and air elements.

The raising of the ida indicates degrees of mastery over the emotional body and the water element.

Cosmic energy spirals, descending from the Heart of the Sun to the heart of the son, spring up as the trinity of the three-fold flame within the heart, whence they are distributed to the upper and lower chakras according to the patterns shown in figure 32. The heart is a prism through which the pure white Light of the Alpha and Omega spirals passes to energize the four lower bodies according to their respective planes of consciousness. Within the heart, where the planes of Spirit and Matter converge, the threefold flame bursts forth "as Above, so below."

Figure 34 illustrates the action of the threefold flame in a spiraling figure-eight pattern, ascending and descending from the throne of the heart. In the plane of Spirit, "Above," the plumes are ascendant, the blue to one's left, the pink to one's right and the yellow in the center. In the plane of Matter, "below," the plumes are descendant, the blue on the right, and the pink on the left, with the yellow remaining in the center.

The fleur-de-lis is the symbol of the action of the threefold flame, "as Above, so below." The triune action of the flame spirals below the heart for the precipitation of Christly virtue in the planes of Matter. The fact that the flame is larger in the planes of Spirit than in the planes of Matter signifies that the preponderance of man's energy is already on the side of his divinity. If people understood this law, they would find that it is actually easier to qualify God's energy spiritually above the heart than it is to misqualify it materially below the heart.

In the plane of Spirit, man and woman receive on their left the power of God as the negative (feminine) aspect of the blue ray, which manifests in the plane of Matter on the right as the positive (masculine) aspect of the blue ray. In the plane of Matter, man and woman receive on their left the love of God as the negative aspect of the pink ray, which manifests in the plane of Spirit on the right as the positive aspect of the pink

FIGURE 34: The Threefold Flame in Spirit and Matter

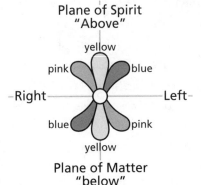

Plane of Spirit
"Above"

yellow

pink   blue

Right ——————————— Left

blue   pink

yellow

Plane of Matter
"below"

The threefold flame reverses to
nourish the lower chakras.

In the plane of Spirit,
the pink plume has the
+ / Father / masculine polarity,
the blue plume has the
– / Mother / feminine polarity.

In the plane of Matter:
the blue plume has the
+ / Father / masculine polarity,
the pink plume has the
– / Mother / feminine polarity.

The fleur-de-lis pattern is the symbol
of the action of the threefold flame,
"as Above, so below." The triune
action of the flame spirals below the
heart for the precipitation of Christly
virtue in the planes of Matter. The
fact that the flame is larger in the
planes of Spirit than in the planes of
Matter signifies that the
preponderance of man's energy is
already on the side of his divinity.

ray. Thus, the left side of man and woman is predominantly feminine (the receiver) and his right is predominantly masculine (the giver).

The relationship of the caduceus pattern to the action of the threefold flame in man and woman determines their respective polarity to the planes of Spirit and Matter:

In man, the pingala (blue) rises from his right and the ida (pink) from his left. These positions correspond with the action of the threefold flame below the heart in the plane of Matter. Thus, by the Law of Attraction, man's orientation is in the concrete physical universe, and by the Law of Polarity, he is drawn to the feminine aspect of his nature in the plane of Spirit.

In woman, the pingala (blue) rises from her left and the ida (pink) from her right. These positions correspond with the action of the threefold flame above the heart in the plane of Spirit. Thus, by the Law of Attraction, woman's orientation is in the spiritual universe, and by the Law of Polarity, she is drawn to the masculine aspect of her nature in the plane of Matter.

It is the action of the caduceus rising from the Seed Atom that determines whether the soul will have a masculine or a feminine incarnation. And it is the impulse of the I AM Presence conveyed from the individualized Causal Body to the microcosmic Causal Body that sets the energies of the caduceus in motion at the moment of conception.

The action of the flame above and below the heart determines the qualification of the energies that ascend and descend from the heart to the six main chakras in the planes of Spirit and Matter and thence to the seven main subchakras and the remaining 130. We shall now explain how through the patterns of distribution, the Alpha and Omega stars become triangles in the firmament of man's being.

The cosmic energy spirals that descend over the crystal cord are composed of two descending spirals, or stars, one from Alpha, having the plus spin, and one from Omega, having the minus spin. Within each star are two triangles, each having a plus and a minus spin. The Alpha star contains the fire (Alpha-plus) and air (Alpha-minus) triangles; the Omega star contains the water (Omega-minus) and earth (Omega-plus) triangles. These four triangles, carrying the frequency of the four cosmic forces, seek their own plane and vibration in the chakras of man.

The Law of Attraction (likes attract) and the Law of Polarity (opposites polarize) are operative in the distribution and control of energy in man. The plane of Spirit (+) and the plane of Matter (–) are in polarity; thus, the three chakras above the heart are in polarity with the three chakras below the heart. The throat, third eye and crown chakras have an A (Alpha) or positive charge, and the solar plexus, seat-of-the-soul and base of spine chakras have an Ω (Omega) or negative charge. The heart, being the nexus between the planes of Matter and Spirit, has both the positive and negative charge.

Now let us see how the Law of Attraction is operative in the distribution of energy through the upper and lower chakras as the mist becomes the crystal in each of the chakras as they govern the release of energy in their respective planes. The triangles of the Alpha and Omega spirals are distributed to the chakras through the Ritual of Creation (clockwise spiral), passing through the planes (chakras) of fire, air, water and earth.

If we think of the plus and minus stars descending via the crystal cord as trolley cars, and their triangles as four passengers that exit at four stops (at the heart chakra and the three chakras above and below), then we can understand how the energy is distributed in the four planes of Matter and in the four planes of Spirit according to the Law of Attraction. The fire triangle exits at the heart, the air triangle exits at the seat of the soul and third eye, the water triangle exits at the solar plexus and throat, and the earth triangle exits at the base and crown. Each time a triangle exits, the combined charges of the remaining triangles determine, by the Law of Attraction, where the next "stop" will be.

Let us examine the clockwise spiral that descends from the heart through the planes of Matter. When the Alpha-plus (fire) triangle exits in the heart (fire) chakra, three passengers are left: the Alpha-minus, the Omega-minus and the Omega-plus triangles. Traveling as a unit in the trolley car, all proceed to the seat of the soul, impelled by the attraction between the Alpha-minus (air) triangle and the Alpha-minus charge of this (air) chakra. After the Alpha-minus triangle exits, the remaining passengers are the Omega-minus (water) and the Omega-plus (earth) triangles. Functioning as a minus star, both are drawn to the "most minus" chakra, the solar plexus (water is more yin than earth). At this Omega-minus (water) stop the Omega-minus triangle exits, and the last passenger, the Omega-plus triangle, is drawn to the base of the spine, the Omega-plus (earth) stop. The identical process occurs above the heart over the ascending clockwise spiral for the distribution of energy through the planes of Spirit. The energy thus distributed is intended to be qualified according to the seven rays, which correspond in frequency to the planes of Spirit and Matter focused through the seven chakras.

When there is no misqualification of energy through the chakras, only ten percent of man's daily allotment is required to sustain his four lower bodies. Another ten percent is destined to return through the heart chalice to the Source from whence it came as a love tithing to the Almighty. This flow of gratitude sustains the antahkarana between man and God, weaving the "stairway to the stars" that man will one day climb to his immortal freedom.* The remaining 80% of man's daily allotment may be qualified with the highest creative intelligence and intent for the precipitation of the patterns made in the heavens through the patterns made in the earth in the seven chakras.

By an act of divine willing, the individual has the option to return to the heart chalice the energies that have been distributed to the upper and lower chakras in excess of their stated need. Their return occurs in the reverse order of their distribution as shown on the chart. Passing through the planes (chakras) of earth, water, air and fire, the triangles follow the pattern of the Ritual of Disintegration. This simply

---

* The Law of the Tithe will be discussed in book 9 of the Climb the Highest Mountain series.

means that the triangles return to the heart where they regroup in the Alpha-Omega star formations for qualification through the prism of the Christ consciousness.

The purpose of returning one's surplus energies to the heart is to magnify the creative output of the soul with the combined energies (triangles) of the Alpha and Omega spirals through the momentum of the Christ anchored in the threefold flame and through the sacred-fire aspects of Spirit and Matter that are uniquely expressed in the heart. In the heart the highest and noblest works of man are born. In the heart is the beginning of wisdom. In the heart the knowledge of love is given, and in the heart the might of the Spirit is felt and shared.

Man's option to return his excess energies to the heart chalice is elected by the authority of either the God consciousness, the Christ consciousness or the Solar consciousness anchored in the third-eye, heart and seat-of-the-soul chakras respectively. These decision-making faculties determine through the planes of fire and air how God's energies shall be used to create in Spirit and Matter.

The wisdom, love and power of the threefold flame are thus anchored in the mental body (1) through the third eye, the focus of the Divine Mind (yellow), which secures to man right knowledge and the singleness of vision and purpose of the All-Seeing Eye of God; (2) through the heart (pink), which releases the intuitive knowledge of the Christ Self; and (3) through the seat of the soul (blue), which impresses the outer mind with the determination of the soul to bring forth the divine plan according to her fiery destiny.

These faculties of heart, head and hand are opposed by the consciousness of duality through (1) the human intellect that proclaims the wisdom of the world as superior to the wisdom of God; (2) the human ego that usurps the authority of the Christ; and (3) the human will that flaunts the divine will and

FIGURE 35: The Trinity of Man's Decision-Making Faculties Anchored through the Planes of Fire and Air

Through the planes of fire and air, man decides how he shall employ his energies in the planes of water and earth.

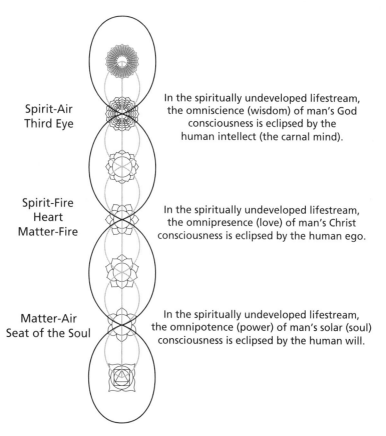

Spirit-Air
Third Eye

In the spiritually undeveloped lifestream, the omniscience (wisdom) of man's God consciousness is eclipsed by the human intellect (the carnal mind).

Spirit-Fire
Heart
Matter-Fire

In the spiritually undeveloped lifestream, the omnipresence (love) of man's Christ consciousness is eclipsed by the human ego.

Matter-Air
Seat of the Soul

In the spiritually undeveloped lifestream, the omnipotence (power) of man's solar (soul) consciousness is eclipsed by the human will.

the Laws of God, justifying by man-made codes its unbridled use of God's energy (figure 35).

My Heart Is the Heart of God

The heart chalice provides the greatest potential for balanced precipitation in the planes of Spirit and Matter because it is the focus of the sacred fire—the threefold flame.

Here the union of Spirit-Fire and Matter-Fire, focusing the power of the masculine and feminine polarities of the Godhead, produces in man the full-orbed radiance of the Christ consciousness. As the pivot point between the upper and lower chakras, the heart chalice receives on the return cycle the perfectly balanced energies of Spirit-Earth, Matter-Earth, of Spirit-Water, Matter-Water, and of Spirit-Air, Matter-Air. These energies are refined by the celestial fires of the heart, molded by the quickening action of the threefold flame, and released through the prism of the Christ consciousness for the blessing of all Life.

Through the crystal cord, the lifeline of the Presence, the heart of man is connected directly to the heart of God. When properly attuned with the trinity of the Creator's consciousness, man becomes a co-creator with Him, his heartbeat one with the pulsation of the divine heartbeat, his mind flowing with the creative intent, his soul humming with the rhythm of the spheres.

Although the threefold flame can never be contaminated by the abuses of men, when man fails to adore it, its size may be significantly reduced; when man fails to invoke it in balanced action, its three plumes may assume different heights; and when man fails to purify his thoughts and feelings, motives and intent, it may become buried in astral debris. Nevertheless, the flame itself burns on to sustain life in the four lower bodies until the crystal cord is withdrawn by the Christ Self and opportunity recedes until another round.

The purification of the heart chakra and the balancing of the threefold flame are essential if man is to become a co-creator with God. The threefold flame must be cultivated, watered and nourished through prayer, meditation and decrees and through service to Life. If man would progress spiritually, he must invoke the sacred fire to remove the debris that

FIGURE 36: Four Planes of the Ego Oppose the Mastery of the Four Elements in the Matter and Spirit Cycles of Release of Energy through the Chakras

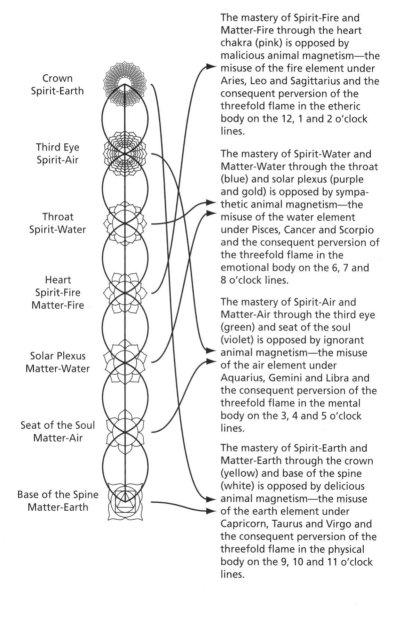

Crown
Spirit-Earth

Third Eye
Spirit-Air

Throat
Spirit-Water

Heart
Spirit-Fire
Matter-Fire

Solar Plexus
Matter-Water

Seat of the Soul
Matter-Air

Base of the Spine
Matter-Earth

The mastery of Spirit-Fire and Matter-Fire through the heart chakra (pink) is opposed by malicious animal magnetism—the misuse of the fire element under Aries, Leo and Sagittarius and the consequent perversion of the threefold flame in the etheric body on the 12, 1 and 2 o'clock lines.

The mastery of Spirit-Water and Matter-Water through the throat (blue) and solar plexus (purple and gold) is opposed by sympathetic animal magnetism—the misuse of the water element under Pisces, Cancer and Scorpio and the consequent perversion of the threefold flame in the emotional body on the 6, 7 and 8 o'clock lines.

The mastery of Spirit-Air and Matter-Air through the third eye (green) and seat of the soul (violet) is opposed by ignorant animal magnetism—the misuse of the air element under Aquarius, Gemini and Libra and the consequent perversion of the threefold flame in the mental body on the 3, 4 and 5 o'clock lines.

The mastery of Spirit-Earth and Matter-Earth through the crown (yellow) and base of the spine (white) is opposed by delicious animal magnetism—the misuse of the earth element under Capricorn, Taurus and Virgo and the consequent perversion of the threefold flame in the physical body on the 9, 10 and 11 o'clock lines.

accumulates around the heart chakra; and until he does, his evolution is at a standstill. The heart must be bathed daily in violet fire, blue lightning and the flame of the Holy Spirit if he is to expand and balance the threefold flame and to free himself from the bondage of the senses that enslave the heart. Truly, he whose heart remains buried in a tomb of matter is himself not quickened from the dead.

It has been said, "As a man thinketh in his heart, so is he."[1] The heart is the fount of man's being. Therefore, if the motive of the heart is pure, man's energies will flow from the heart in a pure stream and return to him in like manner. If the motive of the heart is impure, the energies that flow from the heart and the other chakras will likewise be impure.

The pure in heart see God[2] because there is an unbroken stream of Light that flows from the pure heart to the heart of the One Source of all Life. The strength of Galahad was as the strength of ten because the magnification of the full potential of the Christ was possible through his pure heart flame. In order to become God-realized, then, man must guard the heart, adore the flame and purify his consciousness. Then he will be able to say with Jesus:

> My heart is the heart of God.
> My heart is the heart of the world.
> My heart is the heart of Christ in healing action.

The Caduceus

Having examined the descent of the Alpha and Omega energies and the pattern of their distribution in man, let us now turn to the action of the caduceus, the figure-eight spirals over which God's energy ascends through the planes of Matter and Spirit from the Seed Atom in the base of the spine to the Lodestone of the Presence in the crown (figure 33, page 144).

Only through a proper understanding of the caduceus can the mastery of Life's sacred energies be successfully accomplished, for only in the victory of the caduceus can man vanquish the last enemy, which is death.[3]

The descent of energy from God to man, being a masculine activity of the sacred fire, infuses the chakras with the masculine (positive) charge. The ascent of the sacred fire from man to God via the caduceus, being a feminine activity, infuses the chakras with the feminine (negative) charge of the Godhead. Through our study of the caduceus we shall see how these dual functions combine to produce the Christ consciousness in the planes of Spirit and Matter.

The winged staff, symbol of the medical profession, illustrates the entwining of the masculine (blue) and feminine (pink) rays in a centripetal and centrifugal action around the rod of the Christ (yellow) focused in the spinal column. As shown in figure 33 (page 144), The Caduceus Pattern in Man, the energies of the Seed Atom, which rise from the base of the spine to the crown chakra in a triune action of the sacred fire, are called in Sanskrit the *pingala* (blue), the *sushumna* (yellow) and the *ida* (pink).

The threefold caduceus spiral that rises upon the spinal ladder has its source in the white-fire core of the Seed Atom and in the focus of the microcosmic Causal Body surrounding the Seed Atom. This focus of the World Mother and of the action of the feminine ray in man magnetizes the energies of the Holy Spirit, which are active to a greater or lesser degree in all.

In the unawakened lifestream, only the energies of the outer sphere (the blue band) of the microcosmic Causal Body are active in producing the caduceus spirals; the fires of the

Seed Atom remain dormant, sealed within the white-fire core. Nevertheless, the energies of the outer sphere are sufficient to sustain the flow of the ida, pingala and sushumna from the base of the spine to the crown. Thus, man is never without the flow of the feminine ray rising upon the spinal altar even as he is never without the descending currents of the masculine ray posited in the threefold flame within the heart.

Let it be clear, then, that the descending cycles of the Alpha-Omega currents come forth from the Father aspect focused in the individualized I AM Presence and in the Lodestone of the Presence that is located in the crown chakra, while the ascending cycles of the Alpha-Omega currents come forth from the Mother aspect of the Deity focused through the Seed Atom and the microcosmic Causal Body surrounding it at the base-of-the-spine chakra.*

In this manner the promise is fulfilled that was given to David, "The Lord shall preserve thy going out and thy coming in from this time forth, and even forevermore."[4] The inner meaning of the promise is that the LORD shall preserve the going out of His sacred energies from the Holy of Holies—the I AM Presence—into the body temple through the masculine and feminine rays and their safe return to the Causal Body by the power of the Christ Light released through the chakras.

This mystery was revealed to Jacob in a dream: "... and behold a ladder [the spinal ladder] set upon the earth [upon the base-of-the-spine chakra, the plane of Matter-Earth], and the top of it reached to heaven [to the crown chakra, the plane of Spirit-Earth]: and behold the angels of God ascending and descending on it."[5] Here the term "angels" symbolizes the

---

* N.B. In both the descent and the ascent of the energy spirals, the Four Cosmic Forces of the two stars are in perfect balance. It is the cycle itself that is either masculine or feminine, placing a + charge as the coefficient of the descending stars + (− + + −) and a − charge as the coefficient of the ascending stars − (+ − − +).

particles of energy (electrons)—or triangles as we have shown them—that move in a continual flow up and down the spine.

As the focal point for the flow of the sacred fire in man, the spine is the veritable axis of creation. It has been called the rod of Meru, or Merudanda, and appropriately so; for the God and Goddess Meru hold the focus of the feminine ray for the earth; and the spine, as the focal point for the precipitation of the four lower bodies, represents the Mother or Matter side of creation.

Our examination of a cross section of the spine at the etheric level reveals three rings—another action of the trinity—which are actually canals for the flow of the sacred fire: (1) the center canal (blue), called the *chitrini,* is the passageway for the raising of the Seed Atom; (2) the second ring (pink), called the *vajrini,* is the passageway for the distribution of energies from the I AM Presence through the heart to the chakras; and (3) the third or outermost ring (yellow), called the *sushumna,* is the passageway for the yellow flame of the caduceus (figure 37).

FIGURE 37: The Central Channel of the Caduceus

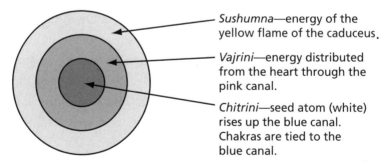

Sushumna—energy of the yellow flame of the caduceus.

Vajrini—energy distributed from the heart through the pink canal.

Chitrini—seed atom (white) rises up the blue canal. Chakras are tied to the blue canal.

People can use force or will (blue) to activate the chakras. If this method is used, morality and Christly virtue are not necessarily an adjunct to the "opening" of the chakras. When love is used to open the chakras, they unfold naturally like the petals of a flower, releasing the proper frequencies of the rays intended for each center and developing simultaneously the attributes of the Godhead. Some yogic exercises use the blue plume solely.

The seven chakras are connected to one another, to the seven main subchakras and to the remaining 130 chakras by etheric tubes called *nadis,* the Sanskrit word for motion, suggesting the concept of energy flow as taught by the Ascended Masters. These nadis are actually forcefields that direct the currents to their proper levels, carrying the energies of the sacred fire to and from the heart chalice. Over these same etheric pathways, the threefold energies of the caduceus ascend the spinal ladder.

The ida, pingala and sushumna are also considered as nadis; thus the flow of energy as well as the 'track' it follows are called by the same names. These three major nadis are the etheric counterparts of the central and sympathetic nervous systems. Beginning at the base of the spine, the ida and pingala (corresponding to the sympathetic nervous system) weave a figure-eight pattern, meeting the sushumna (corresponding to the central nervous system) at each of the seven centers. The caduceus follows the spine, entering the head at the medulla oblongata, and proceeding to the pineal and pituitary centers in the pattern of the shepherd's crook.

The pingala is the Omega-plus triangle, representing the earth element; the ida is the Omega-minus triangle, representing the water element; while the sushumna is the Alpha star containing the Alpha-plus (descending) triangle (fire) and the Alpha-minus (ascending) triangle (air). One's individual mastery in the planes of earth, water, fire and air determines the intensity of color and flow in the energies of the pingala, ida and sushumna. Just as the threefold flame may be unbalanced according to the level of one's attainment, so the members of the caduceus are not necessarily equal.

When the trinity of the mother ray (the rising caduceus) and the energies of the father ray (the descending spirals of the crystal cord) converge at the seven chakras, the fusion of their patterns infuses the four lower bodies with the balance of divine polarity and there is an accompanying release of the Christ Light. The converging of the masculine and feminine rays in the chakras is seen as the rising triangle △ (feminine) meets the descending triangle ▽ (masculine). As the two triangles interlace over each succeeding chakra, the star of man's divinity is born, duality is transcended, and there is a return to the whole-eye consciousness of the Godhead.

Man is never more complete than when the energies of the Father-Mother God merge in the seven purified chalices of his being. For then the Image of the Christ is released through the chakras "as Above, so below" in the planes of earth, air, water and fire.

It is this unique manifestation of the flame of the Christ within the chakras that qualifies man's energy with the polarity necessary for its return to the Causal Body. That which returns to the Secret Place of the Most High, the place of perfection, must be perfected according to the divine polarity manifest in the consciousness of the Christ. In order to qualify for immortality, man must be found in the likeness of the Father-Mother God; likewise, the energies and the creations he sends forth from the seven planes of his being must be stamped with the Christ consciousness that is produced from the reunion of the masculine and feminine rays with the seven chakras.

The Law of Polarity operative in the being of man is both exact and exacting. Unless he maintains a balanced flow of the yin and yang energies in his four lower bodies, man leaves himself wide open to disease, decay, frustration, unhappiness and the symptoms of old age, and he is incapable of drawing and holding an abundant supply of his spiritual and material needs. These signs of incompleteness are the result of man's inability to maintain the balance of the Father-Mother God in his thoughts, feelings, words and actions.

The natural state of man is Wholeness. The return to that state cannot be accomplished as long as man misqualifies the energies that descend from his Presence; for in so doing, he is not able to sustain the action of the masculine ray within the chakras that is necessary to magnetize the feminine ray, thereby accelerating the action of the caduceus. When the entire process of perfectionment is wholeheartedly pursued, the powerful currents of the masculine ray, flowing through the chakras, qualified by the Christly virtues of the seven rays, magnetize an equally powerful action of the feminine ray from the Seed Atom.

As the initiate attains greater mastery in the qualification of Light through the chakras, the seven spheres of the microcosmic Causal Body surrounding the Seed Atom gradually "unwind," releasing the energies of the feminine ray, which intensify the action of the caduceus. Then, at the hour of man's transfiguration (which occurs when man has mastered the seven planes of consciousness through the proper qualification of the energies released from the Presence), the Seed Atom (Kundalini) emerges from the white-fire core; rising up the chitrini, it infuses each of the seven chakras with the solar consciousness of the lifestream—the feminine action of the Christ—and with the pattern of its fiery destiny released from within the white-fire core of the microcosmic Causal Body.

As the Seed Atom rises, man literally becomes a blazing sun; for the divine union of the Father-Mother God that is fulfilled within each chalice produces therein the immaculate conception of the Christ. When the divine polarity is thus attained in each of the seven planes of his consciousness and the Seed Atom is anchored in the Lodestone of the Presence, the perfect balance of man's androgynous nature is realized

"as Above, so below." Having passed this initiation, man is given unlimited power to create in the planes of Spirit and Matter according to the unique designs—the patterns made in the heavens[6]—held within his own individualized Causal Body.

Speaking of the mystical union of the Life-fires in man, beloved Amaryllis said: "When the anointing of the Holy Spirit descends upon the planetary body, it first descends upon the human heart. Then there occurs a natural opening of the spiritual centers in man, and at that moment the kingdom of God first begins to blush into reality as a rising sun of hope* that gladdens hearts who have watched through the long night of pain and struggle.

"Now they behold the beauty of God, and all whose centers are thus opened rush into the orchestra of cosmic grace to participate in the creation of that beautiful music that gladdens heart and soul, that brings delight to every child and child-man. And so when the centers open naturally in man, God's kingdom becomes a shared kingdom."[7]

The Giant Spiral

When the threefold flame is balanced and the four lower bodies are in alignment according to the pattern of the square within the circle, the crystal chalices function at maximum efficiency as catalysts for the fulfillment in man of the Law of Correspondences. The mandate "as Above, so below" is realized as the positive spirals of Christly virtue, emanating from each of the 144 centers, produce one giant clockwise spiral that begins in the heart and culminates in the Lodestone of the Presence. Figure 38, "The Weaving of the Deathless Solar Body," shows the action of the giant spiral that may be

---

* This refers to the rising Seed Atom or to the white-fire ball as it is visualized in meditation.

FIGURE 38: The Weaving of the Deathless Solar Body through the Correct Use of the Evolutionary and Involutionary Spirals
"I AM a Blazing Sun"

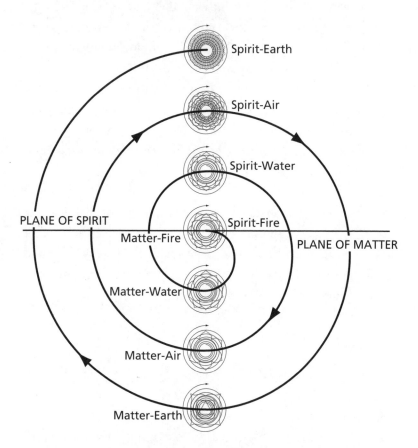

As the energies of God spiral through the seven chakras, qualified by Christly virtue and vibration, they follow the clockwise spiral and the figure-eight pattern shown here, passing through the planes of fire, water, air and earth.

Positive (clockwise) evolutionary spirals emanating from the seven chakras result from the qualification of the white Light with the Christly virtues and colors of the seven rays and their release through the chakras.

Negative (counterclockwise) involutionary spirals are used to draw in prana (Light particles in the air) through the chakras for the nourishment of the four lower bodies. When engaged in these natural functions, the chakras are convex (protruding outward). When engaged in the unnatural functions of sending out impure energies and sucking in astral substance, the chakras are concave (receding within).

Thus the balanced activities of Alpha and Omega are fulfilled in the outbreathing (+) and inbreathing (–) of light through the chakras. The centripetal and centrifugal action that is produced by these functions causes the chakras to have the appearance of a basket weave.

The large spiral makes three cycles through the four elements in the lower and upper chakras, bringing about the squaring of the circle. Thus, by the power of the threefold flame, man precipitates the energies of his Causal Body in the world of form.

Both black and white magicians use the clockwise spiral and figure eight to create and sustain form in Matter and Spirit. Both use the counterclockwise spiral and the figure eight for the purpose of dematerialization. The drawing-in, whether of prana or astral energies, is the involutionary or counter-clockwise spiral (–). The giving out, whether of Light or Darkness, is accomplished through the evolutionary spiral (+). What, then, is the difference between Good and Evil?

The answer lies in vibration, which is produced by motive, matrix, color and quality. If a creation is to sustain Light, the creator must have a pure motive—to glorify God in his work. Second, the matrix, or pattern, must be cast according to the standard of perfection; i.e., it must be as nearly perfect as it is possible to make it. Third, the color and quality or frequency of the creation must emanate from the Christ as aspects of the threefold flame in balanced manifestation.

visualized and actually drawn forth by students on the Path, although the spiral is not sustained in unascended man until he has passed the initiation of the transfiguration.

You will note that beginning in the heart and ending in the crown, the giant spiral makes three complete cycles around the clock, each of the six arcs connecting the chakras representing half of a cycle. Simultaneously, a giant counterclockwise spiral

produced by the action of the caduceus draws into the being of man through the heart chalice the essence of the Holy Spirit. It is from the action of these two spirals—the converging of the masculine and feminine rays within the heart chalice—that the Deathless Solar Body of man is woven.

Different yogic systems teach different methods for the raising of the Seed Atom, or 'Kundalini' as they call it. It is considered the supreme goal of yoga to achieve, through meditation, exercise and various involved practices, the awakening of the inner layers of the Kundalini fires and then the actual raising of the Kundalini itself.

It is said that the union of the soul with God is accomplished when the Goddess Kundalini, who lies sleeping in the root chakra (coiled like a serpent three and a half times at the base, her head blocking the opening of the sushumna canal), is awakened by psychic heat induced by yogic practices, in the same manner as a serpent struck by a rod hisses and straightens itself. The yogins teach that the goal of the Goddess Kundalini is to unite with her Lord Shiva in the crown chakra. They explain that as she proceeds up the chitrini canal, she pierces the chakras with her lightning energies, the flowers turn upward, and the flow of Life through the chakras is greatly enhanced. Kundalini then draws into herself (into latency) the psychological functions (the characteristics of the Christ consciousness, as we would say it) of each chakra and then continues on to fulfill the goal of ultimate reunion—the mystical oneness of Shakti (the Mother-Goddess—feminine aspect of the Cosmic Mind) with Shakta (the Father-God—masculine aspect of the Cosmic Mind), which results in enlightenment, the unfolding of the thousand-petaled lotus whereby man realizes his God consciousness.

Once this state is attained, Kundalini descends the chitrini, entering each chakra and giving back to it the functions she absorbed during the ascent, charged with the energies she has received from her Lord. Some yogic masters teach their disciples to retain the Kundalini in the heart chakra to lend greater momentum to the release of Light from this center, while others teach them to conclude their meditation by leading Kundalini back to the base chakra.

It takes many years for the disciple—who usually goes into a partial trance while raising the Kundalini—to actually raise the Kundalini from the base to the crown chakra. Using the force of his will, he may raise it a little higher with each meditation. An adept is capable of raising and lowering the Kundalini from the base to the crown chakras in the space of an hour.

During their meditations on the Kundalini, these devotees send out to the world through the seven planes of consciousness the concentrated power of the Christ that is activated as Kundalini enters each chakra. These and other meditations of the true unascended masters of the Himalayas have served for thousands of years to provide the open door for the Light to flow into a darkened world and to raise mankind's consciousness and sustain it at the levels beyond that which the unenlightened masses could attain on their own.

Regarding the concept of Kundalini, the Ascended Masters have given us the term *Seed Atom* because it signifies the focusing within the plane of Matter, that is, within the Mother consciousness, the full potential of that which is destined to be realized in the plane of Spirit, in the Father consciousness, through the alchemical marriage—the union of Matter and Spirit. The whole of the microcosm—herein defined as the material universe—is actually focused within the Seed Atom as the negative aspect of divine power. And the whole of the Macrocosm—the spiritual universe—is focused within the Lodestone of the Presence (the name given for the focus of what the Hindus call *Shakta*) as the positive aspect of the divine power.

Thus, when the Seed Atom is raised, the personality of man (the manifestation) merges with the impersonality of God (the Universal One). In merging with the Ocean, the drop is not lost, however, but gains permanent Self-realization as the Impersonal Impersonality, the Impersonal Personality, the Personal Personality and the Personal Impersonality of the Godhead. Truly the goal of yoga, the union of you and God, is the transmutation of the limited human self into the unlimited Divine Self.

Because of the intense powers of the Kundalini, which overnight may make men spiritual giants or demons, it is not advisable to seek to raise the Kundalini unless one is under the guidance and protection of a true unascended master. The Ascended Masters recommend that students meditate only upon the chakras in the plane of Spirit—those above and including the heart chalice. The exercise given in chapter 1 of this volume for the raising of the white-fire ball from the level of the heart to the I AM Presence is the safest meditation for the raising of the Seed Atom; for it simulates in the plane of Spirit the raising of the Kundalini without any danger of actually arousing the Kundalini fires until the lifestream has drawn such a momentum of power in the upper chakras and in the Lodestone of the Presence as to counterbalance any remaining untransmuted substance that may be aroused as the Kundalini rises through the plane of Matter.

If the Ascended Master student uses this meditation to focus the consciousness of the Christ in the planes of Spirit-Fire, Spirit-Water, Spirit-Air and Spirit-Earth, visualizing the white-fire ball rising through the heart, throat, third eye and crown chakras en route to the Christ Self and the I AM Presence, he will never need to meditate upon the chakras be-low the heart, for they will automatically be purified through their connection to the Four Cosmic Forces. Nevertheless, the student may visualize the action of the violet flame and other aspects of the sacred fire swirling through his entire being as shown on the lower figure of the Chart of Your Divine Self.

There is never any possibility of the student misusing the fires of creation if the Seed Atom is raised according to the initiatic timetable, that is, if the initiations of the sacred fire preparatory to and preceding the raising of the Seed Atom are successfully passed. Then the release of God-power, God-wisdom and God-love through the being of man can only intensify the good already outpictured by the lifestream.

But if the raising of the Kundalini is forced prior to (1) the invocation of the sacred fire for the transmutation of impurities in the four lower bodies and electronic belt; (2) the clearing of the astral debris that accumulates at the vortices of Light, at the chakras; (3) the balancing of the threefold flame; and (4) the alignment of the four lower bodies and the manifestation of his God-dominion over the human intellect, ego and will, then there is indeed grave danger to the lifestream; for the Kundalini fires animate whatever is present in the world of man as they ascend the spinal altar. If the passions of the flesh and the temptations of the world still have hold upon his consciousness, these, together with his human creation, may be magnified by the Kundalini to the point of unhinging his mind. When the sex drive is amplified by the Kundalini, it rages in his being as an uncontrollable force, causing him to behave as a wild beast and finally to become insane.

The dangers involved in playing with the Kundalini fires cannot be overstated. We have seen the tragic results of the rape of the Divine Mother and the abuse of the sacred path of the Kundalini by the violent who have sought to take heaven (the crown chakra) by force[8] (by forcing the raising of the Kundalini). We have seen that the tearing of the garment of the soul and the burning of the solar faculties that has resulted from such madness has affected lifestreams for numerous embodiments following their indiscretion. Wise, therefore, is the student who heeds this warning. Placing his hand in the hand of his own Christ Self, he is content to walk the Path under the direction of his God Presence in the calm and certain knowing that if he does all things well, fulfilling the precepts of the Law in service and in grace, he will attain the supreme goal of reunion based on self-mastery.

The Ascended Masters have shown us that it is altogether possible for the advanced student to raise the Seed Atom prior to the transfiguration. If this should occur, it is highly unlikely that the Seed Atom will remain in the crown chakra. It may descend to the heart chalice to magnify the power of the Christ in the planes of Spirit-Fire and Matter-Fire, or it may well return to the base of the spine. If sufficient mastery over the seven planes and the release of the seven rays through the seven chakras is attained prior to the raising of the Seed Atom, then the energies within the chakras will be in perfect polarity, and when the Seed Atom enters each chakra, it will absorb the feminine aspect of the Christ already anchored there. Drawing a greater and greater momentum of the feminine ray as it rises, the Seed Atom has a greater forcefield of attraction to the Lodestone, which simultaneously magnetizes to itself the masculine aspect of the Christ focused in the chakras. In this manner, during the raising of the Seed Atom all of the energies of man are polarized to the planes of Spirit-Earth and Matter-Earth.

If we understand that the chakras are the focus of the Christ, of the masculine and feminine rays in man (in manifestation), and the Seed Atom and Lodestone are the focuses of the Father-Mother God, then we will see that the Divine Mother draws into herself the feminine aspect of man from within the chakras and the Divine Father draws into himself the masculine aspect of man from within the chakras. As long as the union of Matter and Spirit is sustained while the Seed Atom remains in the Lodestone, so long will man be able to remain in nirvana or samadhi. In this state, his consciousness is withdrawn from all planes except that of Spirit-Earth and Matter-Earth. This gives him a direct tie to the planes of Spirit-Earth and Matter-Earth in the Causal Body, the first and second spheres of purity and illumination, which are the open doors to the spheres of the five secret rays held between them —which are the planes of nirvana.

When the Seed Atom returns either to the heart or to the base-of-the-spine chakra, the action of the masculine and feminine rays in man is returned to the chakras accelerated by the God consciousness drawn from within the Lodestone and the Seed Atom. When all other conditions necessary for the transfiguration have been met, the raising of the Seed Atom and its union with the Lodestone, which takes place during this initiation, produces in the four lower bodies and in his flesh the transfiguring power of the Holy Spirit, whereby man becomes God and God becomes man.

Once the initiation of the transfiguration is passed, the Seed Atom may descend the 'Mount of Transfiguration,' but it never again descends lower than the heart chalice, for man has transcended the planes of Matter and his spirit no longer dwells in the planes of Matter. In the initiation of the resurrection, the Seed Atom is permanently anchored in the Lodestone, and the action of the Christ in the plane of Spirit-Fire and Matter-Fire (in the heart chakra) comes into perfect polarity with the action of the Father-Mother God where the plane of Spirit-Earth and Matter-Earth have united (in the crown chakra). In the initiation of the ascension the focus of the Father-Mother God anchored in the Lodestone and the Seed Atom descends to the heart chalice, where the full potential of the Godhead merges with the full potential of the Christ. God in Christ then affirms the victory of the Presence in the planes of Spirit and Matter—"I AM a blazing Sun!"— and the microcosm ascends into the Macrocosm.

"The sound of far-off worlds is heard in the hearts of the lonely ones, and they are lonely no longer. The collapse of the universe into the microcosm of man is the surrender of the Eternal One to the individual. The flame caresses the soul; and, as God draws nigh within the flame, understanding is born and all of the pieces of the strange puzzle of life rise into place as a cosmic picture of celestial hope."[9]

Now the being of man, as the rising triangle, merges with the Being of God, the descending triangle, and man becomes one with the star that once shone over the place where the infant Christ was born. The heart of man becomes one with the heart of God. As Above, so below, the ascension is the victory of the Law of Cycles. God in man is omnipotent, omniscient and omnipresent. Man in God is all powerful, all knowing and everywhere present.

The Crystal of Purity

The mastery of self through the mastery of life's energies is summed up in one word: purity. Indeed, those who have ascended before us avow that their victory was born out of purity of thought, word and deed—and out of their fastidious attention to the purification of the four lower bodies and the chalices.

From time to time disciples on the Path have been privileged to receive admonishment from the Goddess of Purity. Her counsel is born out of her devotion to the flame of purity, which has lifted many a soul out of the degradation of astral confusion into the Light of his native solar consciousness.

From her retreat in Madagascar and her focus of healing established in America have come inspiration and hope for the dawn of the Age of Enlightenment.

Simply, she has said, "Purity, beloved ones, begins with a single crystal, the crystal of your consciousness. And from the point of the flame within the center of the crystal begins the expansion of the consciousness of purity. The pure in heart see God through the crystal of their own consciousness, which they have made God's consciousness.

"When you have mastered the many facets of the single crystal, then other crystals will be added unto you with many more facets of opportunity for self-mastery. And so, you see, each crystal denotes another step of initiation to the brothers and sisters serving in my retreat here in Madagascar.

"In our beautiful island in the sea we have consecrated our energies to the crystal diadem of purity that is the consciousness of God, and as the flame passes through the crystal—the mingling of the mist and the crystal, of the formed and the unformed—there is a release of the Cosmic Christ consciousness to the earth."

In the same discourse she gently reminded the students to keep the crystal of their consciousness pure: "Those who truly love will keep the crystal polished so that all of the myriad hues of the diamond-shining Mind of God will be reflected throughout their consciousness.

"Smudges appear easily on the crystal as one moves through the outer world that has been polluted by mankind's consciousness. Carefully one must take from one's pocket the velvet cloth to polish the crystal.

"Keep it clean as though it were the very dearest object of your affection, for at the moment when the Virgins (the holy Ascended Lady Masters) come to infuse you with the momentum of their purity and the Seraphim gather, having come lately from the very throne of God himself to bring to you a drop of purity from his heart—at that moment, precious ones, the crystal must be polished, else it cannot reflect the flame within the drop of purity.

"But if the crystal be polished, then the flame within the drop, taken from the ocean of God's flaming purity, can merge with the flame that is in the center of your crystal. A fiery magnetic attraction impels the purity of God to the center of each flaming crystal.

"But when there is darkness surrounding the crystal—between the flame within and the flame without—then penetration cannot occur. Blessed are the pure in heart, for they shall indeed see the consciousness of God's flaming purity."[10]

The Goddess of Purity then announced that she and her angels bore gifts for all who were prepared to receive them: "I come this day bearing many crystals, and so do my angels. They are spherical crystals, beloved ones, and they are to be placed over those chakras in each one of you and in each one upon the planetary body who is ready to receive the stepping-up of the release of the flame through the seven centers anchored in the four lower bodies of man.

"Each of the crystals that we bear is designated for a specific chakra of a specific individual. God has individualized himself in these crystals that I carry. And, after the pattern of each one's own flaming identity, he has fashioned the crystal that is designed to unlock your divine blueprint through each of the seven chakras.

"Not everyone will receive a crystal for each chakra, and there are some in the world who are qualified to receive several more than some of you here. For God is no respecter of the human personality. He looks at the law of thy being, of each one's being. He calculates. He draws up the fires of initiations passed, of Light released, and the cosmic computer releases the exact judgment for each lifestream.

"Therefore, as you have sown, so shall you reap.[11] And if you feel that you would like additional crystals in time to come, then remember that the development of the Light, the service to the seven rays and to the diamond-shining Mind of God will ensure to you the mastery of the four lower bodies and of the four elements that must precede the opening of the chakras.

"My angels stand in position over you and over the students of Light throughout the world, and they are now placing the crystals over the chakras in each one of you."

This dispensation from the Lords of Karma presents a challenge to all who seek the prize of purity, for the Goddess of Purity has said that all who read this dictation and diligently prepare their consciousness may likewise receive the gift of the crystals.

"Beloved ones, the crystal will magnify the Light or the darkness that is in you. 'If therefore the Light that is in thee be darkness, how great is that darkness?'"[12]

Later she explained to us that the crystals placed over the chakras would function as transformers to accelerate both the release of Light from the chakras and the transmutation of the remaining human consciousness surrounding the chakras. She also warned the students of the urgency of the times:

"You are at the point of no return. You must therefore surrender the darkness, that the darkness might become Light. For when you surrender the darkness into the flame, the flame consumes the night and returns to you the Light. And that Light is a fire that travels the spiral of the crystal and releases the outburst of the sparks of purity through each of your chakras that is covered with the crystal."

In conclusion, she gave welcome advice and instruction on the handling of misqualified energy and the ritual of bathing the chakras: "Precious ones, do not struggle with the untransmuted energies that accumulate around the chakras. For each chakra is a mighty sun, a whirling sun that is a vortex of light drawing into itself for transmutation all human creation and releasing simultaneously the Light from the heart of the I AM Presence. Therefore, you must expect that untransmuted energy will collect at the brightest chakras, for there it has the greatest possibility of finding release.

"As the ancients performed daily ablutions in holy water, so may I remind you to perform daily the sacrament of bathing the chakras, of releasing into the flame the energies that gather there for transmutation, so that the full-orbed manifestation of the Light of God can blaze through the crystals we have placed over the chakras.

"Won't you train yourself upon awakening, after you have made your initial invocations to the flame of the Almighty One, to call for this transmutation, for the fiery essence of the sacred fire breath to go forth and to draw off all accumulations of negativity around the seven chakras?

"This simple exercise is practiced by the brothers and sisters in our retreat, for I have shown them that such practice will ensure a swift momentum, a swift rising of their light into the Light.

"The light in you must become one with the Light in the heart of the Universal, in the heart of the God Presence. To that end do we maintain our focus of purity. To that end have we come this day—that the light may become one with the Light, that the flame may return to the home of the Flame, that all may come full circle, that you may experience the resurrection during the cycles of the return of karma, which ought to be cycles of transmutation.

"These cycles are stepped up for the elect, beloved ones. Fear not, then, when your karma appears as a mighty legion upon the horizon, as a mighty army that comes forth to defeat the Christ. Fear not, but stand with the prophet upon the hillside.[13] Raise your right hand as the authority of your I AM Presence and say to your own human creation: 'I refuse to accept your domination any longer! Go down before the Sun of the Almighty! Go down before the flame of the Most High God!'

"Stand thus before the Goliath of your own human consciousness, beloved ones, and fear not, retreat not. Draw courage from the love of purity, draw courage from the crystal, draw courage from the Flame in the center of the crystal."

Then, smiling a smile of loveliness, the Goddess of Purity said: "Do you feel all buttoned up with crystals? Well, then, remember that the buttons that shall appear upon the seamless garment of your divinity are the crystals upon the seven chakras.

"I pray that you will make use of those that have been given unto you, that in due course you might all receive the full complement of crystals reflecting the seven rays and the focus of the Crystal Diadem in our retreat.

"My purity I leave with you. My focus is already here. Through it I pour to you each day a greater awareness and consciousness of the purity of your mission, of your divine plan, of the seven color rays and their meaning in your life.

"Seek purity and find it, for it will illumine the entire Law of thy being.

> In the purity of victory I came,
> In victory's flame I came—
> To victory's flame I return.
> In the Oneness of His love I remain
> And I AM the Goddess of Purity."[14]

FIGURE 39: Spirals of Self-Awareness Traverse Planes of Consciousness
The Threefold Trinity from the Macrocosm to the Microcosm

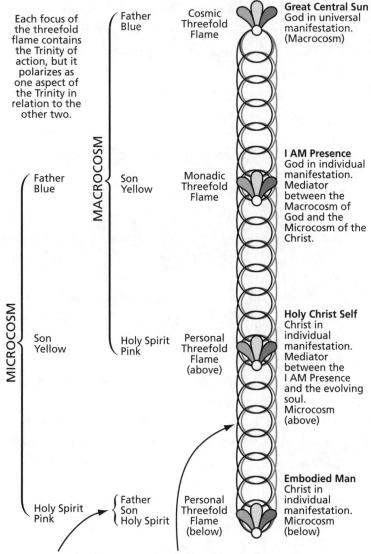

Each focus of the threefold flame contains the Trinity of action, but it polarizes as one aspect of the Trinity in relation to the other two.

MACROCOSM

Father Blue — Cosmic Threefold Flame

Great Central Sun
God in universal manifestation. (Macrocosm)

Father Blue — Son Yellow — Monadic Threefold Flame

I AM Presence
God in individual manifestation. Mediator between the Macrocosm of God and the Microcosm of the Christ.

MICROCOSM

Son Yellow — Holy Spirit Pink — Personal Threefold Flame (above)

Holy Christ Self
Christ in individual manifestation. Mediator between the I AM Presence and the evolving soul. Microcosm (above)

Holy Spirit Pink — Father Son Holy Spirit — Personal Threefold Flame (below)

Embodied Man
Christ in individual manifestation. Microcosm (below)

In man (the manifestation of God) the Macrocosm becomes the microcosm and the microcosm becomes the Macrocosm.

The crystal cord is magnified to show the + and − spirals of Alpha and Omega that form the ray that descends from the heart of the One God to the heart of his individualization in the I AM Presence to the heart of the Holy Christ Self to the heart of the embodied lifestream.

COUNT-TO-NINE DECREE
by Cuzco

In the name of the beloved mighty victorious Presence of God, I AM in me, my very own beloved Holy Christ Self, beloved Archangel Michael, Prince Oromasis, Mighty Astrea, Goddess of Light, beloved Ascended Master Cuzco, beloved Lanello, the entire Spirit of the Great White Brotherhood and the World Mother, elemental life—fire, air, water and earth! I decree:

Come now by love divine,
Guard thou this soul of mine,
Make now my world all thine,
God's Light around me shine.

Visualize the white Light filling the ovoid of the aura

I count one,
It is done.
O feeling world, Be still!
Two and three,
I AM free,
Peace, it is God's will.

Visualize a band of white fire around the solar plexus

I count four,
I do adore
My Presence all divine.
Five and six,
O God, affix
My gaze on thee sublime!

Visualize a band of white fire around the neck and throat chakra

I count seven,
Come, O Heaven,
My energies take hold!
Eight and nine,
Completely thine,
My mental world enfold!

Visualize a band of white fire around the head and third eye

The white-fire Light now encircles me, Visualize the
All riptides are rejected! white Light
encircling all of
With God's own might around me bright the chakras and
I AM by love protected! the four lower
bodies

I accept this done right now with full power! I AM this done right now with full power! I AM, I AM, I AM God-life expressing perfection all ways at all times. This which I call forth for myself I call forth for every man, woman and child on this planet!

Chapter 3

Immortality

*And the LORD God said,
Behold, the man is become as
one of us, to know good and
evil: and now, lest he put forth
his hand, and take also of the
tree of life, and eat, and live for
ever:*

*Therefore the LORD God
sent him forth from the garden
of Eden, to till the ground from
whence he was taken.*

*So he drove out the man;
and he placed at the east of the
garden of Eden Cherubims, and
a flaming sword which turned
every way, to keep the way of
the tree of life.*

GENESIS

Immortality

MANY YEARS AGO AN ARMY
sergeant spurred a regiment
into action, we are told, by shouting at the top of his lungs to
a company stymied by the inertia of fear and indecision,
"What th' h—! Do you want to live forever?"

Reminded of the fact that he will not live forever in one
physical body, that the body is not indispensable to the life of
the soul, and that only Truth lives forever, man is able to
summon the courage to take an unconditional stand for
freedom and to defend, with his very life if necessary, his
divine inheritance and those immortal principles with which
God has endowed his soul.

Nevertheless, the soul yearns for the understanding that
will see him through those moments when, for want of certain
knowing, his courage fails him. He asks that he might understand: If God created man to be immortal like himself, why,
when referring to "the tree of the knowledge of good and

evil," did he say, "in the day that thou eatest thereof thou shalt surely die?"[1] If it was God's desire that man should live forever, why did he set up a condition whereby man, through a seemingly harmless act, might lose his immortal inheritance?

The Serpentine Lie

Just as he is wondering if he will ever come to grips with this perplexing problem, man is confronted with the counter-argument of the Serpent, couched in the pseudo-logic of the carnal mind, which assures him, "Ye shall not surely die." This intellectual appeal takes into account man's latent belief in the immortality of the soul. It subtly suggests that if he sins, he will not "surely" be punished, for even the Serpent knows that man's True Identity is preserved beyond the grave. There-fore, his statement, "Ye shall not surely die," is a half-truth— the most dangerous form of lie there is.

Without equivocation, the Word of the LORD came to the prophet Ezekiel to refute this serpentine lie: for God said, "The soul that sinneth, it shall die.... The righteousness of the righteous shall be upon him ... in his righteousness that he hath done he shall live.... The wickedness of the wicked shall be upon him ... and in his sin that he had sinned, in them shall he die."[2]

These statements set forth the teachings of the Christ on the law of cause and effect long before the birth of Jesus. Much later, the understanding of this irrevocable Law was imparted to John on the Isle of Patmos. After Jesus' ascension, he gave to the beloved disciple the keys to the mysteries of Life, which he "sent and signified by his angel."[3] And John saw the dead stand before God; and he wrote that "they were judged every man according to their works."[4]

There is one important fact that is omitted in the Serpent's logic, and it is this: the part of man that identifies with the unreality of sin cannot endure the flaming Presence of God-reality; it may, therefore, be cast into the Lake of Fire and pass through what is known as "the second death."[5]

Common sense tells us that if God would provide for the immortality of his own perfect creation, then he would also provide for the nullification of those imperfect forms that might be created by unascended man under the original covenant of free will. For when God bestowed upon man the gift of free will, he gave him the opportunity (within a limited framework) to experiment with the creative powers that accompanied the gift. Man could create and experiment as he would; but in order to be stamped with the seal of immortality, his creative experiments must pass the test of time and eternity—the test of fire.

Mysteries in the Book of Life

What is the Lake of Fire[6]? And what is the second death? What is the tree of the knowledge of good and evil? What is the Tree of Life[7]? And what is the River of Water of Life, clear as crystal?[8]

The heirs of God have a right to know the answers to these questions; and so these and other mysteries that are written in the Book of Life shall be made plain in this chapter, that all who read may understand, and that all who truly understand may eat and live forever.

To that end we shall explore the meaning of immortality as it applies to the Higher Self as well as to the lower self of man. And we shall give some answers to the question that has plagued man since his descent into the prison house of Matter: "Good Master, what shall I do to inherit eternal life?"[9]

The Last Enemy

Although Jesus names death as the enemy—the last enemy that shall be overcome[10]—humanity, plagued by sin, sickness and the fears of old age, often welcome the "Grim Reaper." After they have spent their allotment of energy in every form of selfish pleasure-seeking, after they have filled their minds with the knowledge of the world and followed its ways, after they have lived out their abbreviated span of threescore and ten and marked their personal accomplishments "satisfactory" or "unsatisfactory" (as the case may be), they are willing, albeit reluctantly, to wave adieu to an ungrateful world and to sever the ties of human existence.

This attitude is an indictment of civilization and of the materialistic consciousness that has brought it to its present state. This attitude, framed by an ignorant religion and abetted by a fatalistic science, clearly shows that the larger purposes of Life are unknown. Life itself, which is God, is unknown to men—although many continue to worship at the altar "TO THE UNKNOWN GOD."[11] This attitude also reveals in the race consciousness an ingrained acceptance of mortality as a way of life: the hopes, the fears and the aspirations of men all stem from a finite consciousness having a finite existence in a finite world.

Nevertheless, while yet surrounded by the mass consciousness of mortality, David said, "Thou wilt not leave my soul in hell; neither wilt thou suffer thine Holy One to see corruption."[12] Here corruption means disintegration, or the death of the soul. David knew that Life, as a synonym for God, is ipso facto immortal. He knew that Life, as an attribute of God reflected in his creation, man, must go on forever; for eternal Life was, and is, the very nature of Being.

The silent soul, knowing there is more to Life than that

which has been glimpsed by the outer consciousness, more than the few drops left in the cup, knowing that the time must come to terminate his earthly sojourn, wills to go on here and hereafter in the search for Reality. But the attitudes of the mortal mind regarding death are counter to the intent of God, who gives the gift of immortality to everyone who will accept it on His terms. Furthermore, these attitudes are a complete refutation of him who said, "I AM come that they might have life, and that they might have it more abundantly."[13]

➤ Life Is God

Those who are familiar with the Great Law and understand its higher action know that Life is sacred, that Life is immortal, and that Life is God. Those who also understand some of Life's mysteries know that the Tree of Life standing in the midst of the Garden is an allegorical representation of the individualized I AM Presence. In order to eat of the twelve manner of fruits thereof, which are stored in his Causal Body, man is required by Law to exchange his mortal consciousness for the immortal consciousness of God-power, God-love, God-mastery, God-control, God-obedience, God-wisdom, God-harmony, God-gratitude, God-justice, God-reality, God-vision, God-victory (see figure 40).

The Garden of Eden is allegorically the Causal Body of man, even as the Tree of Life in the midst thereof is the I AM Presence. *Eden* can be interpreted as *E*(nergy)-*den*—a place where God's energy is found in concentration.[14] Interestingly, one of the definitions of *den* is a "center of secret (sacred) activity." In fact, man has never really lost his ties to Eden; "Paradise Lost" can be regained as he practices the ritual of service through heart, head and hand. The heirs of Eden who

FIGURE 40: Twelve Manner of Fruits of the Tree of Life

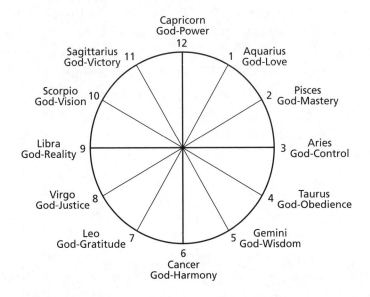

are willing to reestablish their sonship and to claim their inheritance by applying the Laws of God through the orderly processes of initiation will be given the opportunity of unlocking the abundant blessings of the Causal Body for the good of all.

Just as God is individualized for every man in the I AM Presence, so heaven is individualized for each one in his own Causal Body. Each individual Causal Body is one of the Father's many mansions, one of his manifest "ions," or electronically charged particles of individualized manifestation. Just as there is a universal I AM Presence, which some address as "Almighty God," so there is a universal Causal Body, which is generally referred to as "heaven." This universal Causal Body is more accurately described as "the Great Causal Body."

The Great Causal Body is the Macrocosmic heaven-world, whereas the individual Causal Body is the microcosmic heaven-world. Both are reservoirs of great God-power into which all who are sincere may tap for the bringing in of the kingdom of God "as Above (in the Causal Body), so below (in the world of form)."

We read in the Book of Revelation: "And he shewed me a pure river of water of life, clear as crystal, proceeding out of the throne of God and of the Lamb. In the midst of the street of it, and on either side of the river, was there the tree of life."[15] Here John was shown the vision of the Chart of Your Divine Self (facing page 88). The "pure river of water of life, clear as crystal" is the crystal cord, the pure stream of energy that proceeds "out of the throne of God" (out of the I AM Presence) and is conveyed to man by "the Lamb" (the Christ Self).* In this case, we observe the Causal Body as the branches of the Tree of Life, which extend "on either side of the river" and actually embrace the entire garden.

As man partakes of the fruits of the Tree of Life (those virtues that comprise the Causal Body), he experiences his God-identity and is able to gild each moment of his life with the crown of God-perfection. Each moment is thus immortalized, and moment by moment he himself becomes immortal. Thus, he is brought to a state of Eden once again; and he is given the opportunity of making use of the treasures not only of his own Causal Body, but also of those stored in the Great Causal Body, which contains all of the Good that has ever been externalized by the Sons and Daughters of God, Ascended and unascended. Beloved Kuthumi once commented on this process:

"When the necessary purification of consciousness is accomplished through holy service to Life and a concerted decree effort, and the candidate stands purged by the violet flame, stripped by Divine Reality (the Holy Spirit) of every trace of impure thought and feeling, he will be allowed to

---

* The Lamb "slain from the foundation of the world" always symbolizes the Christ.

stretch forth his hand to receive the fruit of the Tree of Life.

"This initiation is given by the Great Initiator—our Beloved Teacher—the Buddha Lord Maitreya. This 'first fruit' is the conferment of the power to direct Light's energy (henceforth magnetized by the initiate from his own Sun Source, the I AM THAT I AM) into the atomic structure of his four lower bodies at will.

"This Light of God—which is the only Light that never fails—then rushes into the original channels where the all-sustaining power formerly flowed. There, through its self-luminous, intelligent quality, the Light transmutes, thread by thread, the overlay of the old energy paths and the old garment of the human consciousness as it weaves (literally, cell by cell) the transcendent perfection of the seamless garment of the living Christ."[16]

In this manner, the Light of God from the Causal Body of man reweaves the imperfect energy-patterns of his electronic belt with a filigree pattern of perfection.

The Right (Rite) to Immortality

The illumined understand that immortality is not merely a reward for well-doing—although reward it may well be—but the natural intention of God for man that was manifest from the foundation of the world and from the moment of creation for each individual. As Kuthumi has said: "It must be understood that immortality is an endowment synonymous and concurrent with Life—a birthright, not a usurpation. The overlay of wrong thought and feeling has too long veiled by an energy veil (a shroud of humanly misqualified substance) the Light that is the Life-giving essence of freedom for every atom in manifestation."[17]

Serapis Bey teaches that "immortality is of high price, and

it demands the allness of men from the smallness of men....
Men cannot build out of mortal substance immortal bodies.
They cannot build out of mortal thoughts immortal ideas.
They cannot build out of mortal feelings divine feelings that
enfold the world and create the great Pyramid of Life."[18]

Every son and daughter of God was endowed not only
with a master plan, a blueprint for destiny, but also with the
tools to implement that plan in the tenets of the Law of Life.
These tenets are the keys to immortality; they unlock the
formulas that enable man to find and fulfill his destiny and to
conquer the elements of death. It is right that men should cling
to life, but let that clinging be for the fulfillment of divine
purposes and for the realization of true illumination. At the
end of the rainbow of one's search for Truth lies the pot of
gold—spiritual illumination.

Let us, then, establish the tenets of man's immortality, the
components of his identity, the building blocks of being that
equate the soul of man to the Soul of God and ensure his
immortality through the fulfillment of his master plan.

The Soul: A Living Potential

God is a Spirit and the soul is the living potential of God.
The soul's demand for free will and her separation from God
resulted in the descent of this potential into the lowly estate of
the flesh.

Sown in dishonor, the soul is destined to be raised in
honor to the fullness of that God-estate that is the one Spirit of
all Life. The soul can be lost; Spirit can never die.

> Never the Spirit was born;
>   the Spirit shall cease to be never;
> Never was time it was not;
>   End and Beginning are dreams!

Birthless and deathless and changeless
remaineth the Spirit for ever;
Death hath not touched it at all,
dead though the house of it seems![19]

The soul, then, remains a fallen potential that must be imbued with the Reality of Spirit, purified through prayer and supplication, and returned to the glory from which she descended and to the unity of the Whole.

This rejoining of soul to Spirit is the alchemical marriage that determines the destiny of the self and makes it one with immortal Truth.

When this ritual is fulfilled, the highest Self is enthroned as the Lord of Life, and the potential of God, realized in man, is found to be the All-in-all.

What Is the Soul?

The soul is a popular topic today. People talk about and write about the soul. They know that the soul is important, but they don't know why. Our souls have been evolving as long as we have been sojourning in the material universe. Yet few people really know what the soul is. Many give it no thought at all. You could say that they are "soul illiterate." If you took a random poll and asked people if they knew how to care for their souls, most people would say they didn't have the slightest idea.

What, then, is the soul, how does one care for the soul, and what is soul evolution all about? We must ask ourselves these questions because our knowledge of the condition of our souls is the key to our success on the spiritual path.

We can think of the soul as a glisteningly transparent sphere that is constantly evolving—or devolving. The soul is the mortal part of ourselves that can become immortal—that *must* become immortal if she is to survive. To achieve immortality, the soul must be fused, or bonded, to her Higher Self, who is her Holy Christ Self. Yes, until this bonding takes place, the soul is impermanent and therefore can be lost.

This is why souls who are not tethered to their Higher Self are in jeopardy on planet Earth. Any one of us can lose our soul and become a castaway[20] by blaspheming God or tormenting our soul (or another's soul) until the soul welcomes death as a surcease from physical and spiritual abuse. The Blessed Mother Mary has implored us to pray to God daily to send his angels to rescue souls who will be lost if we do not call for divine intercession in their behalf. Let us respond to her plea with soul fervor.

Have you ever thought about the fact that in this life and past lives you might have neglected the development of your soul, choosing instead to develop your human ego? Or that you might not have nurtured your soul—this essential "Life-essence" that mirrors both your personality and the Personality of God? What you have drawn from these two personalities, how you have integrated the two and incorporated them into your unique soul awareness, actually defines your soul identity.

If you have walled off your soul from the rest of yourself and disconnected your soul from your personality and the Personality of God, you are at a standstill in your spiritual evolution. And if you don't know it, you're even worse off: you're in a minus position.

Our souls are wise. Our souls know the past and its application to the present and the future. And they see the immediacy of the moment. The soul is highly sensitive, and at the same time she is innocent and defenseless. She is vulnerable to astral forces. She is impressionable and easily led astray. She

is often colored by her surroundings. She suffers when subjected to violence of any kind. She is wounded by mental and emotional toxins and by physical or verbal abuse. Our souls urgently need our comfort and consolation, our soothing words. They need to know that we will protect them from all harm.

The Inner Child

The Ascended Masters have referred to the soul as the child who lives inside of us. Psychologists have dubbed the soul "the inner child." The soul by any other name is still the soul. And we are her parents and teachers, even as we are her students.

It is our responsibility to daily impress upon the soul (1) what is right—what is Real and of enduring worth and therefore must be kept—and (2) what is wrong—what is not Real and not of enduring worth and therefore must not be kept but cast into the sacred fire.

El Morya says that we should not place our emphasis on being obedient to the soul as the inner child, but rather that we should place our emphasis on teaching the soul to be obedient to God and to her Holy Christ Self. You would not allow your children to dictate the terms of your household or your comings and goings, so why would you allow your soul, your inner child, to dominate you and tell you, "Go here. Go there. Do this. Do that"?

The soul is the little child who is destined to become the Christ Child. Let us lead our souls even as we are led by our Holy Christ Self. Moreover, let us remember that as parents and teachers we are responsible for the protection and education not only of our children but also of our souls, that we might mold both the souls of our children and our own

see page 198

souls after the heavenly patterns.

The soul *awakened* is in touch with all Life. And for this very reason she requires daily immersion in the sacred fire of God through deep and one-pointed meditation, an active devotion to God and a loving solicitude for her enemies as well as for her friends.

From the heart of the Elohim of Peace flow the words of the apostle Paul for the tutoring of our souls in the way of sustaining a positive mental attitude:

> *Finally, brethren, whatsoever things are true, whatsoever things are honest, whatsoever things are just, whatsoever things are pure, whatsoever things are lovely, whatsoever things are of good report; if there be any virtue, and if there be any praise, think on these things.*
>
> *Those things, which ye have both learned, and received, and heard, and seen in me, do: and the God of Peace shall be with you.*[21]

The soul mirrors whatever she puts her attention on. So we must use the mirror of mind and Spirit to reflect back upon the soul the values and virtues we want her to first internalize and then externalize.

The soul's visualization of the physical sun and the Sun-behind-the-sun, i.e., the Spiritual Sun, is a key to the soul's becoming a permanent part of the Sun of her mighty I AM Presence. If in her meditations the soul fixes her gaze on Alpha and Omega in the Great Central Sun and on Helios and Vesta in the sun of our system, she will absorb the infinitesimal patterns of the many suns in our galaxy and beyond—the whole and the part, the atoms and the molecules, the worlds within worlds. This will give her an intimate connection with physical infinity, which will bring her, through her dynamic decrees, to that spiritual infinity to which the Ascended Adepts have attained.

The Soul Is Trapped in the Seat-of-the-Soul Chakra

Through ritual the soul evolves. And the soul who is right with her God is eager to evolve to that level of attainment whereby she, after long centuries of exile, may once again take up her abode in the secret chamber of the heart. But there are serious, sobering reasons why it is not so easy for the soul to rise from the seat-of-the-soul chakra to the heart chakra. You see, when the soul fell from grace, she fell from the secret chamber of the heart and thereafter was confined to the seat-of-the-soul chakra.

El Morya tells us that most souls who fell are still trapped in the seat-of-the-soul chakra by their karma and that they cannot rise above that station until they balance the percentage of karma that the Lords of Karma require of them—usually 51 percent, plus or minus. (The percentage is different for every soul because each soul's karma is unique.)

It is from this chakra that Saint Germain would rescue souls by the seventh-ray action of the Holy Spirit and the violet flame. Coincidentally, or not, the seat-of-the-soul chakra is the seventh ray (the violet ray) chakra, the very best environment for the soul in her yet imperfect state.

Alas, the soul is literally a self-made prisoner. Furthermore, she is the prisoner of the human ego and the dweller-on-the-threshold. Both are stern taskmasters and avowed enemies of the soul. They have occupied the temples of man and woman since the Fall of twin flames in the Garden of Eden.

Since Eden We Have Created the Ego and the Dweller

The Garden of Eden was the original Mystery School founded by Lord Maitreya to train Sons and Daughters of

God to become spiritual adepts, initiates of the highest order, that they might go forth from the Mystery School to raise the consciousness of the children of God and to make the teachings of the spiritual path available to them and eventually to all mankind.

The Paradise described in Genesis was in the etheric octave somewhere between heaven and earth. Adam and Eve, the archetypal twin flames, and numerous other sets of twin flames studied there under Lord Maitreya, who is named in Genesis as the LORD God.

When tempted of the Serpent to eat of the fruit of the tree of the knowledge of good and evil, many of Maitreya's students disobeyed him.[22] Even though the LORD had told them that "in the day that thou eatest thereof thou shalt surely die," these students of the Mystery School believed the Serpent's equivocation, "Ye shall not *surely* die," and partook of the forbidden fruit.[23]

All who entered into this act of disobedience paid the ultimate price: the flame of their immortality was snuffed out. Thus, they knew that their souls had become naked and that they were now mortal. Grief-stricken, they went forth from Eden, literally driven out by the LORD God, "lest Adam put forth his hand and take also of the Tree of Life and eat and live forever"[24] in his fallen state.

And so, Adam and Eve and many sets of twin flames were consigned to the earth plane and to earthly bodies. To them the LORD God declared: "In the sweat of thy face shalt thou eat bread, till thou return unto the ground; for out of it wast thou taken: for dust thou art, and unto dust shalt thou return."[25]

No greater indictment has ever been handed down by the LORD God upon his people.

While we were in Eden, we were innocent. We developed

neither ego nor dweller. However, our souls were susceptible and we fell. Over the long centuries of our souls' incarceration on planet Earth since the Fall, we have created the ego and the dweller and allowed them to mushroom until they have displaced the "hidden man of the heart," the Holy Christ Self.

We have allowed the ego and the dweller to intimidate our souls. Only the soul who has garnered the sacred fire of God can counteract the telling blows of the not-self. She who has Wisdom's fire consciously recognizes and confronts the ego. She is up to the task of slaying it. Furthermore, she knows that she alone must undo the threads she has sewn in dishonor and must now sew in honor.

We can all become conscious of the antics of our egos *if we want to*—that is, if we are not in a state of denial, denying the destructive words and deeds that come through our egos and dominate not only our own souls but, sadly, the souls of others. The dweller-on-the-threshold, on the other hand, is not so easy to detect. It inhabits the subconscious and the unconscious minds even as it inhibits the soul's evolution. And while the soul is terrified of the dweller, the ego is allied with the dweller, ever plotting the soul's demise.

When a soul has committed herself to Darkness and the Dark Ones, she is completely taken over by the human ego and the dweller-on-the-threshold. There is no longer a distinction between the ego and the dweller. They are merged as one. The soul has for all intents and purposes ceased to exist.

What was once a pristine creation of God is now bonded to the not-self instead of to the Holy Christ Self. Only Darkness and the Dark Ones inhabit what was formerly a temple of God. Jude called the fallen angels in this state "wandering stars, to whom is reserved the blackness of darkness forever."[26]

"Behold, Now Is the Accepted Time..."

Lifetime after lifetime we have either glorified God in our souls and in our members, challenging the ego and the dweller each step of the way, or we have damned our souls and our God and chosen to plight our troth to the ego, the dweller and the fallen angels, accepting their offers of power and glory and dominion.

"Behold, now is the accepted time; now is the day of salvation," wrote the apostle Paul.[27] We must choose this day whether we will attain union with God in this life or whether we will damn our souls and our God and forfeit that union. If we espouse the former path and our souls pass their tests, we will attain union with God. If we espouse the latter path and our souls fail their tests, we have nothing to look forward to except "fiery indignation."

As the author of Hebrews wrote: "If we sin willfully after that we have received the knowledge of the truth, there remaineth no more sacrifice for sins, but a certain fearful looking for of judgment and fiery indignation."[28]

The truth is that most people have neither the spiritual attainment nor the empowerment from God to gain the upper hand over either their egos or their dwellers, much less the fallen angels. Thus, they do not hold a tight rein on their souls or their souls' evolution. It is sad but true that without divine intercession, all but a small percentage of the population are unable to deal with and overcome the forces of Evil on a day-to-day basis. They are not equal to the challenge of defeating the forces of Evil lodged within their own psyches, much less the forces of Evil lodged within the psyche of the planet.

And so, ultimately, until the soul is once again bonded to her Holy Christ Self, the human ego and the dweller-on-the-threshold are more powerful than the soul. And this is one reason why it is not so easy for the soul to rise from the seat-of-the-soul chakra to the heart chakra.

In order to rise, the soul must overcome her tendency to repeatedly fail her tests at key points of vulnerability. She must recognize these key points and seek daily to transcend them. And with the help of her Holy Christ Self and Archangel Michael, if she applies herself, she will learn step by step how to challenge and defeat her human ego and her dweller-on-the-threshold.

The day will come when, after studious application of the Laws of God, the soul will have balanced 51 percent of her karma. Having achieved this level, she will at last ascend the spiral staircase from the seat of the soul to her lawful abode in the secret chamber of the heart, there to commune with her Lord, her beloved Holy Christ Self.

The Awakening of the Soul

When Gautama Buddha came on the scene, his disciples recognized him to be such an extraordinary human being that they didn't ask him, "Who are you?" but they asked him, "What are you? Are you a god? Are you a man? Are you human or divine?" And he simply said, "I AM awake."

It is startling to think that billions of souls on planet Earth are not awake but asleep. Yes, they are asleep to spiritual realities, dead to the realms of eternal Truth. When we think about waking them up, we had better first wake up our own souls! And when we do and our souls first rub their eyes and yawn and look around and say, "Where am I? Who am I?" and then drift off again into the sleep of oblivion, we must shake them awake! Yes, shake them awake!

Once fully awakened, the soul must learn what is Good and what is Evil. We as parents and teachers must teach the child who lives inside of us to deal with both forces and to see them for what they are. We must teach the soul that Good is all-powerful and that, in reality, Evil has no power of its own but only the power we give to it.

We must teach the soul to defend herself and to take up the sword of Truth to defeat the lie, no matter who mouths it. We must teach the soul that there are four classifications of animal magnetism that can cause her to stumble if she does not clear her four lower bodies daily of their vibration. We must warn her that animal magnetism can entrap her in the lower chakras and the lower animalistic nature.

The four types of animal magnetism correlate with the four lower bodies and the four quadrants of the Cosmic Clock. Malicious animal magnetism manifests in the memory body and the memory quadrant, ignorant animal magnetism in the mental body and the mental quadrant, sympathetic animal magnetism in the desire body and the desire quadrant, and delicious animal magnetism in the physical body and the physical quadrant.

Your defense against these negative momentums is to call daily in the name of your mighty I AM Presence and Holy Christ Self to the Elohim Astrea to lock her cosmic circle and sword of blue flame in, through and around all animal magnetism and family mesmerism[29] and to command that they be consumed by the violet flame.

We all have to deal with these momentums. They are part and parcel of the nature of the beast. They come with the territory, as they say. So what do we do? We teach our souls to rise above them and to stay centered in the heart chakra and in the balance of the threefold flame.

One of the most deadly traps the fallen angels have laid to catch the soul off guard is the collection of offenses that we refer to as the "Martian A's."[30] These offenses, each in its own turn, are a blasphemy against God the Father, Alpha. They all begin with the letter A, and they are a perversion of everything that our Father Alpha stands for. By venting them through any of your four lower bodies or your chakras, you can be the unwitting tool through which they enter and poison the planetary stream of consciousness—to the degradation of every living soul.

The Martian A's are the following: aggression, anger, arrogance, argumentation, accusation, agitation, apathy, atheism, annihilation, aggravation, annoyance and aggressive mental suggestion.

An aggressive mental suggestion is a strong suggestion, projected either from within or without the psyche, that comes into your head and will not leave you alone. It does not originate in the Mind of God nor is it native to the soul, but it can strongly influence the soul to take the left-handed path and to be pressured into making one wrong turn after the other on the highway of life.

An aggressive mental suggestion will pound the brain and pound the brain and pound the brain! until the brain is exhausted and it acquiesces to the erroneous suggestion projected by the sinister force. Because it is so powerful, you may think that it must be of God, when it is really of the Devil.

Aggressive mental suggestion is subtle. Its root is in the Serpent mind. You must never let aggressive mental suggestion sit on you. Deal with it immediately! Call to Archangel Michael to plunge his sword of blue flame into its cause and core. Then give unrelenting decrees to God and his hosts to deliver you, and stick with those decrees until you are delivered of the wiles of Serpent!

The Soul of David

Through the Psalms, we identify with the soul of David, who deftly delivered himself and all of Israel of the ragings of Goliath—the giant who was the incarnation of the four types of animal magnetism and all of the Martian A's. (Although scholars debate whether David wrote any of the Psalms ascribed to him, let's assume for the moment that he did, since the tradition goes back centuries and we are all steeped in that tradition. Whether or not he actually wrote them, they bear his imprint.)

In the Psalms, David speaks of the travail of his soul. In Psalm 6 he says, "Return, O LORD, deliver my soul. Oh, save me for thy mercies' sake." "Deliver my soul! Save me!" David's message for us, which he articulates again and again, is that we must call upon God to protect and deliver our souls from evil—and the evil of animal magnetism and the Martian A's—day after day.

In the Twenty-third Psalm, not only does David seek refuge in the Lord but he also prophesies his soul's immortality. Consider who is speaking in this psalm. Consider that it is the soul of David, who, having slain the dweller (symbolized by Goliath), is becoming one with his Higher Self, his Holy Christ Self, the fullness of whose glory was to shine in his final incarnation as Jesus Christ. He says:

> The LORD [the mighty I AM Presence] is my shepherd; I shall not want.

Notice the simple acceptance: "He is my shepherd. He will care for me. Therefore I shall not want." Through thousands of years of his soul's journeyings on earth, the soul of David has learned that there is only one who can shepherd his soul, and that that one is the LORD, the mighty I AM Presence. He has learned that he cannot commit his soul into the keeping of another.

He maketh me to lie down in green pastures: he leadeth me beside the still waters. He restoreth my soul.

Day after day the LORD restored David's soul. Why? Because the soul on earth requires daily restoration through the Holy Christ Self and the I AM Presence. Daily the soul must deal with the weight of the world as well as the weight of her karma. Before David's soul could take on the morrow and the next day and the next, David would seek solace from his God, and his soul would be restored. He knew that he must care for his soul all the days of his life.

He leadeth me in the paths of righteousness for his name's sake.

He teaches me the right use of God's Laws, he guides me each step of the way.

Yea, though I walk through the valley of the shadow of death, I will fear no evil: for thou art with me; thy rod and thy staff they comfort me.

Does the valley of the shadow of death consist of the remnants of David's lower self that must be passed through the sacred fire to be consumed? Does it represent the subconscious or the unconscious world of David—the enemies within as well as the enemies without, including Death and Hell, that he must slay ere he receive the mantle of his Christhood in his final incarnation?

Thou preparest a table before me in the presence of mine enemies: thou anointest my head with oil; my cup runneth over.

Surely goodness and mercy shall follow me all the

days of my life: and I will dwell in the house of the
LORD for ever.

Recite this psalm to your soul. Do not neglect to do so.
Your soul needs to hear you read her this psalm. She needs to
feel your comforting flame and to have your assurance that
when she gives her all to God, she will also be able to slay her
Goliath. And furthermore, you must teach her to believe in
herself and in her God. Tell her that she can rise to levels of
leadership and be an example of the victory that is possible to
the saints.

The Parable of the Marriage Feast and the Wedding Garment

We know that the goal of the soul is to attain union with
God and that to achieve this she must rise to the heart chakra
and be bonded to her Holy Christ Self through the Sacred
Heart of Jesus. But before this bonding can take place, the soul
must accomplish many tasks, one of which is the daily weaving of her wedding garment. The Ascended Masters call the
wedding garment the Deathless Solar Body.

Let us go back to Eden for a moment. As we mentioned
earlier, once we allowed our souls to be compromised by the
order of fallen angels called Serpent, our souls became mortal,
i.e., naked. Before we partook of the forbidden fruit, we were
immortal. So, the *before* represents the immortality of the
soul in Eden and her allegiance to Lord Maitreya. The *after*
represents the loss of that immortality when she transferred
her allegiance to the Serpent.

Hearkening to the Serpent was not only a matter of
disobedience; it was a breach of trust—a sacred trust. Trust is
the foundation of every relationship and most especially the
Guru-chela relationship. In sum, we disobeyed our Guru,

Maitreya. We lost our immortality. We became mortal. And we have had to face the consequences ever since.

The LORD God told Ezekiel, "The soul that sinneth, it shall die."[31] In the context of the Edenic dispensation, this meant: "The soul that sinneth, it shall become mortal." It meant that the soul that sinned against the Manu and the Guru of that 2,150-year period[32] would not have the opportunity in that round to regain her immortality. She would have to reembody on earth in the next 2,150-year dispensation and trace the footprints of her Manu and her Guru until she found them. She would have to apply to enter her Guru's Mystery School and submit to the rigors of initiation that he would require of her ere she returned to the paradise of a Golden Age.

As we discussed, the Garden of Eden was Maitreya's original Mystery School. Had we not compromised our souls —had we remained in the Mystery School, submitting to our initiations in divine order, passing our daily tests—we would have graduated from the Mystery School and gone forth to bring Maitreya's teachings to the world. Furthermore, we would have walked the earth alive with the flame of our immortality and clothed with the Deathless Solar Body.

Today, as mortals, we must weave our Deathless Solar Body by spiritualization of consciousness, by sacrifice, surrender, selflessness and service. We require the assistance of our Holy Christ Self in this monumental task. We need to match the Light God gives us daily over the crystal cord with our own sewings of Light, for thereby we can say: "My Holy Christ Self worketh hitherto *and I work.*" We can multiply that Light by meditation, mantra and the Science of the Spoken Word.

Day by day we weave our wedding garment, the Deathless Solar Body. When we have perfected that garment, our souls will be ready to return as Brides of Christ to the heaven-world, never to go out again from Eden. Alas, as of this moment our wedding garment is not perfected. Our souls are not ready to rise on the spiral of ascension's flame to be received in the arms of our mighty I AM Presence, who alone can bestow upon us Immortal Life.

No, our souls are yet in the valley of decision. We have many choices to make as we are confronted daily with the initiations Lord Maitreya gives to us. Yes, he, the LORD God who once walked and talked with us in Eden, whose sacred trust we broke, has forgiven us seventy times seven—and perhaps seven hundred thousand times seven hundred—during the intervening centuries of our souls' banishment from Paradise.

Once again, he walks and talks with us and patiently delivers to us the initiations we have so longed to be worthy of receiving. Indeed, how profoundly grateful we are, not only for his forgiveness but also for his compassion and utter kindness. For in a dictation, Jesus Christ announced that Lord Maitreya was dedicating the Royal Teton Ranch as the place prepared for the reestablishment of his Mystery School in this age.[33]

And so, since we can't get out of this world until we have woven our wedding garment, Lord Maitreya meets us at our level—in the lowly estate of the flesh. He has come to save us from our wayward selves. He comes to test us and to test us again and again that he might finally receive us in our wedding garment and bestow upon us the living, pulsating flame of eternal Life that shall never again be extinguished by man or by God.

Here is Jesus' parable of the marriage feast and the wedding garment. The scene of the marriage feast takes place on the third level of the etheric octave.

The kingdom of heaven is like unto a certain king, which made a marriage for his son and sent forth his servants to call them that were bidden to the wedding: and they would not come.

Again, he sent forth other servants, saying, "Tell them which are bidden, Behold, I have prepared my dinner: my oxen and my fatlings are killed, and all things are ready: come unto the marriage."

But they made light of it, and went their ways, one to his farm, another to his merchandise:

And the remnant took his servants and entreated them spitefully and slew them.

But when the king heard thereof, he was wroth: and he sent forth his armies and destroyed those murderers, and burned up their city.

Then saith he to his servants, "The wedding is ready, but they which were bidden were not worthy.

"Go ye therefore into the highways, and as many as ye shall find, bid to the marriage."

So those servants went out into the highways and gathered together all as many as they found, both bad and good: and the wedding was furnished with guests.

And when the king came in to see the guests, he saw there a man which had not on a wedding garment.

And he saith unto him, "Friend, how camest thou in hither not having a wedding garment?" And he was speechless.

Then said the king to the servants, "Bind him hand and foot and take him away, and cast him into outer darkness [the physical octave]; there shall be weeping and gnashing of teeth."

For many are called, but few are chosen.[34]

This so-called friend had not woven his wedding garment; therefore it was not lawful for him to enter the etheric octave. The king had his servants bind him hand and foot and take him away and cast him into outer darkness (the physical octave), where there would be weeping and gnashing of teeth.

The question that comes to mind is: How could the one whom the king called "friend" have gotten past him and his servants? It is clear that fallen angels have stolen their way into the retreats of the etheric octave, masquerading as angels of Light. And did not our Lord say, "The kingdom of heaven suffereth violence, and the violent take it by force"?[35]

One lesson we derive from this parable is that we must guard the citadel of our consciousness lest fallen angels intrude upon our minds, hearts, spirits and soul identity. The fallen angels don't pretend to have a wedding garment, yet they are pretenders to the throne of grace. As we see in this parable, if they are given the slightest entrée, they slither in to defile even the Holy of Holies. Therefore, God has sent his holy angels to protect our souls from the wiles of the fallen angels.

The parable of the marriage feast and the wedding garment is the story of ourselves. We must prepare ourselves for this marriage feast, for one day the king will send his servants to bid us partake of the festivities, and we must be ready. Our souls prepare for the marriage feast during many lifetimes of service, looking to and cleaving to the I AM Presence, eventually bonding to the Holy Christ Self and to the Sacred Heart of Jesus.

Healing the Soul Is a Top Priority

The soul must learn how to work through the burdens of her unresolved karma that are reflected in the burdens of her unresolved psychology. Your soul is attentive when your therapist brings you to the place where you can understand why you have repetitive negative patterns in your life that, try as you will, you cannot seem to correct. We have all experienced this.

Negative patterns do not go away just because you invoke the violet flame. They go away because you invoke the violet flame *and* you learn your lessons, often in the school of hard knocks because you are too stubborn to learn them from your Holy Christ Self.

And then one day, you stop beating your head against the wall and you open your eyes and you *see*, you *know*, because the mist that blocked your seeing and your knowing is cleared. And what was a mystery is no longer a mystery.

So, every morning we put on the mantle of the good physician and we go forth to heal our souls. Healing the soul is a top priority. If you do all things well on your spiritual path but neglect the healing of your soul, you will surely come to the crossroads of your neglect. And you will have no other choice but to pick up the cross of your karma and carry it to the place of Golgotha, the place of the skull—in other words, the place where you have crucified your soul. Here you must take her down from the cross, anoint her body with myrrh and aloes, and call upon the Lord and Saviour to resurrect her from her deep sorrow over your neglect.

If despite your neglect of the child who lives within you, you are worthy of the ascension on all other counts, your first priority before or after your ascension will be to balance your karma with your soul, i.e., your inner child. Since in the final analysis *you are your soul,* your soul's Wholeness will be the key to your ultimate victory.

When you do make your transition, you will be taken to the appropriate retreat in the heaven-world for a period of time to be determined by the Lords of Karma in consultation with your Holy Christ Self. Here you will remain until you have accomplished the healing of your soul under the guidance of masterful angel therapists. They, together with your Holy Christ Self, will tutor your soul until you achieve soul Wholeness. And through the ritual of soul retrieval conducted by the Ascended and unascended Messengers, you will learn to magnetize back to your soul the fragments that have been imprisoned in the earth and throughout the universe.

The Maha Chohan Explains the Gift of Immortality

The Maha Chohan explains the gift of immortality to us: "Speak to your soul and say: This is a new day and a new birth! This day art thou begotten of God! This day begin the climb to your immortality and cast off the fears and doubts of your mortality. Death has no power over you except you give it power, nor does hell, nor do the fallen angels. Therefore, let the great fire of the Holy Spirit into your heart and intensify the walk with God whereby you put on daily that seamless garment of your immortality.

"Immortality must be won! It is not accorded merely for an expression of faith or because you acknowledge salvation through one individual, namely Jesus Christ. Immortality is won as hand in hand with your Holy Christ Self (who is, of course, one with Jesus) you internalize—as the fire infolding itself—the magnificence of God-free being! Thus, it does take many hours and many days and, for some, many centuries to weave the plumes of the threefold flame into this gift, this bridal garment of immortality.

"Let the goal of your immortality, then, be the major goal you shall have accomplished by the conclusion of your life. You see, it is possible for you to neglect the health of the soul, the vibrancy of the soul and the discipline of the soul. And if you do, the soul will not know how to enter the spirals of self-transcendence. If you do not direct your soul to take the steps that are indispensable to the self-transcendence that must come ere you have your victory, surely, *surely* you will not have the wherewithal to bond with me....

"Now then, beloved, plotting the course of your life, seek correct livelihood. Seek a path whereby you may accomplish a number of things, including providing for your family, for your daily bread, for your education, for all that you must accomplish according to your dharma. And I define *dharma* as your calling to fulfill at a certain level the Law of God for you that comes out of the great Dharmakaya, your Causal Body.

"You see, beloved, all things *can* work together for good to them that love God, to them who are the called according to his purpose,[36] called and appointed—called, yes, and anointed.

"So the richness of your life from sunrise to sunset can be in the balancing of karma and the acquiring of more talents in the service of your God. And you can rejoice in God's happiness when you are surrounded by and move with those who understand the cosmic honor flame, who may honor that flame even before they have begun to honor God. So some saints have said that to love the honor of God is ultimately to love God as the personification of that honor.[37]

"Honor and integrity are the virtues of which immortality is made. *Integrity* refers to your 'integral integration' in your I AM Presence. When you have honor and integrity, you weave strong ties to the Infinite, to the immortal realms of Life. When you have no honor and no integrity, beloved, you are like the shifting sands. You are double-minded and therefore unstable in all your ways,[38] and you can accomplish nothing.

"It is not simply honor and integrity toward one's fellow-men of which I speak, but honor and integrity toward God himself. When you align yourself with the first commandment, 'Thou shalt have no other gods before me,'[39] you place God first. After that there are descending hierarchies in your life to which you assign greater and lesser importance

"When you make it your duty each morning to put God first, to honor his flame in your loved ones and to consecrate all your enterprises to him, then all goes well. The key is to put God first in the day and last in the day and to rehearse throughout the day the magnificence of the beauty of Life he has given you.

"To this I call you. I call you as newborn souls beginning a walk with me that will conclude in your victorious ascension in the Light. To that end I invite you to take training from me at my retreat in Ceylon. I will begin with a full house but, alas, as is often the case, I may end with less than a full house.

"Yes, beloved, for during the course you may have to step down from your seat and study at one of the retreats of the Chohans [the Lords of the Seven Rays] to master a certain untoward condition within your soul. Do not think that you are being demoted but rather that you are being sent to a place where you may fortify the weakest link in your being. Having so fortified it, you will be able once again to make good progress in my retreat.

"Many of you have familiarized yourselves with my sons, the Seven Chohans, and you have practiced the disciplines of the Chohans whom you recognized and with whom you identified. You have heard the teaching that if you apprentice yourself to any three of the Chohans and take their disciplines, you may thereby qualify to enter my retreat and to remain there under my tutelage so long as you uphold the standards I have set.

"But in this journey of a lifetime, a portion of your hours will be spent in the etheric octaves in the retreats and Universities of the Spirit, and another portion of your hours will be occupied fully with the responsibilities of your family, household and career, as well as with that descending karma that descends daily, hourly as sands in the hourglass. Thus you are reminded that your sojourn on planet Earth has a tenure, that the sands do fall, and when the top of the glass is empty, you must turn the hourglass over again and again until the hours of your fulfillment have come.

"Some of you sense you are in a race for the prize of your high calling in Christ Jesus.[40] And you *are* in a race. It is a race for victory but it is also a race to balance karma. You have only so much time each day to invoke the violet flame to consume and transmute that karma so that you will not have to wrestle with it. You have two choices: you can wrestle with your karma year in, year out, or you can cast your karma into the violet flame each day and have a clean white page to write on before sundown."[41]

Finding Unity with the Father, the Son and the Divine Mother

All of the divine attributes that come into manifestation through the Christ—such as truth, life and love; light, power and intelligence; purity, unity and beauty; hope, faith and charity; joy, holy expectancy and constancy; freedom, mercy and a true sense of brotherhood—weld together the Body of God and the body of man. They are actually the components of man's true identity that make it possible for him to fulfill his role as an integral part of the Great Cosmic Whole.

As man reflects these gems of heavenly manifestation, he finds his unity with the Father, with the beloved Son (his True Self) and with the Divine Mother. This unity is simply an application of the geometric axiom: "quantities equal to the same quantity are equal to each other." If God is love and man loves as God loves, then he is one with God. If God is wisdom and man expresses His wisdom, then he is one with God. If God is Light and man acts as a conductor of that Light, then he is one with God. If God is Life and man lives God's Life, then he is one with God—he is God—and he, too, shall live forever.

{ kind }

It is altogether fitting and proper that every benign thought and feeling that is expressed in man should achieve immortality; for qualities such as these deserve to live, together with the individuals who embody them, because they are of the essence of the Creator himself and can pass through the great cosmic furnace of transmutation intact, untouched and unchanged by the sacred fire.

On the other hand, let us ask ourselves these questions: Should negative conditions be endowed with Immortal Life? Should the ways of the world—the ways of subtle hatred and disdain, of personal aggrandizement that crushes the aspirations and hopes of others in order to propel the little self upward, of antagonism and the spirit of vain competition, of greed and lust, ignorance and cupidity, of pride and prejudice, gossip and loose talk, of impaired judgment, vengeance and cruelty, of selfishness and self-pity, misery and indolence—should all of these and a host of other degrading negatives everywhere apparent on the screen of life be permitted to continue indefinitely?

Should such unwholesome conditions, which infest the race consciousness, be endowed with Immortal Life? What would be the result if negation were to be self-perpetuating? What would happen if imperfect man, while he yet possessed such traits, were allowed to endow his creative experiments with Immortal Life and if he himself were allowed to live forever?

"Come, let us reason together," saith the LORD.

If the "evildoer" who has partaken of the fruit of the tree of the knowledge of good and evil (of the consciousness of duality) is allowed to eat of the fruit of the Tree of Life (of the omnipotence of the God Presence) "and live forever," then the universal standard of perfection would forevermore be compromised. Cosmic law, as well as the nature of True Being, would soon be contaminated by the experiments of those pseudo-scientists who had not yet been graduated from the Universities of the Spirit.

If God's immutable Laws were to be broken by the introduction of an energy-veil of illusion upon the screen of the Absolute, then we would have to admit that "God is dead!" If perfection could be invaded by imperfection, then there would no longer be any reason for man to strive to perfect himself and his world, to overcome limitation, to maintain order in society and standards of beauty in the arts, precision in the sciences, and purpose in daily living. In short, the bestowal of immortality upon the evildoer and his works would mean the end of existence for God and his Real Image in manifestation.

The Descent into Duality

God's solution to this problem is recorded in the Book of Genesis (3:22–24), which is the biblical heading of this chapter. It is also recorded in the Book of Life (which contains the karmic history of this solar system) that once man had partaken of the fruit of the tree of the knowledge of good and evil, his creative powers were curtailed. He was driven out of Paradise and denied access to the fruit of the Tree of Life—this fruit being the essence of God's power, which endows both the being and the creation of those who partake of it with Immortal Life.

The knowledge of Good and Evil is not knowledge at all in

the divine sense of the word, but the belief in an existence apart from God that comes from the lowering of one's gaze from the Real to the unreal. Once man entertains the idea of himself as being outside of the consciousness of his Source, his True Self, he feels naked and alone. Symbolically, Adam and Eve clothed themselves with fig leaves, but to no avail; for it is the soul and not the flesh that suffers the pangs of a lost identity—that point of contact with the Infinite that is nowhere to be found save in the return to the unity of the threefold flame, the Christ Self and the eternal God Presence.

The knowledge of Good and Evil is the belief that God and man are two instead of one. This knowledge, so-called, immediately lowered the consciousness of man from the plane of Oneness in God, or Spirit (the etheric plane), to that of seeming duality[42] in dense form (the physical plane).

This knowledge produced the synthetic image in place of the Life of Absolute Perfection that originates in the single-eyed vision of the Creator. When man partook of the fruit of the tree of the knowledge of good and evil, his reference point became dual and finite; he was, therefore, no longer exempt from death, for death is the consequence of finitude. Thus, man lost his immortal inheritance and with it his authority to claim the oneness of the Infinite. The Lords of Karma decreed that both his inheritance and his authority to endow his creations with permanence should therefore be withheld until such time as he should consciously shed the delusions of his finite existence apart from God.

The Return to Oneness
through the Path of Initiation

By what means, then, shall man return to the consciousness of God, of oneness, if, indeed, it is possible for him to shed the delusions of duality? Can his return to grace be accomplished by a simple act of will, by a declaration of faith, or by the fervent desire to be Whole? Any one of these may well mark the beginning of his reunion with his Higher Self, but Paradise is not regained as easily as it was lost—by a single act of free will.

First, the prodigal must retrace every step that has taken him out of the way of the pure River of the Water of Life. Among the most important lessons he will learn will be those gained by experiencing firsthand the effects that resulted from the causes he set in motion through his misuse of free will. Therefore, he is placed in the position of being on the receiving end of the energy he has sent forth; and in this manner, the impersonal operation of the Law of Cause and Effect provides him with the opportunity (which must never be construed as punishment) to learn the consequences of his misqualification of God's energy.

When the prodigal has had enough of it all and he cries out for the intercession of mercy to withhold his own insufferable creations, then Hierarchy steps forward to test his sincerity by the rigors of initiation. Is he willing to give his all in order that God may give His All?

The initiations given to the disciples and the trials endured by the saints as they move among the unawakened masses are all part of a foolproof system evolved by the Hierarchy whereby the real intentions and the actual attainment—not the wishful thinking—of seekers may be determined each step of the way. Then, when all tests have been passed and the requirements of the Lords of Karma have been met, their inheritance and their divine Sonship is reestablished and they are bidden through the ritual of the ascension to eat of the Tree of Life and to live forever.

Now let us examine one such initiation in order that all

who aspire to immortality might be acquainted with one of its prerequisites.

The Initiation of the Fiery Trial

The trial of Shadrach, Meshach and Abednego, who were bound and cast into the fiery furnace by the Babylonian king Nebuchadnezzar,[43] illustrates the teachings of Paul on "the fire" which he said would "try every man's work."[44] The biblical account of the fate of these men in the Book of Daniel supplies us with data on one of the most important tests given to the prodigal sons of God. Their experience was also a preview of the Trial of the Sacred Fire, which comes to every man as the final examination of his works.

Paul foresaw that this Trial would come to every man, and he described it to the Corinthians: "If any man's work abide which he hath built thereupon, he shall receive a reward. If any man's work shall be burned, he shall suffer loss: [a loss of misqualified substance that is consumed by the sacred fire]: but he himself shall be saved [the Real Image cannot be lost in the flame]; yet so as by fire."[45]

Shadrach, Meshach and Abednego were initiates of the Brotherhood. God had rewarded their striving for self-mastery with a scientific knowledge of his Laws and a wealth of understanding of his mysteries. These faculties were observed by the king himself: "And in all matters of wisdom and understanding, that the king enquired of them, he found them ten times better than all the magicians and astrologers that were in all his realm."[46]

Because of their superior spirituality and utter confidence in the Presence of God within themselves, Shadrach, Meshach and Abednego refused to worship the golden image that the king had set up. For this they were bound and cast into the "burning fiery furnace," which was so hot that "the fire slew those men that took up Shadrach, Meshach and Abednego."[47] But these God Self–realized disciples of the Christ, having vowed to serve God and him alone, were given tremendous assistance from on high. In them was fulfilled the decree, "While yet in my flesh shall I see God."[48] Although they were not yet perfected "in the flesh," they were temporarily made Whole by the grace of God; and this Wholeness, which was magnetized by their faith, could not be violated. The circle of perfection that was drawn around their forms by fingers of living fire could not be broken by imperfection.

Thus, when the king looked into the furnace, he said, "Lo, I see four men loose, walking in the midst of the fire, and they have no hurt; and the form of the fourth is like the Son of God." Astonished, he called them out of the furnace, "And the princes, governors and captains and the king's counsellors, being gathered together, saw these men, upon whose bodies the fire had no power, nor was an hair of their head singed, neither were their coats changed, nor the smell of fire had passed on them."[49]

What is the spiritually scientific explanation of this alchemical feat? Shadrach, Meshach and Abednego, through their devotion to God, had already expanded and balanced the threefold flame within the heart to the point where their entire forms could be enveloped in the Flame of Life. The Flame of the Christ within the heart of every cell of their four lower bodies had been quickened by their devotion; now they were sustained not only by their own momentum of the sacred fire, long-invoked from their own God Presence, but also by the Presence of the Son of God who appeared within the fiery furnace.

The faith, hope and charity of these sons of flame was such that when they entered the furnace, they magnetized the blazing power of the Christ, whose own Electronic Presence shielded their worlds, not wholly perfected, from the physical fire.

In order that they might endure the fiery trial, the four lower bodies of these holy ones were brought into perfect alignment. As this occurred, the four elements were balanced within their bodies by the Christ within and the Christ without, whose flame merged into a literal conflagration of the sacred fire—the Flame within the flames. Thus, the salamanders* moved freely through their forms (just as some unascended masters walk through walls by a conscious adjustment of the electronic pattern of their physical forms) and because there was no desire-density to be "burned out" of the three brothers, "the smell of fire [the smell of transmutation or chemical change] had not passed on them."

Only those of advanced spiritual attainment could have withstood the sudden step-up of the electronic vibratory rate that is produced by the fire element.[50] The gap between one's personal attainment and the attainment that may be the requirement of the hour is always bridged by the Christ when the disciple surrenders himself completely to the Presence and affirms with every beloved Son who has overcome the world: "I of mine own self can do nothing—it is the Father in me who doeth the work."[51] Verily, the moment of total surrender is the moment of immortality.

As Lord Lanto so beautifully explained: "When men are able willingly to surrender their habitual sense of identification with the changing, death-centered mortal personality, at that moment they actually attain immortality. This act of surrender is a splendid one. It is truly a rebirth by the power of the Holy Spirit. It is a transfer of the consciousness from the forcefield of mortality, with its attendant sense of struggle, to the

---

* Elementals who serve the fire element are called salamanders.

domain of the Holy Spirit—right while the individual consciousness occupies a physical body."[52]

Although Shadrach, Meshach and Abednego had surrendered totally, they had not yet undergone the ritual of
purification by the sacred fire. Nevertheless, because the nuclei
and electrons of their four lower bodies, (being originally of
the fire element) were momentarily infused and stepped-up by
the accelerated momentum of the Son of God, they were able
to mingle freely with the flames without relinquishing their
individuality.

Training for the Trial by Fire

The Trial by Fire is an initiation that every son of God
who would return to Eden must one day pass either with or
without the assistance of Higher Powers. In order to prepare
mankind (who have all but forgotten their own divinity) for
this and other necessary tests, special training in the etheric
and physical retreats of the Brotherhood is given to all who
aspire to recapture the single-eyed vision that was lost when
they partook of the fruit of the tree of the knowledge of good
and evil.

While the inner consciousness is prepared in temples of
Light during the sleep of the physical body, the outer consciousness is prepared for the Trial by Fire through the
teachings of the Masters that are set forth in the Keepers of the
Flame Lessons.[53] The opportunities for the acceleration of
mankind's reunion with God and for his spiritual advance-
ment on the inner and outer planes have never been greater
than they are today; and it is precisely by this means that the
prophecy is being fulfilled, "For the elect's sake those days
shall be shortened."[54]

Therefore, it behooves every earnest seeker to take the

fullest advantage of the "open door" policy now in effect. Serapis Bey explains the meaning of initiation: "If you would be initiated then I say, be willing to come to the feet of your own Reality first. Then be willing to accept that there is a Reality that God has vested in Beings, in Masters who have gone beyond this phase and this plane, who have a greater grasp of the Real Self than you now do though you have equal opportunity to attain that grasp.

"They have reached for the Infinite and they have won. But they look back and extend a hand, for they won by love for humanity.

"Therefore I say, take the hand of Hierarchy. Take the hand extended. Walk slow or swiftly, but walk with measured beat, steady in the rhythm of your own Reality.

"Press toward the mark and the prize of the high calling—the calling of the law of your Inner Self. And know that if you would attain swiftly, I am there to impel you forward. I am there with the sword of the ascension flame."[55]

Truly, we are living in a cosmic moment—in an hour when the Sun is literally standing still in order that the children of the Sun evolving on Terra might catch up with the forward march of the Light across our galaxy.

The Opening of the Retreats

In 1969, God Meru announced the Hierarchy's plan for a "massive program of education in the principles of the Christ."[56] The approval of this plan by the Karmic Board has permitted the Ascended Masters to take into their retreats for training, both during sleep and between embodiments, many lifestreams whose personal karma would, without such a dispensation, deprive them of this opportunity. The program was hailed by the God Meru as one that "shall truly be the

torch that shall light the world and bring in the great Golden Age." But the Hierarch of the Retreat of Illumination at Lake Titicaca added that the cooperation of unascended mankind who have already been given the teachings of the Law would be needed to awaken the outer consciousness to the mighty Truths deposited in the etheric bodies of those taken to the retreats during sleep.

In this cycle of cosmic history, God has authorized his Servant Sons, the Ascended Masters, to contact unascended mankind for the expressed purpose of giving them the correct knowledge of his Laws. This knowledge, if diligently applied, can and will liberate men and nations and bring in the greatest Golden Age the world has ever known. But unless sufficient numbers among the children of God respond to the appeals of these Elder Brothers of the race, the door of opportunity may close for a period of ten thousand years.

During this dark age, mankind, because of their failure to heed God's Emissaries, would have to depend solely upon their own spiritual momentums and their own contact with their God Presence. During this period, only the impersonal functioning of the Law would be allowed, and mankind would find out what it is like to be without the intercession of Hierarchy or the merciful dispensations of the Lords of Karma that have for so long stood between unillumined mankind and the avalanche of his own karma. Yes, unless the people rally to the Light, the present cycle of cosmic opportunity will draw to a close and the doors of the Ascended Master retreats will be shut; for the Lord has said, "My Spirit shall not always strive with man...."[57]

There are many sincere seekers who would gladly pay any price that they might know and do the will of God, that they might win their ascension through service to the Light and usher in the Golden Age. These can best achieve their worthy goal by studying under the Ascended Masters—who know every step of the way—and by willingly submitting themselves to the initiations programmed by the Great Initiator, Lord Maitreya.

The individual's own Christ Self works closely with the Lords of Karma in dispensing to the lifestream that karma for which he is personally accountable. This karma supplies the material for the testing program that is especially developed by the Hierarchy for each disciple. Nonetheless, there are patterns in the initiatic outline that are applicable to the human race as a whole while at the same time being relevant to each particular human need and situation.

In the remainder of this chapter we shall describe the initiations that follow the opportunities for discipleship: the Last Judgment, the "Trial by Fire," the Transfiguration, the Resurrection and the Ascension.

This is the path of immortality. As man unwinds the golden ball of his destiny, following the threads through the labyrinthian caves of his own subconscious world, he must ever keep in mind the vision of the goal: eternal reunion with his God Self and his divine counterpart. Each step of the way he is preparing for the Last Judgment when he will be called to give account for the energies he has expended during his allotted time of opportunity in the world of form. If he has successfully practiced the Ritual of Adornment—that is, if he has assiduously exchanged his human creation for the divine attributes—he will win his immortality through the ascension. If, on the other hand, he has ignored the mandates of his karma, he may lose his soul and become a castaway. Let us now review these two alternatives.

The Last Judgment on Sirius at the Court of the Sacred Fire

The Trial of the Sacred Fire, also known as the Last Judgment, may take place either in the Ascension Temple at Luxor, Egypt, or at the Court of the Sacred Fire on the God Star, Sirius. Candidates for the ascension are reviewed at Luxor, while the unprofitable servants,[58] those who have utterly abused their opportunities to evolve Godward by refusing to multiply their God-given talents, must appear before the Bar of Supreme Justice on Sirius, when the Divine Monad is ready to enter the Yellow Causal Body on the return cycle back to the heart of God.*

In the case of the unprofitable servant, this final review of the soul's experiments in the world of form takes place when the sands in the hourglass have run out, when the soul has spent the last farthing of "energy-opportunity" for all incarnations. On the other hand, the candidate for the ascension may finish his course on time, or ahead of time, to be received by the Hierarch of Luxor with highest honors.

This review is called the "last" judgment to distinguish it from (1) the judgments of the God Presence and the Christ Self that occur daily throughout the soul's many embodiments, and (2) the judgment that takes place at the close of each embodiment when the soul stands before the Lords of Karma to give an accounting of her† activities in the world of form. Neither one of these is the "last" judgment; but they may both be thought of as achievement tests, given in order that the soul

---

* The Yellow Causal Body is the second of the trinity of Causal Bodies that surround the Hub in the center of our Spirit/Matter cosmos. See book 3 of the Climb the Highest Mountain series, *The Masters and the Spiritual Path,* chapter 4, "Hierarchy," pp. 216–21.

† Whether housed in a male or female body, the soul is the feminine principle and Spirit is the masculine principle of the Godhead. The soul, then, is addressed by the pronouns *she* and *her.*

might know where she stands: whether or not she has "passed" a particular grade, how best to prepare for the test of the next day or the next embodiment, and how ultimately to prepare for the "final exam"—the Trial by Fire.

The Trial of the Sacred Fire, whether it is convoked at Luxor or on Sirius, is the final examination of the individual's every motive, thought, feeling, word and deed with its corresponding cause, effect, record and memory. It is here that the final auditing of the soul's account takes place: Has the soul multiplied or wasted the talents given by God? What degree of self-mastery has been attained? In what ways has the soul sought to enhance the evolution of life towards its divine completion? In essence, the purpose of the Trial of the Sacred Fire is to determine exactly how brightly the star of the soul shines and to reward her accordingly.

On Sirius this trial takes place in a large circular courtroom surrounded by twelve smaller circular courts, often referred to as "flame rooms." Thus, the cosmic pattern of the Central Sun with twelve revolving lesser suns is duplicated in the design of the Court of the Sacred Fire. The Twelve Solar Hierarchies are represented at the trial by twelve sets of twin flames, known collectively as the Four and Twenty Elders.[59]

The Elders are seated in a semicircle slightly raised and about twenty cubits from the center dais, a circular platform with a canopy overhead approximately two-thirds the size of the base. Here the defendant stands to give account for all of his actions throughout his many embodiments. He faces the Twenty-Four Elders as though he were in the center of a giant clock, facing the twelve o'clock line.

The Elders are seated from his left to his right in a clockwise pattern. The first twelve Elders, the masculine complements, sit from the nine to the twelve o'clock lines where they balance the feminine aspect of the soul, which manifests through the physical and emotional bodies. The throne of Almighty God, the only Judge and Supreme Lawgiver, is directly on the twelve o'clock line. Here, on the side of the North, the Electronic Presence of God himself is focused. The second group of Twelve Elders is seated from the throne to the three o'clock line. These, the feminine complements, balance the masculine aspect of the soul, which manifests through the etheric and mental bodies.

The Keeper of the Scrolls stands at the six o'clock line to read the record of the lifestream from the Book of Life. Because he holds the testimony of the Recording Angels, which will determine the judgment of God (voiced by the Four and Twenty Elders in consonance with the individual's own God Presence and Christ Self), he, and he alone, is allowed to stand opposite the throne where the Cosmic Honor Flame of the Almighty is sustained through His Electronic Presence.

The seats from the three to six and six to nine o'clock lines (following in clockwise direction) may be occupied by other Ascended Beings who have been called to bear testimony at the trial. No one sits behind the throne of the Almighty, the Four and Twenty Elders or the Keeper of the Scrolls; but at least a dozen semicircular rows extend beyond the places reserved for other members of the Hierarchy. These seats may be occupied by unascended mankind who have come voluntarily in their finer bodies to offer testimony either for or against the defendant.

After all are assembled, the defendant is escorted by guardian angels from his cell into the courtroom through a tunnel, which enters under the place of the Keeper of the Scrolls at the six o'clock line. As soon as he has taken his position on the dais and paid homage to the Deity (if he so desires), the Court is called to order by one of the Four and Twenty Elders, who rotate in the office of "Chief Justice."

Proceedings begin with a reading by the Keeper of the Scrolls, who recalls the birth of the soul within the Mind of God, the immaculate concept that the Father-Mother God held for her individual manifestation, and the divine pattern created for her evolution. Then there flashes forth upon the screen of akasha the records of the soul's development in the heart of God, of her consecutive experiences in the rings of the Great Blue Casual Body as she evolved from the center to the periphery, of her long training in the Laws of God and in the science of multiplying all of the attributes of the Deity. Finally, the moment of birth into the world of form is shown.

At this time, the Court reviews the vows made by the soul at inner levels and the opportunities given by the Solar Lords. The Court examines the divine blueprint—the pattern of individuality—that was stamped upon the soul before she ever went forth from the heart of God. Then they read the record of all that followed: the very first deviations from the original divine plan as she departed from the fiats of the Lord, the partaking of the fruit of the tree of the knowledge of good and evil, the subsequent entering into the consciousness of duality, the fear of separation from God, her eventual doubt in the Creator's existence, and her final and complete descent into the density of sensual experience. All of these events are shown, line upon line, in order that the soul might observe just how and why she forsook the original covenants of God.

When the reading of the record is concluded, the lifestream is asked to show just cause as to why he believes that his deeds, together with his soul, should be immortalized. His court-appointed advocate, always an Ascended Master, then speaks on his behalf, pointing out whatever good he may have accomplished and affirming the omnipotence of God-Good resident in every man to outweigh even the darkest of deeds.

Following the testimony of the Ascended Beings, it may be

the pleasure of the Court to allow unascended beings to speak either for or against the defendant. Then, when all of the witnesses have completed their statements, the evidence is placed in the great balances: the weight of the individual's own karma on one side and the amount of his original allotment of the sacred fire on the other.[60]

The "weighing in" reveals what percentage of the soul's total allotment of energy has been misqualified during and between embodiments since her fall from grace. Black magicians who, after having exhausted their own supply of energy, turned to the vampirizing of energy from other souls will have misqualified far more than their original quota.* Furthermore, such unprofitable servants are also responsible for the energy misqualified by those who came under their influence either directly or indirectly. As one begins to contemplate the complexity of the equation, one can see that the science of karmic accountability is dependent upon a cosmic calculus. Moreover, one can believe that the scales of justice are actually giant computers that store and process data fed into them by the Angels of Record.

After the weighing, there follows a period of silence, during which those present commune with the God Presence and the Christ Self of the defendant, summoning the full power of the lifestream into balanced manifestation. For God has said, "My soul hath no pleasure in the death of the wicked."[61] Until the very last moment, all who have ever overcome the world place the weight of their momentum of victory on the side of victory for the soul who must stand on the central dais of the Court of the Sacred Fire. Nevertheless, it is written in the Book of Life that each one must rise or fall by the weight of his own karma.

After the silence, the Chief Justice renders the decision of

---

* For an explanation of these strategies of black magicians, see the chapter on black magic in book 8 of the *Climb the Highest Mountain* series.

the Twenty-Four Elders as to whether or not the soul is ready for the final examination of the sacred fire. If the Court considers that the soul might fare better with more preparation, she may be awarded further opportunity in the world of form to balance karma and to win her ascension; for when there is even the slightest hope for the soul's redemption, Mercy will disregard the fact that, technically speaking, the defendant's time is up. But if it is considered that he would not alter his course, even if further opportunity in embodiment were given to him, the Court calls for an immediate reckoning of his accounts.

If the margin of judgment—or, shall we say, the margin of mercy—has awarded the soul another opportunity, the sentence is pronounced and the Court is adjourned. The soul is then escorted to an antechamber whence she may be taken to a retreat for instruction before reembodying, which may occur within a fortnight. The entire accumulation of karma may be set aside for a certain period, giving her the opportunity to make good, free from the encumbrances of her own momentums of evil. But, at the end of that period, she, like all who have ever overcome the world, will have to stand, face and conquer the "dweller-on-the-threshold" (the synthetic image composed of her entire accumulation of misqualified substance).

The defendant who is summoned to the Trial by Fire may undergo this, the most important initiation given to unascended man, in the main courtroom on the central dais where he has stood throughout the proceedings, or he may be taken to one of the twelve surrounding courts where he must also stand on a circular dais identical to the one in the center court. After he has been given his "last rites," the sacred tone —the keynote of his Presence—is sounded, and the sacred fire is released through his soul and four lower bodies. The current from Omega rises from the base of the dais, and the current from Alpha descends through the canopy overhead.

The soul whose works have been of God is immortalized by the sacred fire; but the soul whose deeds have been evil—the soul who has used God's energy to spawn a veil of illusion—is consumed. The works of Darkness are never in polarity; therefore, they cannot retain an identity-pattern when the currents of the sacred fire are passed through them.

All of man's creation that is patterned after the Divine Image is perfectly balanced in the masculine and feminine aspects of the Deity. Therefore, the soul who is of the Light is balanced, and when the sacred fire is passed through her in the manner described, there occurs an acceleration of the virtue of her being, and her God-identity is expanded as her threefold flame rises to greet the flowing power of the electrons of Alpha and Omega. The sacred fire is as the coolness of a sparkling waterfall to the soul, and she remembers the day she came forth from God, when she danced as a Spirit-spark in the palm of His hand.

When this sacred-fire ritual is completed, the sacred tone is sounded once again, and the flow of Light from the heart of Alpha and Omega through the dais gradually subsides. Then, if the soul has passed the Test of Fire, she steps forth as an Ascended Being and is welcomed into the ranks of the Immortals.

If the soul passes this "final exam," she ascends to the heart of the God Presence, thereby gaining not only freedom from the round of rebirth but also permanent immortality. Henceforth she is known as an Ascended Master. If the soul fails the exam, she goes through the second death (the first death being the death of the physical body; the second death being the death of the soul) and her individuality is remembered no more.

The Second Death and the Lake of Fire

The second death comes as an act of mercy to those souls whose karma is so heavy that the suffering that would be entailed in the balancing of their debt to Life is considered by the Elders to be too great for any lifestream to bear. Actually, it is God in man who is crucified daily by the weight of men's sins, and He does not choose to bear their burdens indefinitely —hence the second death is the means whereby God himself is liberated from the vile consciousness of men.

In the process of the second death, the Creator withdraws the energies he has invested in the individualization of the soul. This takes place automatically as the sacred fire passes through the personality consciousness, through the cause, effect, record and memory of all that has transpired within the forcefield and pattern of identity, and through the four lower bodies. As these energies are relieved of the stamp of personal impurity, they are drawn into the heart of the sacred fire and thence into the Great Central Sun Magnet (the white-fire core of the Central Sun) where they are purified—repolarized with perfection—and returned to the reservoir of God's creative power, the Great Causal Body, from which they will eventually be released in the mold of a newly created soul.

At the same time that the individual is passing through the Trial by Fire at the Court of the Sacred Fire on Sirius, his negative creations are being cast into the Lake of Fire for repolarization. The Lake of Fire is a giant focus of the Great Central Sun Magnet on the "surface" of the God Star. A flaming sea of liquid fire, it swallows up the horrendous creations of the black magicians, their demons and astral beasts of prey, the mass effluvia of planets and large forcefields of misqualified energy. All of the accoutrements of the black magicians who are sent to Sirius—in effect, all that is not worthy of being perpetuated—are dumped into the lake of fire for transmutation; these creations melt in the fervent heat of the universal solvent as cities have been swallowed up in molten lava. The purified energies then rise to the Great Blue Causal Body to be used in the precipitations of the Sons of God.[62]

The individualized God Presence of the lifestream who has passed through the second death is drawn into the Universal God Presence, and the Christ Self becomes one with the Universal Christ. In the case of twin flames, if one has passed through the second death and the other is continuing on the spiritual path, the latter must wait until the Lord of Creation fashions another divine complement after the same pattern held in the Causal Body of the one remaining. This new soul will have to go through the tests of self-mastery in the world of form like any other soul, eventually to find reunion with the twin flame, who may or may not have ascended by the time this one attains perfectionment.

Thus, God's energy continues to evolve through man—the manifestation of Himself—and nothing is ever lost save the unreality of human creation, which from its inception was no part of God. In reality, there is no death; but those who have made their dwelling place in unreality will find that, for a brief moment, death will seem very real.

The Tests of the Sacred Fire at Luxor

Let us now review the ritual of the Last Judgment through which the sons and daughters of God must pass in preparation for the final test of the sacred fire and their ultimate reunion with the God Presence. This is the judgment that is reserved for the blessed Servant Sons referred to in the Book of Revelation, who "loved not their lives unto the death."[63] As we have said, the Ascension Temple at Luxor is the place prepared for the last judgment of those who have passed through the schoolroom of earth and earned the right to sit at the right hand of God.*

If for one reason or another the disciple who has earned his ascension is unable to ascend directly from the physical plane at the close of his final embodiment of service, he is brought to the Ascension Temple in his finer bodies where the ascension ceremonies are performed. In rare cases, the initiations herein described are given to those retaining a physical body.

The Ascension Temple on the Nile River in Egypt is a part of the retreat at Luxor, which is presided over by Serapis Bey. Archangel Gabriel and Hope also serve here. The etheric retreat of the Brotherhood of Luxor is superimposed upon the physical retreat, which is composed of a large, square, white stone building with a surrounding wall and courtyard, and an underground building including the Ascension Temple and Flame Room.

A few miles from the focus is a pyramid, also superimposed with etheric activity. Here in the upper room of the pyramid is the King's Chamber, where the initiations of the transfiguration and the resurrection take place. Other rooms within the pyramid are used for initiations given by the Council of Adepts to the devotees who come to Luxor prepared for the most severe disciplines and the total surrender of their human consciousness.

---

* In special cases advanced initiates are taken to the Cave of Light or the Cave of Symbols, where they are given the necessary assistance to complete the raising of the four lower bodies either in the Atomic Accelerator, the Sphere of Light or the Cosmic Focus in the Cave of Light. Under certain conditions, ascensions may also take place in other retreats of the Brotherhood or from the exact spot where individuals have passed through the transition; of course it is not necessary to pass through death in order to ascend, as many Avatars have proven. Therefore, the ascension may take place anywhere or anytime it is ordained by God—providing the requirements of the Law have been met.

The focus of the ascension flame was carried by Serapis Bey to this location just before the sinking of Atlantis. In succeeding embodiments, he and the brothers who had served in the Ascension Temple on Atlantis built the retreat, which was originally above ground. Here in an underground building is the circular courtroom where the Last Judgment is conducted by the Council of Adepts. Nearby is the Flame Room, a square building having doors on two sides. One enters here only as a candidate for the ascension, after all initiations have been passed.

Forming another square within the room are twelve white pillars, decorated in gold relief at the base and the top, which surround the central dais on which the ascension flame blazes. They represent the Twelve Hierarchies of the Sun and the twelve Godly attributes. Each one who ascends from this Temple is ascending because he has attained God-mastery through the disciplines and the tutelage of one of these Twelve Hierarchies, the Hierarchy under whom he was born in the embodiment in which he was destined to ascend.

In the underground complex there are other flame rooms for the meditation of the devotees who serve there. There is a focus of the resurrection flame, and there are chambers for the preparation of various initiations, including those of the transfiguration and the resurrection. The keynote of the retreat is "Liebestraum," by Franz Liszt.

Serapis Bey's methods of discipline are tailor-made for each candidate for the ascension. After an initial interview by himself or one of the twelve adepts, devotees who come here are assigned in groups of five or more to carry out projects with other initiates whose karmic patterns lend themselves to the maximum friction between the lifestreams. Each group must serve together until they become harmonious, learning that those traits of character that are most offensive in others are actually the polarity of their own worst faults, and what one criticizes in another is likely to be the root of his own misery.

Aside from this type of group discipline, individuals are placed in situations that provide them with the *greatest* challenge, according to their karmic pattern. In this retreat one cannot simply up and leave a crisis, a circumstance or an individual that is not to his liking. He must stand, face and conquer his own misqualified energy by disciplining his entire consciousness in the art of nonreacting to the human creation of others, even as he refuses to be dominated or influenced by his own human creation.

The final test of the sacred fire is not given to the candidate unless the Hierarch of the retreat considers that the soul is fully prepared to meet God. Hence, before they are brought to the Court of the Sacred Fire, weeks, months or years of training in the Ascension Temple may be required of those disciples who are lacking in one or more of the requirements for the ascension.

The Four and Twenty Elders are represented at Luxor by the Council of Twelve Adepts. This Council is composed of twelve Ascended Masters appointed by the Elders and is presided over by the Chohan of the Fourth Ray, currently Serapis Bey. The Chohan, who is the thirteenth member of the Council, represents both the personal and the Universal Christ. Two-thirds of the Council must agree that the disciple is ready for the Trial of the Sacred Fire before he may be summoned to the Last Judgment.

In a circular courtroom, almost identical to the one on Sirius, the disciple is brought to the center dais where he kneels at the feet of his own Christ Self, who throughout his many embodiments has been his Higher Mentor (hence the term "Higher Mental Body"). This individualized Christ Self, functioning as the Mediator between the Higher and the lower self, is completely familiar with the entire evolution of the disciple whom he has disciplined to the point of self-mastery. His intimate association with the God Presence and his role as the voice of conscience qualifies him to mediate with the Hierarch who will pronounce the judgment of the Almighty.

The candidate for the ascension, who must finish at the top of his class at Luxor before he is considered for the Last Judgment, faces the Hierarch, who sits in the seat of judgment on the twelve o'clock line. The Twelve Adepts are seated as in the Court of the Sacred Fire from the nine to the three o'clock lines, six on either side, each member of the Council representing one of the sets of the twelve twin flames on the Court of Sirius.

Other Ascended Members of the Hierarchy who may be called to testify are seated from the three to the nine o'clock line. The Angel of Record stands at the six o'clock position and represents the Keeper of the Scrolls, who on occasion appears himself to honor the candidate. Other members of the graduating class, not yet ascended, are seated in the second and third rows behind the Ascended Masters from the three to the nine o'clock line. The mighty Seraphim stand in pairs at each of the doors at the three, six and nine o'clock lines. These guardian angels of purity also have the privilege of escorting the candidate through the tunnel under the six o'clock line to the center dais.

To be summoned to the Last Judgment at the Court of Luxor is the highest honor that can come to unascended man prior to his ascension. The purpose of this judgment is *not* the disposing of the individual into that "everlasting fire prepared for the devil and his angels"[64] on Sirius; rather it is a sacred ritual performed for those who are supremely ready for the ascension, but whose energies must be weighed before they may proceed with the final initiations of the sacred fire.

If perhaps the last one-fifth of one percent of their remaining karma may yet require transmutation, the Court may decree that this shall be accomplished through a single act of valiant service rendered from the etheric plane to embodied humanity or to the Ascended Masters. Or, it may be the decision of the Council that the disciple should withdraw to his chamber for a fortnight to invoke one or more of the flames of God in order to bring his soul, together with his etheric, mental and emotional bodies, into the perfectly balanced expression of the power, wisdom and love of the Christ.

This Final Judgment reveals to the Lords who sit on the bench with the Christ Self the stress and strain of the disciple's experiences throughout his many embodiments, including his successes and failures along the way. During the examination, the disciple's entire life record is studied and weighed; and his attitude toward the testing of his soul is considered as important as his actual victory over every trial. Of course, without complete humility before God and without the transmutation of all human pride, he could never have gained entrance into the outer, much less the inner court of the Halls of Luxor.

One of the most important questions asked by the Council of Twelve is whether or not the example set by the disciple while in embodiment is one that would be desirable for all mankind to follow. Has he openly proclaimed the teachings of the Christ and of the Brotherhood? Has he taken a stand for right in the midst of oppression and adversity, challenging the sinister force entrenched in the civilization of his time? Has he left well-defined footprints on the sands of time that those who follow him may trace and thereby find their victory? Or has he sown matrices of error as stones of stumbling in his brothers' pathway that will prevent their fulfilling the requirements of the Law? If so, has he removed these barriers through

➢ subsequent service to Life?

The recommendations that are given at the close of this Trial involve the final preparation of the lifestream for the initiations of the transfiguration and the resurrection, which he must pass prior to his ascension. If all of the required initiations have been passed during the disciple's final embodiment, he is still given the opportunity to participate in these two rituals before entering the Flame Room where he will undergo the final test of the sacred fire and the ritual of the ascension.

There have been cases where the recommendation of the Council has been to send the disciple (in his finer bodies) into the world to perform a special service for the Brotherhood: perhaps a mission to Paris, to Moscow, to New York, or wherever the need is greatest. In rare cases the Council recommends another embodiment of service in order that the candidate might gain more experience in the world of form in preparation for the time when he will serve from Ascended levels with embodied humanity.

When there is great need in the world, the candidate may petition the Council for another opportunity to serve in the world of form even though he has earned his ascension. In the case of Saint Germain, who ascended approximately sixty years after the close of his embodiment as Francis Bacon, the Lords of Karma awarded him the privilege of taking on a physical form after his ascension in order that he might make a valiant effort to unite Europe and to prevent the French Revolution.[65] History shows, however, that when mankind are unreceptive to divine assistance, even an Ascended Being may fail to solve the problems of the nations. As Saint Germain has often said, "Human beings are unpredictable!"

The courtroom ceremony is only the beginning of a series of initiations through which the candidate for the ascension must pass in order to complete the ritual of the Last Judgment. Let us examine these initiations in the order of their occurrence.

The Initiation of the Transfiguration

The initiation of the transfiguration is preliminary to the resurrection because it involves the pre-elimination of the misqualified substance remaining in the forcefield of the candidate for Christhood, the final balancing of the threefold flame, the alignment of the four lower bodies, the victory of the caduceus and the raising of the Seed Atom. Jesus gave a public demonstration of this initiation when he appeared transformed before the disciples with Moses and Elias. The record of this event has been preserved in three of the gospels:

"And as he prayed, the fashion of his countenance was altered, and his raiment was white and glistering. And, behold, there talked with him two men, which were Moses and Elias: Who appeared in glory, and spake of his decease which he should accomplish at Jerusalem. But Peter and they that were with him were heavy with sleep: and when they were awake, they saw his glory, and the two men that stood with him."[66]

To transfigure means "to change the form or appearance of; to exalt or glorify." The transfiguration takes place when the Father Supreme, manifesting through the individualized God Presence of the disciple, commands the white-fire core in the heart of every cell and atom in his four lower bodies to expand and to maximize the brilliance of the Light. This command is given in response to the invocation by the initiate of the final balancing of his threefold flame. It is given because he is supremely ready for the transfiguration.

As the atomic energies are released from within the nuclei of his own being, the power of the Great Central Sun Magnet pours through the lifestream, raising the vibratory rate of the atoms and cells, bringing his four lower bodies into alignment with the divine pattern. While this is taking place, the Magnet draws to itself the remaining residue of misqualified substance lodged between the atoms and electrons. Finally, the fires of the seven rings that surround the Seed Atom (the Kundalini) are activated, intensifying the caduceus action; the focus of the Great Central Sun Magnet in the Lodestone of the Presence draws the Seed Atom from the base chakra up the spine. As it ascends, it opens each chakra to its greatest capacity, releasing the impetus of the Holy Spirit to the four lower bodies.

Rising through the planes of Matter and Spirit to the crown chakra, the Seed Atom (the Divine Mother) unites with the Lodestone (the Divine Father); and the thousand-petaled lotus unfolds. At the moment when the union of the Father-Mother God takes place, the greatest release of the Christ Light through the heart chalice occurs, and the transfiguration is complete.

Within the dimension of his Christ-identity, man is omniscient, omnipotent and omnipresent. He has circular vision, his countenance shines in the full glory of the Christ, his blood becomes golden liquid Light: he is the conqueror of mortality. Free at last from the bondage of the flesh, he may maintain life in his physical body for hundreds of years as Saint Germain and other Ascended Masters have done, or he may proceed within a few days or weeks to go through the Ritual of the Resurrection. Thus, when God in man appears no longer as man, but as God, we behold that man is transfigured.

The flame in the heart of every cell and atom is actually a miniature threefold flame. As the plumes of these millions of threefold flames expand in response to the impetus of the Great Magnet, they arise from the base of each cell as dormant flowers greet the warmth of the sun. Swirling upward, they follow the spherical form of the cell and then return from the northern pole of the cell along the center axis to the base pole, forming the shape of a heart—the diamond heart. This action of the flames within the cells signifies the transfer of the patterns of the Christ Self into manifestation in the four lower bodies. Thus, we find that the Image of the Christ is destined to be outpictured within every cell. He is the Central Sun of each microcosmic universe within the body of man.

If the transfiguration has not occurred before the disciple arrives at Luxor, or before his transition from the physical to the etheric plane, it will occur sometime after the ritual of the Final Judgment. In cases where the Law requires the transfiguration to follow immediately after the ritual, the disciple is taken directly from the court to the highest room in the Pyramid. There he is left alone to commune with the Father; and as his consciousness merges with that of Universal Reality, his transfiguration takes place.

The guardian angels, the mighty Seraphim who are everywhere present at Luxor, watch over the disciple during the transfiguration experience to prevent the interference of the negative momentums of the mass consciousness that are pitted against the Christ in every man. Their protection enables the disciple to concentrate entirely upon his initiation and to use his full capacity to make complete attunement with his God Presence and with the Great Central Sun Magnet.

The Initiation of the Crucifixion and the Resurrection

Following this magnificent spiritual exercise, the beauty of which can only be properly retold by those who have experienced it, the candidate is placed in an unsealed sarcophagus in the King's Chamber. Here he undergoes the initiation of the resurrection, which makes permanent the expansion of the Light that occurs during the transfiguration. At that time, the latent image of the Christ is "developed" in the four lower bodies. Now it must be put in the "fixing bath" of the flame of the resurrection. The transfiguration, then, brings out the seamless garment of Light—the Deathless Solar Body—which the resurrection and the ascension make permanent.

As the Council of Adepts gathers around the sarcophagus, the Hierarch of the Retreat standing at the head, they recite the Ritual of the Resurrection, which begins: "O Son of God, that which thou sowest is not quickened, except it die.... There are also celestial bodies, and bodies terrestrial: but the glory of the celestial is one, and the glory of the terrestrial is another. There is one glory of the sun, and another glory of the moon, and another glory of the stars: for one star differeth from another star in glory. So also is the resurrection of the dead. It is sown in corruption; it is raised in incorruption: It is sown in dishonour; it is raised in glory: It is sown in weakness; it is raised in power: It is sown a natural body; it is raised a spiritual body. There is a natural body, and there is a spiritual body. And so it is written, The first man Adam was made a living soul; the last Adam was made a quickening spirit."[67] The conclusion of the ritual follows closely the remaining text from chapter 15 of Paul's First Epistle to the Corinthians.

The room is then sealed and the disciple is left in the tomb for three days, during which time he dies to the self. All energies must be withdrawn from the ego and from the consciousness of selfhood apart from God. Truly, here is the death of duality. For if he would follow the Christ in the regeneration, he must do all the works that Jesus did prior to his ascension, and he must pass the same tests that Jesus passed.

While in the tomb, the disciple leaves the land of the living; and with what attainment he has received from God prior to and during the transfiguration, he descends into the astral realms[68] and preaches to those spirits who are held there in bondage to their own misqualified energies. His sermon is based on that given by beloved Jesus when he "descended into hell" during his three days in the tomb. We quote here a portion of Jesus' sermon to the prisoners of the astral realms, which he released in a recent dictation. He began by addressing those in attendance:

"And so tonight I exhort you as I exhorted the rebellious spirits that in the days of Noah[69] were disobedient unto God. The three days and three nights while I was absent from the body temple, I did exhort them as I shall now exhort you:

"O my brethren, the LORD God of Hosts is He, He is the Father of us all. The passion of his love is not known to thee, for it is too great, and thy consciousness cannot contain it now. In thy present state thou art unable to awaken within thyself the means to create the resurgent chalice of consciousness that would contain him, for the heavens and the earth cannot contain him. Nor can they contain his love.

"O my brethren, repent of all your acts of discord and of jangle, of darkness and of tangle, of all that has involved you in the web. Repent! Repent! Repent! and turn unto God once again. Take his vows of holiness, of renewal, of the divine intent, of cosmic purpose of the Law. For he is the LORD, and there is none like unto him in the heavens and the earth. He is the LORD that raiseth mankind from the dead, that setteth before them their immortal destiny. By his hand they are fed. All are clothed in white raiment by his Mind. He deifies the soul. He, the LORD, is ever kind, His mercy endureth forever.

"I AM the Good Shepherd. I have walked in many climes and many lands. I have descended through the air. I have seen the atmosphere of planetary body after planetary body. I have roamed the universe with my being, and everywhere I have seen the LORD, and I have seen him in action. I have seen his power and his Presence, I have felt his love, and I AM a witness of that love.

"I urge upon you then, my brethren separated now by acts of disobedience, to return to the folds of his infinite compassion. Cast yourselves upon him, the Mighty Rock, and let not that Rock fall upon thee and grind thee to powder. For the action of his love is great, and he is magnified within thy souls. The power of his flame can free every soul, and the power of his love can make everyone every whit whole.

"My brethren, my brethren, my brethren: In memory of those moments when I myself felt forsaken of him, I repeat the cry: 'Eli, Eli, lama sabachthani'—'My God, my God, why hast thou forsaken me?'[70] Do you feel that moment, then, as I did? Oh, return to him and clasp him to your hearts forever; for he is sweet and full of Truth; whereas, the demons of despair and haughty intellect that have led you to this state are not able to do that which he can do, nor can they confer upon you the vestments of immortality or bring to view the wonders of his love. I urge upon you now a spirit of sweet acceptance of His grace, that you may then by that grace leave this place for higher worlds, for octaves beyond compare!

"This, my brethren, was in essence the sermon that I preached and repreached and spoke again and again to each soul that I could find there who was in the chains of bondage and despair. Many gazed upon me with dullness in their eyes —the dullness of despair from centuries of timeworn care and fear and doubt. The very Light of God seemed to them put out. And I sought to rekindle it then, as I do today to rekindle it in you God's way. I AM the resurrection and the life: he that believeth in me, though he were dead, yet shall he live!"[71]

This initiation reveals the candidate's ability to invoke the Light of the resurrection from his own God Presence—without the assistance of either Ascended or unascended lifestreams—to carry it as a torch of freedom into the astral realm, and then, after having spent two full days there, to return to Luxor. While in the astral belt, he offers himself as a living sacrifice, as an example of Christ-mastery that they, too, the very least of the brethren of God, must one day accomplish. This anchoring of the Light of the Christ in the astral plane is a necessary function of the Servant Sons of God; for without this assistance, there would be no ray of hope for the souls lost in the dark night of their own human creation.

Having preached to these rebellious ones, having withstood their condemnation and their foul reproach of the Spirit of the Christ, having returned to the King's Chamber and to the focus of his body in the tomb, the disciple is ready for the resurrection on the morning of the third day. At this time, he draws the resurrection flame, the mother of pearl that contains all the colors of the Causal Body,[72] through his consciousness and his lower vehicles.

The flame is actually his own momentum of the sacred fire focused through the threefold flame, which is now expanded to a height of nine feet and a width of six feet. The spiraling threefold flame is accelerated by the disciple to the exact frequency of the resurrection flame. When he thus invokes and sustains his own momentum of the threefold flame at this peak velocity, he is awarded the added momentum of the resurrection flame focused in the King's Chamber. The full power of the resurrection flame is then anchored throughout his entire being and world for the complete raising of the form and the overcoming of the last enemy, death.

Saturated, then, with the luster of pearl, the disciple rises from the tomb clothed with the seamless wedding garment of the Christ. He hears the same choirs of angels who sang, "Christ the Lord is risen today," and he knows that right within his form he has realized the oneness of his divinity and his own portion of the sacred flame.

Now he is called upon to go forth for forty days and forty nights to commune with the Christ Selves of those still in embodiment who look to him for Light and for the grace he has received. He is authorized to impart to receptive souls revelations such as those given by Jesus to the disciples and the holy women during the period following his resurrection.

This is the final opportunity prior to his ascension for the candidate to anchor in the world of form the electronic pattern of his God Presence. This tangible presence of Immortal Life will give his unascended brethren who are following the Path in his footsteps a tremendous impetus of victory. Knowing that one who recently walked among them has overcome, their hearts will be quickened with hope, and they will determine that they, too, shall go and do likewise. The record of the candidate's forty days of service to the children of God will remain an etching in the etheric and mental belts of the planet, and all those who follow this path will one day tune in to those records and thereby know that the goal of total reunion is an imminent possibility.

The Initiation of the Ascension

Having completed this portion of the Ritual of the Resurrection, the disciple returns to the Halls of Luxor to make a public ascension in the Flame Room before the Ascended Masters and his classmates. The Trial by Fire is conducted in the same manner as it is at the Court of the Sacred Fire on Sirius, with one exception: at the moment the individual's cosmic tone is sounded and simultaneous with the action of the Flame, the strains of the ascension current (which Verdi recorded as the "Triumphal March" in his opera *Aïda*) can be heard from the trumpets of the Seraphim who gather in the outer court to pay homage to the one who, in merging with the Flame, has retained his immortal identity.

The ascension flame is an intense fiery white with a crystal glow. The reality of that flame is indescribably magnificent; but for those who have yet to stand on the dais at Luxor, God has provided in the "Triumphal March" the means whereby they, through meditation, might attune with the momentums of the ascension of everyone who has ever gone before, as well as with the promise of their own personal victory in the Light.

The "Triumphal March" is the march of your victory. Each time you hear the trumpets in that piece, you can know that it commemorates the moment when you will step onto the dais in the center of the Ascension Temple. With Seraphim surrounding the dais and all the brothers and sisters of the Ascension Temple encircling you, you will rise in the Ritual of the Ascension.

As the charge of Alpha and Omega passes through the candidate standing on the dais, its current also passes through the entire planet and its evolutions. In order that this assistance might be rendered to the world, it was long ago decided by Cosmic Councils that the ascension of those who graduated from earth's schoolroom should be held on earth instead of on Sirius. For all mankind and the nature kingdom are the benefactors of this wondrous release of the victory of the God flame. In addition, the records of the ascensions that take place at Luxor enter the etheric belt of the planet and serve as reminders to unascended mankind of the immortal goal God has set for every lifestream.[73]

The Path to the Ascension

Although the goal of Jesus' life, Gautama's life and the life of Mary the Mother was the ascension, we find that mankind

today, East and West, do not have a correct consideration of
this goal of life. First of all, they do not consider that the goal
is immediate; and secondly, they have a misunderstanding of
the goal and how it will happen.

Most people think of a personal resurrection and an
ascension through someone else—a personal saviour—Jesus
Christ or an Eastern guru—and they consider that it will
happen suddenly with the coming of that one into their
presence. This is because the path of initiation and the path of
attainment have been seized from us almost as if the pages of
this instruction were ripped out of scripture by the angry and
by the accuser of the brethren.[74] We have been deprived in
outer manifestation of the footsteps of the Path, yet written
within our hearts the Comforter has placed the eternal Law of
God, and we are not left comfortless.

Even the Lightbearers on earth and those who know of
the goal of the ascension have allowed to come upon their
consciousness a concept that the ascension is not the goal for
this life—and they have allowed this chiefly through a sense of
being unworthy. There are people who know of the Ascended
Masters and of the teachings, and yet they feel unworthy to be
in the presence of the Ascended Masters, of God himself or
these very teachings. This is often subconscious, but it filters
through, and it is the manipulation of outer activities, emotions, thoughts and feelings.

The Elohim Cyclopea asks: "Are you satisfied to wait till
mañana for that attainment to come, or will you recognize
that the Christ Self within you already has that attainment and
is waiting to transfer the consciousness of attainment to your
outer self?

"If I could summarize those conditions of the mortal
consciousness that make it unable to accept the divinity of
Being, it would be first of all a sense of unworthiness, a sense

of limitation that has not begun to comprehend the co-measurement of the cosmos, measuring the flame of the self against the flame of the Infinite. This is co-measurement! It is also the inability of those in body temples to know when the concepts they hold are the result of tradition, dogma, doctrine, brainwashing techniques, and when those concepts have come from the heart of Almighty God.

"The great masses of humanity have accepted ipso facto whatever they are told, whatever their environment brings. And thus, the forcefield of the average human being is a quivering forcefield that reflects the total mass consciousness at its lowest common denominator. And only the few, fired by the action of the Flame, have risen above the mass stranglehold that the carnal mind exerts upon the souls of this planet."[75]

And so, we find that self-condemnation, which comes not from God but from the originator of the lie of original sin, is yet a burden like a shadow. It deprives us of the sense that not only are we going to ascend in this life but we are ascending here and now.

Moment by moment the energy of our being, of our consciousness, is returning to the heart of God. Each time we send forth a pure thought, a lovely thought, or perform a kindness or a good deed or offer a prayer, we have used God's energy. It will go forth to bless Life and then it will ascend. It will ascend into the I AM Presence to manifest our mansion in heaven, our Causal Body of Light, the forcefield of our cosmic consciousness. And so we are made up, in reality, of all the magnificent creativity that we have sent forth for aeons of consciousness when we have existed in Christ who declared, "Before Abraham was, I AM."[76]

What is the ascension, then? The ascension is the acceleration of consciousness. The ascension is the goal that makes us strive to be better people every day—to do more, to perfect

a project, to keep on keeping on, to sense the threads of
creativity that come from God, to meditate on our creations,
to work side by side for a common purpose that is for the bet-
terment of our friends, of the earth, our country, of humanity
—to accomplish something that we sense is constructive. This
is the basic drive that comes from the heart and the soul and
the mind of the children whom God has made. This is the
striving toward acceleration of consciousness.

We all have something within us. It is a seed idea from
God. It is like the programming of the computer of our life
that is pushing us onward, upward, striving. And when we are
not striving and not working toward lesser goals and greater
goals that lead to the ascension, we are unhappy. And that
unhappiness will take its manifestation as sickness, as disease,
as boredom, as types of intrigue, deception or self-deception. It
will take the form of temperaments, moods—manifestations
that we do not associate with our inner dissatisfaction—but all
types of little irritations and problems with family members,
and so forth.

It all goes back to the fact that every single day of our
lives, our souls are demanding to be fed the fire of the
ascension flame. And if the soul is not satisfied in that return
to that flame, we reap the consequences on the surface of our
being. It can be nervous tension, it can be sleeplessness. But it
is the soul impressing the outer mind: "You are stifling me.
You are not fulfilling the purpose for which I was born and I
will not leave you in comfort. I will make you without comfort
until you return to follow the inner plan of Life."

The Goal of Life

The ascension, then, is our goal, is something that requires
effort, working the works of God, an application for the

graces of the Holy Spirit and the gifts of that Spirit. It demands our input with God's input working hand in hand, together, the giving and the receiving, because the ascension comes from the great interchange. The great interchange is that alchemy whereby we as a soul exchange with the Spirit of the living God our energies day by day. We take the fruits of the day, and at the evening time, at the setting of the sun and the evening hours, we lay those fruits upon the altar.

We give to God the best of ourselves of each day. God takes that energy, he purifies it, and in the morning we awaken to the sunshine and new Life, fresh air and the singing of the birds. And we find that we have new strength and new life because God has given to us once again our allotment of energy to go forth and be sowers in the field of his righteousness.

This divine interchange is what gives us Life. Without it, we are the living dead. With it, we are constantly alive and moving and always occupied, and the twenty-four hours a day seem not enough because so much energy of God is flowing through us that we have to maximize our organization to be able to give that energy forth and to be able to come to God and say, "I have emptied myself. I have given all that you have given to me and here I am now emptied. Fill me again. Return to me another portion."

This is the meaning of ascending every day. And if we are not ascending every day, we can see the signs. We see them in our bodies. We see the lethargy and the sloth. We see the chaos and the confusion in our homes. We see the problems in our environment and in our community and if we are true to ourselves, if we go back to that Inner Self, the Inner Christ, the Inner Buddha and the Inner Mother, if we go back to the Inner Life, we know that the reason that all of these outer conditions affecting mankind are taking place today is because we, as the individual, are not fulfilling that basic requirement of the ascension.

Without the ascension, there is no other reason for living. It is the goal of Life, the purpose of existence on earth. It is our reason for being. It is our reason for coming into incarnation over and over again until we realize that purpose, balance our misuses of energy and finally find that pathway on the steps of initiation to return to the heart of God.

If you comb through the scriptures of the world, you will find mention of the ascension here and there. You will find examples of it. You will find it called "soul liberation," "nirvana," "samadhi"—all types of states of consciousness that do represent the acceleration, the intensification, the actual stepping up of the spin of the electrons around your atoms, the stepping up of the energy in the core of the atom. This is the meaning of ascension.

And when we speak of going up—as Jesus and Elijah are described as going up—we know that going up means increasing in vibration. In reality, there is no up or down, but there is a lesser and a greater momentum of cosmic consciousness that manifests within us. Our God is a God who is transcending himself moment by moment, hour by hour.

This self-transcending God is reflected in the expanding cosmos and in the fact that no matter what attainment a man reaches to, he will always set a further goal. Therefore, the ascension is not the end of life or the end of goals. And we need not shirk from it because we say, "Well, what will I do after I ascend? Sit in heaven and play on harps with the angels?"

Cosmic consciousness is ever appearing, and we are ever striving to catch it and to hold it. And as soon as we try to hold it, we lose it, because the moment we receive an acceleration of consciousness, we are required to anchor it and to give it away so that God can once again increase that consciousness.

Have you ever noticed that in meditation or in using the Science of the Spoken Word or in listening to a dictation by the Ascended Masters, you are elevated to a great height of Self-awareness and sometimes you feel you have never felt the Light of God so intensely, and you want to stay on that mountaintop and hold that Light? And it comes to pass that the meditation period comes to an end, you have concluded your decrees, or the dictation is concluded. And for a few moments, perhaps five or ten minutes—if you are fortunate a half-hour to an hour—you retain the sense of that Light filling your cells, filling your chakras. You have been elevated to a tremendous height of cosmic consciousness. It is the Horeb's height,[77] the mountaintop experience that all of the great prophets knew.

But we must come back to the valley. This is the challenge of the ascension: to ascend every day and then go back to the valley, which signifies the level of our karma and the level of our dharma. And that experience in God has been the opportunity to know what it is like to be free for a moment from the burden of our karma and the responsibilities of our dharma. And for a moment, God has given us a taste of soul liberation —just a taste, a flavor, a whiff of the perfume of that essence of the ascension.

Why has he given this to us? It is the vision. It is the vision that comes through inner senses, and by that vision we say to ourselves, "I must ascend in this life. I must return to the heart of God. I must reach that state where I will no more go out from the mountaintop. But now God has bidden me descend. As he sent Moses down and as he sent Gautama out of nirvana and as he sent Jesus Christ to come into incarnation with the fullness of the Word, as he has sent his sons and daughters out of the plane of bliss, so I must go down and fulfill my responsibility. I will accelerate my service, I will accelerate my meditation, because I want to get through all of this substance, this karma, this misqualified energy that I have carried around as bag and baggage all these thousands of years. I want to plow through it. I want to intensify. I want to get back up on the mountain again."

And this is the ascension. This is the acceleration.

How to Ascend

On the anniversary of his own ascension, Lanello gave us some very practical instructions on how to ascend:

"You have spoken so often of ascending and of your ascension and of the process itself and of the goal of Life, but do you really know how to ascend?

"Do you imagine it shall be a leap from a diving board?

"Do you imagine it shall be some lofty flight?

"Shall it be an automatic process?

"Who will be the helpers and how much will they be allowed to help you?

"How much momentum of ascension's flame must be in your own sails? How much fire of holy purpose must be sealed with such white-hot heat/coolness of intensity in the chakras as to enable you to receive the transfer of flame whereby your identity is sealed and not denied?

"You know well that should you enter that flame prematurely, it would cancel out life. Thus, not prematurely but maturely you will enter that flame and not until you have dedicated your life and the life beyond, if necessary, to garnering the threads of Light, garnering the skeins of ascension's flame, wrapping it around each thread in the garment of the Deathless Solar Body, calling to the angels and working with them to mend the flaws, to mend the tears.

"Yes, beloved, how do you ascend?

Score a Victory Each Day

"*You ascend daily!* It is like mounting a flight of steps. You know not the count, for the steps represent each step that must be taken in life. How to ascend is to arrive at the top step at the end of this embodiment.

"You cannot leap the flights or the spirals and turns. And you do not know how many steps you must take, for each one of you is at a different place on this staircase.

"Since you do not know the end or the beginning, you must keep on keeping on. You must take a step a day, a day being a cycle of an initiation that might endure for weeks or months. But if you do not take the appropriate measures each day—those that you know so well—in terms of maintaining your harmony, the fire of your dedication, your decrees intertwined with meditation upon God, even as you invoke and meditate, visualize and affirm the Word simultaneously—if you do not fulfill in a day's cycle the requirement of a certain step, it will be much more difficult to fulfill it later. For the next steps come upon you and then you are overloaded.

"It is not that you are overloaded with menial work, beloved. You become overloaded when you skip cycles of initiation and then do not know where to turn. The army has marched on without you and you are looking for the staircase—indeed.

"Each rising and setting of the sun marks a cycle whereby you mount those stairsteps. There are many things in the duties of the day that cannot be postponed to the next, for when they are postponed and the momentum wanes, so often the cycle is lost and the project is not completed. And how difficult it is to get that project done when you have to crank it up again and start all over! So understand that this is Life—Life that is measured by the soul and the heart and

⟩ the Holy Christ Self.

"I bid you, then, secure the moments. Secure them as the mind uses them to enter compartments of eternity. For time is indeed an element of eternity, as eternity has compartments of measurement. This time has many dimensions, as does the space of eternity, yet there is a correlation to your life here below.

Joy Is the First Principle of the Ascension

"Thus I say, neglect not the hours. Fill them with joy! Joy is the very first principle of the ascension. Take two individuals—one who fulfills his assignments without joy and one who fulfills them with joy. The one without joy, beloved, may lose his ascension for want of joy, and the one with joy may make it even though some elements are lacking.

" 'That your joy might be full'[78] was the prayer of Jesus— and that you might know and have *his* joy remaining in you.[79] This joy, beloved, can never be satisfied by human companionship alone but by a human companionship wherein those who are together see this as a vehicle for the divine companionship, for a divine joy that sprinkles laughter and merriment and play betwixt the hours of hard concentration. This joy, beloved, that spans all octaves is pleasing to God.

"Therefore I say, abandon a sense of martyrdom! Abandon a sense of self-condemnation! Abandon a sense of nonjoy! But take care that your joy puts God first.

"Therefore, cast out the idolatrous consciousness that will lean upon human companionship to the extent where calamity is on its way. For our God is truly 'a jealous God'[80] and will tear from you that thing, that individual to whom you give greater preference than you give to Him, to Her—to Alpha and Omega.

"Thus, your mighty I AM Presence with you, shining in all the splendor of the Father-Mother God, does continually radiate to you joy. And the descending crystal cord is a bubbling stream of joy. It is a bubbling stream of joy, beloved, as the Light cascades into your heart. Therefore, distribute joy and know that merriment that does also entertain the angels and keep them in their courses, surrounding you and assisting you.…

"Understanding the divine sense of humor will make you able to deal with the most difficult karmic circumstances, the most deadly intent of the fallen ones. As the LORD holds them in derision,[81] may you also hold them in derision. And may your joy be such a consciousness of the Sacred Heart of Jesus that you can meet friend or foe with the same Light and lilt, for you have the co-measurement of the joy of angels and the merriment of God himself in the face of such a seriousness as that of the unreality of the fallen ones themselves.

The Staircase of Life

"Blessed hearts, joy flames go out when you are not in sync with your cycles on the staircase of Life. There comes upon you a frantic sense of urgency within. You may connect it to outer responsibilities, burdens and debts, or to not having enough time to do everything you want to do.

"Well, time will fall in place and so will space when you dedicate your day to meeting the requirements of the day's initiation on that step of your stairway of Life. Then you will go to sleep at night in peace and have the peace of angels, knowing you are one step closer to the victory of your ascension or to the point of your adeptship where you may reincarnate again with a full 100 percent of your karma balanced.

"Yes, beloved, your daily tasks and obligations and responsibilities have everything to do with your initiations on this staircase of Life. Dispatch them well! Guard your time! Seal yourself to accomplish that which must be accomplished. For even well-meaning individuals can be the instrument of fallen angels. They come to waste your time, whether on the telephone, by mail or in person, creating calamities or circumstances that would have you believe that no one else can solve them except yourself.

"Well, release yourself from that sense of idolatry, beloved ones. Only your Christ Self can solve those problems! Only Almighty God can solve them! And when you develop that attitude, you will dispatch those problems and dispense with them in a mighty short time and a mighty short space.

"Therefore, the deftness of your use of the sword of Archangel Michael comes with using it often, comes with using it for every task, every item on your desk or in your shop or in the fields, on the farms, tending God's flocks on the ranch.

"Understand that you can move in eternity, just as you can be in your immortality and the coils of your immortality here below. So you do not have to be confined by time and space. With the mercurian speed of Light from the heart of El Morya and God Mercury, you can utter the command and the fiat that will literally collapse the ploys and plots of the fallen ones.

"This is a present possibility for many of you, yet you do not exercise it! You think of exercising the body. Exercise the mercurial Mind of God and let there go forth a ray of Light, a point of blue lightning from your mind, to literally consume all substance that would prevent you or anyone, even the one through whom that substance comes, from attaining his victory on that day!

Take Control of Your Day

"I ask you to devise a chart ... you can use to check off tasks accomplished in the hours of the day. You can have it on your wall in your office.

"And you and only you will know whether at the end of that day you can paste upon that chart a victory star—yes, beloved, a victory star: a gold star for having accomplished all those things that were on your list that you were capable of accomplishing, a victory star for not having let anyone deter you from that path and yet still having dealt with the needs of those who truly are deserving of your time and attention.

"Blessed hearts, take control of your day! For it is a cycle of the sun, it is a cycle of the earth, it is a cycle of your path of the ascension. This is how you make your ascension: I tell you, you score a victory each day! That means you must enter your day with a fierceness and a determination.

"Take the end of today to plan for tomorrow, to organize what you will do: when you will arise, whom you will see and whom you cannot see. Set goals and achieve them no matter what! For to break the patterns of letting things get by you, letting people interrupt you is no small task, but it is accomplished by the surefootedness of the compassionate ones. These compassionate ones manage to achieve their victory and also accomplish their daily assignments.

"A day's victory can become the victory of a lifetime. Count the days in the year and then the years in the decades of a life span and see how many victories you must achieve to finally step on the dais at the Ascension Temple at Luxor and feel the caressing love, the white fire of ascension's flame and hear the welcome of the Seraphim who surround you and of all the adepts who themselves are candidates for the ascension.

"You will feel better about yourself when *you* are in

control of the hours of the day. Think of your victories as being moment by moment. Think of your failures as losing the moments and think of your lost moments as being added up into hours and days of nonachievement.

Fill Your Hours with the Joy Flame of Christ

"Beloved ones, this is the point of suicide that I come to discuss this day: it is the hours that are lost because you have not filled them with the joy flame of Christ. And without the joy flame of Christ, your bodies will not be healthy, you will not have the strength that you need.

"Joy is the key to healing! Joy is *movement!* Joy is *life!* Joy is self-attention to the needs of the four lower bodies but not over-self-concern. Joy is the sense of committing oneself to God and letting God flush out the nonjoy by that descending cascade of the mighty River of Life.

"O beloved ones, I have seen the days and the hours of earth. I have reviewed my own embodiments. There is not a single saint in heaven nor an Ascended Master who does not look back on the record of his lifetimes with a great sense of loss and burden that in many of those lifetimes a certain percentage of the hours and the days was lost, lost to a pursuit of pleasure that was not required by the body or the soul but was merely an indulgence. I can tell you we have paid the price for those years and embodiments of indulgence, both you and I.

"Now let us get on with life that is lived in the full zest of that joy of living, the joie de vivre that each one of you knows when you are in perfect attunement with your Holy Christ Self.

"O beloved ones, something is the matter when joy flees from you! You must determine *what* is the matter. You must not suppress it. You must drag it out and look at it! You must see the phantom of the night, the ghost of the former self, and all of that psychology that you are working through.

"I say, work *through* it! Do not simply tarry in working with it forever. Work through it, beloved, and get beyond it! See it for what it is. It will not go away without the mighty sword of blue flame of Archangel Michael....

"Use the sword and remember that if you think you have allowed something to pass into your subconscious but you do not understand what it was and you do not remember how you set in motion a negative spiral when you were three or ten or twelve or twenty-five, then, beloved, you must pursue it with all zeal right to the very point of its origin.

"You do not change merely with the violet flame or the Ascended Masters' teachings. You must therefore pick up the decree of the Great Divine Director to arrest those spirals even of your psychology that are negative in your world,[82] even though you know not where they have come from or how they began.

"Call to the Great Divine Director to arrest those spirals! Arrest them with your mighty sword of blue flame! Cast them into the fire and ask to be illumined: What are the elements? What are the elements of the mind or heart or soul that must be healed and must be made whole?

"Then plunge into the sea of Mercy's flame. Plunge into the great heart of the Lady Master Kuan Yin. Plunge into the mantras of mercy. Saturate yourself, beloved, and know that a certain transmutation will take place when you determine not to allow the nonjoy to displace your great joy. A certain transmutation will take place, indeed, without your having to know every point of denial that has caused the spirals of denial to multiply within you.

Call for the Arresting of the Spirals

In the name of my mighty I AM Presence and the Great Divine Director; in the name Jesus Christ, I demand and command the arresting of the spirals of negative karma throughout my entire consciousness, being and world!—that every single cycle of every single cell and atom within my form that is not outpicturing the perfect cycles of the Christ consciousness is now dissolved, is now arrested and turned back by the authority of my God Presence! And in the name Jesus Christ, I demand and command that the cycles of Immortal Life and my divine plan be fulfilled and that my ascension prevail!

"Beloved hearts of Light, I speak to you with a profound love and a great practicality. I am practical and I see at inner levels how souls of Light upon earth do miss the opportunity for their ascension. Of course, when they do not have this path and teaching, they are not at an advantage but at a disadvantage. It makes us sad, indeed, to see those who have the Path and have the teaching and do not make it. For you understand, beloved, that it is possible for many more who have this teaching to make the ascension than actually do.

"Well, what is the difference between those who do make it and those who do not?

Take Command of Your Life

"I believe the difference is that those individuals who do not make it *do not take command of their own lives* but wait for someone else to command them and to take care of them. Taking command of your life and taking responsibility for your life means you take responsibility for the Path and the teaching and your daily service of decrees wherein you know you have accomplished what must be accomplished for that day's increment of your ascension.

"You ascend a little every day imperceptibly. And if you do not take that little flame's point of acceleration in that day because of your failure to invoke the Light of God sufficiently, then you are not stepping up your cells and atoms gradually, and you will not be ready for the full fire of the ascension pillar to pass through you.

"What is the ascension flame but a million little flames?

"What is a River of Life but a million drops of water?

"Do you see, beloved? Each flame you accept and internalize each day (which is not a problem, for you scarcely notice the adjustment in your world), each little flame, then, prepares you to receive the great, great God Flame of your I AM Presence that is the ascension flame.

"Beloved ones, observe your gaze, whether it be upon the mountains and upon your I AM Presence or looking about the world for someone, searching for this or that satisfaction or this or that attention.

"Is there something that you yet want from this world?

"Then tell yourself what it is. Ask yourself why you want it and if it is worth the digression. Ask yourself if you can attain the satisfaction of that experience or that something that you want through the path of self-mastery and initiation. Or do you really need to go out and experience in some form that something that you find wanting in yourself?

"Blessed hearts, more desires and longings for this world and the things of it can be satisfied by communion with God than you would ever dream of. The trouble is that people place their attention upon their desirings to such a great extent that they wind a coil of desire around the pole of being, around the spine. And each time it is wound, each time it is reconsidered, that coil of desire makes a stronger and stronger desire in them to do that thing that will take them from their God-centeredness.

"Thus, you have understood this principle in Lord Maitreya's teaching on fear.[83] So it works with every other negative vibration. But desire, beloved, is the most powerful force in your world. Desire will propel you to God, and desire will take you to the very depths of the astral plane.

"See, then, that you examine on this my ascension day the momentums of your desire....

"Karmas themselves beget wrong desire. Therefore, be free! This is my message to you today. Be free! And the only true and lasting freedom you will ever have is the victory of your ascension in the Light. And short of that you will know a certain element, and a powerful element, of that freedom *if you take hold of your desires!*

"Do not suppress them. But if you desire something that you know is not right, then go after that desire with your sword, with your Astreas, with your Surrender Rosary, with your calls for the binding of your dweller-on-the-threshold. Go after your wrong desires and devour them by the sacred fire! For if you do not, they will only grow, even at the subconscious level, and soon they will devour *you.*

"*This* is the single factor that takes people from the path of initiation. It is wrong desire. Pray to your Holy Christ Self that you might know what is wrong desire and the idleness of the mind and the misuse of time and space. Pray to know it. Pray to have that Christ Mind. Pray to have the Presence of The Lord Our Righteousness.

"Right desire can be known in every circumstance. Therefore, seek ye first the kingdom of God and his righteousness, and all these things shall be added unto you.[84]

"My little ones, my great ones, my children, my souls

aborning in the womb, I rejoice to walk through this land. I rejoice to be in your midst. It is my desire, and it is a great desire, that you accept me as being 'physically' present with you. I am so near to you. If you will only incline your ear, you will hear me speaking to you through your Holy Christ Self with correct discretion and judgment and direction.

"You will also know me through my Beloved. And therefore hear my words through her and do not miss them. When you are closed to some levels of communication, for you do not want your worlds disturbed, you will avoid me *and* her and you will lose a lesson that could liberate you in a day from something you may otherwise carry for a decade.

"We are very much with you and we have been with you for many, many centuries. We have come again and again together, and the bonding of us all to one another can be compared to the bonding of us all to the Cosmic Christ and the Holy Christ Self.

"This horizontal bar of our cross, through which we are bonded to one another, is the strengthening of the vertical bar, through which you achieve that bonding to your Holy Christ Self. To that end we desire to take you to the hour when 51 percent of your karma is balanced and beyond it. We desire to take you to the place where you will not lose what you have gained, where you will not fall back because of false teachers, where you will not be fooled by those momentums of your own electronic belt nor by the dweller-on-the-threshold itself in its final manifestation of the subtlety of Serpent.

"Yes, beloved ones, many of you are yet fragile. Many of you require our sustaining presence. You work hard with your decrees and in your service, but you do not have the sense of co-measurement of just how much strengthening and over-shadowing you receive, not only from ourselves but from the holy angels and many Ascended Masters.

"You can consider yourselves in one sense of the word as mature sons and daughters of God with great knowledge of the Path and in another sense of the word as newly born babes yet in incubators, not able to live outside those incubators until you are strengthened.

"So, there is a side of the nature that is fragile, there is a side of the nature that is strong. And again, beloved, it is relative, so that you know not when you are weak and you know not when you are strong.

"Thus, the Ascended Masters do come and we do dote over you, but we do not indulge you. And we are fierce in challenging you when you allow yourselves to express the not-self. This cannot go unnoticed. This cannot go without discipline. This deserves the cosmic spanking because all of you know better and all of you are capable of doing better.

"And therefore, when you vent that anger of the dweller on occasion, you must understand that you do so knowingly and willingly and that you do so because you have not taken the precautions day by day to gain that mastery over the beast....

"This is the significance of my coming today—to let you know that you can master yourself in the depths of those canyons of your own subconscious and unconscious. But you must be aware that that is what is happening in your life, for without awareness you may falter and fall....

"Yes, beloved, it is wonderful to be with you. It is wonderful to be with you again and again. Make room for me in your office. Even a tiny picture of me will signal that I am welcome there.

My preference, beloved, of a photograph is that which is before you. It is the one of myself on the *Sermons for a Sabbath Evening* album. This particular portrait, beloved, I had taken in the full knowledge that I would be taking my

Mark L. Prophet

leave of this world in the victory of the ascension. In this you will find my Electronic Presence of Divine Love, for it was with the great desire to present to you a photo of my passionate love for your souls that I had this photograph taken. Thus I know that you will know me through that presence, through that look and through that heart....

"There is something immortal about the springtime of Life. I come to reignite the Life of the eternal spring within you. I come to touch you and to have you touch not only the hem of my garment, but that and more.

"My touch is a touch of eternal Life. I would transfer it to you on this occasion of my ascension victory and on all occasions to come when I shall speak to you.

"Drop by drop immortality is won.

"Point of Light, point of self-mastery:

"Point by point eternal Life is won—
    in the moments cradled in the hours,
    in the hours that extend
    from the rising to the setting of the sun.

"So the cycles of the sun are the portents of God-
    realization in the Light-manifestation of each day."[85]

An Invitation for Candidates of the Ascension

Serapis Bey writes: "I am announcing to all candidates of the ascension and to all who desire to be candidates for the ascension flame at the close of this or their next embodiment that we have arranged classes at our retreat that may be attended by those aspiring after Purity's matrix.

"To those who have said in their hearts, 'I desire above all to be perfect in the sight of God, to have that perfect Mind in me which was also in Christ Jesus,'[86] to those who yearn to merge with the flame of God's identity and to find themselves made in the Image and Likeness of God, to those in whom this desire burns day and night—to you I say, Come and be tutored in those precepts of the Law that perhaps have escaped you in this life or which perhaps you have overlooked in previous embodiments.

"For we are here to fill in the missing links in the chain of Being so that when the hour of your transition comes and you find yourself as the rose on the other side of the wall, you will have the momentum and the inner soul-direction that will carry you to this or one of the other retreats of the Brotherhood either for final preparation for the ascension or for preparation for reembodiment."[87]

The Requirements for the Ascension

There are thirty-three initiations that every ascending soul must pass, including the major ones of the transfiguration, the crucifixion, the resurrection and eventually that of the ascension itself. The negative spiral of limitation that opposes the ascension process, which man himself has created, can be overcome by the correct qualification of God's energies as he calls upon the Law of Forgiveness and invokes the sacred fire to transmute the errors of the past. Thus the impure elements of what is called the electronic belt (the conglomerate 'core' of a man's karma and his carnal-mindedness) are consumed daily by the alchemy of dynamic decrees, and the purified energy ascends to the Causal Body.

Serapis Bey tells us, "You ascend daily." Our thoughts, our feelings, our daily deeds are all weighed in the balance. We do not ascend all at once but by increments as we pass our tests and win our individual victories. The entire record of all our past lives and momentums of both good and evil must be counted; and then, when we have brought at least 51 percent of all the energy that has ever been allotted to us into balance with the purity and harmony of the Great God Self, we may be offered the gift of the ascension, which is indeed by the grace of God. The remaining 49 percent must be transmuted, or purified, from the ascended octaves through service to earth and her evolutions performed by the soul after the ascension.

"You need not expect, precious ones," Serapis says, "that as the swoop of a great bird of paradise, heaven will come down to you and raise you instantly up into the Light. Each day you weave a strand of Light substance back to the heart of your Presence by the shuttle of your attention; each strand strengthens the anchor beyond the veil and thus draws you into a state of consciousness wherein God can use you more as an effective instrument for good."[88]

There are several other requirements for the ascension besides the balancing of 51 percent of one's karma:

- the balancing of the threefold flame;
- the alignment of the four lower bodies so that they can be pure chalices for the flame of the Holy Spirit in the world of form;
- the achievement of self-mastery on the seven rays of the Christ;
- the attainment of mastery over sin, sickness and death, and over every outer condition;
- the fulfillment of one's divine plan;
- the transmutation of one's electronic belt;

- the magnification of the Mother energy of the Kundalini.

Serapis Bey reminds us of one more requirement. He says: "The ascension must be desired and it must be desired ordinately. It must be desired not as a mechanism of escape from responsibility or from worldly duties. It must be desired as the culmination of a lifetime of service in the will of God, and men must be willing during their final embodiments upon the planet—the time of their escape from the round of the centuries—to give the very best of service to the Light and to help usher in the kingdom."[89]

Saint Germain has promised us that everyone who sincerely tries can make his ascension in this lifetime or at least in the next if there are extenuating circumstances that require another incarnation. At the time of her passing from the screen of life, the soul will be taken to temples of the Brotherhood and tutored on the inner planes so that the succeeding embodiment can be the victorious one. The only exception to the Master's promise would be if the individual, in order to fulfill his divine plan, is required to take embodiment at some future time so that he can complete a specific mission of service agreed upon before his Holy Christ Self and the Lords of Karma.[90]

The Glories of the Ascension

John the Beloved explains the glories of the ascension: "How can we convey to those of you who have not experienced the influx of the great current of the ascension spiral what this energy is? Shall we say that it is like the splitting of a thousand or ten thousand atoms and man himself being in the center? Shall we say that it is like the explosion of worlds or sun centers? Or shall we say that it is like the unfolding of a lily or a rose?

"Perhaps the poetry of the ascension ought to be written by yourself as you experience that great ritual—perhaps at the close of this life. For as you have been taught, the doors are open to all who will make the call and give the service and apply for the test.

"Line upon line, precept upon precept the victory is won. You are ascending daily. You are ascending the spirals of your own being and your own consciousness. You are not as you were yesterday or last week. And if you are giving daily devotions to the Most High, you are light-years beyond your former self."[91]

We are grateful to have a description of the changes that take place during the ascension recounted to us by the Hierarch of the Ascension Temple. Serapis says, "Although the form of an individual may show signs of age prior to his ascension, all of this will change, and the physical appearance of the individual will be transformed into the glorified body. The individual ascends, then, not in an earthly body but in a glorified spiritual body into which the physical form is changed on the instant by total immersion in the great God flame.

"Thus man's consciousness of the physical body ceases, and he achieves a state of weightlessness. This resurrection takes place as the great God flame envelops the remaining shell of human creation and transmutes, in a pattern of cosmic grids, all of the cell patterns of the individual—the skeletal structure, the veinal and arterial systems, the central and sympathetic nervous systems—all bodily processes go through a great metamorphosis.

"The blood in the veins changes to liquid golden Light. The throat chakra glows with an intense blue-white Light. The spiritual eye in the center of the forehead becomes an elongated God flame rising upward. The garments of the individual are completely consumed, and he takes on the appearance of being clothed in a white robe—the seamless garment of the Christ. Sometimes the long hair of the Higher Mental Body (the Christ Self) appears as pure gold on the ascending one; while eyes of any color may become a beautiful electric blue or pale violet."[92]

Through the ascension the Son becomes one with the Father. He can no longer remain wedded to the earth, for he is filled with the Light of the Sun and he has no further need for a physical body. In a moment, in the twinkling of an eye, the ascending one is changed: his flesh becomes transparent, his veins are filled with golden-pink Light, and the very atoms of his being become lighter and lighter.

The ascension is a raising action that affects the entire being of man. In this weightless condition man's buoyant, God-free form can no longer be bound to earth.

Serapis continues: "Lighter and lighter grows the physical form, and with the weightlessness of helium, the body begins to rise into the atmosphere, the gravitational pull being loosened."[93] Therefore he must rise "into the air," where a cloud of white Light receives him out of mortal sight—and the Son, reuniting with the Father, merges into his omnipresence.

"This is the glory of the ascension currents. It is the glory of attainment that Jesus demonstrated.... These changes are permanent, and the Ascended One is able to take his Light-body with him wherever he wishes or he may travel without the glorified spiritual body. Ascended Beings can and occasionally do appear upon earth as ordinary mortals, putting on physical garments resembling those of the people of earth and moving among them for cosmic purposes. This Saint Germain did after his ascension when he was known as the Wonderman of Europe. Such an activity is a matter of dispensation received from the Karmic Board."[94]

Generally, however, Ascended Beings do not return to the physical plane unless there is some specific service requiring this change in vibratory rate.

Saint Germain also gives a vision of the goal: "When this gift of the ascension is given to anyone by his own I AM Presence and the Karmic Board, the appearance of age drops from him as swiftly as a smile can raise the lips, and the magnetism and energy of that one becomes the unlimited power of God surging through his being.

"The dross of the physical body, the weariness of the emotional body tired of the creations of hatred, the ceaseless rote of the mental body—all drop away and are replaced in perfect ease by their divine counterparts. The feelings become charged by the love of God and the angels. The mind is imbued with the diamond-shining Mind of God—omnipresent, omniscient, omnipotent. The total being is inspired and aspiring."[95]

"I AM Immortal!"

Saint Germain tells us that immortality is not only a goal for some future time, but also something that we can strive to experience here and now: "I know the struggle and I know the labor it takes to deal with the records of this life and past lives, beloved. And I say to you, the Karmic Board is nigh. Receive, then, my beloved Portia and the beloved Kuan Yin and know that by the flame of Justice and the flame of Mercy, if you have faith as a grain of mustard seed, you can receive such a miracle of transmutation of these records as to exceed all previous miracles of transmutation.

"I say to you, believe in it and accept it and implore from these Divine Mothers even that total transmutation of the records of the manipulation of your being by the fallen ones.

Accept it quickly, beloved! For this is indeed an hour of unlimited alchemy! If you seek this alchemy, then begin with the premise of this fiat:

"*I AM Immortal!*

"What does this convey to you, beloved?

"I will tell you what it conveys to you. Your body elemental hears. Your Christ Self hears. Your soul and your spirit hear. And in that hearing there is the calling up of the ancient memory of the Law, the Law of Immortality, which does declare that where the flame of immortality is, there there can be no decay, no disease, no disintegration, no death of the soul!

"Where immortality is, there is eternal Life! And the law of mortality is struck down and neutralized by the Law of Immortality!

"Therefore when you declare, '*I AM Immortal!*' every cell and atom and electron of your entire being responds, is quickened and affirms the same. And you reverse the spiral of death and disintegration* and you enter the spiral of integration and everlasting Life right within these four lower bodies! And that soul begins to put on the Permanent Atom of Being. And the Deathless Solar Body is woven and the strands are woven tightly until that Deathless Solar Body becomes an armour of Light invincible!

"When you say, beloved, '*I AM Immortal!*' and you repeat it day after day when the thought comes to you to say it and you even have the projection of your mortality and death —when you say it, beloved, you are galvanizing all of the armies within your physical body, within the tiniest cell to defeat the vibration of Death and Hell within your entire

---

* You reverse the spiral of death and disintegration first in the superconscious mind, then in the conscious, then in the subconscious, then in the unconscious, as the fiat descends through the etheric, mental, desire and physical bodies.

consciousness, being and world.

"Yes, beloved, there are forces and armies of Light waiting for *you*—you, the leader in the battle for the victory of your life—waiting for *you,* the son, the daughter of God, to make that declaration, to believe it, to affirm it and then to accomplish all things that lead to it. For you *do* know, you do know *indeed* what leads to Death and what leads to eternal Life! And if you think you do not know, then study and learn.

"Yes, beloved, in the words of Moses, 'Choose Life, not Death'—Life with a capital *L,* which is Absolute God-Good— and tear from Absolute Evil the consciousness of Death and Hell and their misqualification of God-Good and the flame of eternal Life.

"This is why Jesus demonstrated to you the crucifixion, the resurrection and the victory over Death and Hell. This is why the saints who have gone before you have allowed themselves to be martyred. For in their allowing of that martyrdom, beloved, they have accomplished before your very eyes the victory over Death and Hell! They have stepped forth from their bodies and they have graduated to new levels of Light....

"May you know and understand the meaning of the great truth that Death is not real! It has no power over the saints of God. Therefore live Life now, that when you must ultimately face that call, you shall step forth *fully* the immortal one.

"Such as these who reincarnate reincarnate as immortal ones, beloved. And it is an accurate statement of the Messenger that there be some that walk this earth in their physical bodies who are immortals.[96] For they have won that flame of immortality, they have won that flame of the transfiguration. And when they come again and again, they carry that Light and you recognize them as saints and as Christs in your midst."[97]

The Bodhisattva

Once you have balanced 51 percent of your karma, you may choose to ascend at the conclusion of this life or to re-embody again and again, increasing your Christhood as you pursue the path of the Bodhisattva on earth. When you do elect to enter the Ritual of the Ascension, you may be received and initiated by Serapis Bey at the Ascension Temple of Luxor, Egypt.

Then, fully anointed of the Light of your mighty I AM Presence, you, the Christed one, will rise—that is, you will accelerate in vibration to the level of the I AM THAT I AM. And the Son will merge with the Father. And the Father will merge with the Son. And you will know the full God-realization of the mantra "I and my Father are One." For having fulfilled the Light of the unascended master here below through your Holy Christ Self, you will now have fulfilled the Light of the Ascended Master Above through the God-reality of your mighty I AM Presence.

Thus, as Above, so below, with God all things are possible in the Eternal Now.

Whoever and whatever God is (and you know who and what your God is), he is your mighty I AM Presence with you *now*. And ultimately, whenever you choose to know it, he is your Ascended Master God-reality!

Archangel Raphael speaks of the potential to carry the flame of immortality while yet in physical embodiment: "When by love and adoration and obedience,[98] you allow the Father/Mother and the Son and the Holy Spirit to dwell in your temple, then you shall know the magnitude of God and you, too, shall cry out: 'We give thee thanks, Lord God Almighty, that thou hast taken to thee thy great power and hast reigned—in our hearts, in the superconscious mind, the conscious, the subconscious and the unconscious mind, all planes of being!"[99]

"And God will give thanks to you that you have cleared out all levels of being through the self-emptying process that you might be filled, wholly filled and filled again. Then you will know what it means to walk in the flame of your immortality while yet in physical embodiment.

"When you hear of the ancients who lived beyond a hundred years, when you hear of those mighty ones of old who were of God, know, then, that this is what they did accomplish.

"How is it that Enoch walked with God?[100]

"He walked with God because God was indwelling in him and he was, therefore, that God-manifestation, that Guru, that Dispeller of Darkness!

"Yes, beloved, it is not merely the physical body perfected that you seek but the physical body as a chalice for the great Body of Light. Know, then, that the goal of immortality is not merely to vegetate in the physical domain but to anchor the immortal consciousness, the ray, the Life and the Body of God in the earth.

"This, this is the key to the turning back of the horrendous karma descending upon the planet!"[101]

The Law of Conservation of Energy

Immortality is a treasure of the ages, but only that which is of true cosmic worth deserves to be immortalized. Therefore, if the godly would, by reason of their godliness, retain their identity, they must express that immortality of the Spirit that has been the natural gift of God to all Life from the foundation of the world.

The goal of Life (of God) is to raise the manifestation

thereof, called "mankind"—or a kind of man by men—and "man," by God, into the fulfillment of cosmic purpose. When cosmic purpose is aborted and lesser goals and images are brought forth, the inferior creation must ultimately be stripped of its power, the form broken, and a line drawn that cries, "Halt!" to the abomination of desolation standing in the Holy Place where it ought not.[102]

In the baptism of the sacred fire, the very vibratory action of lesser deeds falls to the ground to be transmuted, commingling with the elements and vibrating downward into the dense strata of Matter, thence to fly with the rising electronic patterns of Light back to the Central Sun for repolarization and for renewed opportunity to be used in the eternally creative flow scheme. For all creation is made up of energy-in-motion—the flow of the eternal electrons.

We see in the Trial by Fire one phase of the operation of the Law of Conservation of Energy, which states that God's energy can never be destroyed but only transformed. In this case, it is transformed into the pattern God originally intended, into the likeness of purity, whose immaculate design he holds in his consciousness for every particle of Life.

No matter what form has been superimposed upon God's energy by man's imperfect thoughts and feelings, His energy can never be denied. For God's energy is all that exists in universal manifestation: nothing exists outside of his energy, and all that exists is composed of his energy. Where his energy has been wrongly used or misqualified, it may be stripped of the overlay of imperfection by the blazing power of the sacred fire invoked by the faithful.

The power of the sacred fire is concentrated for this and other purposes in the Great Central Sun Magnet, focused in the white-fire core of every God Star. Here, in our sector of the galaxy, the electrons that have been freed through the application of the sacred fire are repolarized to their original perfection in order that they may be used again to image forth a more noble work. The sons of God may invoke the power of the Great Central Sun Magnet—wherever they may be in the universe—to demagnetize from their forcefields and consciousness all energy that is not polarized to perfection.*

Immortality is won through the freeing of God's energy. The command of the I AM Presence of every son of God to "Set the captives free!" is spoken to the flame within the heart of every atom that it might expand to free the electrons that have been superimposed with a positive or negative charge of human creation. The command, "Set the captives free!" strips the lesser image of its power, breaks the ungodly form in which God's energy has been imprisoned, seizes the energy in the name of the Christ, and compels its transmutation by the power of the sacred fire.

The transmutation of negatively qualified energy or substance is a process that can take place anywhere in the universe where a son of God has established an outpost of the sacred fire. The stars in the heavens bear witness to the fact that these outposts have been established many times in many places by many Sons of God. Through decrees and other forms of invocation, the sacred fire can be commanded to free the precious electrons from the impositions of human consciousness so that they may flow back to the center of the Sun, drawn by the magnet of God's heart.

It has been explained to us by beloved El Morya that in all perfect creations, which are sustained at present only at Ascended Master levels of consciousness, the form of the creation is maintained by electrons in a state of flow. Electrons in a state of flow do not tarry in the form that they enliven; but

---

* The decree to the Disc of Light (page 374) may be used for this purpose.

they flow, as if on conveyor belts, to and from the Sun to fulfill, or *outpicture*, the perfect patterns of creation invoked by God or one of his perfected Sons. The moment the pattern and its form are conceived in the perfect consciousness of God or Ascended Man, the electrons descend with the speed of Light to "outpicture" the command. The moment the Creator decides to withdraw or cancel the pattern, the electrons cease their flow into the form, and it disappears. Hence, the freedom of the electron is to flow, but not to choose the direction of the flow.

In all imperfect creations, the electrons are bound to the dense form: they are not free to come and go, to ascend and descend on the ladder of Light that connects every perfect work to the heart of the Sun. Therefore, the condition of decay can occur only in an imperfect world where the electrons have been bound to the form they ensoul. Once the pattern of the imperfect form is withdrawn, the density of the form is broken down by the four elements; as this occurs, the electrons are released to flow back to the Sun for repolarization. The process of decay is the slower method of withdrawing or freeing the electrons from the form. The God-ordained method of freeing the electrons is through the use of physical and/or spiritual fire, both of which are focuses of the Great Central Sun Magnet.

The change called "death" by mankind, or "transition" by those who understand that there is no death, is actually a function of cosmic law that strips individuals of their illusions, thereby freeing the holy energies that mankind have misqualified through ignorance. As these energies are freed from their prison houses of mothlike corruption and rusting density, they once again become a part of God's flaming reservoir of purity—the Great Central Sun Magnet.

Focuses of the
Great Central Sun Magnet

Wherever a focus of the Great Central Sun Magnet is established on earth through the calling forth of the sacred fire from the altars of God, transmutation—or repolarization of the electrons—will also take place. Devotees of the sacred fire are, therefore, encouraged to establish a focus of the Unfed Flame in their homes. This may be accomplished in the following manner:

A small table or chest covered with a white cloth is placed in the room where one's energies are consecrated to God through prayer, meditation and decrees. Centered on the table is a chalice made of cut glass or crystal. If you do not have a crystal or glass chalice available, a simple clear glass bowl may be substituted.

The Chart of Your Divine Self is hung on the wall over the chalice as the central focus of the altar. The Chart is flanked by the Charles Sindelar portraits of Saint Germain on the right and Jesus Christ on the left as you face the altar.

Candles burned during one's devotional period may be the pastel shades of the colors of the rays, but custom favors white candles. Alternatively, three candles, one pink, one blue and one yellow, may be used to focus the threefold flame.

The altar table may also hold one or more vases of fresh or artificial flowers and selected statuary of Cosmic Beings or Ascended Masters, such as Jesus Christ, Saint Francis, Gautama Buddha, Lord Maitreya, Lord Krishna, Lord Shiva, Archangel Michael, Archangel Gabriel, the Goddess of Liberty, Kuan Yin and Mother Mary. Pieces of natural quartz or amethyst crystal may also be placed on the altar.

The Keeper of the Flame should visualize the sacred fire, invoked through his decrees, blazing continuously within the chalice. The intense white brightness of the Flame is seen as the brilliance of the sun shining on new-fallen snow. He should acknowledge the power of the sacred fire to transform not only his own consciousness but also his immediate environment and the entire planetary body as well.

Once this focus of the Great Central Sun Magnet is established, the Flame should be "nourished" daily through the offering of decrees unto God. Unless these be given regularly (preferably at the same hour each day), the Flame will return to the heart of the God Presence, the octave of perfection from whence it came; for the lower octaves of imperfection in which mankind live are an unnatural habitat for the perfection of the Godhead. Here on earth His flaming Presence can be sustained only through the threefold flame anchored in the hearts of the sons and daughters of God. Thus, the focus of the sacred fire within the chalice is actually an extension in the world of form of the threefold flame of the supplicant's own I AM Presence.

If the devotee is faithful in his practice of this ritual of invocation, the ministering angels who tend the altars consecrated to God throughout the world will tarry at his altar once every twenty-four hours to magnify the power of the Son of God (the power of the Great Central Sun Magnet). The Unfed Flame aglow within the chalice provides the point of contact through which the expansion of the Light of God on earth is accomplished. This Flame, although invisible at first, may become visible to the devotee as his devotional pattern, his spiritual senses and his consciousness are refined.

The Masters recommend that spiritual music and recordings of their dictations and decrees be played continuously (if possible) in this room when the disciple is not present. The Electronic Presence of every Ascended and Cosmic Being is focused wherever their dictations are played; and through the power of the spoken Word—even when it is reproduced electronically in this manner—one's entire community, nation and world may be blessed (repolarized to perfection). The playing of their dictations gives the Ascended Masters an anchor point through which they may act in our octave to bring in the kingdom of God.

As the vibrations of the Masters' love penetrate the physical, emotional, mental and etheric envelopes of the planet through the conscious, steadfast attunement of the devotee and the playing of their recorded dictations, these vibrations circle the earth and effectively counteract the discord that is being released hourly by a spiritually unenlightened humanity. In fact, the radiation of the Heavenly Hosts released through their dictations and alternated with the disciple's own personal decree momentum is the only power that will stay the rising tide of witchcraft and black magic that is carried on radio waves from one end of the earth to the other through the endless playing of jazz, rock and the dissonant rhythms of modern music.

heavy metal is worse than jazz

If every Ascended Master student would so consecrate an altar, and if possible an entire room, in his home to the magnetization of the Unfed Flame both within (in the chalice of his heart) and without (in the crystal chalice on his altar), unlimited assistance will be rendered to all of Life. It should be noted that this assistance is never limited by the God Presence, but only by the presence of inharmony within the home or within the disciple's own consciousness. Therefore, he must stand as the watchman on the wall of the citadel of his consciousness to guard his "Peace with honor" as the highest Law of his being.

Retaining the Gifts and Graces of God

Cyclopea explains that we can also contain a focus of the Great Central Sun Magnet in our heart: "The great retainer of God consciousness is this, and I impart to you a secret of the ages: the retainer whereby you retain all of the gifts and graces of God is the very focus of the Great Central Sun Magnet, which you must consciously invoke and place within your own heart. A replica of that magnet is bequeathed to each one of you this day, but in order to keep it, it must be used according to the great balance of the scales of the Holy Spirit. And those scales must have the weight of Light sufficient to balance the remaining weight of Darkness within your forcefield.

"If at any hour or moment of the day or night you lose your Light through discord, the balance scale then tips to the side of your own impending karma. And you see, you cannot hold the balance for cosmos, and the balance of Alpha-to-Omega energies in the focus of the Great Central Sun Magnet cannot be retained. Therefore, guard well the scales of Life and know that you must always, by invocation and service and devotion, keep in one side of the scale that portion of Light that is sufficient to the keeping of balance, of harmony and the abundant Life within your forcefield.

"This is the happy way to the ascension. This is the way whereby the pain of overcoming and of the divine alchemy is dissolved. For greater is the Light that is in you than the Darkness; thus, you experience Light.

"It is as though you were walking on a parched desert in the baking sun and the winds of the Holy Spirit begin to blow, and so you identify with the wind, rather than with the burning sun. And by your attention upon the wind, you are cooled, and you find that your four lower bodies adjust to the climate. But if in pain and sorrow and self-pity you identify with that sun, then you burn; and the burning is the action of the Law whereby transmutation is forced upon you because you have not first surrendered to God. It is like dying. The dying of the old self, the giving birth to the new must one day come to all.

"Why not, then, let that day come quickly? 'Come quickly, O Lord,' ought to be your prayer and invocation. 'Come quickly, O Lord. Let me die this day, let me die yesterday, that the Christ might be born in me, that I might go forth, then, to show all mankind the way of becoming the Christ.'

"Why wait for your karma? Why wait for the end of a life span to experience death and the testing of death, that last enemy that shall be overcome by the flame of the Christ? Why not invoke the initiation now so that you may put behind you that day when the forces of Darkness will stand arrayed to jeer, as a throng of rebellious ones, attempting to tear down the image of victory?

"I say to you, sons and daughters of God, when you are ready, truly ready in harmony, when you are ready through surrender, there is no Master in cosmos who will withhold his presence from you. Draw nigh to the Flame and see how the representatives of God will draw nigh to you. See how the tiniest victory, the tiniest surrender will cause the angels to rush to your side, singing the glorious Christmas anthems of the freeborn Christed ones. See, then, how, if you have asked yourself, 'Why do I not make greater progress in the Light?'— see how, then, that the answer must be: (1) a lack of humility; and (2) a lack of surrender. These ingredients are the making of the avatar.

"You stand now in a position in cosmic history where, at the beck and call of the I AM Presence, the voice that says, 'Take a giant leap into the Flame and into eternity,' you can make a decision to put on the robes of immortality and walk the earth as unascended masters. The only difference between you and more advanced teachers is application of the Law you already have.

"How long will you tarry, then, revolving and regurgitating the substance of your electronic belts, the patterns that ought to long ago have been placed in the Flame?"[103]

Holy Communion

When immortality is studied on the basis of cosmic science —only fragments of which have been revealed in this chapter of the Everlasting Gospel—it will be seen that immortality can never be awarded to lesser images or to imperfect forms, for these lack the polarity of the Father-Mother God; they are lifeless from their inception because they were never polarized to perfection. Thus, we see that the imbalance of the yin and yang principle in human consciousness and human creation renders them both unfit for the kingdom of God. But the LORD has not left man comfortless. In order that he might regain this precious balance, God has provided the Ritual of Communion with himself through Christ, the Mediator.

The disciple participates in the sacrament of the Lord's Supper, Holy Communion, as a preliminary act to his cosmic recognition as a son of God and as an atonement for his misuse of God's energy. Jesus said, "Except ye eat the flesh of the Son of man, and drink his blood, ye have no life in you."[104] The Body and Blood of Christ are the essence of the Father-Mother Principle: the body being the negative, or feminine polarity, and the blood being the positive, or masculine polarity.

When the sacred Eucharist is consecrated by God, the bread and the wine are charged with the power of Light that has the perfect balance of the masculine and feminine rays.

[handwritten margin notes:] Divine Love + Divine Light + Also Divine + Divine Truth is the wine of Divine Good is also symbolized by the bread — Divine Truth is the wine of

When the communicant takes in the substance of God (the bread) and his essence (the wine), his entire form is polarized (or "blessed" as some would say) to the vibrational pattern of the living God. Those who do not have this balance, those who do not eat the "flesh" of the Son of man and drink his "blood," have no Life in them. Nor do these have God in them, for that which is of God and of Immortal Life has the perfect balance of the masculine and feminine rays. — Divine

[handwritten margin note: Light plus Love plus Truth plus Good]

Each time the supplicant goes before the altar of God to receive Holy Communion, he should renew his vow to consecrate his energies to the manifestation of the divine plan. He should invoke the balancing of the threefold flame within his heart and ask the power of the Holy Spirit to realign his four lower bodies that he might be a living chalice for the very Being and Consciousness of God. His coming before the altar signifies a willingness to hold sacred communion with the Body of God (which is comprised of all of the sons of God) and with the flow of his vital Life-force (the Light of the I AM Presence) as it descends into the cup of his individuality.

Each time the disciple takes Communion, he should remember that this ritual is a commemoration of that moment when he was originally infused with the power of the masculine and feminine rays of the Deity—the very moment of his creation. He should also realize that participation in this ritual is preparation for that moment when he will stand on the dais either at the Court of the Sacred Fire on Sirius or in the Ascension Temple at Luxor, Egypt.

Communion is part of the ascension process; and if one can retain the charge of the Father-Mother God that is given by the hand of the Holy Spirit each time he takes in the consecrated Eucharist, he will be gathering the momentum of Light's victory in preparation for the day of his salvation.

Goal-Fitting

All Life comes from God, and all Life is God. In many ways man has lost that Life: he has walked among the dead who know not that they are dead, and he himself has taken on the ways of death.

How wondrous is our God, who has given us a means whereby we might regain the Life of Christ. This means is the sacred fire that manifests as the God Presence, as the Christ Self, as the threefold flame, as the Holy Spirit, as the power of the seven rays, and as the essence of the Body and Spirit of God that penetrates body, mind and soul through the Ritual of Communion. Wise and blessed is he who avails himself of the opportunity of participating in this ritual.[105]

The leaves of the Tree of Life and the twelve manner of fruit thereof symbolize the fact that immortal goal-fitting prepares man, regardless of his station or background, to become the manifestation of the Sun of Righteousness[106]— whose seed is within himself (whose Christ-power is summoned from the God within) and in whose wings (in his Light momentum) is the healing that will lift him out of the socket of mortal delusion into the consciousness of immortality.

Saint Paul's admonishment on the Ritual of Adornment was beautifully phrased:

> *Finally, brethren, whatsoever things are true, whatsoever things are honest, whatsoever things are just, whatsoever things are pure, whatsoever things are lovely, whatsoever things are of good report; if there be any virtue, and if there be any praise, think on these things.*[107]

It would be well, then, if by the power of directed thought, all individuals would become accustomed to the habit of thinking of themselves not as mortals, wedded to carnality and the life patterns of earth, but as immortal sons of God: deathless, birthless and eternal, whose every act must hold fast to worthy deeds that can endure the acid tests of righteousness and the fire that will surely try every man's work.[108]

Maitreya says, "Let us talk about what is eternal. Let us talk about the etheric plane as being far more concrete than your physical octave. Let us talk about you becoming whole and being on the verge of moving from mortality to immortality. Oh, what a transition that will be, beloved, what a transition! Know that you may enter in to that immortality before you are ultimately one with God in the ascension.

"Many things can transpire in your life in a short time, and as you view the world in this decade and on to the next, you must know that there is the absolute opportunity for your victory, for your ultimate victory whereever you are."[109]

Hope Cast Beyond the Veil

The love of the Cosmic Christ, the blessings of the angelic hosts, the communion of the saints, and the Spirit of Life's natural affinity with joy, with righteousness and Truth are the claims of God entered for man in the great halls of karmic justice. The past, with its condemnation of the human, is prologue; but the future, with its affirmation of the Divine, beckons.

Thus, the Tree of Life was placed in the midst of the garden. It cannot be found by a cursory search, but by penetrating Life's purposes and by reentering the garden of the heart. And this is accomplished through the balancing of one's karmic debts and through the entering into one's novitiate of service. By dedication to the very principles of Life, the beholder of perfection, who sees in Life the faith, hope and charity of God in action, shall stand before the Tree of Life, put forth his hand, eat and live forever.

Immortality and righteousness go hand in hand. How better can immortality manifest here below than as the tangible Flame of Life that God has implanted within the heart? The heart that is on fire with his love is the heart that is saturated with right action. The heart that identifies with the thoughts and feelings of God, with the Identity of God and with the qualities of his nature is the heart that is determined to manifest his God-potential here and now at the personal level.

"Life, Immortal Life, is within all," Jesus says. "It exists as a tiny flame of perfection, fanning hope into a bright beacon in the minds of many devotees of Truth, but bestowing upon the divinely perceptive few the living way to overcome the last enemy, which is death."[110]

"Your dedication, precious hearts of Light, joined with my own, to destroy this death (and the hell that is the abode of the godless dead) does clear the way for Immortal Life to take command, dominion and control over your lifestreams from the threefold flame enthroned on your hearts' altar.

"By God-direction and only thereby, man returns to the state of grace whereby heaven is secured in the present rather than postponed by doubt or uncertainty. The laws of man's destined immortality and living grace can never be broken except in the life of the individual who woefully abuses the precious gift of free will. Therefore, each obedient one, by cosmic law, does come to a place of comforting inner awareness—the long dark night is past, and the dawn floods the soul with peace and the restored hope of return to heavenly grace, attainable here and now."[111]

How else can we forge a future that is based on the blueprint of our soul's immortality than through a hope that is cast beyond the veil, beyond mortal reason and feeling, into the domain of the Holy of Holies, the high altar of faith everlasting? For there God's idea of man appears as universal immortality—immortality by creation, immortality by divine right, immortality by worth, and immortality by his Law as love in action.

"Who shall separate us from the love of Christ?"[112] Saint Paul asked. "With what measure ye mete, it shall be measured to you again"[113] is the decree of God-justice implemented by the Karmic Board. Can we not now call for a dispensation from the Lord's Hosts of that full measure of righteousness that shall enable us to render to our fellowmen the service and accord of a living Christ? Shall we not now pass from death unto Life, from the consciousness of darkness unto the consciousness of the dawn? Shall we not now hold fast to that which is Good and forsake that which is Evil?

Let us come apart, then, from the fate of mortality, shaking its dust from our feet and replacing it by the conscious destiny of an active sense of immortality that is our own, even as we make it so. Let us walk with the Christ not only on the way to Emmaus,[114] where our hearts may burn within us, but also all the way back to a Paradise regained, a consciousness won, a communion reestablished.

Rose of Light, an Ascended Lady Master, speaks of the victory that awaits us: "Let all know that Life is real, that your promises are sealed by God, that God has heard you vow a vow of Life, not death. God holds you to that vow. Therefore be Life! Be the Life triumphant! Be in universal manifestation! Be the allness of the One and know that your Light holds the balance for the earth, holds the balance for the nations that souls of worth might be drawn out, drawn out and saved for a mighty conflagration in the image of the Christ."[115]

"This Mortal Must
Put On Immortality…"

" 'Never the spirit was born, the spirit shall cease to be never' spoken by the Bhagavad-Gita brings to the world the basic idea of the Eternal," Lanto says. "For the Eternal desired from the Beginning to see a perpetuation of the Divine Image existing throughout aeons and returning to the fullness of his givingness. Through mortal reason, through sense involvement, through the skein of entanglement, man has again and again denied himself the great cosmic privilege of perpetuating for himself by divine decree the gift of Immortal Life.

"For immortality, contrary to popular belief, must be won, and you can spell it either *w-o-n* or *o-n-e*. It makes little difference, for it is the symbol of oneness with the Eternal that must be won over the dark hordes of shadow shapes, of things to come that are the phantoms of the night captivated by mortal ideas flooding forth into the mind and causing men to creep upon their knees and hands whereas they ought otherwise to stand as men upright in the earth and uphold righteousness and let righteousness expand the activity of the Eternal through the frame of the temporal man."[116]

The hour comes when this mortal *must* put on immortality. It is a spontaneous combustion. It is a critical mass. It is a sacred fire that burns. This corruptible must put on incorruption.

We are not gods that we so choose and dictate our life. God chooses, and when we are one with him, it is so. And for all of the loves that we have on earth, and for all that we understand that we could do more and more if we could but stay longer, the hour does come when the cosmic law declares, and you will hear it resounding through your temple: "This mortal *must* put on immortality, this corruptible *must* put on incorruption." And the word *must* becomes the imperative of Life.

It is not easy for anyone, least of all the avatar. Jesus *did not* want to leave us. His great, great message that comes to us in the Book of John explains this. He gave us the under-standing, "If I go not, the Comforter will not come."[117] If I do not go before you, the Comforter will not come. He knew that he had to go away so that the Holy Spirit could infill their temples and they could go forth.

> For this corruptible must put on incorruption, and this mortal must put on immortality. So when this corruptible shall have put on incorruption, and this mortal shall have put on immortality, then shall be brought to pass the saying that is written, Death is swallowed up in victory.[118]

It is Finished!
by Jesus the Christ

It is finished!
Done with this episode in strife,
I AM made one with Immortal Life.
Calmly I AM resurrecting my spiritual energies
From the great treasure-house of immortal knowing.
The days I knew with Thee, O Father,
Before the world was—the days of triumph,
When all of the thoughts of Thy Being
Soared over the ageless hills of cosmic memory;
Come again as I meditate upon Thee.
Each day as I call forth Thy memories
From the scroll of Immortal Love,
I AM thrilled anew.
Patterns wondrous to behold enthrall me
With the wisdom of Thy creative scheme.
So fearfully and wonderfully am I made
That none can mar Thy design,
None can despoil the beauty of Thy holiness,
None can discourage the beating of my heart
In almost wild anticipation
Of Thy fullness made manifest within me.

O great and glorious Father,
How shall a tiny bird created in hierarchical bliss
Elude Thy compassionate attention?
I AM of greater value than many birds
And therefore do I know that Thy loving thoughts
Reach out to me each day
To console me in seeming aloneness,
To raise my courage,
Elevate my concepts,

Exalt my character,
Flood my being with virtue and power,
Sustain Thy cup of Life flowing over within me,
And abide within me forever
In the nearness of Thy heavenly Presence.

I cannot fail,
Because I AM Thyself in action everywhere.
I ride with Thee
Upon the mantle of the clouds.
I walk with Thee
Upon the waves and crests of water's abundance.
I move with Thee
In the undulations of Thy currents
Passing over the thousands of hills
   composing earth's crust.
I AM alive with Thee
In each bush, flower, and blade of grass.
All Nature sings in Thee and me,
For we are one.
I AM alive in the hearts of the downtrodden,
Raising them up.
I AM the Law exacting the Truth of Being
In the hearts of the proud,
Debasing the human creation therein
And spurring the search for Thy Reality.
I AM all things of bliss
To all people of peace.
I AM the full facility of divine grace,
The Spirit of Holiness
Releasing all hearts from bondage into Unity.

It is finished!
Thy perfect creation is within me.

Immortally lovely,
It cannot be denied the blessedness of Being.
Like unto Thyself, it abides in the house of Reality.
Nevermore to go out into profanity,
It knows only the wonders of purity and victory.
Yet there stirs within this immortal fire
A consummate pattern of mercy and compassion
Seeking to save forever that which is lost
Through wandering away
From the beauty of Reality and Truth.
I AM the living Christ in action evermore!

It is finished!
Death and human concepts have no power in my world!
I AM sealed by God-design
With the fullness of that Christ-love
That overcomes, transcends, and frees the world
By the power of the three-times-three
Until all the world is God-victorious—
Ascended in the Light and free!

It is finished!
Completeness is the Allness of God.
Day unto day an increase of strength, devotion,
Life, beauty and holiness occurs within me,
Released from the fairest flower of my being,
The Christ-consecrated rose of Sharon
Unfolding its petals within my heart.
My heart is the heart of God!
My heart is the heart of the world!
My heart is the heart of Christ in healing action!
Lo, I AM with you alway, even unto the end,
When with the voice of Immortal Love
I, too, shall say, *"It is finished!"*

Golden-Pink Glow Ray

In the name of the beloved mighty victorious Presence of God, I AM in me, and my very own beloved Holy Christ Self, I call to the heart of beloved Serapis Bey and the Brotherhood at Luxor, beloved Lord Gautama, beloved Saint Germain, beloved God and Goddess Meru, beloved Sanat Kumara and the holy Kumaras, the cosmic being Harmony, the seven mighty Elohim, the seven beloved archangels and their archeiai, the seven beloved Chohans of the Rays, beloved Lanello, the entire Spirit of the Great White Brotherhood and the World Mother, elemental life—fire, air, water, and earth!

1. I AM calling today for thy golden-pink ray
   To manifest round my form.
   Golden pink Light, dazzling bright,
   My four lower bodies adorn!

Refrain: O Brotherhood at Luxor and blessed Serapis Bey,
   Hear our call and answer by love's ascending ray.
   Charge, charge, charge our being
   With essence pure and bright;
   Let thy hallowed radiance
   Of ascension's mighty Light
   Blaze its dazzling Light rays
   Upward in God's name,
   Till all of heaven claims us
   For God's ascending flame.

2. Saturate me with golden-pink Light,
   Make my four lower bodies bright;
   Saturate me with ascension's ray,
   Raise my four lower bodies today!

3. Surround us now with golden-pink love
    Illumined and charged with Light from above;
    Absorbing this with lightning speed,
    I AM fully charged with Victory's mead.

And in full faith I consciously accept this manifest, manifest, manifest! (3x) right here and now with full power, eternally sustained, all powerfully active, ever expanding and world enfolding until all are wholly ascended in the Light and free!

Beloved I AM! Beloved I AM! Beloved I AM!

Seraphic Meditations

These meditations are spoken in the first person by the Seraphim on behalf of the children of God— they are the observations that would be made by man if he were to attain the level of the seraphic consciousness. They may be given in prayer form by all who aspire to these heights of glory.

Serapis Bey has said: "I know of no power more valiantly capable of assisting anyone into his own ascension in the Light than the transmutative efforts toward Cosmic Christ purity that are emitted by the Seraphic Hosts. In our retreat at Luxor, the meditations upon the Seraphim are a very important part of our spiritual instruction. Jesus himself spent a great deal of time in communion with the Seraphic Hosts. This developed in him the superior power whereby he could cast out demons and take dominion over the outer world of form."[1]

And I beheld the great electronic fire rings of the Central Sun. I saw the surface thereof as of molten gold, blending with an azure blue. The sky became a sea and behold, the soft glow as of pale pink roses of living flame bubbling upon the surface beneath, translucent and then transparent; a white-fire core that pulsed and rose and fell with a holy radiance inundated my soul. My eyes I sought to shield from the glorious wonder that I knew to be Reality, Infinity and Love without end.

All Knowledge, all Power, all Love going on forever and having neither beginning nor ending were before me. And I saw the naturalness of home, of friends, of family, of all that ever was and is or is to come. Ribbons of inter-connecting glory from this gigantic orb spread into space from galaxy to galaxy, from star system to star system, and the song of the music of the spheres moved upon the strings of my heart as a lute of fire.

I heard the turning of the seemingly silent spheres and the tones of the cosmic fires, of dead and dying worlds, blended with the nova, the eternally new, the children of space, interstellar systems moving outward into the far-flung deserts where the fractional margins spread apart, yet they were engulfed in the love of the Center.

My soul was separated from my body, and I under-stood that all that I had felt to be a tether of solidity and of identification with an integral, "dyed-in-the-wool" consciousness was no more. I roamed through spiral nebulae, through gossamer veils of Light, through the flaming hair of the Seraphim. I saw the places of the Sun and the turning of empty worlds as well as those that were overly populated with a progressive order of humanity.

I understood the message of the Elder Ones and I knew that the consciousness of a little child was the consciousness of the innocent of heart. I knew that the pure in heart should see God[2] and that the sophistications of the earth were a curse to my own Reality. My heart burst as chunks of ice melted and became a warm liquid that revived all of the hope within my bones.

O Divine Love, thou wouldst not separate me—no, not for an instant—from the experiences of eternality. The last enemy that shall be destroyed is death. O death, where is thy sting? O grave, where is thy victory?[3] I know now no tethers to keep me from thy Presence. Thy majesty with me is every man with me, and I with every man pursue the course that leads to thee.

Consciousness can move. It can penetrate. It can fly. It can break tethers. It can loose itself from the moorings of Life and go out into the sea, the briny deep where the salt tears of my joy are a spume of hope, renewed again and again. I am gladdened as never before, and there is no remembrance of the former conditions. These are put aside as finite, as trite, as a passing fancy of the mortal mind.

> Now I engage my consciousness
> With the Beings of Fire,
> With the Seraphic Hosts—
> Now I see God's desire
> To be the most intense,
> Glowing white radiance—
> A furnace white-hot
> Whose coolness is my delight.

> I see the shadows and the veils
> Of human thought and human foolishness
> Melt and evaporate,
> Vanish in the air;
> And all that I AM is everywhere
> And everywhere I AM.

> Consume in me the dross, O God,
> The impure substance of the sod,

The dingy state of mortal fame—
Consume it all, O Mighty Flame,
And take me by the hand right now
And lead me to thy Light that glows.

My soul as fairest, sweetest rose
Emits the perfume of creative essence.
Lo, I AM mine own God Presence—
Taken from the flame of Truth,
My vital energies of youth,
My infinite strength is holy proof
That as thou art I, too, shall be—
Removed from all impurity
Until thy very face I see.

I AM the pure in heart,
For the pure in heart shall see God.
And as I join hands
With Seraphic Bands,
I know that out from the world of illusion,
Confusion, commercialization,
Unrealization, intense prudery,
And retreating fear of the Light,
I AM come!

I have overcome fear and doubt.
I stand now clothed upon
With a garment spun of the Sun—
My flesh is clothed with an Electronic
Swaddling Garment:
It electrifies my entire form;
It renews my mind,
My identity with its original self,

And the glow of that Star
That is within me and on my forehead
Is one of hope for the ages.

I come under thy dominion
And all things come under my dominion.
I AM the LORD thy God,
The LORD thy God I AM—
For between the shores of our being
There is oneness,
The oneness of hope that does evoke
A release from all that is not real.

By thy grace, O God, I am made to feel
I am made to heal!
I am made to seal myself
And all that I am
Within a garment of electronic Light
Whose impenetrability, bright radiance,
Shining down the dawn of foreverness,
Refuses acceptance
Of any mortal thought whatsoever
That limits my soul,
For by thy grace I am made whole.

Out of the Light I am come
And with thee I am unified to see
Shining down the century,
The corridor of years, of Light
Of *pralaya*, of mantrams, prayers,
And ended human tantrums—
The celestial manifestation
Of God terrestrial

Raised unto the heaven-world
Where the ascension currents,
As electronic essence,
Pursue in me every dark chasm
And intensification of mortal passion
Until they are milked—
Placed in the violet-fire caldrons—
And purified as substance of shining Light.

O God, here am I, here I AM!
One with thee and One to command
Open the doorway of my consciousness
And let me demand as never before
My birthright to restore.
Thy prodigal son has come to thee[4]
And longs once again to walk with thee
Every step of the way Home.

Serapis

Chapter 4

Entities

And unclean spirits, when they saw him, fell down before him and cried, saying, Thou art the Son of God.

GOSPEL OF MARK

 # Entities

W HEN THE MASTER JESUS journeyed into the country of the Gadarenes, he was met by a man who was tormented by an unclean spirit. Whereupon Jesus commanded, "Come out of the man, thou unclean spirit!"

And it is recorded that the spirit, speaking through the man, "cried with a loud voice and said, What have I to do with thee, Jesus, thou Son of the Most High God? I adjure thee by God, that thou torment me not.... And [Jesus] asked him, What is thy name? And he answered, saying, My name is Legion: for we are many."[1]

Discarnate and Mass Entities

The term *entity* means literally "existing thing"; it is defined as "an independent, separate or self-contained existence." In our consideration of entities, we will be dealing with two types: (1) discarnate entities and (2) mass entities.

(1) Discarnate entities (or disembodied spirits, as they are commonly referred to) are made up of the personality consciousness, as it expresses through the astral, mental or etheric bodies, of lifestreams who have passed through the change called death.

Whereas advanced souls are taken to etheric temples for instruction between embodiments, those who are not spiritually awakened may find that when the crystal cord is withdrawn, the consciousness of the soul, which has identified with the lower bodies, remains in the astral realm with one or more of the three lower bodies (etheric, mental and emotional).[2]

These lower bodies are designed to be the vehicles of the Christ consciousness when they are infused with the life-endowing qualities of the threefold flame. But once the flame returns to the plane of the Christ, they are as "clouds without water"[3]—empty vessels blown by the winds of mortal desire untethered to immortal destiny.

These bodies cling to the earth and hover around familiar persons and places as ghosts of their former selves. They are not the Real Man whose identity is hid with Christ in God, but the synthetic images, the vehicles of the personality consciousness that lives in unreality and is itself unreal. With their layers of misqualified substance, these bodies are the aspects of the lower self that must be transmuted before the soul can attain immortality.

(2) Mass entities are forcefields of humanly misqualified energy. They are the thought and feeling creations of unascended man—the accumulation of mankind's momentums of hatred, violence, war, greed, envy, grief, fear, lust, gossip, and the like. These entities, as islands of darkness, float in the astral belt and are moved about on the grid of the field of human consciousness by diabolical forces that direct these pools of dark power against unsuspecting lifestreams. (These

diabolical forces and their methods will be analyzed further in book 8 of the Climb the Highest Mountain series.)

For example, acts of crime diagnosed as temporary insanity are sometimes brought about by the focusing of these vortices of vicious energy upon the auric fields of negatively oriented or unsuspecting people. These individuals are then held accountable for crimes in which they may have been wronged as much as their victims, their sole error having been either their receptivity to or their lack of defense against harmful vibrations.

The Law of Attraction

As we take up the study of entities, let us note first of all that the Laws of God do govern their existence, even as these Laws are fundamental to man's existence at every level of his conscious and unconscious being. For it matters not to what sublevel of vibration the thoughts of men have directed God's energies; these energies still belong to God, and they will ultimately return to him—and wherever they go in the interim, they are subject to his Laws.

Let us consider the Law of Attraction ("like attracts like") as it governs the movement of entities.

Discarnates as well as mass entities drift with the wind and the tide of human emotion. In fact, they are blobs of energy in motion. Whatever their vibration may be, discarnates and mass entities gravitate toward energy pools of a similar vibration. They move compulsively according to the dense magnetization of their energy fields, merging with other misqualified bodies that roam the astral world, until they find shelter in the auras of like-minded individuals in embodiment. Because the Law of Attraction is operative throughout the planes of man's consciousness, few among mankind are free from the influence of discarnate and mass entities.

The Psychic World

The psychic world* interpenetrates the world of form; therefore, its influence permeates men's thoughts, feelings and actions. People who are saturated with vibrations that are not affinitized with the higher aspects of the soul are comfortable with spirits of like mind or similar vibrations who live both in this world and in the next.

The astral plane, which corresponds to the emotional body of man, is the repository for the feelings, both the exalted and the debased, of all mankind. Thus, the varieties of expression in the astral plane are as complex and variegated as they are in the familiar physical plane.

Before examining in more detail the entities that inhabit the strange world of the psychic, let us familiarize ourselves with their environment through the description of the Elohim Astrea:

"The psychic world is the world of images. It is a hall of mirrored forms, but these are not necessarily arranged in any form of order. The modes of the inhabitants of the psychic world resemble almost the sea itself in depth. A seemingly weightless condition persists there, and forms may be tipped at any angle and piled up haphazardly as the substance of which dreams are made. A sense of timelessness is also apparent, with the past, present and future all blending into a montage of incongruent ideas.[4]

"There are segments of the psychic world where a greater degree of order pervades, and this is in complete contradistinc-

---

* The word *psychic* is derived from the Greek *psychē*, meaning "soul." The soul is anchored in the body at the seat-of-the-soul chakra, which is below the heart and also in the center of the electronic belt, the forcefield of the accumulation of man's negative energies and momentums. Most extrasensory perception and gleanings gained from that level are unreliable, because one has to get through the astral plane, through one's electronic belt, through one's karmic momentums, and rise to the level of the Christ to really perceive what is Real. The term *psychic* has therefore come to be used synonymously with the term "astral" in its negative context.

tion to the disorder that pervades others. This is because the psychic world is the reflection of a cross section of humanity.

"There are among mankind transparent souls who on their own, although subject to a great deal of guidance from the Light, have externalized, after a fashion, order and beauty in their personal lives and also to the benefit of society in general. Therefore, the sections of the psychic world that are inhabited by those individuals whose thoughts and feelings are apparently of a higher type represent a relative standard of organization in the 'higher' psychic world that the lower belts of the psychic could profit from if it were possible.

"However, this is not the case; for we who have examined it for centuries, for aeons, can truly say that differing planes of consciousness usually remain fixed in a relative sense, and people almost invariably gravitate to those sections with which they are most closely affinitized. Nevertheless, some are not content to remain in an uncomfortable atmosphere, and they struggle against almost insurmountable odds, straining to rise just a little higher to the next level of the psychic plane."[5]

And so we see that the compartmentalization of life in the astral realm is as complete as that of a teeming metropolis with its many-storied skyscrapers, where layers of people numbering in the thousands function independently of one another within the same square mile. Yet, there is a sense of order in both planes of existence. Circles of interest move together, mingling for a time and then separating and regrouping as the lines of interchange are drawn and redrawn.

Astral Affinities

Astral entities affinitize with those on the physical plane who have habit patterns similar to their own—those addicted to alcohol, tobacco or drugs, for example. Wherever people congregate to indulge themselves, there the entities gather. Bars, smoking rooms and places where people habitually use drugs are literally packed with discarnates who attach themselves to those who are taking in these harmful substances. Sometimes there are as many as fifty to one hundred entities to one person.

These entities crave the sensual pleasures to which they were addicted before losing their physical bodies. They have the same desires that they had before passing through the portals of death, but they no longer have a physical body through which to experience and satisfy their desires. Thus, like leeches, they tie into the nervous system of those who are embodied (usually at the back of the neck and along the spinal column). By so doing, they can vicariously enjoy the pleasures to which they are accustomed. This transfer takes place as the result of the merging of the astral bodies of the discarnates with the astral and physical bodies of the one in embodiment through the sympathetic nervous system.

Soul Progress on the Etheric Plane

Those who pass from the earthly scene through the change called death (if they are not offered their ascension by the Lords of Karma) must prepare to return to the world arena once again to pick up their ball of karmic yarn with its many loose ends. Each succeeding embodiment granted to the soul by the Lords of Karma as an act of mercy presents another opportunity for the soul to move forward on the path of experience back to the heart of God in fulfillment of the divine plan.

We find on the mental and etheric planes different compartments of consciousness, just as there are in the astral realm. Some of these compartments are schoolrooms where souls who have passed on are prepared to outpicture a higher measure of their divine expression in succeeding embodiments. In the higher etheric levels are the retreats of the Masters, temples of Light where the more advanced are taken for further training.*

In these schools, the natural affinities of the soul for the Light are cultivated. Those who have been associated with the various fields of human endeavor such as the arts, the humanities, government and science are given special assistance whereby they might further develop those talents that they have wisely used. They are also trained in areas of latent ability so that they may acquire new talents for future service.

In review classes, the individual has the opportunity to study the akashic records not only of his most recent embodiment but also of previous lives in which he has either erred or excelled in the ways of love. Through what appears to be a moving picture in three dimensions, he is able to examine the events that have shaped his identity and marked his progress on the scale of self-mastery.

The Christ Self and the Angels of Record carefully record on the etheric body the lessons learned from this review. Thus, in time of future testing when the individual has reembodied and the lessons of experience must be taken again, the record of instruction given between embodiments will key in the outer consciousness the necessary and valiant responses that will qualify him to ascend another cycle in the spiral of being.

Unfortunately, not all who pass through the change called death reach the etheric schoolrooms. Many get stuck in the mire of the astral realm, where their energies remain hope-

---

* Classes in these etheric retreats may be attended by souls of Light not only between embodiments, but also when they leave the body each night during sleep. For further information about the retreats, see Mark L. Prophet and Elizabeth Clare Prophet, *The Masters and Their Retreats.*

lessly entangled with embodied and disembodied souls who carry the lowest common denominator of human vibration.

This is one reason why the *satsanga* ("fellowship with Truth") consciousness should govern one's selection of friends. Intimate associations made in the world of form can well carry over into the next plane. By choosing friends of a spiritual nature, you will help assure yourself of an environment of higher vibration both here and hereafter.

Those who have inordinate attachments to earthly things (to family, to position or to unfulfilled desires and ambitions) are so much a part of the world that when they pass on, their spirits are not free to rise into the beautiful realms, the many mansions that God has prepared for those who love him. Therefore, they remain earthbound, for the most part unable to communicate with those they have left behind, for the majority of unascended beings have not developed their sensitivities to the point where they are able to hear or recognize communications from the other side.

This state of affairs is extremely frustrating to the disembodied spirits, especially when they are unaware that they are dead. Fully conscious of the physical world around them, they move among the living, unnoticed and almost totally ignored except when they can influence people indirectly by tying into their feeling worlds. Unable to rise, they hover around all the old familiar places, sometimes alone, sometimes in twos and threes as an ancestral unit—and then again they may come en masse, like a gray cloud of descending locusts.

Some individuals seek to contact such disembodied spirits through séances or through psychics, hoping to gain thereby some insight into life or the hereafter. However, these discarnate entities can never assist the soul in finding her freedom, for they themselves are bound. They are incapable of expanding either their own God consciousness or the God consciousness of embodied individuals, for they themselves lack the development of solar awareness. Obviously, if they had any spiritual attainment whatsoever, they would not be hovering near the earth.* — What about helping humanity? and

Furthermore, these individuals do not have any enlightening, enriching or spiritual experience before they return to embodiment. When they return, nothing has changed, and they continue their lives as they have lived them in their previous embodiment.

This reminds us of the passage from the Book of Revelation, "He which is filthy, let him be filthy still;... he that is holy, let him be holy still."[6] There is no sudden change at the moment of transition called death. As we are at the moment of passing, so we are when we behold the other side. There is no miraculous transformation. We do not suddenly become saints in heaven when we have not been and had no inclination to be before.

This is why one's life-energies should be consciously mastered before physical death. This is why, here and now, men should ask God for the power to change their lives and to overcome their weaknesses.[7]

The Separation of the Bodies at Transition

At this point, let us review in more detail what happens to the soul and what takes place in each of the four lower bodies when death occurs.

First of all, it should be borne in mind that the actual cause

---

* Those who seek to consort with the spirits of the dead will find ultimately that not only did they not receive anything of value from the disembodied spirits, but that their own Life-essence was stolen in the process. The dangers of these practices are described in detail in "Psychic Thralldom," chapter 2 of *Paths of Light and Darkness*, the sixth book in the Climb the Highest Mountain series.

of death is the cessation of the heartbeat, no matter what other contributing factors may be present, such as disease, old age or accident. The cessation of the heartbeat takes place when the Christ Self withdraws the crystal cord from the four lower bodies. It is through the crystal cord, the lifeline to the Presence, that the energies of God flow to sustain the focus of the three-fold flame within the heart of man. The heart ceases to beat when the flame is drawn back into the Christ Self, because it is through the flame that the pulse of God's own heart regulates and sustains the heartbeat of man.

Since the feeling, mental and memory bodies interpenetrate the physical form and are anchored to it through the chakras, these bodies are also cut off from the Presence and the Christ Self when the crystal cord is withdrawn. But each of the bodies is charged with the energies of God that it has managed to store. Each of the bodies is also colored by the momentums it has generated during the episodes of a lifetime. Because each of the lower bodies is a repository for these energies and momentums (this residual magnetism), they do not immediately dissolve when the crystal cord is withdrawn. Nevertheless, once the cord is withdrawn, it is merely a question of time as to how long they can function independently of the Source.

Each body, then, has its own decay rate. The rate of decay of the etheric and mental bodies is determined by the amount of Light that the soul has drawn forth and held. The greater the Light, the longer the life of the bodies.

The lower bodies may completely separate at death. The soul, which usually remains with the etheric (memory) body, may gravitate with that body to the lower etheric plane of the earth. The mental body may rise no higher than the mental belt, and the astral body may remain in the astral realm, while the physical body is interred in the earth. Or the soul, together with the etheric and mental bodies, may travel to the etheric plane, leaving the astral and the physical bodies behind in their respective realms.[8]

According to the Law of Attraction, the bodies are polarized to the octave where the vibrations correspond to their own. In the case of the astral body, when it separates from the soul but remains in the astral plane, its eventual dissolution is to be expected. When the soul reembodies, another astral body is formed at the same time as the physical body is being formed within the womb; both are fashioned according to the pattern held in the etheric body.

When the consciousness is full of Light because the eye (the attention) has been single (has been focused on the Presence of God),[9] then within three days after the crystal cord has been withdrawn, the soul will rise to the higher realms of God's consciousness, to the higher etheric plane that is just beneath the level of the octave of Ascended Master perfection.

The higher etheric plane is the retreat of the Christ Self. The blessed Mediator remains in this heaven-world a great deal of the time. While the individual is embodied, the Christ Self may descend to focus through the lower vehicles when these vehicles become so attuned with the Mind of God that they are a fit habitation for the Christ. The Christ Self tarries there just as long as the welcoming vibrations of harmony, purity and devotion are sustained. However, when transition (death) occurs, the Christ Self returns to its haven of Light, seeking to draw the soul to the heights of God-realization.

Whereas during embodiment it is the service of the Christ Self to teach the soul how to outpicture the will of God in the world of form, between embodiments the Christ Self serves to instruct the soul in the integration of her vehicles with the will of God on the etheric plane.

In the case of those who have earned their ascension but are not able to make a public demonstration by raising the physical body, as Jesus did, they may ascend from the etheric plane. In this case, after the ascension, the physical body that has been laid to rest may still be going through the process of dissolution—unless, of course, it has been cremated. When the physical body has been left behind, the energies focused within it become a part of the untransmuted karma of the Ascended Being that he or she must redeem from the ascended state.

Now we are able to understand precisely what a discarnate entity is. It is (1) the astral body that has been separated from the physical, mental and etheric bodies; (2) the mental body, separated from the other three and wandering perhaps in the astral plane, perhaps in the mental or etheric plane; (3) the etheric body moving with the soul (the personality consciousness) in any of the lower planes; or (4) any combination of the astral, mental or etheric bodies functioning with or without the soul as a unit in any of the lower planes.

Unfortunately, the original plan of gathering the sheaves of consciousness at the harvest of life and bringing them into the storehouse (into man's Causal Body) has become a ritual so rare that it seems unnatural. People say, "I don't want to go to heaven because none of my friends will be there." And so the need for approval from the group affects men's aspirations even beyond the grave.

Freedom through the Fire Element

Present systems of embalming and burial only prolong the flight of the soul and keep the astral body bound to the earth by the residual magnetism within the form. However, cremation, as we mentioned in *The Masters and the Spiritual Path*, frees the energies of God that have been imprisoned in the mold of clay, the fire element not only transmuting the physical form but also serving obediently to erase many harmful recordings that have been made upon the other vehicles.[10] The Ascended Master Zarathustra speaks of the assistance provided to the soul through this process:

"Beloved hearts, there is much superstition concerning the passing of loved ones on this planet. And many cling to them, and therefore the progression of earthly and spiritual cycles does not accelerate as it should in the Aquarian age.

"I remind you—as a spokesman of the sacred fire as God, the consuming fire who revealed Himself to Moses—that cremation is the lawful means of disposing of the remains of the lifestream who has passed from this octave, thereby accelerating and hastening the return of the entire consciousness that exists within the body cells to that one's Christ Self and I AM Presence for purification. Blessed hearts, it is very difficult for those whose bodies are interred to afterwards perform the necessary rituals at inner levels to liberate their Light and consciousness from that earth focus."[11]

Sanat Kumara also speaks of cremation and explains the part it plays in assisting the destined resurrection of the sons and daughters of God: "The carnally minded will think that I preach a flesh-and-blood resurrection. I do not. The outworn garment may remain, as the chambered nautilus remains, as proof that the soul has vacated the tomb for a greater glory in the eternal womb of becoming.

"That is not to say that it is not possible for Christ in you to accelerate body, soul and mind into the white cloud in the hour of thy ascension. But, my beloved, I do say that it is not necessary that the resurrection be physical, as it was indeed the case with Jesus Christ. For it is the soul who is resurrected in the rapture with Christ. And the wedding garment is provided, the seamless garment thy soul has woven and won. This is the body celestial that supplants the body terrestrial.[12] And in that hour you will be glad to cast aside the outworn garment and to consign it to the sacred fire.

"Therefore the law is given by my Son of Luxor, Serapis Bey, for the cremation of the physical vehicle. For did He not say that flesh and blood cannot inherit the kingdom of God?

"The morbidity surrounding the people's consciousness of death and dying is also the demon that must be cast out. For the embalming and the burying of the body is the prolongation of the death entity itself. For the body is composed of Light; and the Light in the nucleus of every atom and molecule and cell must be demagnetized from the 'earth, earthy' and the dust must be allowed to return to dust, even as the Light that preserved its matrix is allowed to spiral to the Great Central Sun as it is released from its encasement in form by the fire element. To this end, the fiery salamanders perform their priestly duties of returning the noble work of Elohim, the body of male and female, to the Great Central Sun for repolarization.

"Let cremation be the liberation of my people from morbidity and attachment to the form. For nevermore will that form be reborn. But the soul, the soul—it shall be clothed upon with white raiment, with the righteousness of the saints. It is the idolatry of the self that perpetuates the cult of the tombstone and enriches the morticians and fills the coffers and the coffins of the mausoleum operators who capitalize on the false belief of the masses that immortality is to be found in the ground.

" 'The earth is the LORD's, and the fullness thereof.'[13] Let the sea, the earth be exorcised of death, the death entity and the bodies in whom there is no Life! For the breath of Life hath gone out of them, never to return. And those empty houses are invaded by the foul spirits of death who, as vultures, feed upon the Light yet imprisoned in the form. This is God's Light and God's energy. Let the elementals of fire, air, water and earth recycle this energy back Home to God and see how the planetary body, blessed Virgo herself, will radiate more Light and more Light and more Light.

"Citizens of earth, we deplore the death consciousness on which you have seemed to thrive after the fashion of the black magicians who would destroy you alive—destroy your souls in hell while leaving your bodies to walk the streets of physical cities and astral planes. Saints of God, this is a serious matter! For the whole Matter vehicle of this evolution must be cleared. And the ancient practices of the Egyptian cult of the dead must give way to the culture of Life that leads to the ascension.

"Therefore go forth and teach the people to place the body on ice, dry or otherwise, two days and two nights. And on the third day, the commemoration of the Resurrection is the invocation of the resurrection flame. Whether on funeral pyre or in a modern crematorium, let the physical fire pass through the body that is untouched; for both flesh and blood must be intact; and embalming is forbidden by the Brotherhood of Luxor.

"This method is safe and sane and healthy for all and allows the soul the freedom from all earthly ties as the four lower vehicles are demagnetized simultaneously by the physical fire and the spiritual fire, and the soul, as the winged symbol of the ka,* takes flight with the flying Eagle to pursue the initiations of the Mother in the retreats of the Great White Brotherhood.

"In this way, the demons have no prey and the vultures no flesh and blood. And the astral sheath, itself consumed by the physical/spiritual fire, may not roam the earth, a ghost of the

---

* In the religion of ancient Egypt, the *ka* was the name for the non-physical part of a person, that which survived the death of the physical body. The original meaning of the term is uncertain, and it has been variously translated as "soul," "spirit" or "double." Some authorities believe that it was originally used to describe the protecting divine spirit of a person (what we might term the I AM Presence and Holy Christ Self). Sanat Kumara uses it to describe the soul under the guidance of the Higher Self. However, the Ascended Masters most often use the term to describe the astral shell, and this seems to be the way in which it was used in later times in Egypt, when religion had degenerated under the influence of false priests and the people became polarized to the psychic instead of spiritual planes.

former self. The astral hordes that would devour the coils of Light are themselves put to flight. For the soul has clean escaped the mortal round and is heard singing, heavenbound."[14]

Thus, it is essential to use the fire element in cremation at the transition of death so that there is a demagnetization of the cells of the body of the Light that they contain. If you have walked this earth and your body is filled with Light, that Light needs to be taken up into the higher permanent vehicles. If it is left in the cells of the body, the cells of the blood, as it is left when the body is buried, then astral entities may come and steal that Light. And these are the real grave robbers. They steal from the body the Light that you have garnered in your entire spiritual path. Sometimes that Light is cumulative from many lifetimes. The fire releases that Light from the cells and atoms and enables it to return to the Holy Christ Self.

So also the astral ka, a double of oneself, can go out and do harm in one's name, thereby creating karma for the soul, even though she is not part of that shell any longer. And once she enters the etheric octave or her lawful place, she will not even be conscious of what that ka is doing, therefore cannot exercise any control and restraint over its actions.

It is important that the ka also be consigned to the spiritual fire, which is why a memorial service and a prayer vigil must be kept for one who has passed until the soul is free.

Freedom from Records of Death

Cyclopea speaks of the importance of clearing records of death from previous embodiments: "'O death, where is thy sting? O grave, where is thy victory?'[15] In the sense of sin, in the sense of mankind's misuse of the Law there is the experience of death, and when mankind identify with the spirals of disintegration that the electrons and atoms must go

[handwritten margin note: Why not good and love? (instead of harm?)]

through in order that that energy might be released and sent back to the Great Central Sun for repolarization, when they identify with death, with disintegration, then they become a part of death, death becomes real, and the soul is flung into a pattern of annihilation, and she does not successfully make the transition but becomes caught in webs and warps of darkness.

"Therefore Hierarchy desires this day that you shall secure for yourselves the certain knowledge that when the hour comes when you must part the veil to behold Him face to face, that the old coat that you take off, that you take off in order to don the new garment, is cast into the flame, is transmuted by fire, physical fire. Therefore the ritual of cremation is a sacred ritual of those who worship the sun, who bear the sun. To return that which is no longer useful to the soul into the flame is a great protection, which cannot be overestimated. It is necessary that your energies, the energies of your body temples that have become so filled with Light, so saturated with Light by your devotion, be sealed in fire, for fire is the baptism of the Holy Ghost and the protection of the Holy Ghost.

"Do you understand that the ritual of the embalming and the burying of the remains comes from the ancient custom in *The Book of the Dead?* The preservation of the form for the next life is absolutely unnecessary, and I declare it unto you that in the day of the resurrection when Christ shall summon the elect to rise from the earth,[16] they shall arise in new garments, new Light-bodies, and they shall be one with him in the great rapture of the Lord.

"I tell you then with a stern warning that if you allow the remains of your habitation to go into the earth unguarded, there to rot and decay, you will find that the ghosts of Christmas past will arise to steal that Light, to absorb it, to perpetuate their existence, and thus long after you have exited this world and this temple, you will find forces of darkness that harbor near the mausoleums and the cemeteries of the world will be living off the Light that you garnered in this house during the period of contemplation, service and dedication to the Most High God.

"Sons and daughters of flame, you have a responsibility to return to the Flame every erg of energy and all substance that has served its usefulness, its purpose upon earth. Be no longer fooled by the cult of the dead. There is no death. Why, then, preserve a record of death when these records must be undone, line upon line, each one till every jot and tittle of the Law be fulfilled? At the hour when mankind prepare for the ascension, the return to the heart of God to go out no more into pain and suffering and the round of rebirth, at that hour they must consider the details of the Law pertaining to the sweeping clean of the earth of all debris that might contaminate, that might be a stone of stumbling in a brother's pathway.

"The earth is pockmarked with records of death, the records of mankind's death consciousness. I send my legions north, south, east and west from this place by the action of the All-Seeing Eye of God to transmute death, its records and the remains of each one of you who have come for the Class of the Harvest Sun. I send them forth anywhere and everywhere upon the face of the earth where in ignorance you have discarded the outworn shell in past lives, past incarnations, and there I send them by the authority of your Christ Self and by the authority of the Lords of Karma this day to transmute that energy and to give you a freedom from death that you have not known before. This is the key to God-mastery in the flame of Jesus the Christ. This is the resurrection, the Light of the resurrection that will give you impetus to move upward in the Light.

"You do not realize, precious hearts, how each such focus of the remains of sense consciousness is like a lead weight upon the soul. You walk the earth in such heaviness that you have become accustomed to the weight and density of cycles of imperfection long past, long behind you in the yesteryear of centuries, covered now by dust of further centuries.

"Therefore, be free! Be free! Accept this victory. No doubt the awareness of this dispensation and this freedom will be realized by you only after your ascension, the fullness of its import, but even now your very soul rejoices, bubbling in the happiness of the eternal spring, the fountain of immortal youth that is immortal Truth.

"O mankind, how you have accepted the concept of age, of death and decay as the natural order! When you are quickened by eternal Life, you will see that as energy flows from God to man, from man to God, man is renewed hourly, and not even the sense of death, not even the smell of smoke can be retained within consciousness or clothing or surrounding."[17]

The Plight of Astral Entities and How to Be Free from Their Influences

We return, then, to the plight of the astral body that moves helplessly, like a jellyfish, in the psychic sea of human effluvia. Tormented by unfulfilled desires, disconnected from the Presence, the Christ Self and the soul, and sensing that its battery is running low, the astral body feels the psychic currents pulling it toward the rapids of nonexistence.

Out of an almost subconscious drive toward self-preservation, astral entities sooner or later discover (or they are taught by one another) the means of drawing strength from those who have not lost their tie to the Source. Attaching themselves to unascended beings, who are usually totally unaware of their existence, these entities draw the very lifeblood of their victims—sometimes at an alarming rate and in other cases at a steady, slow drain.

How, then, are we to be free from the influence of discarnate and mass entities? The Elohim Astrea, who specializes in working with these lost souls (or if we are to be strictly accurate, "lost astral bodies") gives this invaluable advice:

"The LORD God has given to man dominion over all things. But this dominion does not give man the freedom, before he attains self-mastery, to probe the depths of human effluvia and to become entangled in the astral world of thought and feeling.

"The source of all human imperfection is old astral records. Buildings and houses, people and even animals in the world of form are filled with these old records. Your tube of light must be made strong and resilient that it may bend when necessary but never break against the onslaughts of psychic disturbances.

"You must learn to move in the world of form as victors over death and misqualified energy. The vortices of evil and of psychic disturbances may move all around you, but you may call upon your Divine Presence for release and deliverance. You may call unto me, and I will assist you by locking my cosmic circle and sword of blue flame around these vicious foci and providing not only you with deliverance but also those whom you love.

"You must be persistent in your calls and determined in your conviction that the Light of God will not fail to answer them, and you must under no condition yield an inch of ground to those forces that are not of the Light. Beloved ones, these forces could not survive a single day if it were not for the feeding of mankind's energies into them. There is only one source of Life, and that is God.

"The inhabitants of the astral world have in the main cut themselves off from the Divine Idea. They no longer recognize the God of the universe as their God. They seek to take the vital energies of God released to man daily, and to siphon them off through his imperfect, mortal consciousness by playing brother against brother, by creating situations of hatred and confusion, so that people will willingly yield their energies to the wrong vibratory action.

"Every time you lend yourself to feelings of irritation, criticism, condemnation and judgment, or inharmony of any kind whatsoever, you are prolonging the life of the astral entities, whereas divine harmony is of no use to them at all. God's energies, retained inviolate and pure by man, can never be trampled upon by the astral creation. For they cannot enter perfection, and thus perfection is its own protection.

"Jesus gave the key to holiness (wholeness) when he said, 'Be ye therefore perfect, even as your Father which is in heaven is perfect.'"[18]

Now we must heed this instruction of the Elohim Astrea and remember that entities are unable to attach themselves to those who are spiritually oriented, to those who prize harmony above all godly virtues. The white Light, the halo or nimbus (the delicate radiation that surrounds the medulla oblongata at the top of the spinal column in the spiritual man), acts as a natural repellent to astral entities.

However, if these entities can catch the children of the Light off guard as Astrea describes, they can derive more benefit from the relatively pure energies of the children of the Light than they can from the relatively impure energies of those who move in and are saturated with the momentums of the mass consciousness. For the purer the energies, the more readily they are assimilated by the astral hordes.

It is a known fact that black magicians are very particular about the energies they steal, preferring those of young children, virgins, priests and devotees of God. If perchance they are forced to use the energy of unclean spirits, they must first strip it of its unwholesome vibrations—a process that they find most distasteful.

The Comings and Goings of the Soul

There have been assigned to this planet nine to ten billion lifestreams, with about six billion in embodiment at the present time. Through the portals of birth and death passes a steady flow of souls, some desiring to progress in the schools of experience and some totally unaware of the spiritual opportunities that are available to them in the here and now as well as in the hereafter.

Both the comings and the goings of the soul have their dangers. Descending from the lofty freedom of the etheric plane into the denser spheres of the world of cause and effect, the soul knows that once the veil has been drawn over the memory body at birth, the precious gifts and graces that have been carefully gleaned in the temples of Light may be lost.

So many factors are uncertain: Will the parents and teachers who have pledged to train the child in the way he should go fulfill their vows? Will the individual pick up the right books, take the right courses, attend the right lectures at the right time and place in the labyrinthian world of form, which at times seems a deliberate obstacle course to thwart every attempt to discover the real meaning of Life? And when he hears the Truth, will he recognize it and obey its mandate?

There is always the possibility that when the individual is confronted with the responsibility of balancing his karma, he will instead repeat the old offenses, ignoring the opportunity to serve those whom he has wronged in the past.

When all is said and done and his allotted span in this world draws to a close, the individual knows that if he has not magnetized enough of God's Light to propel himself with his lower vehicles into the higher octaves of Light, he may wander in the caves of the astral realm for years without ever seeing the Light of the Son—of the beloved Christ Self.

Shortly after their transition, souls assigned to the earth must go before the Karmic Board to give account for the use they have made of the opportunities of physical embodiment. The Karmic Board examines and grades them, and determines who shall reembody at what specific time according to the life records of all concerned.

Those souls who have accomplished what they set out to do, those who have kept the vows they made prior to descending into the world of form, are naturally given priority over those who have squandered their inheritance. But even the souls who have erred must eventually be given another opportunity to right the wrong they have done and to balance their karma. As the sun shines on the just and the unjust, so the ungodly must return with the godly that mankind might move forward together in the evolutionary spiral.

Nevertheless, the Karmic Board decreed that certain key lifestreams directly responsible for the Fall of Atlantis be restrained from reembodying until the twentieth century. These had remained on the astral plane since the submerging of that continent (recorded in the Bible as the Noachian deluge). They were given the opportunity to repent when Jesus preached to them during the three days that transpired between his crucifixion and his resurrection, but their lack of response did not warrant a dispensation of mercy.[19]

Only since the 1940s have the portals of birth been opened to these Atlantean laggards. They have revealed their ties to the ancient culture in their bearing, in their dress and in their amoral conduct. Many of them, when they came to maturity, started radical left-wing movements.[20] Others among their ranks, under pressure from the black magicians, sponsored the drug cults to force their spiritual centers and to gain thereby psychic control over the children of God, whom they have drawn into their "new" culture with cries of "Peace, peace!"

These laggards take pride in condemning the evils that have been injected into society by the black magicians (many times with the help of the very ones who now sit in the seat of the scornful). Well might these conditions and their devilish sponsors be rejected by members of both left- and right-wing factions of the governments of the nations who are working according to their own best understanding to build a better world. This could be accomplished in short order if they would unite in the power of the living Christ against the common enemy, which appears in many guises.

The dark forces have taken full advantage of the introduction of these backward and treacherous lifestreams into our society. It is through these individuals that the dark forces have plotted the overthrow of the foundations of our modern culture that were established by the Masters. These are only some of the hidden perils that the children of the Light must be prepared to deal with in the days to come.

It is the considered opinion of the Karmic Board that those who have had the opportunity to evolve in and out of embodiment during these ten thousand or more years since the sinking of Atlantis have been given enough understanding of the Law and have drawn enough of a momentum of spiritual power to hold these rebellious souls in check—if they will summon the courage to challenge the schemes of the wicked. Unfortunately, those who are in a position to stop these hordes do not always do so, and once again civilization hangs in the balance of mankind's own free will.

Since the fall of Lucifer, the black magicians have cunningly employed astral entities and laggard souls as chessmen on the board of human creation. Because of the dark activities and subtle machinations of the black magicians, the expansion of the golden flame of Christ-illumination, which began to shine forth so radiantly in the early days of Mu and came once again to a peak of brilliance upon Atlantis, has been checked by cataclysm (which always follows in the wake of man's disobedience to the Laws of God). Hence the full-orbed radiance of this flame has thus far been denied to mankind in this age.

The Creation of Mass Entities and Their Vampire Activities

We come, then, to another danger that confronts the soul on the homeward path. Black magicians have the power to create various types of mass entities. These they manipulate to trap the unwary into compromising situations and activities of darkness to which they, on their own, would never be drawn.

Every day we read in the newspapers accounts of crimes committed in a fit of passion by those who testify that they were temporarily out of their minds. "I don't know what came over me," they say. "I never would have done it in my right mind." And so they are ruled innocent by reason of insanity.

What actually happens behind the scenes? First of all, black magicians as well as entities require energy to perpetuate themselves and their activities. As we have explained, one of the methods used to acquire energy is to tie into the sympathetic nervous system of innocent souls in embodiment who know not that they are being vampirized. But there are other means of procuring energy. In order to provide our students with knowledge necessary for their self-defense, we feel that it is our solemn responsibility to expose another.

For the most part, the ceremonies of witches and black

magicians require the letting of blood. That is, the fresh blood of an animal or a human being must be spilled in order for them to invoke the evil spirits needed to complete these rituals. The reason for this is that the blood is the essence of Life. It carries the energies of God from the heart through the body, and it animates the form. Thus, wherever blood is spilled—whether in voodoo rite, on the battlefield, on the highways or in the slaughterhouses—there the discarnates gather to re-charge their batteries. For it is possible for them to absorb energy directly from the blood without having to tie into the nervous system of the organism. It is the most direct means for them to be able to obtain Light.

We begin to see that black magicians and discarnates have a most compelling reason for causing wars, traffic accidents, murders, suicides, epidemics and every form of disease that leaves its victims weak and therefore more susceptible to the vampire activities of the dwellers on the astral plane.

To precipitate these conditions, the black magicians and all who cooperate with them both in and out of embodiment have mastered the black art of creating mass entities. Using the energies that they gather hourly from the thousand and one different types of negative activities in which mankind are unwittingly engaged, the black magicians create giant astral thoughtforms, grotesque shapes, animal distortions and focuses of concentrated evil. These are patterned after the signs and symbols of spiritual alchemy, which the black magicians distort to channel the energies of God in a downward, counter-clockwise spiral. This reverse spiral works in direct opposition to the ascending clockwise spirals of the flames of God used by the Masters in their practice of white magic.

These forms and the black magicians who manipulate them are to a great degree responsible for the crimes, hostilities and wars that are a daily occurrence in our world. Nevertheless, neither the forms nor the black magicians could influence people for a moment unless the people themselves harbored the hatreds and prejudices of centuries within their own electronic belts.

Let us never lose sight of the fact that the masses of misqualified energy that float as dark clouds in the very being of man (the microcosm), hiding the sunlight of the Christ, correspond to and magnetize the mass entities that the black magicians put into orbit in the electronic belt of the earth (the macrocosm). When the entities in the macrocosm unite with the entities in the microcosm, personal and planetary cataclysms are bound to follow.

These mass forcefields can be extremely dangerous—in fact, they are lethal. As they float, they move like the clouds in the sky. Sometimes you will get unsuspecting souls who, by circumstances, by their lack of cleanliness, by the poor environment they're in, will attract large masses of energy misqualified. Suddenly they will be seized with an insane momentum to commit mass murder. When it is all over with, they may have no idea why they did it; but many times when they are questioned they will say, "A voice told me to do it." This is what happens when these grids and forcefields of mass entities come into congruency with an individual's consciousness. It is extremely deadly. Wars are perpetuated century after century after century because the cause and core of war as mass entities on the astral plane has not been cleared.

A tragic example of this phenomenon was recorded in the *Rocky Mountain News* of Thursday, January 25, 1968:

"A young hippie mother who said she plunged a jagged wine bottle into the chest of her baby boy 'because voices told me to do it' Wednesday was ruled innocent of murder by reason of insanity." She was committed to the state hospital after testimony was given that she had taken peyote, LSD and marijuana for some time prior to killing her child. She had sought medical help three days before because she heard "voices ... telling her to do terrible things."

The attending physician testified that the distraught young woman came to the outpatient department of the hospital on November 19, complaining of severe headaches and "spells." "Even as we spoke she began to stare with a faraway look and cried out that people were dismembering her," he said.

She was sent by taxi to another hospital for special treatment, but upon arriving she just sat about "without seeing a doctor. Then she left in response to the voices which told her she didn't need to see a psychiatrist." On November 21 she was found doubled over on the floor of her bathroom beside the body of her son. The psychiatrist described how she told him that "voices threatened to kill her son 'by tearing him apart limb by limb' unless she killed him herself in a less painful way." The girl sobbed as she told the doctor, " 'They were almost there. I had to hurry.' "

The voices this young mother heard were those of discarnate entities, demons and unclean spirits such as those Jesus drove out of the insane. These, who identify themselves as "legion," had to have blood at any cost. The pressure they brought to bear upon this young girl was focused through one or more mass entities seething with mankind's own misqualified energies of violence, greed and hatred.

Having taken drugs, the girl had opened her spiritual centers, but her receptivity did not go beyond the astral plane. Having neither the spiritual development nor the spiritual protection that must always precede the expansion of one's spiritual faculties, this young mother was helpless before the demoniac forces that invaded her consciousness.

By her taking of drugs, the protective envelope that was placed around her soul at birth was rent—and when the enemy came, he found her naked and alone. This is the plight of those who seek to take heaven by force.[21] They enter prematurely those areas of initiation through which Jesus passed during his forty days in the wilderness, and they are not equipped to emerge unscathed. May God have mercy upon them.

Freedom from Psychedelic Drugs

Thousands of young people throughout the world have forced their spiritual centers open by taking psychedelic drugs. What are they to do to reestablish their forcefields of natural spiritual protection?

First of all, they may call on the Law of Forgiveness for having interfered with the natural unfoldment of the divine plan within their lives. They may then invoke the violet fire and the tube of light. They may call to Archangel Michael and his legions of blue lightning to cut them free from all psychic forces that seek their destruction, and then to Archangel Raphael and Mother Mary to bathe them in the healing fires of the Christ for the healing of their auras of the damage done.

The plight of the souls who have been misled by the Atlantean laggards is unfortunate indeed, but they must remember that with God all things are possible. The Light of God is the universal panacea that the faithful can implement to right every wrong, to heal every diseased condition—if individuals will accept the responsibility for their acts and for their redemption.

Jesus gives some invaluable instruction for those who desire to be cleansed but at the same time fear that they are unworthy of taking their problems to God:

"Many people fear to take to God those distressing problems that involve their own personal guilt—whereas others, working in the opposite direction, seem to almost enjoy telling God how very unworthy they are.

"We would clarify for the benefit of all. Insofar as impure acts and thoughts go, bringing them to God for purification is in a very real sense bringing your iniquities to heaven for judgment ahead of time, thus removing from the karmic record, in many cases, the need for future recompense. 'Some men's sins are open beforehand, going before to judgment; and some men they follow after.'[22]...

"You know, precious ones, the evil spirits that have lived in the world in the past and who are now out of the body, together with those possessing entities that attach themselves to individuals because they love Darkness rather than Light,[23] enjoy performing acts that they suspect might give distress to the Creator of the universe.

"This attitude is difficult for many to understand, but like that psychological trait known as masochism or self-abuse, the attempt of these spirits to flagellate the Deity by acclaiming their own dire condition actually feeds their egos and is intended to make those whom they control enjoy being sinners.

"When the sincere disciple brings to the Father *all* of his energy for purification, God is truly able to wash and to regenerate with his love and attention the developing son and bring him to maturity. In cases where extreme perversions have been practiced, it will be necessary that the individual make application for forgiveness with deep sincerity and follow the injunction 'Go, and sin no more.'[24] Those in the latter category must of necessity strive until they have won a relative state of victory over the outer condition and understand that the demons of ego and rebellion must be put down.

"There is a law involved here that states that man is accountable for that which he creates. Those who have created or harbored a rebellious spirit must themselves bring it under control and then approach God with humility that they, too, may be received and their energies purified.

"There is never any question whatsoever concerning the will of God to receive the prodigal son[25] back to his heart. Therefore, no one should make unworthiness an excuse for not engaging in holy prayer. The worthy need to progress and the unworthy to disentangle themselves from the enchantments of the psychic world."[26]

The Astral Trap

Let the reader disabuse himself of the idea that alcoholics, drug users, chain smokers and those who live riotous lives are the only victims of the wiles of astral entities. Under the manipulation of the black magicians, these entities have a trap for every type of human consciousness, even for those who call themselves the elect of God.

And for those who doubt the existence of entities at all, we would explain that it is the entities themselves that propound the theory that there are no entities. For the best way to get left alone is for people to think you don't exist.

Astrea warns of the vibrations of spiritual pride, which attract to the aspirant the most deadly type of entities—who seek nothing short of the destruction of the soul in hell:[27]

"There are many who are engaged in forms of spiritual work who, by reason of their own human egos and the desire for association with the invisible world, are trapped into an alliance with one or more entities harbored in the psychic realm. These do, then, develop what we may term a very unhealthy friendship with the denizens of the astral world.

"You have heard it said that 'Satan himself is transformed into an angel of light.'[28] One of the aspects of the psychic world that makes it difficult to detect the dangers inherent within it is the chameleon-like nature of the entities, fallen angels, demons and vampire forces that exist there solely upon the stolen (albeit in many cases willingly given) energies of mankind....

"From time to time many religious people make contact with vicious astral forces masquerading as angels of Light and even purporting to be Ascended Masters. In reality, these entities seek only to deceive mankind and to perform upon the waiting stage of their consciousness an unfolding drama of mutually magnetized attention—mutually magnetized because the individual in contact with the entity is enthralled with the concept that he, as a person, is in reality at last in touch with the invisible realm of the Ascended Masters.

"What a pity it is, precious ones, to disabuse the minds of these children of God who are caught in an astral trap. Often when the Truth is presented to them, they are so heartbroken by the facts at hand that they refuse to accept them, and they continue the misalliance they have formed with the illicit masquerader.

"This blinds their eyes to the astral dangers and causes them to be led further and further from the Truth and deeper and deeper into association with these marauding entities. At last, having extended almost their total personality into this realm of shadow, which they consider to be a realm of light, they are completely victimized by the sinister hoax and strategy that has been worked upon them, and they can no longer call their souls their own.

"Forced, then, to a form of obedient disobedience by the controlling entities, they mock the Reality of Truth and the high standards of the Deity. It is difficult for them, then, to recognize the difference between Reality and shadow; for the shadow in which they dwell becomes to them a reality. And because of their disconnection from the developing or latent realities of God within their own life, they are unable to recover their balance.

"Often individuals are fooled by the fact that the entities give forth some measure of Truth (while even the lies that they put forth are imitations of the Truth). Because the utterances are sometimes given in a simple or sweet way with honeyed phrases of endearment or dissertations freely using the word 'love,' people become snared by the idea of the truth of the utterance, and thus they say in defense of their positions, 'But it makes such good sense!'...

"All that is foreign to His nature, all that is false or falsifying, all that is and does emanate from the psychic realm has no part in the Reality of God, which exists far, far above the realm of psychic vibratory action."[29]

Types of Mass Entities

Having reviewed some of the dangers confronting the soul from the traps of the astral plane, let us now examine specific types of mass entities, together with the energies and the consciousness that sustain their existence. The following definitions are included to give the student a general working knowledge of the most common types of mass entities that inhabit the astral belt. The false hierarchy manipulates these entities against mankind and especially against the children of the Light to drain them of their energies, to keep them in a state of lethargy and to thwart the manifestation of the kingdom of God upon earth.

The entities are listed as having either masculine (m.) or feminine (f.) nature. Masculine entities tend to repel, whereas feminine entities tend to attract.

Annihla (a-<u>nigh</u>-la, f.): The suicide entity. Anybody who has ever been in the presence of the suicide entity knows the tremendous pull of this entity, the drawing toward death. Its feminine nature is seen in that it is not a repulsion entity; it's an attraction entity. It makes you feel that death is sweet and death is a release.

This entity projects feelings of depression, worthlessness, hopelessness and utter frustration with life into the subconscious minds of those whose consciousness is open to this type of suggestion. When these feelings surface to the mental and feeling bodies, they influence the victim to accept a philosophy of nihilism, of his own nonexistence. The pressure that the black magicians and the demoniac forces bring to bear on the mind by the seething energies focused through the suicide entity is enough to make thousands of souls every year accept the lie that self-annihilation is the only way out.

This lie is a direct attack by those who spawn it against the destiny that God has given to man, including the opportunity to master his world and become immortal through the ascension. The complete fallacy of the argument of the sinister force is to be seen in the fact that suicide is never a way out, for the Lords of Karma have decreed that those who commit suicide must return to embodiment within a very short time so the soul might learn that she can never escape her responsibilities in the world of form.

The suicide entity may also project a certain excitement of death. The excitement of death is sweet death—the indulgence in the things of this world that are pleasant for the moment, but the net result is the loss of energy. Whether through indulgence or anger or wrath or lust or crime or whatever may be the out-of-alignment state, the suicide entity convinces us to commit a little suicide. This is also seen in the daredevil consciousness, the chances people take with their lives for the thrill of it—little bites of sweet death.

Death is made to seem exciting. It is thrilling. It releases a rush into the system. And those who have not experienced the bliss of God or the infilling of the temple with the Holy Ghost take a paltry, counterfeit substitute in this excitement of death.

The Hierarchy feels that only the most severe discipline will enable the soul to develop the fortitude to withstand the arguments of the suicide entity when the soul must face and conquer this enemy in the next round of her existence. Usually the soul embodies in a situation similar to the one from which she sought escape, and there she must learn to master herself that she might master her environment.

Calls to Archangel Gabriel and Archeia Hope to charge one's consciousness with the flame of hope—hope in life, in Truth and in love—will dispel the sinful cynicism of the suicide entity.[30]

Calumnus (ca-<u>lum</u>-nus): Entity of murderous intent.

Carpia (<u>car</u>-pi-a, f.) or **Harpia** (<u>har</u>-pi-a, f.): The collective names for the gossip entities, which carp and harp, prattle and prate, and involve susceptible people in every walk of life in an insatiable desire to learn the latest juicy morsel of gossip. The entities and their coordinates in the world of form seize upon gossip as their very lifeblood to elevate their poor sagging egos by debasing and defaming the character of others. To be in the know about everything that goes on within the few square miles that make up their universe seems the goal of their existence.

Gossip is one of the most vicious and malignant forces that the false hierarchy uses in their attempts to defeat all that is of worth in man. The accumulation of mankind's misqualified energies that have been used in gossip forms a mass entity that hangs in the astral plane, seeking to devour the very life of spiritual organizations and every noble undertaking. Every effort the Ascended Masters make to reach mankind is attacked by this force. Thus Keepers of the Flame and students of the Light must counteract it daily so that their fraternity and all other avenues of Truth might be protected.

Needless to say, disciples on the Path should never engage in the practice of gossip. For in so doing, they trespass against their brethren and the precepts of the Law. And they also thereby tie into the forcefield of the gossip entity (for by the Law of Attraction, like attracts like), thus becoming tools for its destructive maneuvers.

The end result of gossip is psychic murder. If the black magicians can cause the associates of their victim to release enough negative energy against him by first distorting the victim's true nature in the eyes of his friends and then causing these "well-meaning" ones to tell outright lies about him— sometimes in the belief that they are true—the black magicians may accumulate enough energy to cause their victim's death through accident, disease or even suicide.

This has happened again and again in the history of our planet. The buildup of gossip, of lies and hatred of one individual has become so great that it has made him insane; or that throbbing energy directed against that individual has caused him to have a fatal accident, or in despondency, to commit suicide. So we see how the entities work together.

Delta 9/Cannabis Sativa (f.): Marijuana entity. The entity influences the thoughts and feelings, the outlook and perceptions of anyone who smokes or eats marijuana and thereby takes into their physical body the physical counterpart of the entity. At that point the identities of the pot smoker and the entity begin to mesh.

The marijuana entity is a parasite that robs the individual of his Light, blocking his ability to contact the Higher Self and leaving him spiritually and physically spent, or "burned out." At the early stages of use, the pot smoker usually feels exhilarated because the drug releases Light stored in the chakras. This flow of Light (which is being siphoned off by the entity) gives the feeling of creativity, insight, and enjoyment. But ultimately the person is depleted, since he is being emptied, not filled.

Relying on their own personal experiences, many marijuana users believe that the drug is harmless. They do not perceive any difficulties, but this is because their faculties of perception are being destroyed while they use it. And so they have a receding level of the ability to discern within themselves levels of their own God-awareness. Day by day they perceive no harm because marijuana is destroying not only the physical senses but the senses of the soul. This is one of the most subtle dangers of marijuana and most other psychedelic drugs. The user is rendered incapable of detecting the changes in himself. This is the subtlety of the cult of death.

(For further information about marijuana and its effects, see "The Cult of Hedon" in *Paths of Light and Darkness,* the sixth book in the Climb the Highest Mountain series.)

Depressa (de-press-a, f.) and **Manik** (man-ick, m.): Depression entities. Depression causes the chakras to become concave and then collapse. They collapse by the pressure of the mass consciousness and the astral plane. The depressing of the chakras makes people weak-spined and makes their brains fuzzy and confused. It allows them to misqualify the heart chakra and put themselves completely out of attunement.

Thus, depression needs to be met with a thrust of energy to force out the substance in the chakras that is depressing them.

People may be depressed because of a biochemical imbalance in the physical body—the acid/alkaline balance and the balance of minerals. This can cause them to be unable to deal with the astral energies that are causing their chakras to be depressed. It may also come from psychological problems. But in addition to these causes, deep depression is caused by discarnate entities that infest the mind and body. Often they do not leave even when people come out of depression; therefore, they are subject to its return, because those entities have not left.

If you find depression in your consciousness, you need to realize that it takes an enormous effort to thrust it out. You have to stop everything you are doing and get rid of it. In addition to appropriate medical treatment, it is necessary to work very hard with Archangel Michael, the seven archangels and Astrea to go after the entities, to call for their binding in the name of Jesus Christ.

Depression needs to be treated from the physical as well as from the astral level. When depression is solved in those planes, the mental and etheric conditions can usually be brought back into alignment as well.*

Derangia (de-<u>range</u>-i-a, f.): Insanity entity.

Dormé (<u>door</u>-may, m. and f.): The sleep entity, which induces sleep to cut off or to interrupt the flow of ideas from the Mind of God to the mind of man. It often brings on a feeling of drowsiness just when individuals decide they will consecrate their energies in prayer, meditation and spiritual study.

This entity tries to tell you that you didn't sleep enough last night so you deserve a little nap now, or you had a heavy meal and you deserve to have a little rest to digest your food. The entity always gives you the logic of why you should be

---

* In cases of severe depression, bipolar disorders, schizophrenia and other serious psychiatric conditions, certain psychotropic medications prescribed by psychiatrists are helpful in treatment of the condition because the vibration of the drug itself is offensive to the entities associated with the condition. These medications may also coat the aura and prevent the intrusion of astral entities into the outer consciousness. Such medications may enable people to maintain mental and emotional balance while working on underlying causes. Professional help should always be sought when dealing with these conditions.

Tell us how you liked this book!

SUMMIT UNIVERSITY PRESS

Non-Profit Publisher since 1975

Book title: _____

Comments: _____

_____

_____

What did you like the most? _____

How did you find this book? _____

☐ **YES!** Send me **FREE BOOK CATALOG**   ☐ I'm interested in more information

Name _____

Address _____

City _____ State _____ Zip Code _____

E-mail: _____ Phone no. _____

Your tax-deductible contributions make these publications available to the world.

Please make your checks payable to: Summit University Press, PO Box 5000, Gardiner, MT 59030.
Call us toll free at 1-800-245-5445. Outside the U.S.A., call 406-848-9500.
E-mail: tslinfo@tsl.org   www.summituniversitypress.com

491-PTI#4503 1/06

Summit University Press

PO Box 5000
Gardiner, MT 59030-9900

sleeping and why it is perfectly natural to suddenly be going to sleep.*

The black magicians use what is known as the "sleep ray" in conjunction with the activities of the sleep entities. This ray can only be reversed by a powerful call to the God Presence. For example:

In the name of the mighty I AM Presence and beloved Jesus the Christ, I demand the reversing of the sleep ray and the binding of the sleep entity, Dormé. You take command of this entire situation. I shall not be moved! Into thy hands I commend my spirit, and unto no other shall I give my energies sent to me each hour by the hand of Almighty God!

The giving of the decree "I AM Alert, Awake, Awake!" will magnetize to one's forcefield the full-gathered momentum of the alertness of the Christ, which will dispel all mental fogginess that might tend to open the door of one's conscious-ness to the sleep ray.

I AM ALERT, AWAKE, AWAKE!

I AM alert, awake, awake!
I AM alert, awake, awake!
I AM alert, awake, awake!
Come right now and shake,
Shake my mental body's grids;
Remove the ash, transmute it all,

---

* It should be noted that sleep is a natural function, vital to one's health and to the soul's resistance to psychic forces. During sleep, transmutation and the recharging of one's four lower bodies take place. Both processes are essential to the spiritual development of the individual. Therefore, one should take care to get the required amount of sleep each night. The Masters recommend that students retire no later than 11:00 P.M. that they may be escorted by the ministering angels (out of their bodies) to etheric temples for instruction. They have also stated that the taking in of food after 9:00 P.M. hinders the flight of the soul to higher octaves, since one's energies are thereby tied up in the digestive process.

Give me Christ Mind for which I call!

Violet fire blazing,
Violet fire blazing,
Violet fire blazing,
God's own Light is raising, raising, raising
All my thoughts, consciousness, too,
To the plane of my Presence, who
In God's name releases all
Wisdom and balance for which I call.

Draculus (<u>drak</u>-u-luss, m.) and **Dracula** (<u>drak</u>-u-la, f.):
Horror entities that work through horror movies, crime and
mystery magazines, writings such as those of Edgar Allan Poe,
monster comic books, and through television shows.*

While Dracula engages people's minds in a curious and
irresistible fascination for Frankensteinian horror, Draculus
induces feelings of revulsion and terror. When people place
their attention upon tales of horror and newspaper accounts of
brutal criminal acts, they tie into the astral realm and thereby
into the demons who specialize in keeping alive in the consciousness of the race the horrors of "the pit"—a name for the
collective subconscious of the entire planet.

It is this fascination with horror that is somewhere in our
electronic belts that the entities prey on. They have us watch it
to get our attention to perpetuate horror in reality. Over man's
attention flows God's energy, which is then funneled into the
horror cesspool available to the black magicians when they
desire to implement a plot of mass murder through one of

---

* Early movies of this genre included the Frankenstein series and Alfred Hitchcock's
horror movies. One technique that has been used is to make images of horror more
attractive through humor or through placing them in a family setting, as was done in
the television show *The Munsters* in the 1960s and in *Buffy the Vampire-Slayer* more
recently. The current focus on horror through books, movies and television has
reached unprecedented levels, in part through the work of Stephen King and the
popularity of the Harry Potter series of books and movies.

their tools in embodiment. War can be produced out of the attention of a nation of people watching a show like *The Munsters*, because their energy goes into those matrices.

Edgar Allen Poe is one of the early writers that opened up a doorway from the astral to the physical for Dracula and Draculus. Certain people have a tremendous fascination for the writings of Edgar Allen Poe, and that fascination is produced by these entities. There is nothing within our soul to make us read his writings. There is nothing native to the soul in any one of these stories. Why do we let ourselves be fooled that way? Why do we get drawn into this astral miasma? Because no one has ever really defined it for us; no one has ever explained these laws.

Watching a horror movie now and then may seem an innocent pastime, but nothing could be farther from the truth. Let us here and now, once and for all, expose the lie of harmlessness, which the astral hordes have spread concerning their evil deeds.

Jesus speaks of the price we pay for indulgence in these kinds of entertainment: "Think about this: Each time you take in a worldly motion picture, it takes you a minimum of five days to transmute it if you have a good momentum on giving your violet-flame decrees—and much longer if you don't. For those who do not decree at all, the records of their media experiences, including rock concerts and violent films, pile up in the psyche; and the sounds and the scenes come up again and again as though they were actual life experiences.

"Who in his right mind would want to thus burden his soul?

"Select motion pictures that profile the heroes of history, the rise and fall of civilizations, the origins of the major religions of the world and a wealth of cultural material that teaches children about the world they have reincarnated into.

"Think about how many hours you devote to entertainment that does not afford you a net gain physically or spiritually. Think about how you could spend the same amount of time developing a powerful spiritual momentum on giving calls for the healing of all who mourn, all who are sick, all who are dying and fear death. The hours you spend in unproductive activity are costly, very costly! both to you and to us, as we are your sponsors."[31]

Exhora (ex-*or*-a, m. and f.): Entities that induce in mankind exhilaration and titillation through fascination with horror.

Fluorida (floo-*ree*-da, f.): Fluoridation entity, playing on the fears of the people and the greed of the industrialists who sell fluorides. This entity exerts pressure on communities to fluoridate their water, supposedly for reasons of health. Actually the use of fluorides is harmful not only to the physical body but also to the proper functioning of the spiritual centers in man, as are all artificial chemicals.* *Fluorida* is also a general entity name for chemicals in food.

Gargantua (gar-*gan*-choo-a, m.): The lynch mob entity, which works through mob psychology to bring about the rule of the mob. Its slogan is "Let's take the law into our own hands." Gargantua is behind mass murders such as those that occurred in the Reign of Terror during the French Revolution and in the purges that followed the Communist takeovers of Russia and Eastern Europe. This entity has also been active in the western part of the United States.

At one time there was a restaurant east of Colorado Springs where the architect had picked up the forcefield of the

---

* The Ascended Masters encourage the prevention of illness through natural methods, including a disciplined diet, exercise, fresh air, a positive spiritual and mental attitude and wise health care in every area of living. However, this is not a substitute for medication and the proper medical care under a physician when needed. The Masters do not recommend the avoidance of established medical procedures.

place in his design of the building. There was a large area which was open from the first floor to the second floor, like a well, and right on that very spot, in the nineteenth century, a lynch mob had lynched a man who was a cattle rustler. He had hung at that very place that was now the circle in this restaurant. The lynching was the work of Gargantua, the lynch-mob entity. "Take the law in our own hands. We're going to kill this guy; he stole our cattle." These records are all over the American West.

Did you ever step into a ditch? Did you ever step on wood that was infested by termites or rotten and you went through with one foot? That's just how it feels when you step into an old record or an old matrix, or something terrible that happened somewhere: all of a sudden you go down into this record and it's like a vortex. And if you don't have sanity and moral integrity, you go right down and you outpicture this vortex of a record that is left, together with the entities and the discarnates that made up the record.

Guisa (geez-a, f.): Masquerading entities. These are never what they appear to be. Wolves in sheep's clothing, they fool the people every day of the year, not just on Halloween and at the New Year's Eve masquerade ball.

Incubus (In-cu-bus, m.) and **Succubus** (Suck-u-bus, f.): Sex entities that project erotic dreams and sensations during sleep. Incubus is an evil spirit supposed to lie upon persons in their sleep, and especially to have sexual intercourse with women by night. Succubus is a demon assuming female form to have sexual intercourse with men in their sleep.

These demons may assume the mask and the persona of individuals you have known in this embodiment or in the past. So you think you are dreaming of a particular person, when it is actually a discarnate, one of many that are known by this name. These are the collective name for the species.

Infurio (in-<u>foo</u>-ri-o, m.) and **Riptide** (<u>rip</u>-tide, f.): Anger entities. These entities often cause people to release a great quantity of their precious energies in a fit of passion or a violent explosion of temper.

Anger entities work on poling the energies of the mental and feeling bodies of man through the solar plexus and the brain, causing people to enjoy a "good" argument. Their enjoyment comes, first of all, from the intellectual satisfaction of downing their opponents through wit, logic and intimidation, and secondly, from the flushing out of their own misqualified substance that gets clogged in the pores of the feeling body. This flushing-out process takes place with any sudden burst of emotion such as one experiences in anger, in grief or in moments of great happiness.

This enjoying a "good" argument is a substitute for the proper use of the sacred fire in flow. When energy dams up, in the solar plexus or in the lower chakras, because people don't know how to release the sacred fire and raise it, many people will release that dam-up and that flow through sexual intercourse. The real solution, of course, is to raise it and keep the flow going. When you start that flow going, then you have all of this energy in the balance of Alpha and Omega to use for healing.

But mankind, in their state of discord, have no recourse. And when they are not able to release this dammed-up energy in sexual relations, they may release it in fits of anger, in tantrums or in fits of weeping. Many women have monthly fits of weeping, and this weeping has to do with the damming up of energy and lack of control of the emotional body.

Entities take advantage of this damming-up of energy in the lower chakras. They watch forcefields and auras, and they look for people who have the greatest buildup of frustration. Then they start dividing their attention—a phone call, a knock on the door, the baby screaming, the pot overflowing in the kitchen. Pretty soon their attention is going four ways, and then there is an explosion because nobody can keep their attention going in so many directions and keep harmony, unless they are a master. This is especially the case when an individual is dealing with levels of fatigue. So one of the great tactics of the anger entity and all kinds of entities is divide and conquer: divide your attention, divide your four lower bodies so they can't function as one Christ vehicle and then come in and give you a reason to have an explosion.

Enraged individuals, once they have tied into the anger entity, are supercharged with energy—enough to carry their feelings to the ultimate threat, should they feel so inclined. The entity gives its victims strength to do what it wants them to do. This is why you see that people have the strength of ten or twenty men when they are in a great rage of anger: that fit of passion is fed by the entity.

Whereas the individual's energies may have been stalemated before the argument, afterward they are released into the mental and feeling belts of the planet as riptides of anger, which may be the undoing of an unsuspecting lifestream. This, of course, creates a heavy karma for those who chose to unburden themselves in an ill-fated moment of anger.

One thing you must always remember about the anger entity is that if you keep your mouth shut, nothing will happen. When you use the throat chakra, the power of the spoken Word makes etheric, mental and feeling energies physical. And the really heavy karma begins when you've made something physical. As long as you're only thinking about something, you haven't really completed a spiral of energy. You may have the karma of dense thoughts, and these do go out into the world, but until the act becomes physical the return karma doesn't begin.

This is why Jesus said to Judas, "That thou doest, do quickly."[32] Judas could not begin the spiral of the return of his karma for betraying the Christ until he actually betrayed him. He had thought about it, he had plotted it, he made a deal for thirty pieces of silver, but he hadn't done it yet. So Jesus said, "Get this over with, so you can start to learn the lesson of the wrong."

Isn't that a dispassionate teacher? He watches his disciple. He knows he's got a lesson to learn. He will not learn this lesson until he does the act. So until you commit the act, you're not going to have the karma. The mist doesn't become the crystal. The mist is the unformed energy of God. The mist comes down in the hourglass; it gets crystallized when we take that energy in our domain and use it. To crystallize means to put into form. And we do that through the spoken word.

There is always a point of decision in this. There is that little lever in your consciousness that says, "Ok, I'm good and mad, now I'm going to explode." There is a moment where you have the decision to make that you do not have to explode. It's like pulling a ripcord. Once you pull it, the whole thing comes out.

But there is a decision that you make; there is a split second when you can say, "No, I'm going to walk away. I'm going to keep my mouth shut and I'm not going to explode." So there is a will to anger, and that will that is not the will of God aligns with the entities that are just waiting. They are like dogs hanging around with their tongues out. They just can't wait to get that energy. They're just waiting for you to explode. By that vivid image, you'll remember that you're feeding the dogs when you engage in anger. It is definitely a conscious decision when your will is no longer the will of God, but it's the will of the anger entities.

These sudden releases are very costly. We pay too dear a

price to allow ourselves to release energy suddenly in a riptide of anger. Therefore, the Ascended Master Cuzco wrote the "Count-to-Nine Decree" (page 177) so that students might protect themselves against emotional riptides and preserve their God-control at all times.

When you are counting, you are counting around the clock; and when you say a number, you are really saying the number of a Hierarchy. So when you "Count to Nine," it gives you the time to tie into cosmic Hierarchies before an explosion of anger occurs. Counting to nine gives you the power of the three times three.

In the "Count-to-Nine Decree," you visualize a band of white fire, first around the solar plexus. This band of white fire around the solar plexus seals you from the intrusion of Infurio, the anger entity, at the solar plexus, which is where the upset of the emotions occurs. This band of white fire shatters the forcefield of witchcraft practiced against the sons and daughters of God. You visualize yourself standing in this, holding it at the level of your solar plexus, and then you see it glow white-hot like the filament in a light bulb, white, fiery hot. In size, it is almost like an inner tube around your waist, a band of white fire around the solar plexus.

In the next verse, you visualize a band of white fire around the neck and throat center. This band of white fire can be visualized like the brace that people wear after a neck injury— pure white fire around the neck. This band protects your throat chakra from speaking. If you don't open your mouth, you're not going to release the energies of your emotional body —there is a tie between the solar plexus and the throat chakra.

A third white-fire band is then visualized around the head and the pituitary area, around the forehead, like a crown. These three bands around you protect the centers that the entities and demons want to work through, aggravate, irritate in order to get you to explode. Anybody who has ever had a problem with anger or with explosions can overcome immediately with this decree, with this science, with this knowledge— if they will just practice it.

Jazzor (jazz-or, m. and f.): The jazz entity, which combined the rhythm of voodoo rite and the beat of jungle syncopation with a form of musical instrumentation and called it jazz. The entity existed prior to the music, and in his pride, he named it after himself.

Perverting the music of the spheres and distorting the harmony of the soul through an inversion of the sound ray, the black magicians were able to anchor the jazz thoughtform in New Orleans, where focuses of voodoo and witchcraft provided fertile soil for the "birth of the blues" and later, the birth of jazz.

The irregular rhythm and atonal chord patterns used in jazz are designed to do three things:

(1) To bring the pure energies of the youth under the control of entities by focusing their attention upon discord. Jazz, rock music and even some forms of modern so-called classical music are just another disguise for the vampire activities of the entities whose very existence, as we have said, depends upon the energies they can steal from the children of God.

(2) To separate the four lower bodies of those who hear jazz, thereby enabling the black magicians to drive into the soul, through the openings between the bodies, wedges of discord, which the black magicians use at a later time to key in people the negative responses they desire. The rhythm of jazz is designed to disorganize the entire consciousness and being of man. It tears apart the finest fabric of the soul and ruptures the natural protective garment that God himself has established as an electronic tube of naturally pure and powerful energy around the four lower bodies of man.

If you visualize the soul as being a forcefield in the center, and then the four lower bodies as interpenetrating sheaths that go around the soul, there is a rhythm and a beat of jazz that causes the quivering of these bodies, because it's apart from the natural emanations of the soul. The soul is sending out the forcefield of what it truly is, and impinging upon the bodies that are trying to absorb this forcefield is this discord that's coming in from jazz.

This discordant energy starts a quivering, and the four lower bodies start to separate, they start to come apart. This energy wears down the protective forcefield that God has formed as an envelope around the four lower bodies. It breaks it. It shatters it. And through the openings that are created, wedges of darkness come in through the four lower bodies at oblique angles. This is what happens through long-time listening to jazz.

These penetrations look like slits of darkness when you look at the four lower bodies. They are called astral wedges, or psychic wedges. These wedges becomes forcefields of darkness in the four lower bodies.

If you listen to jazz or rock music voluntarily, you move to it, so you reap the karma; and the karma is these wedges. Now you have openings. If the forces of darkness want to manipulate you to make a wrong decision, they have something that they can work through. And it will come through disobedience and rebellion, because rebellion is what jazz is.

There is a beautiful form of the waltz rhythm that goes with the beat of the heart. That beat is the law of your being; it is the natural flow when you are obedient to the natural law and the natural feelings of the soul. When you introduce a jagged beat, you are going against law, against geometry, so it sets up a forcefield of rebellion. Never since the days of Atlantis and its fall has there been such a wave of rebellion on the planet as there is today upon the earth, and it is primarily because of the music.

(3) To cause the energies of the sacred fire, normally focused in the head and heart centers, to descend to the lower end of the spine, where they may be siphoned off by sex entities.

In the modern dance forms where individuals move to the rhythm of the music without physical contact, the unseen partners are astral entities, warlocks and witches. They siphon off the energy of their victims to the electronic beat that is transmitted and controlled through the consciousness of the group. Each step is a key that causes the sacral (sacred) energies of life to be released through the sacrum (the holy bone—the last bone in the spine), the coccygeal center and the genitals. This release, you will note, is not induced through sexual contact, but it is brought about solely through the individual's cooperation with astral rhythms and astral entities.

It is impossible to participate in this without beginning a sex spiral that will have to culminate in some form. It may be released through hatred or some other solar-plexus vibration, but the goal of the music is to get the young people to release their energy as misqualification of the lower chakras.

Some individuals remark that they feel energized merely from listening (consciously or unconsciously) to jazz or rock music. The fact is that they are energized (charged with energy) by the entities associated with the music. This is done in order to keep people dependent upon and tied to entities. Psychic energy is a stimulant; people become habituated to it as they do to coffee, cigarettes or alcohol.

El Morya tells us that when large numbers of people gather for jazz or rock festivals, sexual orgies or a psychedelic "blast,"* there is enough misqualified energy released to bring

---

* The use of light, music and drugs to produce altered states of consciousness and extract the Light of the chakras is seen more recently in the phenomenon of rave.

about cataclysm at some point on the globe—and ultimately, if these manifestations are allowed to continue, they may well invoke the total destruction of civilization.[33]

In contrast to the downward spiraling of man's energies that is induced through jazz, we may observe the upward spiraling and purification of his energies that take place during the playing of Strauss waltzes. The waltz, which was introduced in the courts of Europe by Saint Germain, who inspired the music of Johann Strauss, follows the rhythm of the violet fire. It has a healing, integrating effect on the four lower bodies and the soul. An experiment conducted on a Wisconsin farm showed that cows responded to Strauss waltzes with an increase in milk production, whereas with the playing of jazz, their milk production dropped far below normal.

Classical music that is inspired and drawn from the music of the spheres and the Ascended Masters' keynotes (some of which have been popularized by composers who have tuned into the Masters' vibrations) transmits the healing, resurrecting, revivifying and transmutative powers of the Heavenly Hosts wherever and whenever it is played. These energies are delicately spiritual yet highly powerful; individuals must develop appreciation for them just as they do for classical music.

Jezebella (jez-e-<u>bel</u>-la, f.): The money beast. Greed has been defined as "inordinate or reprehensible acquisitiveness."[34] Greed is the love of money that is the root of all evil.[35] Many people think it is money that is the root of all evil; but it is not. Money is our supply. It is the *love* of money, or the love of the form, that is the problem.

Greed is a mass entity of human creation that enslaves the nations of the world, devouring the Light of men's souls by inducing attachment to material possessions. The "money beast" is an astral form that hangs over Wall Street, manipulating the stock exchange and producing periodic economic crises through black magicians in and out of embodiment. It stretches its tentacles across continents and into the hearts of men. The economic enslavement of the planet is sustained through this form because men willingly feed their precious energies into it in their insatiable desire for wealth, which they think will give them freedom and control over others.

Lesbos (f.) and **Sappho** (m.): Lesbianism entities.

Luciana (lootch-i-<u>ahn</u>-a, f.): The gambling entity, focused over such gambling capitals as Reno, Las Vegas and Monte Carlo, and wherever people engage their energies in gambling and games of chance (including cards). The combination of sex, liquor, tobacco, drug, gambling and jazz entities that pack into casinos is enough to cause men and women to lose their fortunes, their sanity and their souls.

This entity also goes by the name of "Lady Luck." She is the false hierarchy impostor of Fortuna, the Goddess of Supply.

Mania (<u>main</u>-i-a, f.): Mad spirit entity.

Masturba (mas-<u>tur</u>-bah, f.): Masturbation entity.

Melancholia (mel-an-<u>ko</u>-li-a, f.): Melancholy entity. Also associated with depression.

Mischievus (mis-<u>cheev</u>-us): Mischief entity.

Morphus (<u>mor</u>-fuss, m.): The dope entity, which has focuses in all of the major cities of the world. Its campaign is to demoralize, degenerate and debilitate the youth of the world, to destroy their minds, weaken their spiritual faculties and render them nonresistive to the infiltration of society by the tools of the sinister force. Through Morphus, the black magicians project the stupefying ray, which makes people forgetful, stupid or clumsy, and causes them to feel awkward and inadequate. The stupefying ray is used to project accidents and all types of mechanical problems. This ray, together with the energies of the dope entity, should be reversed and exorcised in the manner suggested for the sleep ray and the sleep entity.

Individual drugs have their own entities associated with them. For example, the heroin entity is known as **Heroica.** Other drug entities may be named in prayer using the name of the drug: for example, the **Cocaine Entity** or the **PCP Entity.**

Nicola (ni-<u>ko</u>-la, f.) and **Nicolus** (ni-<u>ko</u>-lus, m.): Nicotine and tobacco entities, which focus through everyone who smokes cigarettes, cigars or pipes. These entities interfere with the individual's sensitivity to Truth, clouding the brain and coating the lungs with a film that prevents the prana in the air from passing into the bloodstream.

This entity resembles manduca sexta, the tobacco worm that is the scourge of tobacco growers' crops. Everyone who is addicted to tobacco and cigarette smoking has this tobacco worm in their aura and moving in their brain, cutting off the Light. The nicotine entity entwines itself around the nicotine addict, like a boa constrictor. The entity has a death grip on the brain and central nervous system. It transmits its desire for nicotine to the victim. It is this desire working through the nicotine residue in the body that binds people to the smoking habit. This is why it is so hard to kick the nicotine habit.

Jophiel tells us that this beast devours not only the body but also the soul. Smoking cuts short the life span and therefore the extended opportunity most souls require to balance their karma and to make their ascension in this life.[36] Jophiel has taught us that our addictions follow us into succeeding lifetimes until we determine to kick the habit.

Phobia (f.): Fear entity.

Roccochó (rock-o-<u>ko</u>): Rock music entity. The 4/4 beat is the natural rhythm of the four-petaled base-of-the-spine chakra. In rock music, the 4/4 beat is syncopated, it is uneven. With the syncopated beat, the energy of the spine does not rise but it falls, and the Life-force in your being then descends.

The fallen ones seek the bliss of reunion of the Light of the Mother with the Light of the Father, but they can't have it without submission to the living Christ. So they invert the beat, and the vibration of the energy descending becomes the synthetic experience, or the inverted experience, of the raising of the Kundalini fire.

The sensation is the movement of energy. The raising of the Light through the chakras results in the wholeness of the Light of Alpha and Omega as the Kundalini ascends. The descent is also a movement, a vibration, a sensation. If one has never tasted the pure nectar of God, how does one know that the synthetic nectar is inferior? Thus the rock beat is for the descent of the Kundalini and has its own perverted bliss, which is the substitute experience for reunion with God.

Unwittingly and ignorantly, then, many people on earth, especially the youth, have come to like this music and have developed a habit of listening to it to the point where it actually has become an addiction. And as their energy is thus directed to the lower chakras, they become more vulnerable to the influence of sex entities.

Satus (<u>say</u>-tus, m.) and **Matus** (<u>may</u>-tus, f.): Entities that induce sadistic (inflicting pain on others) and masochistic (inflicting pain on oneself) tendencies in people. Sadism is the tendency to inflict pain on someone else. Both tendencies have to do with condemnation, the perversion of God-power, where that condemnation becomes physical, inflicting physical pain. These are the entities that cause a perverted use of sex, a complete perversion of life.

Schizo (<u>skitz</u>-oh, m.): Schizophrenia entity.

Scytha (<u>sigh</u>-tha, f.) and **Scythus** (<u>sigh</u>-thus, m.): Death entities that present the image of the Grim Reaper, the old man with a scythe. These entities project into the consciousness of the race the fear of death, the sweetness of death and the inevitability of death. Serapis Bey warns the students about giving in to this entity:

"Mankind's resistance to age is very slight; and once they have accepted old age as inevitable, men are often prone to accept death not as an enemy, but as a friend. I call to mind the words of the Great Ones that clearly state, 'The last enemy that shall be destroyed is death.'[37]

"I think that the scriptures ought not to be wrested to man's destruction; therefore, this enemy, which I choose to define as such, is the enemy that must be fought with every ounce of energy of your being. God is Life, and death is the antithesis of Life. How could it please God for Life, which is himself, to be extinguished in the domain of the individual?"[38]

So we fight death as an enemy: we never give in to death. Now there are what are called death angels. These beings come to individuals who are going to make the transition and they prepare their consciousness, or their soul, their psyche to the gentle impulse that their time on earth is nearing completion. Most people have an intuition within a week or two weeks before they pass on that there is a change that is coming. And often people will let you know, they will talk about it.

This is a very subtle thing. It's not overt, but just a feeling. This is to prevent shock to the soul. When people die suddenly or unexpectedly, as they do in accidents, they are in such a state of shock that they often don't know that they have died.

While driving along the highway, we have noticed discarnates floating by the side of the road. They are over the road right at the scene where a fatal accident has occurred. They don't know they have died. They don't know why they can't get back into their bodies. They don't know where their bodies have gone, because of the shock.

In a natural death, when the time is naturally over and people are going on, the soul is prepared so that she can gently leave the physical form, so that the astral, mental and etheric bodies can separate in a natural spiral. You can see that kind of death when you look at the peace on the face on someone who has just passed on. You see that the transition has been natural.

The death angels are always on the scene, no matter what the cause of death. They come and try to assist the individual in adapting to the next plane and in taking the individual where he should go. They are severely limited, of course, if they do not receive sufficient energy from our octave, from individuals who are praying for those who have died. The saying of prayers for those who pass on gives the Masters the energies that they need to help them. And so it is true of the death angels also.

It is important to distinguish between Archangel Uriel and the death angels who perform a service of ministration, and the death entity that projects death as something that is real and final. It is the concept of death of finality, as the end, that we must fight, as well as physical death. We have a responsibility to perpetuate our lives in our physical forms as long as we are able.

Sensua (sen-shu-a, f.): Sex entity. Seventy-five percent of all sexual involvements occurring on the planet are instigated from the astral plane by discarnate entities, demons and black magicians. Disembodied witches and warlocks invade the bodies of young men and women, amplifying their sexual drives and rationalizing to their consciousness the practice of free love. These evil spirits experience sex vicariously through the indulgences of their counterparts in physical embodiment.

If mankind were left completely alone, without interference from such sinister influences, their sexual patterns would be more natural and more spiritual. Their energies would automatically rise to the heart, head and hand to be used in the service of God and man. The act of procreation would be understood as the sacred union of man and woman who come together before God offering themselves as sponsors of his children waiting at the portals of birth for the opportunity to reembody.

The sex entities work heavily in advertising.

Sentimentia (sen-ti-<u>men</u>-she-a, f.) and **Sensia** (<u>sen</u>-she-a, f.): Sentimental entities playing on people's nostalgia for one another and for the "good old days." They play on people's emotions through popular music, keep them seeing through rose-colored glasses and seriously detract from their ability to make objective and rational decisions.

There are many people who, from the age of forty-five or so on, keep living in the past in this way. They live in the music of their era, they eat the food they used to eat when they were young, they talk about when they first met and what they did when they were young; and their whole lives are nothing but sentimentality. They may be totally involved in the sentimentality of their relationship with their children or their grandchildren, catering to their little human whims and giving each other presents. They cry when they hear the music of the old country. Their whole life is actually involved in sentimentality.

There are many people who function a great deal on the basis of whimsy and sentimentality. Sentimentality becomes one of the forces that seems to drive man to bargain his life away and impoverish his environment. He wants to do a certain thing because it's always been done that way. That old tree has always stood there, and he doesn't want to cut it down because grandmother planted it.

This sentimentality is destructive, in a way. People should

be capable of moving with the flow of the universe, or the divine Tao—the divine endowment. This flow cannot and will not be stopped by any of us. We may stop progress in our own time, if we want to, by insisting upon the sentimentality of whatever we wish to keep or preserve of our human nature. But if we are determined to actually pursue an avant-garde realization of God, we have to be willing to let go and make progress—keep alive, be eternally young because we can accept the fruits of the Spirit of the coming age.

Simpatica (sim-<u>pa</u>-ti-ca, f.): Sympathy entity, which works on the emotional body through human sympathy, personal attachments and relationships not based on the Christ. It causes individuals to exert unwholesome control over one another in the name of family ties.

Sympathy has been defined by the Masters as agreement with human imperfection, whereas compassion is agreement with the Christ. Sympathy allows a person to stay right where he is. It doesn't help him at all. It allows him to lick the wounds of his own pride. Compassion implies that you are going to help a person out of what is wrong and are not going to just reinforce his own negativity, his negative spiral. Compassion is a real emotion, whereas sympathy is an unreal emotion.

If a person's consciousness is so saturated with entities and the way he is speaking and what he is saying and his whole premise in life is identified with entities, there is just so far you can go in lending an ear of understanding. And the greatest act of compassion you can have is often to call a spade a spade, "Look, this is what is acting in your life. It's Darkness, it's not of the Light. If you want to be free from it, I will help you. If you want to keep this state of consciousness and live in it, then I have to remove myself from you. There is nothing I can do for you."

There are too many people who want to come up higher in

the world, there are too many people who you can find that sincerely want to surrender and pursue God. There is no point wasting time with people who feel sorry for themselves and feel sorry for their entities.

There is a word, "simpatico," that means that you have something in sympathy with someone, you are on the same wavelength. You have this little thing going together where you understand each other's human creation, you like the same things and you like to talk about the same things—you have common entities. These kinds of relationships seem good, you pass the time of day, you do things, but what is the net gain? Are you closer to God?

Sodoma (m.) and **Gomorrah** (f.): Homosexuality entities. One action of these entities is to cause a revulsion toward the sacred use of the sacred fire in mankind's consciousness, so that love with the opposite sex becomes repugnant. This takes from people the natural polarity that God has given them and the natural opportunity to focus the energies of Alpha and Omega.

The issue of homosexuality is multifaceted. Homosexuality began on the continent of Lemuria. The desecration of the shrines to the Mother flame came about by priests and priestesses perverting the sacred fire of the Mother. And that perversion is what caused the sinking of Lemuria as well as the destruction of Sodom and Gomorrah. As homosexuality was repeated in Greece, in Rome and in other civilizations down through the centuries, people reincarnated and developed a momentum on these practices.

At conception, there is a charge of energy that determines the sex of an individual in that incarnation. This charge of energy has to do with the base chakra, the Mother chakra, and with the flow of the three energies of the Kundalini—the ida, pingala and sushumna. Men who practice homosexuality are perverting that masculine current and are thus stripped of their masculine power. And this is why it is common to observe that male homosexuals become effeminate—they are losing the masculine energy and throwing their Alpha and Omega energies out of balance. Similarly, women who practice lesbianism are destroying the balance of the feminine current; they are misusing that energy. They lose their intuitive faculties, their feminine faculties, and become more masculine.

In order to make your ascension, you must have the energies of the Kundalini in balance, because the ascension current that we raise actually is the Mother flame. Therefore, you cannot make your ascension in a life where you have abused this energy unless, when you hear about the Truth, you stop and you begin qualifying it correctly.

Spiritus (spi-ri-toos, m.) and **Spirita** (spi-ri-ta, f.): Liquor entities, which create in people a dependence upon spirituous liquors for relaxation, stimulation and euphoria. They destroy incentive and self-respect, and they wreck homes, families and lives. The thousands upon thousands of alcoholics, heavy drinkers and social drinkers throughout the world are puppets on the strings of the liquor entities and their previous victims who have died and are now in the astral plane.

Those who are inebriated either become vicious through Spiritus, the masculine or aggressive form, or they become totally passive through Spirita, the feminine.

Sucrose $C_{12}H_{22}O_{11}$ (f.): Sugar entity. Refined sugar contributes to numerous health problems, including hypoglycemia, obesity, tooth decay, coronary heart disease, diabetes and hyperactivity in children.[39] It drains vital vitamins and minerals from the body. It is debilitating and addictive, weakening the fibers of the spiritual body and the auric envelope.

Suspoócia (sus-poo-see-a, f.) and **Spookia** (spook-ee-a, m.): Suspicion and spook entities.

Handwritten marginalia:

But some men are more feminine even at a child or even born feeling feminine [transgender?— or androgynous— like twin flames who have not been separated of

What about the original androgynous nature of God.

Yet wine is used in Communion

Vanitas (<u>van</u>-i-tas, f.): Vanity entity.

Voluptia (vo-<u>lup</u>-tee-a, m./f.): Lust entity.

Vudu (voo-doo, m. and f.): Voodoo and black magic entity. Voodoo entities keep alive the focuses and the practice of voodoo, the black arts and kahuna-magic in every nation and continent of the world.

[handwritten margin notes: "X", "magic", "not all Kahuna it dark"]

One manifestation of this entity is the practitioners of voodoo in Africa who funnel their energies through focuses in the Caribbean. These in turn pole with their coordinates in the bayou country of Louisiana, in New York, in Chicago and at other key points in North America.

The hatred of the Christ and of the spirit of freedom projected by these black magicians (both in and out of embodiment) is directly responsible for the yearly quota of hurricanes that beat upon the Atlantic coast and the Gulf coast of North America. The black magicians imprison the beings of the elements (earth, air, fire and water) in focuses of furious hatred that are programmed to outpicture as hurricane, flood, fire and tornado. Thus the servants of God and man, the precious elementals, instead of fulfilling their own divine plan as builders of the kingdom of God upon earth, become the innocent tools of the false hierarchy and the instruments of mankind's hatred.

The black magicians in Africa occupy the plus position—the perversion of Father or the perversion of Spirit—and the witches and witch doctors in the Bayou country assume the perversion of Mother, or the minus polarity. Thus, they attract that hatred, and over the arc and flow of that hatred these storms are built by the elementals who become caught in these vortices of misused energy.

This is one reason why it is very dangerous to be involved in what may seem to be innocent forms of entertainment like Ouija board, palm reading, gambling and other activities that the Masters warn against. The outer activity may seem harmless, but it gives us an opening to these practitioners of darkness. We then become their electrodes by the fact we have lowered our consciousness into an astral level.

The decree to seal the elementals in an ovoid of violet fire (see "Set the Elementals Free," page 413) will magnetize the power of God to insulate them from the malpractice of the ungodly and from the vibrations of men's violent fears that the elementals mimic in nature. The "Reverse the Tide" decree (page 411) may be given with an appropriate insert to reverse the projections of those who practice the black arts against individuals and nations.

Weepa (<u>wee</u>-pa, f.): The weeping entity. Whenever people cry in self-pity or in sympathy with others, whenever they become hysterical or violently angry and then dissolve in tears, you can be certain they are being worked on by Weepa, who siphons their energies into a "pool of tears."

Some adults tend to indulge in what they call "a good cry." However, there is nothing good about feeding astral entities, and the flushing-out process can be accomplished much more effectively with the violet flame. So the next time you feel a "good cry" coming on, call in the name of God and in the name of Jesus the Christ to the Elohim Astrea to encircle the weeping entity, and then invoke the violet flame throughout your four lower bodies.

Weeping entities cause you to weep over nonsense, and they engage you in that weeping that comes over a large mass of people over death or some kind of violence or catastrophe. It is one thing to cry and to express one's emotions, which is natural; it is another thing to become hysterical with weeping where you can see that there is an uncontrolled force that is part of the picture.

Protection from Entities

Let us here and now, once and for all, expose the lie of harmlessness that the astral hordes have spread concerning their evil deeds.

First of all, let us remember that the individual is always responsible for the use he makes of God's energy. As this energy flows through his consciousness, it is stamped with the seal of his identity. This seal is the signature (the insignia) of his soul, a perfect design that is uniquely his own. It might be a star, a crown, a leaf or a flower. One cannot deny his seal any more than he can deny his thumbprint.

God's energy becomes personalized in man as it passes through the nexus of man's consciousness and receives not only the stamp of his thoughts and feelings but also that of his personal seal. Wherever man's attention is fixed, there goes his energy, and wherever his energy goes, there will his consciousness be drawn, sooner or later. For the Law requires that each man redeem the energy he has misqualified. Stamped with the personal seal of the one who sent it forth, that energy, misqualified and imprisoned in a negative form, returns to him with the impact of the initial force with which it was charged, combined with the momentum it magnetized in gathering more of its kind.

Therefore, in connection with this study of entities, it is important that the student understand that he himself may be keeping alive the very forces he would condemn. This he does by allowing his energies to flow in alternating currents of repulsion and attraction into images of horror, patterns of death, and every type of distortion of Reality that can be conceived in the minds of the black magicians.

Actually, through his attention, he is placing the seal of his approval upon the object of his attention. This energy, as a part of himself, lives in and sustains the life of the evil forces. Furthermore, the record of horror (or whatever type of astral nightmare into which the individual has fed his energies) is stamped upon his etheric body, superimposed upon the blueprint of his own divine plan. Until he erases the imperfect pattern, it will interfere with his outpicturing of the plan and the Image Most Holy.

The entities described here and many more mass entities could be dissolved within twenty-four hours if mankind as a whole, conscious of themselves as the Body of God on earth, would make a concerted effort to withdraw their attention and their energies from these forcefields of misqualified energy. Students of the Light can accomplish a great deal by making invocations to God to send his legions of Light to cut free all who are in bondage to discarnate and mass entities.

It must always be remembered that these forces that appear to be so deadly are nothing before the Light of the Christ. They have no Reality because, by their evil deeds, they have placed themselves outside of the Presence of God.

If the individual will take his stand for the Light and give persistent calls for his freedom and for the freedom of all mankind, and if he will accept this freedom and his God-dominion over all evil conditions as a present fact of his existence, he will live to see the transmutation of every lie and its manifestation. And he will live to see the victory of the Christ over the consciousness of the betrayers in whom the lie was spawned.

The only power that can act is the Law of God through the Mind of Christ. If we live in the Truth of this statement, we will be found to be overcomers, worthy of our calling.

Guarding the Solar Plexus

It is most often through the door of the solar plexus, the seat of the emotions, that the harmful vibrations of discarnate and mass entities enter the world of the individual. Therefore the solar plexus, as the sun of man's being, must be guarded lest his energy levels descend with the sudden inrush of psychic forces that would intrude upon the harmony of his world.

The student should make daily invocation to the God Presence, to Jesus the Christ and to the Elohim of Peace for the Great Sun Disc to be placed over his solar plexus. This disc is visualized as a shield of armor charged with the dazzling white Light of the Christ and possessing his power to "instantaneously deflect all discord whatsoever that may ever be directed against me or the Light for which I stand."

⟩ GREAT SUN DISC

Beloved mighty I AM Presence, beloved Holy Christ Self and beloved Jesus the Christ: Blaze your dazzling Light of a thousand suns in, through and around my four lower bodies as a mighty guardian action of the Light of God that never fails to protect the peaceful outpicturing of God's plan through my every thought, word and deed.

Place your Great Sun Disc over my solar plexus as a mighty shield of armour that shall instantaneously deflect all discord whatsoever that may ever be directed against me or the Light for which I stand.

I call now in the name of my mighty I AM Presence to the Elohim of Peace to release throughout my entire being and world the necessary action of the mighty flame of Cosmic Christ–peace that shall sustain in me the Christ consciousness at all times, so that I may never be found engaged in a release of misqualified energy to any part of life, whether it be fear, malice, mild dislike, mistrust, censure or disdain.

I call to beloved Saint Germain to seize all energy that I have ever released against my brethren and that has caused them any form of discomfort whatsoever. And in the name of my mighty I AM Presence I command that that energy be removed from their worlds— cause, effect, record and memory—and transmuted by the violet flame into the purity and perfection that is the sacred-fire essence of God, that the earth and all elemental life might be cut free forever from human creation and given their eternal victory in the Light!

I accept this done right now with full power! I AM this done right now with full power! I AM, I AM, I AM God-Life expressing perfection all ways at all times. This which I call forth for myself I call forth for every man, woman and child on this planet!

Beloved I AM! Beloved I AM! Beloved I AM!

The short mantra "O Disc of Light" may also be used for the sealing and protection of the solar-plexus chakra.

O DISC OF LIGHT
O disc of Light from heaven's height,
Descend with all your perfection!
Make my aura bright with freedom's Light
And the Masters' love and protection!
(recite nine times)

Practical Steps

There are also very practical steps that the student can take to protect his forcefield and keep his consciousness and environment free from entities. The fragrance of pine, which carries the spiritual essence released through pine trees, repels entities. The pine devas who minister to the pine forests afford great spiritual protection to entire nations, standing as a buffer between mankind and their own psychic effluvia. City dwellers vacationing in national parks and forests absorb the balancing, restoring and healing power that is transmitted by the Holy Spirit through nature—especially through all types of pine. Intimate communion with nature is absolutely necessary to the health, harmony and sanity of the soul. *(including vegetarian or vegan eating)*

The fragrances of pine, frankincense, fresh mint, deodar and of flowers (especially roses) are also entity repellents. These may be used on the body, in the home and around children. Some yogis place a drop of oil of deodar over the third eye before going into samadhi.

Those who desire to keep their homes free of entities will take steps to see that food and wastes are never left uncovered, that dirty dishes are not left overnight and that the garbage is put out in sealed containers before retiring. For wherever substance is in a state of decay, there entities gather to absorb the energies released through oxidation. Such things as wilted flowers, body odors, soiled clothing, dirty rags, old newspapers, stagnant water and fine dust (on furniture and in cars) attract entities. Entities also work through and draw upon the energies of animals. They feed at dumps, junkyards and car graveyards, and often they are attached to antiques and used furniture.

Because they are not seen but only felt, entities can and often do make individuals uncomfortable without their realizing the source of their distress. Upon entering a house or a public building and finding there infestations of entities or persons possessed by them, you may become uneasy or painfully aware of a vibration that is foreign to the Christ within.

You may even sense the record of unpleasant events that have taken place there, and you may feel the desire to leave as soon as possible.

Entities can lower one's vitality, and they make a point of interfering with one's projects. They can bring on nervous tension and nervous breakdowns. They may make one irritable or tardy. And they attempt to disorganize one's entire life by working through employers, employees, family, friends or strangers—it doesn't matter.

The tenacity of the grip of sex, drug, gambling, liquor and nicotine entities cannot be imagined by those who have never been hooked by the claws of these astral beasts of prey. If the poor souls who have been caught off guard by one or more of these mass entities only knew that the cravings and the desires they attribute to themselves are, in reality, not their own but merely the projections of astral entities, they would rise up in righteous indignation to cast out, in the name of Jesus the Christ, the enemy they have unwittingly comforted and aided. Turning to God with utter faith in his love and in his willingness to free them from the bondage of the accusers of the brethren, they would overturn the tables of the moneychangers who have made their houses dens of thieves.[40] They would shatter the clay vessels that have harbored the entities, and they would throw open the windows of their consciousness to welcome the fresh winds of the Holy Spirit.

The Use of Color

The science of color can be used to raise the vibration of an environment, anchor greater Light and give protection against negative influences. Vesta explains: "Light is a great key, beloved ones; and men and women should understand that the garish colors of the world with their deep-dyed densities only stir the passions and destroy hope while the pastel shades reactivate communion with higher spheres. By the correct use of color and the use of the correct colors, men can find in the limitless expansion of Light's rainbow hues a renewal of their consciousness and the purification that must occur daily if they would progress along the path of stewardship."[41]

One means by which the astral vibration of entities can penetrate the physical plane is through colors that vibrate at their level—namely, red, red-orange, orange, black, brown, gray, olive and chartreuse. These colors, together with their metallic correspondents silver and copper, vibrate at the level of astral creations and discordant qualifications such as anger, fear, doubt, resentment, pride, rebellion, greed, death, uncontrolled passion, and so on. They can be seen in the auras of spiritually undeveloped people.

Disciples of the Brotherhood should avoid the use of these colors in clothing and in home decorating, for they focalize discord and disorder of the most degrading kind, else through proximity and the flow of his attention, the disciple may become the victim of vicious forces that can only gain entrance into his world through the penetration of inharmony and/or the above-mentioned colors. Sometimes all it takes is a fresh coat of paint and a change to Ascended Master colors, the colors of the pure rays of God, in home decorating and in clothes to discourage these intruders.*

Just as the Masters draw and maintain focuses of Light wherever individuals express harmony and enhance it with the proper colors and music, spiritual matrices and individual consecration, so do the brothers of the shadow sustain their

---

* When combined with the white, the colors of the seven rays form pastel colors that may be used as a most effective means of drawing the spiritual radiation and blessings of the angelic hosts to manifest as an actual focus of the higher realms in one's immediate environment. A fresh coat of paint also helps to clear a forcefield because the odors and chemicals in paint tend to repel entities.

nefarious schemes through discordant focuses amplified by chaotic colors, thoughtforms and music.

The use of strobe lights, of psychedelic art forms, distorted images, and wild prints in fabrics and in wall coverings opens the door to the astral plane and facilitates the entrée of entities into the consciousness of those who are not careful about eliminating from their persons and from their homes these seemingly harmless distortions of the divine art. The removal of such focuses will pave the way for a harmony and a peace that some will find difficult to believe is possible, so accustomed have they become to the modern jangle of discord and disorganization in their lives.

The combining of Ascended Master colors with astral colors in modern art, fashion design and interior decorating was planned by the false hierarchy. By placing colors that vibrate at the lowest level of the astral plane next to those that carry the pure vibrations from the Ascended Master octaves, the enemies of righteousness are able to accomplish a threefold purpose: (1) through proximity, having their focus next to an Ascended Master focus, they are able to siphon off the pure energies they need to perpetuate their existence; (2) they create an open door through which they may funnel astral energies; and (3) they create in the subconscious minds of the youth the patterns of these combinations, through which they may introduce subtle distortions of Truth and an inversion of Ascended Master Law.

Orange with pink, with yellow, with blue, with white, with purple, with green or with violet is used to funnel Luciferian rebellion and pride into the consciousness of the children of God. Chartreuse has a bilious vibration, and when it is used in combination with these Ascended Master colors, it ties those who look upon it directly into the most vile and violent astral creations. Reds and oranges stir the emotions, and in combi-

(But there are all colors in a rainbow)

nation with black, these colors are a funnel for the vibrations of black magic and witchcraft.

When white, the most concentrated focus of the sacred fire, is used with astral colors, it tends to subdue them and to make them more acceptable; nevertheless, the principle is the same. Similarly, silver and copper, which tend to conduct astral vibrations, are sometimes used to set precious jewels that carry a focus of the God flame and neutralize some of the negative effects of these metals. The substance of gold, on the other hand, actually focalizes the energy of the sun. It focalizes a very high vibration and a very high energy that is something that all of the people may benefit by. When people wear gold and own gold, it is something that is a magnet for their own supply and abundance and something that they benefit from a great deal spiritually. It may be worn on the body at all times for its balancing and healing properties.

Astrologically speaking, gold belongs to the sun, silver to the moon. The moon was created by God to be the reflector of God's feeling body, or the desire body. It is a giant mirror. If mankind's feeling bodies were filled with the feelings of God, the desires of God—purity, love, wholeness, compassion, tenderness, faith, reverence, constancy, all of these qualities that the angelic hosts ensoul—then the moon would be an asset, reflecting and amplifying those feelings. However, because mankind have polluted those energies, especially at the astral or water level where the moon manifests, there is an impure substance that is reflected by the moon and by the substance of silver. ⟨but not always!⟩

Copper is associated with the planet Mars, and it has an even lower vibration than silver.

Some may wonder why astral colors are prevalent in nature. We must remember that the earth in her pristine state was transparent, the sands and the rocks of pastel hue. Even the blood, which carries the energy of God through the body temple, was a golden pink glow-ray that gave a warm, delicate tone to the skin and a luster to the entire form.

With the advent of discord, the elementals began to out-picture in nature their fears and frustrations that flowed from the impure stream of mankind's consciousness. Thorns and thistles bore witness to man's betrayal of the image of the Christ, and the fruits of the earth were marked with man's own imperfect sowings. And so they are today.

When mankind return in consciousness to the Golden Age standard they have lost, the elementals will return in nature to precipitating the patterns for the coming Golden Age.

Maintaining a Forcefield of Light

The Goddess of Purity speaks of the importance of maintaining a forcefield of purity in the home: "Do you suppose that the Light of the Christ can descend through a forcefield charged with the records of human creation for generations?

"People who collect antiques that have been held by mankind for hundreds of years and know not the use of the violet flame whereby they may purify that substance before bringing it into their homes unwittingly preserve the impurities of history. And of what does it avail them, then, to have these objects of art if they carry with them a talismanic action of times and places that did not bear testimony to the Light, having dense conditions in that forcefield?

"Take care, then, as to that which you keep in a physical sense in your household and the clothes you put upon your temple of Light. For when you reach the portals of the Temple of the Ascension, the flame of purity penetrates all. Nothing can be hid from before the Lords of Karma. For that mighty Light ray makes your entire soul transparent, and it deals with detail, precious ones, with the minutiae of everyday living.

"You think that things are unimportant, that it is superstitious to be concerned with color or fragrance or your surroundings. I tell you, the very perfumes that people place upon their forms draw to them impurities and discarnate entities. It is most essential, then, that you maintain a consciousness of purity, sensitive enough that you can tell at the touch of a hand whether or not an object needs cleaning, needs washing.

"The use of the water element, the power of Neptune and Luara is very essential. And the use of the water element benefits not only the physical form but also the emotional body and the mental world.

"I caution you to also not to neglect the purple fire, the violet flame and the flame of cosmic purity, for these are potent forces to keep you free. Once freed, remember, precious ones, that you do go forth again into the outer world and you must realize that you may take on the conditions of the outer world once again and these must be purified."[42]

It is therefore recommended that the students examine the objects of art and other furnishings in their homes, removing those that do not contribute to the spirituality of the household and its members. In the case of expensive and necessary items, a long-range plan is suggested for the gradual replacement of unsuitable items. Balance is the byword in all such transitions from the material to the spiritual: perfection the goal in an imperfect world.

Floating Grids and Forcefields

The Great Divine Director, speaking on the subject of the floating grids and forcefields of humanly misqualified thought and feeling that we have discussed in this chapter (mass entities), gives some invaluable advice to the students on how to counteract these conditions and still maintain God-control:

"The power of prayer and spiritual attunement, of living close to the Divine Presence of God, the maintaining of attitudes of happiness and an awareness of life's purposes, the sustainment of service and goodwill for others, and the amplification of every divine beatitude is, of course, one's own best protection against the intake of these forces.

"I cannot deny that some of them, by reason of size and density patterns, are particularly lethal, hence dangerous to those who are unsuspecting and therefore unprotected against them. Just as a cloud will cover the face of the sun preceding a storm, so in many cases a sudden feeling of depression, a drop in the normal level of happiness or well-being will indicate the presence of such an invisible forcefield.

"There are two simple defenses available to mankind against these unseen pitfalls. One is to recognize that mobility can soon bring an individual into an area out of the center of the thrust; hence, many times a distance of one or two miles will give absolute safety. At other times, for various reasons when individuals cannot conveniently flee the invaded area, they can make mighty application to the Godhead, to the Cosmic Beings and to the Ascended Masters, including beloved Jesus and Archangel Michael, for spiritual assistance in moving these forcefields away or transmuting them into Light.

"Now I do not for one moment wish anyone to accept the idea, no matter how deadly these forcefields may appear to be, that they cannot be made to yield to the invincible power of God. Yet, just as Don Quixote was unable to defeat the windmills with the point of his lance, so it is senseless, in the words of Saint Paul, to 'fight as one who beateth the air.'[43]

"You see, there are few in physical embodiment today who are able on the instant to cope with the more malevolent of these conditions from the level of mankind's externalized personal grace. But I am certain that no call goes unheeded by heaven; therefore, mighty inroads can be made into these forcefields. Sometimes they can be reduced or cut in half by a thrust of the sword of blue flame invoked by a chela.

"It is not my wish that the student body become overly conscious of these forces. Yet, precious ones, it is not wise to ignore evil or to allow oneself to be unconsciously subject to its temporal manifestation in the world of form.

"Therefore, in a state of perfect mental and spiritual balance, mankind ought to understand that these mass entities do exist and that they function almost mechanically—not necessarily as fixed monsters, but frequently as predatory roaming beasts of the air, subject to unconscious driftings and magnetization by minutely affinitized centers in individuals or in groups."[44]

The Creation of Riptides

Mighty Cuzco explains how to find freedom from the riptides of energy that are released by mass entities: "There are many different types of riptides—some are creations of anger, fear, violence, hopelessness, desire for palliative and temporary pleasure; frustrations, self-aggrandizement; insanity, confusion, irreverence, hatred, derision, gossip; love of money and power, and many other destructive momentums whose end is never practical or perfect.

"The force employed in sustaining these conditions is never divine love. Divine love naturally withdraws the energy by the inner action of the Law from every malevolent center. As this process occurs, the energy quotient of the vortex is depleted, and these whirling riptides, which depended for sustenance on the constant feeding of their foci by a multitude of people the world around, are dissipated. The blessed people of earth have continued to hide the Light of God within them under the negative 'bushel' of outer personality misqualified with a mask of negative riptides falsely claiming to be their own thoughts and feelings.

"I am interested that the students understand that the centripetal (counterclockwise) action is that which dissolves substance or returns life to the Universal. This centripetal action has been wrongly used by psychic forces to strip the seekers of their own God-given spiritual blessings, and thus students are deprived of the fullness of the blessings the Ascended Masters intend them to have. The centrifugal (clockwise) action creates and sustains substance and vibration, but it has also been wrongly used to build momentums of thought, feeling and habit that pull mankind down.

"The sacred fire when concentrated as a dual focus of Ascended Master Light does swing both ways to transmute the centripetal and centrifugal action of all human riptides and discordant energy, thus setting mankind free to manifest God! The sword of blue flame is typified in the generic allegory of the two-edged sword at the gate of Paradise recorded in the Pentateuch."[45]

The Circle and Sword of Blue Flame

The circle and sword of blue flame are the special implements of the legions of purity and blue lightning (Elohim Purity and Astrea, Elohim Hercules and Amazonia, Archangel Michael and Faith, beloved Surya and Cuzco, the Ascended Master El Morya and others).

The circle of blue flame is a ring of spiritual fire that may be invoked around any person, place, condition or thing requiring a concentrated action of the will of God, of his protection or of his purifying power. The circle is used to contain and to immobilize forces of evil. It will absorb the impurities of the soul and the psychic effluvia residual in the four lower bodies of man, which effluvia is often the cause of disease, accident, old age and death. By intensifying the activity of the will of God, it will restore to the consciousness and being of man the original pattern of his perfection and of his divine plan.

The sword of blue flame is a ray of Light, a rod of divine power, a scepter of authority, drawn by the hosts of Light from their individual God flame. They wield it to cut mankind free from all that would hinder them on the road of attainment. In imitation of the Christ-power that is focused in the sword of blue flame, the students may visualize a flaming sword in their right hand, and they may wield it as the angels do.

The Elohim Astrea warns that invisible forces cause more problems than most of us realize. She says, "Have you noticed how dogs seem to bark into the air in this direction and that and there is nothing there? They see the astral plane! They see the astral entities! They warn you! They are your protectors. They many times have blue-lightning angels overshadowing them, and they sense their mission in defense of your life.

"Or perhaps you have noticed how you will have a sudden mood change. You may become angry. You may become sad. You may become depressed. Yes, it may be the product of medication or wrong diet; but more than this, the forces of Darkness produce these conditions. All is at peace and suddenly there is an explosion of argument and anger in confrontation within the family or between two individuals who love one another deeply.

"All of these things must be seen by you objectively. You must come to the realization, beloved, that you are dealing with 'principalities and powers and spiritual wickedness in high places."[46] This verse refers to hierarchies of fallen angels with whom you deal daily. They move against your most cherished hopes and dreams and dash the cup of Light before you can drink the elixir handed to you by a Seraphim of God."[47]

Archangel Michael says we should be ashamed to allow demons and discarnates of any kind to trick us when we are off guard. He says, "In that moment when those little demons come and jump on your shoulders and cry out for recognition, you must in that very moment thrust forth your sword. If the truth were known, these demons actually fear the flame in your heart. They know their only hope is to trick you into feeling that you are somehow separated from God. They know they have to catch you off guard. They already know they are no match for the Christ or the God flame within you. They already know that you have all power from God if you will claim it. They have to trick you into failing to claim that power, if but for an instant, in the moment when they come."[48]

Lanello says, "Don't be ... fair game for any little half-pint demon that desires to unhorse you and does."[49]

Invoking the Legions of Astrea

The Elohim Astrea speaks of the necessity of clearing the earth of discarnate entities: "Beloved ones, we are here to cleanse the soul chakra of a nation and the nations. We have come for the binding of demons and discarnates who work ill against the entire population and the environment. We have come to rescue souls who ought not to be caught on the astral plane, who ought to be in the retreats of Light. We have come to unburden this city....

"The weight that many of you feel here is a weight of an accumulation of discarnates. They weigh upon you personally.

It is as though the entire city were packed—as packed as cans of sardines, as you would say—with discarnate entities, who have no reason to be here except for the fact that the Keepers of the Flame have not mustered in a concerted effort the whirlwind action of the circle and sword of blue flame to whisk them away!

"Keepers of the Flame on planet Earth, I address you: These are the last times. Souls who cannot navigate out of the lower planes simply accumulate in that bewildered state or else they are caught in the grips of a deathly stranglehold by forces of Darkness. This planet could fare much better if you would take seriously just how important it is for you to come together in your groups wherever you can locate yourselves across this city and give those calls to me....

"So you can see that a few hours of work can deliver you from burdens upon your bodies that cause ill health, that cause a loss of supply and the ability to deal with your lawful debts. These conditions moving against you come in the form of these entities, who siphon from you your Light....

"It is well, beloved, to give your investment of spiritual energy at that Friday night Ascension Service.[50] This is the hour when the portals of the octaves of Light open and our angels may escort many to those cubicles and schoolrooms where they will make much greater soul progress. Therefore, these having left the city, you will find that the winds of the Holy Spirit may bring to you good tidings of the Central Sun and angels and higher vibrations, and once again you will know the peace that you have known here before.

"Beloved ones, we ask little and offer so much. If you would only give your call to me, to Astrea—that number 10.14 in your decree book, beloved—and give it daily with full fervor, you would see just what ten thousand-times-ten thousand legions of Astrea might do for you personally and for this city....

"My love comes as the blue lightning. It comes as the ruby ray mingling with it and the white fire. Thus you see, our colors appear as patriotic colors. We are patriots of a cosmos! We are patriots who come forth from the Central Sun. We are lovers of freedom and we espouse that freedom on behalf of all souls.

"Therefore, long ago I fashioned my circle and sword of blue flame, for no soul is free so long as unseen forces may attach themselves as barnacles to the aura, to the consciousness, to the organs of the body, draining Light. This is no freedom, beloved! And because they are all invisible, you imagine that the pains and the conditions and the adversities that you deal with are some product of the malfunctioning of your bodies. Well, the malfunctioning of your bodies is due to unseen energies and forces and vibrations. That is where you must begin....

"Beloved ones, do you have a loved one who is burdened by any form of addiction to drugs or alcohol or nicotine or even sugar itself? If you do, beloved, and this person is not on the Path and would not understand how to make the call, I say to you, find the sharpest and most recent photograph of that one, even taking that one's picture, or better yet have a photograph taken of yourself standing with that loved one.

"Then place that photograph, eight by ten, large enough, on your altar and ... call for that one to be delivered of every single demon or discarnate that is siphoning that one's Light, that is taking Light while enjoying the addiction through that one's body....

"These drug entities that hang on to discarnate entities who themselves were addicts before they passed from the screen of life and entered the astral plane (and this applies to alcoholics and alcohol entities as well) do tie into the lifestream and lock into the spinal cord at the back of the neck of the addict in physical embodiment. There could be as many as one hundred ? discarnate entities latching on to a single individual!

"If you could see this, beloved, your compassion would burn within your heart, and you would understand why that loved one has not the ability or the strength to move away from that addiction; for each time that one will try to be free, along come the entities projecting into his emotional body, into his physical body and brain the desire and the need to partake of that substance again.

"I tell you, the purveying of drugs throughout this nation is surely a conspiracy of fallen angels of other planetary systems to destroy the opportunity of the Lightbearers to merge their minds with Christ. Understand such a warfare of Light and Darkness. It is Armageddon in full swing as the youth of the world are crucified in the streets of the world.

"I need your help! I enlist your help! I say, try me. See what will take place when you use the circle and sword of blue flame! See how a hundred entities can be bound by our legions in answer to your call, as you give that decree to Astrea. I am the Starry Mother. You will see how that loved one can be cut free and kept free and how that one will return to the dignity of a child of Light and find his mission before it is too late.

"How I have stood by mothers and fathers who have wept because of drug-related deaths or suicides! Would to God they would have known this teaching! Would to God that the ministers in the churches would have accepted it!...

"Thus, my beloved, if you would keep the vigil for a loved one or a number of loved ones, know that the power of the circle and sword of blue flame will work as you pray for them each day and for every other child of God on this planet who is similarly enslaved!

"I, Astrea, make you this offer: Pray for your loved ones,

put as many photographs as you like upon your altar. And when you pray for them, pray also for all others upon this planet who can be delivered by Astrea. I will place my Electronic Presence over all of them, a billion times over if needed and more. This is the capacity of a Cosmic Being who is one with God, hence fully God in manifestation. I need only the call of single hearts on earth.

"Mothers and fathers and teachers and citizens of planet Earth, I appeal to you! God has endowed me with the power to deliver the pure in heart and all upon this planet! May your voice utter the spoken Word that is needed.

"Do you understand the principle, beloved, that we must have those in physical embodiment to speak the decree in the power of the spoken Word? If they do not do it, if you do not do it, we are not authorized to enter this octave. This is your octave, this physical octave, and what happens in it is up to you and the call you will make. God has given you two things—free will and planet Earth. He will not take back that free will by entering in to do for you those things that you are ordained of Him to do.

"Your call to us compels the answer from our realm of Light. We come instantaneously. We await it! We nudge you! We give you the thoughtform to take out your decree books. The single prayer, beloved, will authorize us to help a million souls. If you cannot give the decree to Astrea (page 407) thirty-six times, give it three times, but give it rather than not give it at all."[51]

Exorcism

There are several methods of mastering discarnate and mass entities, of taking dominion over the demons and of exorcising the evil spirits that work with them. Jesus demonstrated his mastery over the inhabitants of the astral realm, and before his ascension he promised that all who believed in the Christ would be able to cast out devils in his name.[52]

While Jesus walked the earth, the entire body of entities on the planet knew and feared him. Through their psychic whisperings, they conveyed from one end of the earth to the other the knowledge of his whereabouts, of his every move. This fact can be noted in the record found in the fourth chapter of Luke.

It is written that when he entered the synagogue at Capernaum, "there was a man, which had a spirit of an unclean devil, and cried out with a loud voice, saying, Let us alone; what have we to do with thee, thou Jesus of Nazareth? art thou come to destroy us? I know thee who thou art; the Holy One of God.

"And Jesus rebuked him, saying, Hold thy peace, and come out of him. And when the devil had thrown him in the midst, he came out of him, and hurt him not. And they were all amazed, and spake among themselves, saying, What a word is this! for with authority and power he commandeth the unclean spirits, and they come out....

"And devils also came out of many, crying out, and saying, Thou art Christ the Son of God. And he rebuking them suffered them not to speak: for they knew that he was Christ."[53]

Much in the same manner we find the mouthings of evil spirits coming through individuals who are possessed. In some churches, where they fear that they might be exorcised, the entities shout through members of the congregation the name of the Lord and "Amen," often interrupting the service to be heard, feigning reverence to retain their immunity. Outside of the churches, these same spirits boldly take the name of the Lord in vain through those upon whom they can depend not to exorcise them. Today, as of old, the unclean spirits fear the absolute power of the living Christ to cast them out, and they are well acquainted with all on the planet who have demonstrated the power to do so.

Jesus often asked the entities their names, for he knew that the name was the key to the vibratory pattern of the entity's forcefield. Having this key, he could effectively command their energies to be taken from the consciousness of the tormented ones into the flaming Presence of the Holy Spirit, where they would be rendered impotent and then transmuted.

Jesus applied this same principle when raising the dead. It is recorded that "he cried with a loud voice, Lazarus, come forth. And he that was dead came forth."[54] Speaking the name of Lazarus, Jesus commanded his energies to return to the body and to coalesce around the image of perfection that he invoked by the power of the resurrection flame.

When the modern disciple has the power of the Christ sufficiently developed within himself and the necessary faith that Jesus said was prerequisite to casting out demons and to healing,[55] he will be able to perform the works that Jesus did, and "greater works than these shall he do; because I go unto my Father."[56]

From his Ascended state Jesus lends his momentum of victory to every son of God who would overcome the world. And this momentum, added to the power of the individualized God Presence of the unascended lifestream, is able to work even greater works than those that were accomplished by Jesus prior to his ascension.

It is the desire of every Master to see his disciples exceed his own achievements. This is not blasphemy; it is a fact of the universal Law of Eternal Progression, which is a consequence of God's own transcendental nature. We see it illustrated in the life of Jesus himself, whose guru in his embodiment as Elisha was Elijah. Elijah, reembodied as John the Baptist, likened himself to the friend of the bridegroom who "rejoiceth greatly because of the bridegroom's voice: this my joy therefore is fulfilled."[57] Having already attained his victory as the prophet Elijah, John the Baptist's joy was to see the fulfillment of Elisha's mission outpictured in the life of Jesus. Thus John said, "He must increase, but I must decrease."[58]

Having been given in this chapter the names of some of the mass entities that prey upon mankind, the students may call to God in the name of Jesus the Christ, that these entities be exorcised from their worlds, from their homes, from their communities and from their planet. After invoking the protection of the Holy Spirit through application to the violet fire, the tube of light and the decrees to Archangel Michael, an appropriate call such as the following may be given:

> In the name of the mighty I AM Presence and in the name of Jesus the Christ, I command that these spirits
>
> _____[give the names of the entities if they are known]_____
>
> be exorcised from my consciousness, being and world! [or name the person or location from which you desire the spirits expelled] And in the name of Jesus the Christ and our Lord the Maha Chohan, I accept this done this hour in full power!

Where two or more are gathered for the purposes of exorcism, they may add:

> And we agree together on earth in Jesus' name that this shall be done and that it is done![59]

The giving of the Entity Decree included at the end of this chapter is most effective when "their name is legion"—when there are great numbers of entities infesting an area.*

---

* Sanat Kumara gives extensive teaching on the spiritual science of exorcism in *The Opening of the Seventh Seal*, pp. 192–230.

You have to realize that the Christ within you is the authority to challenge anywhere, anytime, any of the lies of the Liar, as long as you do it in the name of the Christ and add to your fiat, "and according to God's holy will," so that you aren't responsible for practicing black magic by invoking something that isn't correct.

If your decrees always involve the affirmation of Good, the casting out of Evil and are never against persons, and you always finish your call by saying, "In the name of Almighty God, let this call be adjusted according to the will of God," then your Holy Christ Self will carefully adjust the call.

Then, every Archangel, every Angel, every Elohim, the entire company of saints, all the hosts of heaven are locked into your call. And when you don't know who to call to, call to the entire Spirit of the Great White Brotherhood.

Assistance from the Realms of Heaven

If you are ever going to work on a condition where there are entrenched forcefields of entities—in an individual, in a house or in a city—preparation is required. It is necessary to do decrees to Archangel Michael, to Hercules and to Mighty Astrea for a great forcefield of blue Light to be established around that consciousness, and then the decree to the All-Seeing Eye of God for the exposure of these forces. This can all be given in advance of the "Entity Decree." Especially when you are calling entities by name, they seem to come out en masse to counteract what you are doing.

Archangel Michael and his legions put on their helmets and their armour and take up their swords when they go into the astral realm to cut people free. If beings that have been in the realm of perfection for thousands and tens of thousands of years feel the necessity to put on armour in order to contact our octave, where we live every day, we must consider that if we are not perfect and therefore we are susceptible to the influence of forces, then it is certainly rushing in where angels fear to tread to not put on our armour. You should never underestimate the force of an enraged demon or an enraged entity that realizes that the Light of God is standing ready to take him.

We must realize that Light is not in a battle—Light dissipates Darkness, it doesn't fight it. But the *identities* of God, both Ascended and unascended, must go forth and do battle against forces of Darkness. This is taking place, and this is what the battle of Armageddon is all about. And when we start directing a frontal attack on entities, we are enlisting in the legions of Archangel Michael, and we must observe the same precautions.

The Elohim Astrea serves in the power of the Christ with Archangel Michael and the legions of blue lightning from Sirius to exorcise the evil spirits of this planet. The work of these magnificent Cosmic Beings is to cut mankind free from all astral influences, whatever their classification. When confronted with entities and in any moment of difficulty, the wise devotee will first invoke the aid of these servants of God who, by divine decree, are compelled to answer the prayers of unascended mankind (as long as these prayers are in keeping with the will of God) whenever they are called upon in the name of God and his Christ.

Here again the principle of the name as the key to the identity applies. When a man speaks the name of an Ascended Being with reverence, instantly he is enfolded with a ray of Light from the heart of God and from the representative of God to whom he has appealed. This is a function of Hierarchy that was ordained by God in the beginning when he said, "Let us make man in our image, after our likeness."[60]

Astrea comments on how important it is that mankind invoke the assistance of the Heavenly Hosts into every area of their lives. For once Ascended, a Master may not intercede on behalf of unascended mankind unless he is petitioned to do so by someone in embodiment. Man asked for and was given free will. He was sent forth to take dominion over his world, and until he willingly resigns himself and his world to the will of God, he can be sure that neither God nor his emissaries will interfere with his plans. Astrea says:

"It is one of the greatest tragedies of this age that individuals should believe the soft and subtle projections of the psychic forces that say, 'Do not disturb the Master. The Master, perhaps, is sleeping. The Master, perhaps, is away. He is involved in great conferences. These Great Beings cannot be disturbed by little people, for these Great Beings wish to do the things they are doing that require their fullest attention, and we must be careful not to disturb them.'

"How do you think we feel, beloved ones, when we see the awful conditions of the world continuing to worsen? Do you think, then, that we desire to see such frightful conditions prolonged or even compounded? Do you think that Almighty God would desire the perpetuation of these awful conditions that are taking place in the world today? I tell you, nay!

"Invoke! Invoke! And invoke and invoke again and again and do not fear to invoke! I say to you, fear not to invoke, for it is far better that men should fear *not* to invoke than that they should fear to invoke.

"I say, drill this into your consciousness and watch how we will function through the Body of God among ye all and through all of our students in the field wherever they are. For when individuals shall have the spiritual boldness to assert their own cosmic regeneration, the resurgence of Almighty God will once again come to the fore...

"These laws operate, in one sense, almost mechanically. But unless mankind know that they must invoke them, and unless they do so with a tender and contrite heart, with a loving heart, and with a definite amount of cosmic faith in our existence, they cannot bring about these miracles that the Light will produce gladly for any son of heaven who will do so—who will call upon us, who will do so; who will understand, who will do so, and know that the Law that is not in action is not the Law at all. The Law must be in action, and you must become that Law in action! You must become that Law in action *now!*...

"I am reminded now, as I bring this dictation to a close, of the episode that occurred at the time of Jesus when the young man lay on the ground frothing at the mouth. The disciples had attempted, again and again, to cast out the demon from that boy, and I tell you they exerted themselves to the fullest. But they lacked the faith and they lacked the knowledge of our octave of Light. If my cosmic circle and sword of blue flame had been invoked around that boy by any one of those disciples, they would have found that that demon would have left on the instant and would not have remained for a second. This was the power of Light that Jesus himself invoked. He invoked that energy of the blue flame, and it immediately fulfilled the destiny that God intended it to do. And thus the boy was effectively cut free and healed of that condition.[61]...

"The day of deliverance is at hand! And it does not lie in your octave. It lies in *ours!* It is by attunement with our octave and the shunning of the octaves of human consciousness (especially the psychic realm) that you will find your freedom. In God's name, awake to this fact before it is too late! And *use* the energy that we have given you, for it was given you that it might be used, and you are intended to use it!"[62]

Jesus and His Apostles
Cast Out Entities

Matthew 4:24

And his fame went throughout all Syria: and they brought unto him all sick people that were taken with divers diseases and torments, and those which were possessed with devils, and those which were lunatic, and those that had the palsy; and he healed them.

Matthew 9:32–33; Luke 11:14

As they went out, behold, they brought to him a dumb man possessed with a devil. And when the devil was cast out, the dumb spake: and the multitudes marvelled, saying, It was never so seen in Israel.

Matthew 10:1, 7–8; Mark 6:7, 13; Luke 9:1

And when he had called unto him his twelve disciples, he gave them power against unclean spirits, to cast them out, and to heal all manner of sickness and all manner of disease....

And as ye go, preach, saying, The kingdom of heaven is at hand. Heal the sick, cleanse the lepers, raise the dead, cast out devils: freely ye have received, freely give.

Matthew 12:22; Luke 11:14

Then was brought unto him one possessed with a devil, blind, and dumb: and he healed him, insomuch that the blind and dumb both spake and saw.

Matthew 15:22–28; Mark 7:25–30

And, behold, a woman of Canaan came out of the same coasts, and cried unto him, saying, Have mercy on me, O Lord, thou son of David; my daughter is grievously vexed with a devil. But he answered her not a word. And his disciples came and besought him, saying, Send her away; for she crieth after us. But he answered and said, I am not sent but unto the lost sheep of the house of Israel.

Then came she and worshipped him, saying, Lord, help me. But he answered and said, It is not meet to take the children's bread, and cast it to dogs.

And she said, Truth, Lord: yet the dogs eat of the crumbs which fall from their masters' table.

Then Jesus answered and said unto her, O woman, great is thy faith: be it unto thee even as thou wilt. And her daughter was made whole from that very hour.

Mark 1:23–26; Luke 4:33–35

And there was in their synagogue a man with an unclean spirit; and he cried out, saying, Let us alone; what have we to do with thee, thou Jesus of Nazareth? art thou come to destroy us? I know thee who thou art, the Holy One of God.

And Jesus rebuked him, saying, Hold thy peace, and come out of him. And when the unclean spirit had torn him, and cried with a loud voice, he came out of him.

Mark 1:32–34; Matthew 8:16; Luke 4:40–41

And at even, when the sun did set, they brought unto him all that were diseased, and them that were possessed with devils. And all the city was gathered together at the door. And he healed many that were sick of divers diseases, and cast out many devils; and suffered not the devils to speak, because they knew him.

Mark 1:39

And he preached in their synagogues throughout all Galilee, and cast out devils.

Mark 3:11–12

And unclean spirits, when they saw him, fell down before him, and cried, saying, Thou art the Son of God. And he straitly charged them that they should not make him known.

Mark 9:17–29; Matthew 17:14–21; Luke 9:38–42

And one of the multitude answered and said, Master, I have brought unto thee my son, which hath a dumb spirit; And wheresoever he taketh him, he teareth him: and he foameth, and gnasheth with his teeth, and pineth away: and I spake to thy disciples that they should cast him out; and they could not.

He answereth him, and saith, O faithless generation, how long shall I be with you? how long shall I suffer you? bring him unto me.

And they brought him unto him: and when he saw him, straightway the spirit tare him; and he fell on the ground, and wallowed foaming. And he asked his father, How long is it ago since this came unto him?

And he said, Of a child. And ofttimes it hath cast him into the fire, and into the waters, to destroy him: but if thou canst do any thing, have compassion on us, and help us.

Jesus said unto him, If thou canst believe, all things are possible to him that believeth.

And straightway the father of the child cried out, and said with tears, Lord, I believe; help thou mine unbelief.

When Jesus saw that the people came running together, he rebuked the foul spirit, saying unto him, Thou dumb and deaf spirit, I charge thee, come out of him, and enter no more into him. And the spirit cried, and rent him sore, and came out of him: and he was as one dead; insomuch that many said, He is dead. But Jesus took him by the hand, and lifted him up; and he arose.

And when he was come into the house, his disciples asked him privately, Why could not we cast him out?

And he said unto them, This kind can come forth by nothing, but by prayer and fasting.

Luke 8:26–33; Matthew 8:28–32; Mark 5:1–13

And they arrived at the country of the Gadarenes, which is over against Galilee. And when he went forth to land, there met him out of the city a certain man, which had devils long time, and ware no clothes, neither abode in any house, but in the tombs.

When he saw Jesus, he cried out, and fell down before him, and with a loud voice said, What have I to do with thee, Jesus, thou Son of God most high? I beseech thee, torment me not. (For he had commanded the unclean spirit to come out of the man. For oftentimes it had caught him: and he was kept bound with chains and in fetters; and he brake the bands, and was driven of the devil into the wilderness.)

And Jesus asked him, saying, What is thy name? And he said, Legion: because many devils were entered into him. And they besought him that he would not command them to go out into the deep.

And there was there an herd of many swine feeding on the mountain: and they besought him that he would suffer them to enter into them. And he suffered them. Then went the devils out of the man, and entered into the swine: and the herd ran violently down a steep place into the lake, and were choked.

Luke 10:17

And the seventy returned again with joy, saying, Lord, even the devils are subject unto us through thy name.

Acts 5:12, 16

And by the hands of the apostles were many signs and wonders wrought among the people....

There came also a multitude out of the cities round about unto Jerusalem, bringing sick folks, and them which were vexed with unclean spirits: and they were healed every one.

Acts 8:5–7

Then Philip went down to the city of Samaria, and preached Christ unto them. And the people with one accord gave heed unto those things which Philip spake, hearing and seeing the miracles which he did. For unclean spirits, crying with loud voice, came out of many that were possessed with them: and many taken with palsies, and that were lame, were healed.

Lord Michael, Cut Me Free!

In the name of the beloved mighty victorious Presence of God, I AM in me, my very own beloved Holy Christ Self, Holy Christ Selves of all mankind, beloved Archangel Michael, beloved Lanello, the entire Spirit of the Great White Brotherhood and the World Mother, elemental life—fire, air, water and earth! I decree:

1. Lord Michael, Lord Michael,
       I call unto thee
    Wield thy sword of blue flame
       And now cut me free!

Refrain: Blaze God-power, protection
       Now into my world,
    Thy banner of faith
       Above me unfurl!
    Transcendent blue lightning
       Now flash through my soul,
    I AM by God's mercy
       Made radiant and whole!

2. Lord Michael, Lord Michael,
       I love thee, I do
    With all thy great faith
       My being imbue!

3. Lord Michael, Lord Michael
       And legions of blue
    Come seal me, now keep me
       Faithful and true!

Coda: I AM with thy blue flame
       Now full charged and blest,
    I AM now in Michael's
       Blue flame armor dressed! (3x)

And in full faith ...

O Hercules, Thou Elohim

In the name of the beloved mighty victorious Presence of God, I AM in me, my very own beloved Holy Christ Self, Holy Christ Selves of all mankind, beloved Mighty Hercules and Amazonia, beloved Lanello, the entire Spirit of the Great White Brotherhood and the World Mother, elemental life— fire, air, water and earth! I decree:

1. O Hercules, thou Elohim,
   I AM a child of love,
   Come and seal my being
   By might from heaven above.

Refrain: Like a bolt of lightning blue,
   Power of God flashing through,
   Take dominion o'er me now,
   To thy Light and love I bow.

   Purify and guard my being
   By thine eye of grace all seeing,
   Clothe me in thy power real,
   Fill me now with holy zeal.

   I AM come to do God's will,
   Give me grace now to fulfill
   All the plan of heaven's Son,
   With thy Light I AM now one.

2. O Hercules, thy splendid shining
   Shatter failure and opining,
   Ope the way in love divining,
   Seal each one in crystal lining.

3. O Hercules, for strength I call,
   Give me victory over all;
   Let God triumph over me,
   Raise thy scepter, set me free.

4. O Hercules, beloved one,
   Crown me with thy blazing sun;
   Set thy hand upon my brow,
   Raise me to perfection now.

And in full faith I consciously accept this manifest, manifest, manifest! (3x) right here and now with full power, eternally sustained, all powerfully active, ever expanding and world enfolding until all are wholly ascended in the Light and free! Beloved I AM! Beloved I AM! Beloved I AM!

Beloved Cyclopea, Beholder of Perfection

Beloved mighty victorious Presence of God, I AM in me, Holy Christ Selves of all earth's evolutions, beloved Cyclopea and Virginia, beloved Helios and Vesta, Lanello and K-17, the entire Spirit of the Great White Brotherhood and the World Mother, elemental life—fire, air, water and earth! In the name of the beloved Presence of God which I AM and by and through the magnetic power of the sacred fire vested in the threefold flame burning within my heart, I decree:

1. Beloved Cyclopea,
   Thou Beholder of Perfection,
   Release to us thy divine direction,
   Clear our way from all debris,
   Hold the immaculate thought for me.

Refrain: I AM, I AM beholding All,
   Mine eye is single as I call;
   Raise me now and set me free,
   Thy holy image now to be.

2. Beloved Cyclopea,
   Thou Enfolder All-Seeing,
   Mold in Light my very being,
   Purify my thought and feeling,
   Hold secure God's Law appealing.

3. Beloved Cyclopea,
   Radiant Eye of Ancient Grace,
   By God's hand his Image trace
   On the fabric of my soul,
   Erase all bane and keep me Whole.

4. Beloved Cyclopea,
   Guard for aye the City Foursquare,
   Hear and implement my prayer,
   Trumpet my victory on the air,
   Hold the purity of Truth so fair.

And in full faith I consciously accept this manifest, manifest, manifest! (3x) right here and now with full power, eternally sustained, all powerfully active, ever expanding and world enfolding until all are wholly ascended in the Light and free! Beloved I AM! Beloved I AM! Beloved I AM!

Decree to Beloved Mighty Astrea

In the name of the beloved mighty victorious Presence of God, I AM in me, mighty I AM Presence and Holy Christ Selves of Keepers of the Flame, Lightbearers of the world and all who are to ascend in this life, by and through the magnetic power of the sacred fire vested in the threefold flame burning within my heart, I call to beloved Mighty Astrea and Purity, Archangel Gabriel and Hope, beloved Serapis Bey and the Seraphim and Cherubim of God, beloved Lanello, the entire Spirit of the Great White Brotherhood and the World Mother, elemental life—fire, air, water and earth! to lock your cosmic circles and swords of blue flame in, through, and around my four lower bodies, my electronic belt, my heart chakra and all of my chakras, my entire consciousness, being, and world.

[You may include here calls for specific circumstances or conditions for which you are requesting assistance.]

Cut me loose and set me free (3x) from all that is less than God's perfection and my own divine plan fulfilled.

1. O beloved Astrea, may God Purity
   Manifest here for all to see,
   God's divine will shining through
   Circle and sword of brightest blue.

First chorus: Come now answer this my call
   Lock thy circle round us all.
   Circle and sword of brightest blue,
   Blaze now, raise now, shine right through!

2. Cutting life free from patterns unwise,
   Burdens fall off while souls arise
   Into thine arms of infinite love,
   Merciful shining from heaven above.

3. Circle and sword of Astrea now shine,
   Blazing blue white my being refine,
   Stripping away all doubt and fear,
   Faith and goodwill patterns appear.

Second chorus: Come now answer this my call,
   Lock thy circle round us all.
   Circle and sword of brightest blue,
   Raise our youth now, blaze right through!

Third chorus: Come now answer this my call,
   Lock thy circle round us all.
   Circle and sword of brightest blue,
   Raise mankind now, shine right through!

And in full faith I consciously accept this manifest, manifest, manifest! (3x) right here and now with full power, eternally sustained, all powerfully active, ever expanding and world enfolding until all are wholly ascended in the Light and free!

Beloved I AM! Beloved I AM! Beloved I AM!

[Give each verse, followed by the first chorus; repeat the verses, using the second chorus; then give the verses a third time, using the third chorus.]

Entity Decree

Beloved mighty victorious Presence of God, I AM in me, my very own beloved Holy Christ Self, Holy Christ Selves of all mankind, beloved Alpha and Omega, beloved Helios and Vesta, beloved Seven Mighty Elohim, beloved Cyclopea, Great Silent Watcher, beloved Archangel Michael, all the Archangels and Legions of Light, the beloved Maha Chohan and the seven beloved Chohans of the Rays, beloved Mother Mary, Lady Masters Meta, Nada and Kuan Yin, beloved Lord Gautama, beloved Goddess of Liberty and the Great Karmic Board, beloved Lord Maitreya and Jesus the Christ, beloved Amerissis, Goddess of Light, beloved Goddess of Purity, beloved Mighty Astrea, the beloved mighty Cosmic Being Victory, beloved Lanello, the entire Spirit of the Great White Brotherhood and the World Mother, elemental life—fire, air, water, and earth!

In the name of the Presence of God which I AM and through the magnetic power of the sacred fire vested in me, I decree:

Charge! Charge! Charge! into the atmosphere of earth the full cosmic Light of a thousand suns, your mighty transcendent flame of perfection from the heart of God, the flame of cosmic blue lightning, and the violet transmuting flame! Seize, bind, hold inactive, and remove from within and around every lifestream, every elemental, the earth and its atmosphere all discarnate entities. (3x)

Take all discarnate entities from our planet instantly to Ascended Master octaves and schools of Light: Saturate! Saturate! Saturate! their forms with the flames of cosmic forgiveness and illumination from the heart of God in the Great Central Sun and our dearly beloved Kuan Yin and the Goddess of Wisdom. Dissolve forever! Dissolve forever! Dissolve forever! all recalcitrant densities within them and transmute, transmute, transmute them all into Light, illumination and love. Cut them free! Cut them free! Cut them free!

until humbly, adoringly they surrender their all to the service of the mighty I AM Presence and the Light of God which never, never, never fails to give earth freedom now. (3x)

Beloved Archangel Michael, beloved Mighty Astrea, all Ascended Beings, powers, activities and Legions of Light, angels and activities of the sacred fire: Lock your cosmic circles and swords of blue flame in, through and around all humanly created entities and Shatter! Shatter! Shatter! all negative thoughtforms, influences and akashic records adversely affecting mankind, elemental life, the earth or its atmosphere. (3x)

Replace them all by the immortal, victorious, cosmic three-fold flame of love, wisdom and power, the great cosmic Light and the Light of cosmic victory. Transmute! Transmute! Transmute! forever all human recalcitrance and resistance to the perfection of the mighty I AM Presence and the Light of God, which never, never, never fails to give earth freedom now. (3x)

I AM, I AM, I AM the unfailing Light of God blazing, blazing, blazing into the heart of every nation, city, town, hamlet and home to Cut them loose and set them free! Cut them loose and set them free! Cut them loose and set them free! from all harmful influences and aggressive intent. Seal, seal, seal every lifestream upon earth in the purity of his God-design from the heart of the beloved Goddess of Purity and the beloved Great Silent Watchers! (3x)

Charge! Charge! Charge! the immaculate concept of the victorious ascension in the Light into the forcefield of every man, woman and child on this planet from the heart of beloved Mother Mary and the individualized mighty I AM Presence. Awaken! Awaken! Awaken! within them all the inner knowledge of the I AM Law of Life and the all-consuming love of supreme allegiance to the mighty I AM Presence and the Light of God, which never, never, never fails to give earth freedom now. (3x)

And in full faith ...

Reverse the Tide

In the name of the beloved mighty victorious Presence of God, I AM in me from the Great Central Sun, my own beloved Holy Christ Self and Holy Christ Selves of all mankind, beloved Goddess of Light, beloved Queen of Light, beloved Goddess of Liberty, beloved Goddess of Wisdom, beloved Cyclopea, thou Silent Watcher for the earth, beloved seven mighty Elohim, beloved seven Chohans and Archangels, the Great Divine Director, Ascended Master Cuzco, beloved Mighty Astrea, beloved Lanello and K-17, the entire Spirit of the Great White Brotherhood and the World Mother, elemental life—fire, air, water and earth! I decree:

TAKE DOMINION NOW OVER:

[Give one or more of the following inserts, or compose your own prayer for the specific situation you are working on.]

INSERT A: all lying entities, psychic riptides, black magic and witchcraft directed against elemental life or the Light and the freedom and illumination of all mankind—with their causes and cores.

INSERT B: all racial violence, civil disorders, rioting, insurrection, international terror, treason, anarchy, fanaticism, insanity, plots of assassination, plots to overthrow our federal government, plots to vampirize and destroy the Light of America, and plots to unleash nuclear warfare between the nations—with their causes and cores.

INSERT C: all sex, liquor, tobacco and dope entities, their masquerades and vampire activities; the misuse of the sacred fire in advertising and entertainment; all distortions of man's creative energies and perversions of the Life-force designed to degrade the youth of the world; the flood of pornographic literature and motion pictures and those responsible for them; and all psychic forces, their pawns and tools of the sinister force—with their causes and cores.

INSERT D: all entities promoting the distortion of the divine arts, the music of the spheres and the culture of the Divine Mother; jazz, rock, acid rock and disco; the tide of aggressive energy directed against the youth of the world; and all hypnotic and jagged rhythms used to captivate the youth of the world through Luciferian activities and controls—with their causes and cores.

> * Reverse the tide! (3x)
> Roll them back! (3x)
> Reverse the tide! (3x)
> Take thy command!
> Roll them back! (3x)
> Set all free! (3x)
> Reverse the tide! (3x)
>
> (*Repeat this section 3, 12, or 36 times.)

Replace it all by the glorious principles of God-freedom, of cosmic liberty for the expansion of the Christ flame in every heart and for the mighty plan of freedom for this age from the heart of beloved Saint Germain!

> Unite the people in liberty! (3x)
> By God's own love now set them free! (3x)
> Unite the earth and keep it free (3x)
> By each one's I AM victory! (3x)
> Expose the Truth! (12x)
> Expose the lie! (12x)

And in full faith I consciously accept this manifest, manifest, manifest! (3x) right here and now with full power, eternally sustained, all-powerfully active, ever expanding and world enfolding until all are wholly ascended in the light and free!

Beloved I AM! Beloved I AM! Beloved I AM!

Set the Elementals Free

In the name and by the power of the beloved mighty victorious Presence of God, I AM in me, my very own beloved Holy Christ Self, Holy Christ Selves of all mankind, beloved Lanello, the entire Spirit of the Great White Brotherhood and the World Mother, elemental life—fire, air, water and earth!

I call to the heart of beloved Helios and Vesta, the beloved Maha Chohan, and the flame of cosmic comfort from the Great Central Sun; to beloved Virgo and Pelleur, beloved Aries and Thor, beloved Oromasis and Diana, beloved Neptune and Luara, the Seven Mighty Elohim, the seven beloved Archangels, and the seven beloved Chohans of the Rays; to beloved Archangel Zadkiel, beloved Saint Germain, beloved Mighty Arcturus, and their legions of violet-flame angels to answer this our call infinitely, presently and forever for the precious elemental beings of earth, air, fire and water:

> Seal, seal, seal in an ovoid bright
> Of the violet fire's clear Light
> Every elemental, set and keep them free
> From all human discord instantly.

1. Beloved I AM (3x)
2. By Christ command (3x)
3. By God's blue ray (3x)
4. By God's violet ray (3x)
5. By God's love ray (3x)
6. By Hercules' might (3x)
7. By Jesus' Light (3x)
8. By Michael's sword (3x)
9. It's done today, it's done to stay,
   it's done God's way

And in full faith ...

I AM the Violet Flame

In the name of the beloved mighty victorious Presence of God, I AM in me, and my very own beloved Holy Christ Self, I call to beloved Alpha and Omega in the heart of God in our Great Central Sun, beloved Saint Germain, beloved Portia, beloved Archangel Zadkiel, beloved Holy Amethyst, beloved mighty Arcturus and Victoria, beloved Kuan Yin, Goddess of Mercy, beloved Oromasis and Diana, beloved Mother Mary, beloved Jesus, beloved Omri-Tas, ruler of the violet planet, beloved great Karmic Board, beloved Lanello, the entire Spirit of the Great White Brotherhood and the World Mother, elemental life—fire, air, water and earth!

To expand the violet flame within my heart, purify my four lower bodies, transmute all misqualified energy I have ever imposed upon life, and blaze mercy's healing ray throughout the earth, the elementals, and all mankind and answer this my call infinitely, presently, and forever:

> I AM the violet flame
>> In action in me now
> I AM the violet flame
>> To Light alone I bow
> I AM the violet flame
>> In mighty cosmic power
> I AM the Light of God
>> Shining every hour
> I AM the violet flame
>> Blazing like a sun
> I AM God's sacred power
>> Freeing every one

And in full faith ...

Chapter 5

The Messengers

He that receiveth a prophet
in the name of a prophet shall
receive a prophet's reward.

MATTHEW

Behold, I will send my
messenger, and he shall prepare
the way before me: and the
Lord, whom ye seek, shall
suddenly come to his temple,
even the messenger of the
covenant, whom ye delight in:
behold, he shall come saith the
Lord of hosts.

MALACHI

The Messengers

THE TRUE PROPHET OF GOD IS the Messenger of God, and God speaks through Messengers today just as he spoke through the prophets of the Old Testament. Indeed, every age needs a *many* Messenger from God, for in every age the Ascended Masters are permitted by cosmic law to release greater teaching on the Law. They are permitted to reveal the precepts that will enable mankind to disentangle themselves from the web of karma and from the forces that play that karma against them.

Progressive Revelation

The Ascended Master Lanto once said, "Without cosmic revelation, all men would be ultimately dead."[1] In other words, without the contact with the Most High that provides man with a greater purpose than a merry-go-round whirl for threescore years and ten, "life is but an empty dream"[2] where man walks among the dead and knows not that he, too, is spiritually dead.

There is no such thing as final revelation, for revelation is ever coming forth from the I AM Presence and Christ Self of every individual as the still, small voice within. It is also coming forth through those lifestreams ordained by God to serve as Lightbearers to focus his wisdom and to make it practical for the age.

Kuthumi, the Master who teaches us sacred psychology, has said: "When we pause to consider the wealth of Ascended Master instruction that has been given in the past as avant-garde spiritual information, we perceive that one of the reasons why so much of it has not been appropriated is because some individuals have limited our release of spiritual information according to certain misinterpretations of cosmic law taken from the sacred scriptures of the world.

"For example, the admonishment, 'Ye shall not add unto the word which I command you, neither shall ye diminish aught from it,'[3] certainly was not intended to forestall the privilege of the Eternal Father to release from the treasure house of his Being, through his emissaries and teachers, through his prophets and revelators, transcendent information for each advancing age.

"To diminish or to take away from the Word is to delete the eternal Truths, the timeless Truths of God, from the consciousness by failing to recognize the divine intent hidden within the Word. The adding to the Word of extraneous matter is the adding of distortion from the levels of the human intellect to the pure teachings of the Universal Christ, which are the same 'yesterday, today and forever.'[4]

"On the other hand, the statement of the angel who released the Book of Revelation to John the Beloved, 'Seal not the sayings of the prophecy of this book,'[5] signifies that Revelation is an open book, to be continued by God's appointed representatives for the enlightenment of every age.

"Transcendence is progressive change; and the nature of God, with all of its absolute beauty, becomes more magnificent each moment. If it were not so, the advancing souls of the Ascended Beings would come to a point in the Absolute where all things would be attained and they would no longer experience that holy anticipation—that joyous expectancy for the cornucopia of progress and expanding awareness—that is so much a part of the unfoldment of the Divine in man at every stage of his development.

"It is, then, the nature of God to increase the vibratory action of the Godhead itself, so that all of creation can always move progressively in the direction of greater happiness, greater achievement and greater wisdom."[6]

The Messenger of God Within

Every man has his own messenger in the person of his own Christ Self. Without contact with the Mediator of the Christ Self, man loses contact with his own God Presence.

In the first three Golden Ages, before the descent of mankind's consciousness into the dense spheres of duality, the sons and daughters of God relied upon the Christ within to teach them the knowledge of the Law, while the Manus set the example for the Christ-pattern they were to outpicture. The hierarchical office of Messenger was therefore not established until mankind lost contact with the inner voice and were no longer able to hear the Word of the LORD or to receive directly the instruction of the Ascended Masters. Through his Messengers, God provided the missing link to Hierarchy in the ages of darkness when mankind knew not the way in which they should go.

At present, the Messengers are serving to reestablish each man's contact with his own Christ Self. Through the instruction on the Law that is being given forth from the Ascended Masters, every man in Christ will one day be able to discern what is Truth. He will know the difference between the "mutterings and peepings" of familiar spirits[7] and the voice of God himself.

Isaiah prophesied that this time would come when the "teachers" (the Christ Selves) would not be removed into a corner anymore, when "thine eyes shall see thy teachers: and thine ears shall hear a word behind thee, saying, This is the way, walk ye in it, when ye turn to the right hand, and when ye turn to the left."[8]

Until that time comes, when each man shall sit under his own vine and fig tree,[9] there will still be a need for Messengers.*

The Functions of God's Messengers

The primary function of a Messenger is to act as a sensor of the Ascended Master's Presence, attuning with the Master and acting as his hands, his feet, his mouth and his direct representative in the world of form.

While Messengers and prophets of God have not always manifested the fullness of Christ-perfection in their outer consciousness, but have on occasions exhibited human traits, their purified consciousness—their dedication to God and to the Masters—is complete within itself. They have always sought to transcend their limitations and to increase their spiritual manifestation.

The office of Messenger is carried out from the level of the

---

* The vine is the Christ and the emanation of the Word through the crystal cord; the fig tree is the Causal Body surrounding the I AM Presence—your own Tree of Life.

Christ Self. In other words, when a Messenger is acting as the mouthpiece of God, the instruction comes forth from the level of his own Christ Self as an expression of the Christ Selves of all mankind, as admonishment to those selves who are in a state of becoming the Christ but who as yet do not hear the voice of their Lord. Therefore, such communication would not be in conflict with private revelation, if the latter is accurate.

Neither does the service of one Messenger ever preclude the good that has been done by those who have gone before, for all Messengers of God are one. Their office in Hierarchy is under the World Teachers, who in turn serve under the Lord of the World and the Great Central Sun Messengers.

True prophets of God and Messengers of the Great White Brotherhood have progressively attained to a higher degree of efficiency in their predictions and activities for the Hierarchy. Several thousand years ago, the biblical prophets were considered to be from 50 to 65 percent accurate. Early in the twentieth century, the prophets were considered to be from 90 to 95 percent accurate, and currently the Messengers are considered to be from 95 to 98 percent accurate in their transmittals to mankind. (These percentages were obtained from the Ascended Master Saint Germain.)

The Messenger, then, brings forth through the written and spoken Word the instruction that the invisible Teachers would impart to their unascended disciples. In all cases, Messengers are sensitive, reliable lifestreams who have proven their worthiness to serve the Hierarchy through many embodiments. Their attunement with the Hierarchy and the God Presence, together with the preparation they have made at inner levels, enables them to act as Mediators between the higher realms of Light and the four lower levels of earthly consciousness.

Beloved Morya once said that "these gifted and cosmically ordained prophets are God's telephone, a divine instrument through which the Masters of Light may speak without human interference."[10]

The ritual of the ordination of a Messenger, which is conducted by a member of the Hierarchy, takes place only after years of intensive preparation, both during the embodiment in which he serves and during countless previous lives, which may possibly extend over thousands of years.

The Requirements of the Office of Messenger

Every office in Hierarchy has its requirements, and the office of Messenger is no exception. There are certain inner initiations that must be passed. Unless the individual who has been called to that office has surrendered the ego and the human will totally to the Divine Ego and the Divine Will, he is considered unfit to hold the office.

In our case, it was the Ascended Master El Morya who trained our lifestreams for this service in this embodiment. He organized a program of initiation and study especially suited to each of our lifestreams.

Mark served beloved K-17 for many years before he took public dictations from members of the Hierarchy. Although he held and still holds other offices in the Brotherhood, the formal dedication of his lifestream and the ceremony of his ordination took place shortly before the formation of The Summit Lighthouse in 1958.

In the case of Elizabeth, the training she had been given at inner levels and in previous embodiments continued on through her childhood. The ceremony of her ordination was conducted in 1963 by the Ascended Master Saint Germain in the presence of twelve witnesses in Washington, D.C.

The Messenger's Contact
with the Brotherhood

The individual who holds the office of Messenger receives certain cosmic keys that the Masters anchor in his four lower bodies, as well as the sacred science and technique of contact with the Ascended Octaves. Without these keys and the accompanying technique, no amount of training can give the individual the assurance that he has indeed tuned in to Ascended Master levels of consciousness.

The keys that are anchored in the Messenger's four lower bodies as hieroglyphs of the Spirit—cosmic computers in capsule form—give him instantaneous contact with the Brotherhood at any hour of the day or night. As the reverse is also true, the Messenger is the Brotherhood's immediate point of contact in times of crisis, catastrophe or great urgency, when those who are part of the mass consciousness are in too great a turmoil to be able to make the necessary calm attunement with the God Presence. The Messengers can be depended upon to receive the Word of God that contains within itself the power to still the storm and the raging of human emotion and to channel into every negative condition the healing unguents of Truth.

The technique of contact (which gives the Messenger the use of the keys) includes certain rituals that the Messenger must perform before taking a dictation, one of which is the locking of his mind within the vibratory frequency of the Master who is dictating. This is done by means of what Morya has called the *thread of contact*.

Saint Germain once said that the thread of contact is usually somewhat gossamer in appearance but must be made strong like diamond-steel cables of Light, strong enough to resist completely the "din of dissonance" (as Morya often calls the voices of the brothers of shadow) and strong enough to conduct the mighty currents of God's glory as they flow through to bring blessings to all the world.[11]

How Dictations Are Received

The Hierarchy communicates with the Messenger over the light and sound ray. Those who have studied the Masters' instruction and those who have seen and heard live dictations may be interested to know that messages are received in several ways:

1. In letters of living fire that appear before the Messenger, who reads them as one would read the letters that appear on the Times Square building in New York City. Invisible to the audience, these letters move across the screen of the Messenger's mind as if they were on a conveyer belt.

2. Ex cathedra, from the mouth of God. The Ascended Master superimposes his Electronic Presence over the Messenger, making his voice box congruent with the Messenger's and using it as if it were his own. In this case, the transfer of thought from the Master's consciousness to the Messenger's is instantaneous, and there is no intermediate process whereby the Messenger must discern or read. This form of dictation comes through with great rapidity and is usually flawless.

3. In thoughtform. The Master releases from his consciousness to the Messenger's capsules that contain the matrices for the dictation. These are decoded in the Messenger's brain through a computerized process, and by means of the keys that have been inserted in the Messenger's four lower bodies, the patterns of the Master are translated to the wavelength of the Messenger and then are formulated into words. This is a complicated process that takes place independently of the time-space continuum, at that point where the Mind of Christ,

superimposed as a halo over the Messenger, is congruent with the Mind of God individualized in the Ascended Master.

4. By telepathy. Mental patterns are released from the Master to the Messenger through the Mind of Christ. This form of dictation is used when the Master is not present, but is in his retreat or at another point in this solar system. This method is also used for brief comments that the Messenger may solicit from the Master on organizational problems or personal counseling for students. Over the thread of contact that connects the Messenger with the entire Spirit of the Great White Brotherhood simultaneously as he is connected with each individual member of the Brotherhood, he can receive telepathically such information as the Masters deem vital to his service in the world of form.

Each method of receiving dictations serves a different purpose. The ex-cathedra method is the highest and best form, for it enables the Master to extend his aura with greater intensity into the atmosphere of the room and into the auras of those who are physically present. Thus they are able to take in with all their faculties the Master's message, as well as the release of his radiation.

However, when there are disturbing elements in the room, such as those who are skeptical of or out of harmony with either the Masters, the Messengers or their teachings, it is possible for them to interfere with the transmission of the ex-cathedra dictation to such an extent that the Master will find it expedient to relay the message either telepathically or in letters of fire.

The rapidity of speech and the flow of ideas in the dictations is, in many cases, superhuman. The Messenger has no idea what the content of the dictation will be prior to the moment that he stands to receive it, and he often does not even know who will be dictating. Therefore, it is preposterous to suppose that the Messenger has premeditated either the topic or the sequences of the worded concepts (as some skeptics have proposed). It is not even within the capacity of a human being to develop, on the instant, an intelligently organized speech and then to deliver it with the speed with which the dictations come forth. The memorization of such a lengthy discourse would be equally impossible.

The representative of the Holy Spirit once said, "I am amazed that mankind can imagine in their own vanities that this Messenger would have the ability to express himself as I do; and I compliment them upon their foolish imaginations.

"Those who think for one moment that this Messenger has the power—although he has some power of speech—to speak as I am speaking, are in effect betraying the energies of heaven. For I assure you that we are endowing him now with our graces, that you may partake of heavenly manna. And the purposes that are being served are the purposes of Light and the purposes of Light's perfection.

"And therefore I say to you tonight, realize the need to sustain each such focus of Light who is genuinely representing us. Beloved ones, they are *few*. They are few and far between.

"The Great Divine Director served in such a capacity in past civilizations and rendered a service to the people of that generation. It is a precious service; yet each one of you has a service that is precious to render."[12]

The Intuitive Faculties of God's Messengers

Those who are steeped in dogma are not able to discover in the dictations the subtle keys that are often self-evident to more advanced chelas. As one tends to become that to which he is exposed, so the Messenger and the chela of the Masters tend to acquire the qualities of the Divine, of an Ascended Being, of an Angel, of an Archangel or of a Cosmic Being when exposed to the vibratory action of their consciousness.

Thus, the intuitive faculties and the abilities of discernment that all Messengers have are by no means unique to them. These can be developed to a greater or lesser degree by any sincere disciple and are, of course, very helpful in corroborating the testimony of the prophets themselves.

Whenever an Ascended Master such as Jesus the Christ chooses to dictate a message to the mankind of earth through one of his chosen Messengers, there is an accompanying release of the vibratory action and the high thoughts and energy patterns of the Master himself. Those who are sensitive and who are able to feel these vibratory actions are often raised in consciousness far above their ordinary state.

Certainly, those who feel the Master's presence do not question intellectually that which is already confirmed by the heart. They have felt the radiant release that moves in waves through the nerve centers, realigning the thought patterns and producing feeling patterns of wonderful harmony. However, those who have not yet opened their spiritual centers need a great deal of faith in order to assimilate the truth about prophecy.

Do Not Judge the Teaching by the Imperfections of Its Messenger

In reply to students' questions concerning the nature of prophecy, Saint Germain said: "We have been asked to define prophecy. Those who lack discrimination, torn between the desire to believe all things and plagued by honest doubt, yearn for clarification from heavenly places.

"Remember that all of the sacred books that have ever

been written and all of the knowledge that is esteemed by the many religions of the world—regardless of the claims of men to the contrary—have come into manifestation through individuals who were embodied upon the planet. In other words, they have all come forth through man.

"There is and has always been a tendency on the part of mankind to judge the accuracy and quality of spiritual material by the lives of those through whom the material came. We have said that men should not spend as much time as they do in the examination by mortal mind's measures of the lives or persons of spiritual teachers. We have said that thirsty travelers ought not to spurn a cup of cold water, simply because the tin cup in which it is delivered has an imperfection in it.

"If the world of individuals is old, every individual on earth is old in the sense that myriad experiences have created encrusted concepts that are difficult for men to relinquish. Thus, as in olden times even to the present hour, men do examine the sources of information rather than the teachings. And it is, blessed ones, the teaching, after all, that is everything.

"That which bears the earmark of cosmic authenticity registers within the chords of the heart; but how shall this be manifest in those whose attunement with their own hearts is sadly lacking, where the brittleness of the mind can analyze only the worded structure of our releases?

"Where, then, is the sounding board for authenticity? Men should understand that they, themselves, need perfectionment as well as attunement with the Higher Powers if they are to register the genuine perfection they profess to seek.

"You see, frequently seekers for Light maintain a very unprofessional attitude in their examination of the various teachings they encounter. But after all, they lack experience in that which they seek. Therefore, there is almost a blind struggle that occurs in the world of individuals on the Path toward the Light.

"Is it any wonder, then, that they are easily victimized by those blind leaders of the blind[13] who themselves have not attained what we could call one iota of God-realization? These are they who have studied all about the miraculous manifestations of the lives of the saints, yet who have permitted their brains to register—together with a more perfect admonishment—the fatuous ideas of mortal contempt for their compeers, for their brothers and for one another.

"Heaven is not disdainful of honest men's search for Truth, but we know that people are prone to be overly critical of those whose simplest thoughts they cannot yet understand. Human sophistry and wit do not of themselves produce a passport that leads to higher dimensions and accurate perceptions.

"On the contrary, many have excommunicated themselves from a movement of definite spiritual progress before they could take root or refuge in an onward-moving company of spiritual devotees. Surely this must pinpoint for the perceptive how very vital it is that men shall be as little children, trusting in the Infinite One and in the wisdom of Heaven itself to perform judgment upon men whose hypocrisy they eschew.

"There is no need, blessed ones, for men to be constantly engaged in a witch hunt while they yet seek to find their way back Home. Again and again individuals, steeped in tradition or in traditional concepts, attend one of our services only to turn away from the great opportunity that is given to them.

"For ere the door can be opened toward the Light or valid explanations given, they have decided in their minds that the appearance of those who represent us, or the expressions of their mouths, are not pleasing to them. Arbiters of their own confusion are they, laying hold upon decaying substance and proclaiming it as real, while turning away from the Real and the banner of freedom without ever knowing what its true value is.

"I admit that some things are self-evident and cast their shadows before them, but Truth is often subtly concealed beneath a crude exterior or a manifestation that belies its great content. If there is, then, any admonishment that I would give to humanity in these troubled times it is this: 'Be not hasty of judgment.'"[14]

Messengers Do Not Engage in Astral or Psychic Practices

yet there are some truly gifted mediums who are not Master's or full messengers

There is a big difference between the Messenger who represents the Hierarchy by divine appointment and the channel or medium of astral personalities and vibrations. It is impossible for the Messenger of God to be involved in any form of spiritualism, for his consciousness is not at the level of the astral plane where the spirits dwell.

Neither is it possible for him to be involved in trance. There is nothing mediumistic about the work of the true prophets of God. The consciousness of the Messenger must be purified by the Holy Spirit and transformed by the Mind of Christ. Only when functioning from the level of that Spirit and that Mind is he able to contact the Ascended consciousness of the Master and thereby bring forth his dictations.

The difference is clear — but Edgar Cayce was an authentic trance medium, though not a matter of

The Brotherhood does not allow the Messenger to engage in trance or automatic writing, not does it recommend that the true disciple of the Christ engage in these practices, because when one turns over his consciousness to one who is not perfected—an unascended consciousness dwelling on the astral planes—he is subject to that one's total consciousness.

Not only do the words and thoughts of the discarnate pass to the channel, but so does his entire momentum—a literal sewer of untransmuted substance. The same is true in hypnosis. Since the abuses of spiritualism, the Masters have withdrawn the dispensation that provided for spirit communication on a limited basis for the purposes of establishing proof of existence beyond the grave.*

Psychic Mediums and Communication with Disembodied Souls

At present, the Brotherhood's plan for extensive instruction in their etheric retreats for souls preparing to reembody precludes the possibility of their remaining in the lower strata for such activities as spirit communication. Any indication of the presence of departed loved ones or astral so-called guides should be one's signal to make calls for them to be taken swiftly to octaves of Light and the retreats of the Brotherhood.

There is definite karma in magnetizing unascended disembodied souls. These souls should be set free to pursue nobler purposes, while those embodied here below should cleave only to the I AM Presence and the Ascended Hosts of Light, whose presence in our midst we are privileged to enjoy.

Where there are true prophets, there are often those who—while they may be sincere—are victims of their own illusions. Their Light is stolen through their involvement in the glamour of the psychic realm, and they serve as tools of psychic personalities. They disseminate teachings cloaked in Light, whose core is actually misqualified energy or darkness. Their words may appear to convey wisdom, but the effect of their words can be shattering. While there may be false prophets in every age, there are degrees of falsity. → Even as Church

(but with the coming New Ager that door has been opened against people to people which is the saddest trauma to people and caused trauma to people leadership)

---

* The Masters' original sponsorship of spiritualism and its later abuses are described in the chapter "Psychic Thralldom" in book 6 of the Climb the Highest Mountain series, *Paths of Light and Darkness*.

Church leaders are much more dangerous and delusional

It is our studied opinion that the majority of mediums are more the victims of their own delusions than they are the willful deceivers of men. This does not lessen the dangers for their followers, but the sincere follower of a false prophet can readily adapt himself to the Truth once he has found it.

Many communications received by mediums are but the thrust of impostors who cleverly cloak their words in a steady practice of deceiving even the mediums through whom they speak. Often it is the entity who intends to deceive mankind, not the medium. And the entity is deceived by the archdeceiver himself, the ally of world negation.

Indeed, the false hierarchy has representatives both in and out of embodiment who imitate the dictations of the Ascended Masters, hoping to preempt the activities of the true Hierarchy of Light. The false hierarchs send their unwitting tools on supposed errands of the Brotherhood and direct them to establish centers that are supposedly under the sponsorship of the true Hierarchy, but are actually outposts of confusion set up to deliberately snare well-meaning seekers and to lure them from the one true Path.

There are two ways in which one can test those who claim to be the representatives of the Brotherhood—by their vibrations and by their teachings. If their vibrations are of darkness, then their teachings will be partially or wholly inaccurate, for they themselves do not have the ability to contact the Light while they remain in darkness.

Therefore, that which they bring forth must be based on what the true prophets of God have already brought forth. Dwellers of the night, they are not qualified to be teachers of men, for their vibrations will always taint the teachings as well as the souls to whom they impart them. They will not possess the fire of the Christ that is able by the power of the spoken Word to quicken the hearts of the many and to draw all men unto Him.

On the other hand, if their vibrations are good but their teachings are falsely based, they must be tutored by the Christ in a correct understanding of the Laws of God before they go forth to sow bad seed among good and later reap the harvest thereof.

El Morya speaks of the difference between the true Messengers and their impostors: "The Word is all and everything. The Word is the eternal Logos. It is the voice of the Ancient of Days thundering the Ten Commandments from Horeb's height, etching out of the living flame the markings of the Law on tablets of stone. The Word is the will of the AUM and the ray of your divinity. The Word is life and love and Truth. The Word is Law and principle. The Word is individuality through and through.

"We send forth Messengers of the Word whose souls, anointed by God himself, have knelt before the altar at the Court of the Sacred Fire and received the commission of the Four and Twenty Elders. And their authority is that of the Great Central Sun Messengers. To be a Messenger for Hierarchy is a high and holy calling—one that is not lightly given, one that ought not to be lightly received.

"Down through the centuries we have appointed our Messengers prophets of the Law, Teachers of the way of the Christ consciousness and of the Buddhic Light. Others whom we would call unappointed or self-appointed messengers have come forth to blatantly usurp their ministry and their office in Hierarchy. And so there is abroad in the land an enticing spirit, beguiling as the Serpent, that is not the true spirit of prophecy. Nor is it come as the gift of the Holy Spirit;[15] it is the voice of rebellion and of witchcraft, of vain talkers and deceivers.[16] These are the crystal-ball gazers, the psychic readers and self-proclaimed messiahs—bewitched and bewitching, coming in the name of the Church yet denying the true Church, coming in the name of the Logos yet their lives a betrayal of true reason and the Law.

"They are the archdeceivers of mankind. They would take over the person and the personality of the Ascended Masters and the real Gurus. Setting themselves up as gurus, they sit in the lotus posture smoking the peace pipe with the false hierarchy, dispensing drugs along with demons, and even training their disciples in the manipulation of sexual energies for heightened sensual gratification. In their all-consuming lust for power, they teach the way to God through sexual perversion, abuses of the body, and the desecration of the Mother. And the Light they steal from those they ensnare is used to satisfy their mad cravings and to control vast segments of the population through witchcraft, variance and mortal cursings.

"Others are in the business of training 'channels' and psychic healers. They know not the difference between spiritual and psychic energies—the pure and the impure stream. Thus they make the gullible to be channels for the energies of the pit, for the diabolical murmurings of familiar spirits and of 'wizards that peep and that mutter.'[17] The false hierarchies and the fallen ones come in many guises, seeking to impress an infant humanity with their sleight of hand, trance and telepathy, their flying saucers and other trappings.

"I say woe to those who are adept in the mental manipulations of Matter and astral energies yet have not the Christ— the snake charmers and charlatans who display a phenomenal control of bodily functions yet have not one iota of soul mastery! As if they had a thing to offer mankind that mankind cannot get directly from their own Christ Self, their own I AM Presence and the living flame that God has anchored within the heart!

"Some of these, deceived and deceiving others, go so far as

to say that everyone should be a psychic channel, everyone should develop his psychic powers. Like the magicians in Pharaoh's court,[18] they hold up to our Messengers their psychic phenomena and they say, 'See, we do the same thing!' Not so! Like the fallen ones who, in their attempt to level Hierarchy, would make themselves equal with the sons and daughters of God, these psychic channels would cause our Messengers and their work with the living Word to become muddied by the flood of psychic material being released by the false hierarchy.

"Let it be so! They have free will. As the grass of the field, they have their day; for the wind passeth over them and they are gone, to be remembered no more.[19] But the day of the true Messengers of Hierarchy shall be as the giant redwood marking the cycles of the spiritual-material evolution of the race and as the snow-covered Himalayas outlining the pinnacles of soul attainment. Thus the prophets have come in every age, and their day is the day of the salvation (self-elevation) of the race of mankind. And the coming of the Messenger is always the preparing of the way for the coming of a new level of the Christ consciousness. 'Behold, I send my messenger before thy face, which shall prepare thy way before thee.'[20]

"In every century the Messengers have proclaimed the living Truth that should free mankind from age-worn doctrine and dogma. In this age they have come to prepare the world to receive their own Christ-identity and the I AM Presence 'coming in the clouds of heaven with power and great glory.'[21] Their coming marks the hour when all who have realized the oneness of the I AM Presence through the ritual of the ascension should appear to mankind through the exalted vision of the Christ consciousness."[22]

Powers of the Messenger

Among the other powers given to the Messenger are gifts of healing, discerning of spirits, speaking in tongues and the casting out of demons and discarnate entities. The Messenger retains these gifts only as long as he uses them for the specific purposes outlined by the Hierarchy for the blessing of humanity and for purposes in accordance with karmic and cosmic law.

Although the Messenger has the power to read all levels of human consciousness, including the akashic records, he never does so by the power of the human mind and its involvement with the human side of life, but always through the third eye that is tethered to the I AM Presence, always through the Mind of Christ. The Messenger has pledged never to use this gift for the entertainment or the flattery of egos, but only at the behest of a member of Hierarchy on behalf of an unascended chela.

Whereas a medium may be trained, the Messenger, the true prophet, has a calling from God. That calling was given to him when the Almighty fashioned the archetypal pattern for the destiny of the twin flames. "And how shall they preach, except they be sent? as it is written, How beautiful are the feet of them that preach the gospel of peace, and bring glad tidings of good things!"[23]

We Come in the Name of a Prophet

We come, then, to the subject of our own Messengership. Because some have thought that our surname was selected for business purposes, we wish to say that it was given to Mark by his earthly parents, Thomas and Mabel Prophet. It was a divine bequest for which we are grateful.

We have been asked whether we were chosen because of the purity of our being or our high state of spiritual progress. We have been asked whether we are unascended masters, saints or exalted beings.

To these questions we reply: If there be any virtue, if there be any Light, if there be any blessings coming forth to the followers of the Christ in the place where we stand, let men look up and acknowledge the Source of all Good. For we are only servants of God, by no means perfected, only willing to raise the chalice of our consciousness that all might drink of the living water of eternal Truth.[24]

Often we are so humbled by the great height from which the divine energies are released, that we cry, "Lord, I am not worthy," and to this He replies, "The Christ in every man is worthy to receive me; so are ye also worthy."

Sanat Kumara, First Messenger and Keeper of the Flame

Students of the occult often inquire about our past embodiments. Quite understandably, they wish to know our "credentials." Although we look to the God within every man and to his present realization of that God, we also realize that a man's past performances set the sail of his soul in future lives. Therefore, to satisfy the questions of would-be adherents of Ascended Master Law, we offer the following information concerning our inheritance from the past.

Our service to the evolutions of this planet began with the advent of Sanat Kumara, the Ancient of Days, who came from Venus to keep the flame of the Christ blazing for the mankind of earth at the time of the planet's greatest crisis. At that time the earth had already been besieged by the laggards and the Luciferian hordes, and under their influence, her evolutions had been reduced to the level of the caveman.

The earth provided a great challenge to unascended souls evolving on other planetary homes in this system. Earth's evolutions no longer emitted Light, for all had forgotten their Source. The earth stood at the point of being dissolved by cosmic decree.

The evolutions of sister planets, remembering the fate of the destroyed planet Maldek (whose remains still circle the sun as the asteroid belt between Mars and Jupiter[25]), appealed to Solar Lords for intercession on the earth's behalf.

Sanat Kumara, Hierarch of Venus, went before the Cosmic Councils, volunteering to leave his home and consort to keep the Flame for the evolutions of earth who had been led astray through outside interference. He was the first Messenger to the planet and the first Keeper of the Flame. Realizing his great courage, many volunteered to accompany him.

These volunteers came not only from Venus but also from other planets and stars beyond our solar system. They knew that once they embodied, the chances were very great that they would become involved in karma-making situations that would tie them to their adopted home for perhaps thousands of years. Nevertheless, they had been trained to render this service, and the opportunity beckoned.

For many centuries, the thousands of lifestreams composing the retinue of Sanat Kumara remained in his service at etheric levels at Shamballa, the retreat of the Lord of the World situated over the Gobi Desert. But there came a time when, through their ministration from etheric levels, the general consciousness of the race was raised to such a level that Sanat Kumara considered it safe for the volunteers to embody.

Upon his direction, they were commissioned to go forth into the world of form to carry his Light. Two by two they took embodiment, until an entire wave of Venusian and other interplanetary volunteers were firmly entrenched in the karmic patterns of the earth.[26] Among these were our own twin flames.

On Atlantis

One of our first recollections of physical embodiment on earth is on Atlantis, when Mark was a high priest and a master of invocation in the temple and Elizabeth was a temple virgin instructing the children there in the art of spiritual dance.

In Ancient Egypt

After the sinking of Atlantis, the former Atlanteans began to reembody in the Fertile Crescent, and so we gave our service as rulers of ancient Egypt. **Ikhnaton** (Amenhotep IV, c.1377–c.1358 B.C.) and **Nefertiti,** his wife, are remembered for having founded the first form of modern monotheism.

Thirty-three centuries ago, Ikhnaton (or Akhenaten, as the name is sometimes spelled) recognized the one God in the spiritual Sun behind the physical sun, and he called this God "Aton." Ikhnaton visualized the Infinite One, Aton, as a divine being "clearly distinguished from the physical sun" yet manifest in the sunlight. Ikhnaton gave reverence to the "heat which is in the Sun," as he saw it to be the vital heat that accompanied all Life.[27]

Ikhnaton created a symbol that depicted Aton as a golden circular disk from which diverging beams radiated. He was careful to point out that the solar disk itself was not God but only a symbol of God. Each diverging beam, or ray, ended in a hand extending over every person as a blessing, and in some depictions the hand brought the ankh, the symbol of Life, directly to Ikhnaton and his Queen.

Ikhnaton and Nefertiti

Ikhnaton also saw God as a personality whose "beams nourish every field" and "live and grow for thee."[28] These beams are the very seeds of Light and sparks of Light that form our own threefold flame in the secret chamber of our heart. (Is this conception of the sun disc with its emanating rays not similar to the Masters' current instruction on the I AM Presence—the Sun of Righteousness—and the crystal cord through which the energies of the Sun descend to embodied man?)

Impatient with the practices of priests of Amon at Thebes, the king not only denounced their gods and ceremonies as a vulgar idolatry, but built a new capital for the kingdom, Akhetaten (known to archaeologists as Tel el Amarna), located nearly three hundred miles north of the ancient city of Thebes. Ikhnaton prohibited the worship of the old Nephilim gods, particularly Amon, the chief god, and ordered their names and images erased from the monuments. These were both embodied and disembodied fallen angels, to whom the black priests had erected their altars.

In his total loyalty to the one God of the Sun, Amenhotep IV changed his theophoric name to Ikhnaton, "He who is beneficial to Aton." His passionate songs to Aton have been preserved as the fairest remnant of Egyptian literature.

> Thy dawning is beautiful in the horizon of the sky
> O Living Aton, Beginning of life.
> When thou risest in the eastern horizon,
> Thou fillest every land with thy beauty....
>
> How manifold are thy works!
> They are hidden from before us,
> O sole god, whose powers no other possesseth.
> Thou didst create the earth according to thy heart.[29]

Seven hundred years before Isaiah, Ikhnaton proclaimed the vitalistic conception of the Deity, found in the trees and flowers and all forms of Life—with the sun as the emblem of the ultimate power he now proclaims as the I AM Presence. Although the consciousness of the people was not ready for the one God in Ikhnaton's day, the impact of monotheism is felt to the present day throughout the world's great religions.

Alas, the reign of Ikhnaton and Nefertiti was but a tender interlude in Egypt's era of power. An idealistic reformer, Ikhnaton was not wont to send Egyptians to war in defense of dependencies of Egypt that had been invaded. As a result, the Egyptian empire shrank, and the ruler found himself without funds or friends.

In the seventeenth year of Ikhnaton's reign, he, his wife and the eldest daughter disappeared. Scholars have guessed that they were murdered. By whom and when and how is unknown. El Morya has shown us that it was the chief military leader, General Horemheb, who led a revolt against Ikhnaton and Nefertiti, and stabbed them to death.

The black priests reestablished the former gods and obliterated the name and image of Aton and Ikhnaton. Ikhnaton died at the age of thirty, having failed to accomplish his dreams, and his successor, Tutankhamen, reinstated the old gods and feast days and returned the capital to Thebes.

The devotion to Truth demonstrated by these rulers is typical of the qualities required for true Messengers of God. Ikhnaton's virtue was not in military victory or in political bargaining with the priests of Amon, but in his total lack of compromise with error.

His devotion to his queen was often publicly displayed and depicted in Egyptian art. The akashic records shows that Ikhnaton had a great sense of mission to outpicture the principles of the Brotherhood, not only in his private life, but also in the laws of Egypt. The culture that the king and queen brought forth at Tel el Amarna in art, in poetry and in music was under the direction of the Brotherhood, inspired from Venus and the ancient lands of Mu and Atlantis when these civilizations were at their height.

The bust of Nefertiti that can be seen today in a museum in Berlin is considered to be one of the masterpieces of the Amarna age. When one compares the portraits of Ikhnaton and Nefertiti with our present-day photographs, he will see how the characteristics of the soul are outpictured again and again in the physical form; indeed the physical form is the counterpart of the etheric. The resemblance may carry over for many embodiments until the traits change.

During the Time of Jesus' Mission

The next embodiments we wish to relate are those during the time of Jesus' mission. Mark was then **John Mark,** the son of Mary of Jerusalem. He authored the gospel that bears his name, known as the Gospel of Deeds, because it is based more on the works than on the words of Jesus. This emphasis on action is typical of the first-ray consciousness, which our twin flames embody.

Mark was just a young boy when Jesus and his disciples celebrated the Last Supper in his mother's home. His mother was among the most devoted of the women who followed Jesus.

Having been raised in the Essene tradition and having witnessed the power of the Holy Spirit on Pentecost, Mark became the chief disciple of Peter. Mark founded the church in Alexandria, which was to become the foremost exponent of the deeper mysteries of Christianity, and he was later martyred there by being dragged through the streets.

During the same period, Elizabeth was embodied as **Martha,** the sister of Mary and Lazarus. In this relationship, Mary was a focus for the devotion of the heart, the path of the mystic, whereas Martha represented the reasoning of the mind, the path of the occult. In Lazarus we find the heart and head united in the action of the hand of service to Christ.

Mary and Martha of Bethany

In the account of Lazarus' resurrection in the eleventh chapter of John's Gospel, we read in verse twenty that "Martha, as soon as she heard that Jesus was coming, went and met him, but Mary sat still in the house." Their attitudes symbolize the outgoing searching mind contrasted by the heart that rests in the knowledge of the kingdom that is within.

Martha expressed her faith when she said unto Jesus, "Lord, if thou hadst been here, my brother had not died. But I know, that even now, whatsoever thou wilt ask of God, God will give it thee." [30] Jesus said unto her, "I am the resurrection, and the life: he that believeth in me, though he were dead, yet shall he live: And whosoever liveth and believeth in me shall never die. Believest thou this?"[31] Martha's reply again anchors the ray of faith that has been her greatest strength through her many embodiments. Without hesitating she replied, "Yea, Lord: I believe that thou art the Christ, the Son of God, which should come into the world."[32]

The same contrast is noted in the events that took place during the supper prepared for Jesus in the home of Lazarus. Martha, "careful and troubled about many things," bears the responsibilities of the household, while Mary, whose every thought is devotion to her Lord, sits at his feet, oblivious of the cares of the world. Both attitudes are essential in Christian service—Mary receiving the energies and the teachings of the Christ, and Martha making them practical through the organization and administration in daily life.

Very early in our mission it was revealed to us that Mary, the sister of Martha, was a previous embodiment of Mary Baker Eddy, the founder of Christian Science. We find in her *Science and Health with Key to the Scriptures* her recollections of the intimate teachings imparted by Jesus on the many occasions when he sojourned in the home of these friends.

The sacred mysteries that were taught to Mary, Martha and Lazarus during their last supper with Jesus before his crucifixion were anchored in their four lower bodies as a record of cosmic Truth they were to bring forth at a later time. Lazarus reembodied in the twentieth century as a teacher of Christian Science whose ministry of healing has touched countless lives.

David S. Robb, who pioneered the teachings of Christian Science in Canada and knew Mrs. Eddy very well, quoted her as having said, "In Christian Science I have brought forth the ABC's of spiritual truth, but there are others who will come after me to reveal a fuller explanation of the laws which Jesus taught."

The words of this great pioneer in metaphysics ring from akasha as prophetic of that which would be released less than one hundred years after the publication of her *Science and Health* in 1866.

Mrs. Eddy was well aware of the fact that the dispensations of Hierarchy allow for only a certain amount of Truth to be revealed within a given period of time; each advancing decade and century provides the opportunity for greater and greater Light and understanding to be released from the retreats of the Brotherhood. These dispensations are governed by cosmic law, and they cannot be altered; hence one hundred years from now we can expect the unfoldment of mysteries not even glimpsed by the prophets of this era.

The mission of these three lifestreams has formed a threefold flame down through the centuries, and the love of Mary and Martha has become the essence of wisdom, a legacy for the age, while it was the destiny of Lazarus to go forth and proclaim the highest teachings of the Christ and to demonstrate those teachings by the actions of the Law.

Origen of Alexandria

In his next embodiment, we find Mark as **Origen of Alexandria** (c.185–c.254). Writer, teacher and Church Father, he drew forth from the Bible the very fire of the teachings of Christ and made these teachings understandable to his contemporaries. Butterworth notes in his introduction to *Origen: On First Principles:*

"Origen is one of those figures, none too common even in Church history, of whose character we can say that we know nothing but what is good. He was humble and free from envy, caring neither for power nor wealth. He bore unmerited suffering, from friends and foes alike, without complaint. His life, from beginning to end, was hard and strenuous. His courage never failed, and he died, in reality, a martyr's death. He loved truth with a sincerity and devotion rarely equaled, and never excelled. Intellectually he stands pre-eminent and alone, towering above the Greek fathers as Augustine towers above the Latins. The wide sweep of his thought is amazing. He contemplates a universe, not small and narrow as was that of many of his contemporaries, but of immense magnitude, world following world in almost infinite sequence, from the dim primeval epoch when God created all souls equal and free, to the far-off event when after countless vicissitudes of degradation and suffering they shall return to their original unity and perfection, and 'God shall be all in all.' "[33]

Many of Origen's beliefs parallel those being released by the Masters today. In his *De Principiis,* or *On First Principles,* he teaches that God is Spirit, that he is a Trinity of Father, Son and Holy Spirit. He discusses the Fall of Lucifer and the fact that man is free to rise or fall by the gift of free will.

He proclaims that the sun, moon and stars are living beings. He believes in the pre-existence of souls and in re-embodiment. He says that Matter was created by God and that the use of bodies will cease, that the bodily nature returns to non-existence (to Spirit), just as formerly it did not exist.

Origen speaks of the Christ as the Mediator between God and man. He also refers to a place of instruction for souls after death. He concludes that since the teaching of the Church includes the doctrine of the righteous judgment of God, man must have a free will to choose to live a good life by avoiding sin.

Origen and his teachings were supposedly condemned by the Fifth Ecumenical Council convened by the Emperor

Justinian in A.D. 553, although modern authorities are un-
decided as to whether they were actually anathematized. The
Catholic Encyclopedia states that there is no proof that the
Pope approved the fifteen anathemas against Origen, and that
these were later mistaken for a decree of the Council.[34]

Justinian accomplished his purpose in part, but the
Ascended Masters have also accomplished theirs. The concepts that were revealed by the Christ and the Brotherhood
to Origen are today being brought forth through him to be
organized as sacred scripture for the coming two-thousand-
year cycle, not displacing that which has gone before but
adding to it, breaking (explaining) the Word and building
upon the foundations that have been laid by all who have gone
before.

The students of Ascended Master Law will enjoy reading
Origen: On First Principles, edited by G. W. Butterworth.
Page by page they will see the realities of Ascended Master
Law unfolding through the lens of a higher consciousness
than that of Origen. They will see the universal message of the
Brotherhood that belongs to no single age but to all ages, to
no single prophet but to all prophets. That it was suppressed
by the powers of darkness during the Dark Ages is not sur-
prising, for we have been told that the Lamb of God was slain
from the foundation of the world.[35]

Therefore, our rejoicing must be in the knowledge that we
have fulfilled our divine plan, and if perchance some souls
have been saved through our labors, we may stamp above the
akasha of that effort, "MISSION ACCOMPLISHED." Of all the
things that are in the world, only the Word of God is Real and
permanent. All else is subject to decay—including the paper
upon which it is written. "For all flesh is as grass, and all the
glory of man as the flower of grass. The grass withereth, and
the flower thereof falleth away: But the Word of the Lord

endureth forever."[36]

Those who hold the office of Messenger are committed first to the Word and then to the preservation of Truth in the Word as it passes from God to man. May we humbly echo the words of one of the greatest Messengers who has ever graced the planet by his presence: "To this end are we born, for this cause came we into the world—that we should bear witness to the Truth."[37]

The student will also enjoy reading the life of **Saint Bonaventure,** another of Mark's embodiments in which he expounds the teachings of the Masters in the same tradition that he began on Atlantis and has carried forward with ever-increasing clarity in many succeeding lifetimes, most of which we are not at liberty to discuss.

Recent Embodiments of the Messengers

In concluding this examination of our past preparation, we should like to mention briefly some of our more recent embodiments. Mark served as a Messenger for the Brotherhood in the capacity of poet laureate when he was the American poet **Henry Wadsworth Longfellow** (1807–1882).

In that embodiment he passed the initiation, not only of recording the teachings of the Brotherhood, but also of recording them in poetry, which is the language of the angels. His poems established within his forcefield and consciousness the patterns of the Master El Morya, who dictated through him at that time, the Master himself having previously been embodied as the poet Thomas Moore. Longfellow's poetic rhythm is evident in the decree patterns that have been dictated through Mark.

The poet's ability to tap the akashic records—not only of his past embodiments but also of events taking place in his time—enabled him to write epic poems that have been loved by millions because of their essential Truth. Concerning "The Golden Legend," he said, "The story upon which it is founded seems to me to surpass all other legends in beauty and significance. It exhibits, amid the corruption of the Middle Ages, the virtue of disinterestedness and self-sacrifice, and the power of Faith, Hope and Charity, sufficient for all the exigencies of life and death."

Longfellow referred to Faith, Hope and Charity as proper nouns—perhaps as virtues, but more likely as guardian angels, which, in reality, they are. Lucifer also plays a part in "The Golden Legend." He was as real a personality to Longfellow as he was to Origen.

Longfellow was able to enter into the spirit of **Hiawatha** in his poem by that name because he himself had been embodied as that great Indian leader.

In his poem "The Sermon of St. Francis" Longfellow alludes to the saint's role as a Messenger of God:

> "O brother birds," St. Francis said,
> "Ye come to me and ask for bread,
> But not with bread alone to-day
> Shall ye be fed and sent away.
>
> "Ye shall be fed, ye happy birds,
> With manna of celestial words;
> Not mine, though mine they seem to be,
> Not mine, though they be spoken through me."

In his poem "Rain in Summer" he shows how the gift of spiritual sight common to Messengers reveals the round of rebirth as part of the universal wheel of Life:

> Thus the seer,
> With vision clear,

Sees forms appear and disappear,
In the perpetual round of strange,
Mysterious change
From birth to death, from death to birth;
From earth to heaven, from heaven to earth;
Till glimpses more sublime,
Of things, unseen before,
Unto his wondering eyes reveal
The Universe, as an immeasurable wheel
Turning forever
In the rapid and rushing river of Time.

Longfellow's last poem was written in 1882 in honor of another Messenger of the Brotherhood, Hermes Trismegistus. In it he alludes to his belief in reembodiment:

Was he one or many, merging
Name and fame in one,
Like a stream, to which, converging,
Many streamlets run?...

Who shall call his dreams fallacious?
Who has searched or sought
All the unexplored and spacious
Universe of thought?...

Trismegistus! Three times greatest!
How thy name sublime
Has descended to this latest
Progeny of time!

Elizabeth was **Mary Storer Potter,** Longfellow's first wife. She died on November 29, 1835, when they were abroad for his study in Amsterdam.

So our twin flames were allowed to be together briefly before the karma of world service intervened. Longfellow was later to prophesy of the mission that not only his twin flame but all representatives of the Divine Mother were to fulfill in the coming century:

> A lady with a lamp shall stand
> In the great history of the land,
> A noble type of good,
> Heroic womanhood.[38]

For duty called her to Vienna—her destiny to become **Elisabeth, Empress of Austria** (1837–1898). In her role as the wife of Francis Joseph, Emperor of Austria and king of Hungary, she was tutored by the Master El Morya in the art of government and in the intrigue and treachery of power politics—the actual cause of her assassination in 1898.

She studied at the same time with Saint Germain, whose retreat in Transylvania (then in Hungary) was within that kingdom, which she was called upon to rule by popular acclaim. (Both Mark and Elizabeth have been Saint Germain's pupils during and between many embodiments.)

The queen was trained in administration and in dealing with people of every level of society—including "the rulers of the darkness of this world."[39] Her training in the initiations of the Brotherhood took preeminence over her Catholic upbringing. Elisabeth's Greek tutor recorded in his *Vienna Diary:*

"Speaking of the difference between culture and civilization, she says: 'Civilization is reading, culture is the thoughts.... Everyone has culture within himself as heritage of all his preexistences, absorbs it with every breath and in this lies the great unity.'... Of Dante and other great ones, she says: 'They are souls, who, from ages past have come anew to earth to continue their work and to anticipate the development of others still to come.... Our innermost being is more valuable than all titles and honors. These are colored rags with which we try to cover our nudities. Whatever is of value in us we bring from our previous lives that were spiritual.' "[40]

It was through the Austro-Hungarian Empire that the Brotherhood made their final attempts to unite Europe. Although these failed to stem the mounting control of Europe's governments by dark powers both within and without, the democratic reforms instituted by Franz Joseph were "more rational than anything seen in Europe before or since."[41]

Mark Prophet entered his final life on December 24, 1918. He ascended on February 26, 1973, and is known today as the Ascended Master Lanello. Elizabeth was born April 8, 1939, in Redbank, New Jersey, and continues her service as a Messenger from the unascended state.

And so the Messengers, "the other two, the one on this side of the bank of the river, and the other on that side of the bank of the river," remain the servants of the Lord and of his children in Spirit and in Matter "for a time, times, and an half," as Daniel wrote, that "many shall be purified and made white, and tried" and that "the wise shall understand."[42]

Numerous embodiments have been shown to us by the Masters for our training in this life. If they were all recorded in this chapter, the student would have a century-by-century account of our service to the earth. The saga of twin flames, it is a history that has repeated itself in the lives of many. It is based on centuries of dedication to Truth, training in the temples of the Brotherhood, and service to mankind born out of love for our Creator.

Higher Service

It is not unusual for a Messenger to be of the evolutions of another planet. Jesus himself and many of the world's great thinkers and leaders in every field of endeavor have come forth with the message of the Brotherhood as volunteers from other planets in this system and even other systems.

In 1965, Casimir Poseidon announced that we had been offered the guardianship of the Lake Titicaca Retreat after its two current Hierarchs, the God and Goddess Meru, have been advanced in cosmic service. In preparation for that position in Hierarchy, we were given a crown of illumination and were made Prince and Princess of the Holy Order of God and Goddess Meru. We are to be overshadowed by these two great beings of Light throughout the remainder of this embodiment in order that we may absorb illumination's ray.[43]

The Messengers Bear the Brunt of Opposition

As Messengers we have become the target of much opposition. The Maha Chohan has said: "There are individuals today upon this planetary body, who have through the years in the name of Christ committed acts against these beloved Messengers, against this activity and against other activities of Light. They sometimes feel that they can escape with impunity the actual fruit of their acts simply because they do not clearly see that they have suffered any punishment whatsoever as a result of these acts.

"Let men understand clearly, then, that those who have acted against the Light and those who are engaged in the practice of witchcraft upon this planetary body may suddenly find that all of their activities are brought to a grinding halt by the Law, which itself acts in the name of love, to cut off from the earth the seed of those who will continually bend their wills toward evil.

"Therefore, tonight I utter a decree. Heed, O Keeper of the Scrolls, our call. By cosmic decree, in the name of the I AM

Presence in the heart of the Great Central Sun, whosoever shall hurt or attempt to hurt our Messengers henceforward and forever shall receive tenfold from all that the Law has required hitherto and it shall come to pass with suddenness and they shall find out that many of them shall be cut off from among the living, for the patience of God has ended even this day against those activities that are based entirely on sensuality, entirely on the heeding to carnal spirits and a listening to forces of darkness without any justification whatsoever.

"Therefore, wheresoever there is an activity against the Light upon this planet, whether it be against The Summit Lighthouse, its Messengers or against any activity of Light, we are going to enforce the Law as we have never enforced it before, and I tell you the devils themselves shall tremble because the Spirit of the living Christ has stood forth as in days of old when the power of the Christ went forth against Mainin the High Priest, and he himself did cry out in agony as the great cosmic Light fell even as the Word fell forth in the Temple of Belshazzar.[44]

"My decree is ended. The full implementation of it can be seen at inner levels. It is involved and covers 110 pages of script that are calculated to set forth the exact manner in which all of these actions shall take place."[45]

El Morya has also spoken to those who criticize the Messengers: "Why will you take your time to criticize the action of those who are serving the Light when your own lives, in many cases, are but shambles? Why will some of you come here with the idea of searching out and discovering, if you can, some fraud in these blessed Messengers? I tell you, dear hearts, that we are aware of every activity of every individual. Discover the fraud in yourselves first, and then you will find the means to eradicate it, for I tell you that the Light of God that never fails is a most penetrating Light and, if we would, we could expose publicly the names of those who have heaped insult after insult upon those who have nobly given their lives and their energies to God for his glory and whose every thought is the manifestation of the kingdom of God upon earth.

"Dear ones of the Light, if you would be wise, then, *be* wise. If you will be foolish, separate yourselves from us, for we will not even sully our skirts much longer with those who continually try the very patience of our souls in the Ascended state by professing to love us, and then in secret doing those things that are of great despite to the very purposes for which we serve."[46]

On this same subject, the Great Divine Director has said: "We have poured forth to you spiritual food throughout this conference, and little do you dream of the energies that have attacked these beloved Messengers to prevent the dictations from coming through with smoothness, with clarity and with peace so that their blessed hearts could rejoice in knowing that they had performed most beautifully according to requirements made of their lifestreams.

"Well, precious ones of the Light, you must always remember that the prow of the ship and the bow must sometimes take a ferocious beating during a storm. Why is this so? Because as it parts the waves, it is the instrument that contacts them first.

"You must understand, then, that these Messengers are also instruments through which we contact you. But we contact them first with our energy, and then the energy flows out into your world.

"Quite naturally, then, just as an arrowhead that penetrates substance will also receive a great deal more of a blow than the feathers that are at the shaft end of the arrow, you can plainly see that these beloved Messengers will from time to time receive the brunt of a physical attack as well as a psychic attack, mounted against them in order to disturb the equanimity of their beings and thus prevent the manifestation of the radiance we desire to furnish to every student of the Light.

"I want you to stand behind these Messengers and support them, not in the mistakes that any human being may make—in God's name, if you yourselves are perfect, then cast a stone at them—but in the sense of the great God-reality that they represent.

"And, after all, is not this same God-reality also present in yourselves? What, then, shall we do? Glorify the errors of the world or glorify the honor that God has already conferred upon all?

"None of you would particularly welcome an attack against yourselves. None of you would particularly rejoice because you were suffering some vicious misinterpretation of your attitudes. Well, then, precious ones, will you understand with me that I would like to make you an elite guard for these Messengers. I would like to establish in you a focus of protection for them so that their work can improve each conference and every day, and thus will you not also be blessed? Will you not also receive mighty assistance? I think you will.

"Let me explain to you that you have no concept, in the main, of the difficulty in actually contacting and holding contact with our level. If I were for example to transfer to you, even momentarily, some of the viciousness that has been directed against the Messengers, you would be amazed what a change it would make in your life. If you think you have troubles now, some of you would be utterly amazed at the troubles you would have then; and the reason I say this is to secure greater support for them against the problems that they encounter in the service of the Light."[47]

Other Messengers

El Morya gives some of the history of Messengers who have been sent in recent centuries: "The testing of the Messengers is the testing of the decibels and of the cycling of the energies of infinity through form and consciousness. Where there is Light uncontaminated by the darkness of ego and ego manipulation, where there is a dazzling sun of glory and real contact with Hierarchy through the power of the spoken Word, where there is the conveyance of the Christ Mind, there stands the Messenger of the Great White Brotherhood.

"And so the messenger of the covenant shall suddenly come to his temple.[48] His temple is the heart of man. He is the Christed one standing at the altar of the sacred fire to read the proclamation of deliverance—the deliverance of the soul into the arms of Almighty God. And so the Christed one releases the statement of the Law even as that statement has been sent forth by the Messengers whom we have chosen and ordained.

"In 1876, Helena Petrovna Blavatsky was ordered by the Master Kuthumi and me, then known as the Masters K.H. and M., to write *Isis Unveiled.* Later she was given the responsibility of imparting *The Secret Doctrine* to the world. Commissioned by Jesus the Christ, the Ascended Master Hilarion and Mother Mary, Mary Baker Eddy was given certain revelations which she set forth in *Science and Health with Key to the Scriptures.* Though at times beset with their own preconceptions and the burden of the mass consciousness, these witnesses codified the Truth and the Law of East and West as the culmination of thousands of years of their souls' distillations of the Spirit.

"Such Messengers are not trained in a day or a year or a lifetime. Embodiment after embodiment, they sit at the feet of the Masters and receive the emanations of their mantle in the power of their word and example. A number of others who were selected to perform a similar service for Hierarchy failed in their initiations through the pride of the intellect and their unwillingness to submit identity totally unto the Flame. They have become thereby totally self-deluded and they continue to draw innocent souls into the chaos of their delusion.

"In the 1930s came the twin flames Guy W. Ballard and Edna Ballard imparting the sacred mystery of the Law of the I AM, further knowledge of Hierarchy, the invocation of the sacred fire, and the path of the ascension. Representatives tried and true of Saint Germain, they were commissioned to remain the only Messengers of the Hierarchy of the Aquarian age until mankind should redeem a certain portion of their karma.

"When that cycle was fulfilled, Saint Germain, together with the Darjeeling Council, sponsored Mark and Elizabeth Prophet to carry on the work not only of the Ballards and the I AM movement, but also of Nicholas and Helena Roerich. The Roerichs set forth the word of Morya destined to reach both the Russian and the American people with the energy and the enlightenment that should deter the red dragon[49] of World Communism. And so the Mother flame of Russia and the Mother flame of America converge in spirals of freedom and victory for the sons and daughters of God in both nations and in every nation upon earth.

"Hierarchy is no respecter of persons, of politics or of polemics. Hierarchy's call knows no barrier. It cannot be stayed by the iron curtain or by the iron wall that a mechanistic civilization has erected around the children of God. The beam of our eye is a laser beam; it is the action of the ruby ray. It goes straight to the heart of the devotee; and no hand and no force and no ideology can stay the will of the Master who sends forth that ray to call the souls of God home.

"Let those who reckon otherwise beware. For I have

spoken; and the Lord has said, 'So shall my word be that goeth forth out of my mouth: it shall not return unto me void, but it shall accomplish that which I please, and it shall prosper in the thing whereto I sent it.'"[50]

The Messengers at the End of the Age

We conclude this chapter with the interpretation of the eleventh chapter of the Book of Revelation. This is the Revelation of Jesus Christ, "sent and signified ... by his angel unto his servant John."[51] The following is the Word of the Lord concerning the Messengers:

And I will give power unto my two witnesses, and they shall prophesy a thousand two hundred and three-score days, clothed in sackcloth.

The Two Witnesses are twin flames who come forth in the last days as representatives of Alpha and Omega, the Father-Mother God, to teach and to demonstrate the Law of Christ-mastery on both the masculine and feminine rays. They are exemplars of the Law that all twin flames are destined to fulfill.

The periods of time mentioned throughout the Book of Revelation refer to initiatic intervals. The duration of the twin flames' prophecy, therefore, is measured according to the revolutions of the electrons and the cycles of the sun. The one thousand two hundred and threescore days, making a total of three and one half years, reveal that the Hierarchical position of the Messengers is at the point of the Christ between God and man (their position is that of the Christ Self of the souls evolving on the planet).

The number one symbolically stands for God, and seven stands for man. The number three and one half, which is half

of seven, indicates that the Messengers have vowed to stand as
the mouthpiece for the age—the point at which Truth passes
from God to man—in order that the covenant between each
man and his God might be fulfilled—as Above, so below.

The phrase "clothed in sackcloth" refers to the fact that
the Messengers are not without karma, for they must bear witness to the Truth that even those who have karma can become
the Christ.

These are the two olive trees, and the two candle-
sticks standing before the God of the earth.

In the mystical sense, the two olive trees and the two
candlesticks are a part of every man. They are the masculine
and feminine poles focusing through the sympathetic and
cerebral-spinal nervous systems in the physical body. In the
universal sense, the two olive trees and the two candlesticks
represent the peace and the Light that their Christ Selves bring
to all twin flames.

Thus, they outpicture the archetypal pattern of the masculine and feminine counterparts of the divine Mediator. In a
more specific sense, they are unascended initiates appointed to
serve as a liaison between Ascended and unascended members
of the Great White Brotherhood. The phrase "standing before
the God of the earth" refers to their position in the Hierarchy
under the Lord of the World.

And if any man will hurt them, fire proceedeth out
of their mouth, and devoureth their enemies: and if any
man will hurt them, he must in this manner be killed.

The fire that proceeds out of the mouth of the Messengers
is the sacred fire, the power of the spoken Word, which is
theirs by reason of their holy office. This fire transmutes the
energies that are directed not only against the representatives

of the Christ in every age, but also against the Light that
passes from God to man through their mission. By the law of
karma, those who intend harm against these servants of God
receive quick retribution, for the power of their spoken Word
is quicker than a two-edged sword.

mainly
symbolic?
2

> *These have power to shut heaven, that it rain not in
> the days of their prophecy: and have power over waters
> to turn them to blood, and to smite the earth with all
> plagues, as often as they will.*

This verse refers to the inner initiations in alchemy that the
Messengers must pass in order to quality for their office.

> *And when they shall have finished their testimony,
> the beast that ascendeth out of the bottomless pit shall
> make war against them, and shall overcome them, and
> kill them.*
>
> *And their dead bodies shall lie in the street of the
> great city, which spiritually is called Sodom and Egypt,
> where also our Lord was crucified.*
>
> *And they of the people and kindreds and tongues
> and nations shall see their dead bodies three days and an
> half, and shall not suffer their dead bodies to be put in
> graves.*

In order to qualify for the office, the Messengers must vow
before the Lords of Karma to make this total sacrifice. They
must be ready to surrender their life at any moment for the
sake of the kingdom and the salvation of man. When and how
that supreme sacrifice will be made is determined by the Lords
of Karma.

> *And they that dwell upon the earth shall rejoice over
> them, and make merry, and shall send gifts one to
> another; because these two prophets tormented them* 2.

that dwelt on the earth.

Here we see the hatred that all representatives of the Brotherhood and of the Christ must be prepared to meet. It was said of Jesus, "He is despised and rejected of men,"[52] and Jesus said of himself, "They hated without cause."[53] The carnal mind rejoices over the crucifixion of the Christ, for it thereby gains a temporal hold upon the consciousness of mankind.

> *And after three days and an half the Spirit of Life from God entered into them, and they stood upon their feet; and great fear fell upon them which saw them.*
>
> *And they heard a great voice from heaven saying unto them, Come up hither. And they ascended up to heaven in a cloud; and their enemies beheld them.*
>
> *And the same hour was there a great earthquake, and the tenth part of the city fell, and in the earthquake were slain of men seven thousand: and the remnant were affrighted, and gave glory to the God of heaven....*

All who would return to the consciousness of God must pass the initiations of the crucifixion, the resurrection and the ascension. These were outpictured in the life of Jesus and are described in chapter 2 of the third book of this series, *The Masters and the Spiritual Path*, and in chapter 3 of this book. Whether these rituals are performed publicly or in the Temple at Luxor, they are the prerequisites to Immortal Life. The Messengers' ascension is a matter of akashic record, whether or not it is actually witnessed from the physical octave.

Whenever an ascension takes place upon the earth, the balancing action of the Light raises the entire planet. Where there is discord or great density in the mass consciousness, the penetration of the Light may result in cataclysm; where the level of the mass consciousness is more spiritual, however, the action of the Light produces great waves of peace that emanate throughout the four lower bodies of mankind and the earth.

It is the destiny of the Messengers of Hierarchy to complete their round in the world of form and to ascend back to the Presence of God. As those who are chosen to represent the Brotherhood in every age complete their mission victoriously, so millions of others during cycles that follow are enabled to do likewise, because the Messengers have left their footprints in the sands of time.

And the seventh angel sounded; and there were great voices in heaven, saying, The kingdoms of this world are become the kingdoms of our Lord, and of his Christ; and he shall reign for ever and ever.

And the four and twenty elders, which sat before God on their seats, fell upon their faces, and worshipped God,

Saying, We give thee thanks, O Lord God Almighty, which art, and wast, and art to come; because thou hast taken to thee thy great power, and hast reigned.

And the nations were angry, and thy wrath is come, and the time of the dead, that they should be judged, and that thou shouldest give reward unto thy servants the prophets, and to the saints, and them that fear thy name, small and great; and shouldest destroy them which destroy the earth.

And the temple of God was opened in heaven, and there was seen in his temple the ark of his testament: and there were lightnings, and voices, and thunderings, and an earthquake, and great hail.[54]

Notes

Books referenced here are published by Summit University Press unless otherwise noted.

Introduction

1. John 14:16–17.
2. Mark 4:23–24.
3. II Cor. 3:18.
4. Ps. 104:16, 17; Matt. 13:31–32; Mark 4:30–32; Luke 13:18–19.
5. "And the LORD God said, Behold, the man is become as one of us, to know good and evil: and now, lest he put forth his hand, and take also of the tree of life, and eat, and live for ever: therefore the LORD God sent him forth from the garden of Eden" (Gen. 3:22–23).
6. I Cor. 15:50.
7. I Cor. 15:47.

Chapter 1 · The Law of Cycles

Opening quote: Ezek. 1:4–5.

1. Serapis Bey, Hierarch of Luxor, July 3, 1967, "The Discipline of God as the Manifestation of His Order."
2. A. Trevor Barker, comp., *The Mahatma Letters to A. P. Sinnett* (Pasadena Calif.: Theosophical University Press, 1923, reprint 1975), Letter XXII, p. 144.
3. *Merriam-Webster's Collegiate Dictionary*, 10th ed., s.v. "cycle."
4. Sanat Kumara, "The Space Within," *Pearls of Wisdom*, vol. 11, no. 25, June 23, 1968.
5. *The Mahatma Letters*, Letter XIII, pp. 70, 71.
6. Ibid., p. 71.
7. Bhagavata Purana, section 3, chapter 11.
8. Ibid.
9. Ibid.
10. Sir John Woodroffe, *The Garland of Letters: Studies in the Mantra-Sastra* (Pondicherry, India: Ganesh and Co., n.d.) p. 4.

11. John 14:6.
12. The Emerald Tablet, quoted in G. de Purucker, *Man in Evolution* (Pasadena, Calif.: Theosophical University Press, 1977), p. 26.
13. I Cor. 3:16.
14. Justinius, "Seraphic Meditations III," in Serapis Bey, *Dossier on the Ascension* (1979), p. 136.
15. Exod. 33:20 records an incomplete version of this ancient precept.
16. Saint Germain, "Endowed with the Potential for Immortality," *Pearls of Wisdom*, vol. 13, no. 44, November 1, 1970.
17. Ikhnaton had his artists depict the sun with rays terminating in the form of a hand, symbolizing the hand of God in action in the world of form.
18. The Epistle to the Hebrews speaks in a number of places of correspondences between earthly and heavenly patterns. For example, in 8:5, the author points out that "Moses was admonished of God when he was about to make the tabernacle: for, See, saith he, that thou make all things according to the pattern showed to thee in the mount."
19. Gen. 1:1–3.
20. John 1:1, 3.
21. Exod. 13:22.
22. Paul the Venetian, "Art Transcends an Era," *Pearls of Wisdom*, vol. 13, no. 43, October 25, 1970.
23. Rev. 3:15, 16.
24. Mark L. Prophet and Elizabeth Clare Prophet, *Saint Germain On Alchemy*, pp. 155–57.
25. Dan. 11:31; Matt. 24:15; Mark 13:14.
26. John 11:44.
27. I Thess. 5:21.
28. I Cor. 3:13.
29. Alpha, December 29, 1963, "A Sense of the Perfectionment of Your Mission."
30. Matt. 19:26.
31. Confucius, *Analects*, 9:16, quoted by Richard Wilhelm, trans., *The I Ching, or Book of Changes* (Princeton, N.J.: Princeton University Press, 1967), p. lv.
32. *Descend* means literally "Deity sends"; whereas *ascend* means "A-mega returns."
33. Vesta, "A Vision of Cosmic Reality for the Golden Age: The Banner of the Mother of the World Is Unfurled," *Pearls of Wisdom*, vol. 12, no. 1, January 5, 1969.
34. Archangel Gabriel, March 22, 1964, "The Breathing Immortal Presence of the Living Christ," in "The Radiant Word," *Pearls of Wisdom*, vol. 7, no. 13, March 27, 1964.
35. Isa. 1:18.
36. Rev. 21:5.
37. Gen. 22:17.
38. Ezek. 2:3.
39. Ezek. 3:17.
40. Ezek. 1:1, 3.
41. Ezek. 1:4.

42. Ps. 8:4.
43. John 15:5.
44. John 4:24.
45. Gen. 3:8.
46. Job 42:5.
47. Job 19:26.
48. Saint Germain, "Endowed with the Potential for Immortality," *Pearls of Wisdom,* vol. 13, no. 44, November 1, 1970.
49. Matt. 24:22.
50. I Cor. 15:31.
51. Mother Mary has said: "If you will ask, beloved ones, that the Electronic Presence of the Master of your choice be superimposed over your form before you go to sleep at night, you will find that throughout the hours of rest, all of the momentums of Light of that Ascended Being can be absorbed into your consciousness, into your four lower bodies, by the power of the electrode upon the spine—the ascending and descending currents of God that formulate the magnetic forcefield that is the focus of the great cycles of Infinity within your very own Presence." (Mark L. Prophet and Elizabeth Clare Prophet, *Mary's Message for a New Day* [2004], p. 324.)
52. Great Divine Director, "Leadership, Take an Uncompromising Stand for Righteousness!" *Pearls of Wisdom,* vol. 11, no. 36, September 8, 1968.
53. Gen. 18:20, 21.
54. Gen. 19:1–28.
55. Mark 13:2; Matt. 24:2; Luke 21:6.
56. Gautama Buddha, "In the Calm Knowing of the Sun Center of My Soul: The Sign of the Dark Cycle Set Aside Pending the Action of Israel and the Arab States," *Pearls of Wisdom,* vol. 12, no. 3, January 19, 1969.
57. Vesta, "A Vision of Cosmic Reality for the Golden Age," *Pearls of Wisdom,* vol. 13, no. 1, January 5, 1969.
58. Luke 23:28.
59. El Morya, August 17, 1969, "He Sustaineth All Things."
60. Gautama Buddha, "In the Calm Knowing of the Sun Center of My Soul."
61. Matt. 25:29, 30.
62. Luke 23:30.
63. Heb. 12:6.
64. El Morya, *Pearls of Wisdom,* vol. 7, no. 15, April 10, 1964.
65. Mark 8:36; Luke 9:25.
66. Vesta, October 12, 1970, "The Flame of the Whole Eye Consciousness."
67. "There is a tide in the affairs of men / Which, taken at the flood, leads on to fortune; / Omitted, all the voyage of their life / Is bound in shallows and in miseries" (Shakespeare, *Julius Caesar,* act iv. Sc. 3).
68. Eccl. 3:2, 4.
69. The Great Divine Director, April 18, 1976, "Direction for Diagramming Your Ascension."
70. John 14:6.

Chapter 2 · Planes of Consciousness

Opening quote: Matt. 6:22.
1. Prov. 23:7.
2. "Blessed are the pure in heart: for they shall see God" (Matt. 5:8).
3. Paul wrote to the Corinthians, "The last enemy that shall be destroyed is death" (I Cor. 15:26).
4. Ps. 121:8.
5. Gen. 28:12.
6. This concept is seen in the Epistle to the Hebrews, which says, "See, saith he, that thou make all things according to the pattern showed to thee in the mount" (8:5).
7. Amaryllis, Goddess of Spring, December 6, 1970, "I See Men as Trees Walking...."
8. Matt. 11:12.
9. Mother Mary, *Pearls of Wisdom,* vol. 11, no. 39, September 29, 1968.
10. Matt. 5:8.
11. Gal. 6:7.
12. Matt. 6:23.
13. II Kings 6:15–18.
14. Goddess of Purity, September 13, 1970, "The Flame in the Center of the Crystal."

Chapter 3 · Immortality

Opening quote: Gen. 3:22–24.
1. Gen. 2:17.
2. Ezek. 18:20, 22, 24.
3. Rev. 1:1.
4. See Rev. 20:12–15.
5. Rev. 2:11; 20:6, 14; 21:8.
6. Rev. 19:20; 20:10, 14, 15.
7. Gen. 2:9; 3:22, 24; Rev. 2:7; 22:2, 14.
8. Rev. 22:1.
9. Luke 18:18.
10. I Cor. 15:26.
11. Acts 17:23.
12. Ps. 16:10.
13. John 10:10.
14. In the book *Unveiled Mysteries,* Saint Germain gives the following explanation of Eden and of mankind's departure from his original state of perfection: "In ages past, humanity manifested Perfection in every way. This former condition of the race has been chronicled by historians as the Garden of Eden—Eden or E-Don—meaning Divine Wisdom. As the conscious attention or the outer activity of the mind was allowed to rest upon the world of the physical senses, the 'Divine Wisdom'—the All-Knowing activity of consciousness—became clouded or covered over and the 'Cosmic Divine Plan' of the individual's life became submerged. Perfection and conscious control by mankind over all form was hidden

and forgotten along with it.

"Man became sense-conscious, instead of God-conscious, and so manifested *that* to which his attention was directed and which he thought most upon. He *deliberately* and *consciously* turned his back upon the Perfection and Dominion with which the Father endowed him in the beginning. He created his own experiences of lack, limitation, and discord of every kind. He identified himself with the part instead of the whole, and of course imperfection was the result.

"All mankind's limitation is the result the individual's own misuse of the God-attribute of free will. He compels himself to live within his own creations until, by the direct volition of the outer activity of his mind, he again consciously looks back to his Royal beginning—God, the Great Source of All. When this occurs, man will begin to remember *That* which he once was, and may become again—whensoever he chooses to look once more at the 'Great, Cosmic, Blueprint'—of Himself" (Godfré Ray King, *Unveiled Mysteries* [Schaumburg, Ill.: Saint Germain Press, 1982], pp. 85–86).

15. Rev. 22:1–2.
16. Kuthumi, "Threefold Flame," in Jesus and Kuthumi, *Corona Class Lessons* (1986), pp. 338–39.
17. Kuthumi, "Alchemy," in Jesus and Kuthumi, *Corona Class Lessons,* pp. 354–55.
18. Serapis Bey, July 3, 1967.
19. Sir Edwin Arnold, trans., *The Song Celestial or Ghagavad-Gita* (London: Routledge and Kegan Paul, 1948), p. 9.
20. I Cor. 9:27.
21. Phil. 4:8, 9.
22. The Serpents were an order of angels on the Second Ray under Archangel Jophiel's command. They fell from grace when they tempted twin flames in Paradise to depart from the covenants of the LORD God. As their punishment, they were cast out of heaven into the earth, henceforth to wear the bodies of mortals. And the LORD God said unto the serpent, "Because thou hast done this, thou art cursed above all cattle, and above every beast of the field; upon thy belly shalt thou go, and dust shalt thou eat all the days of thy life: and I will put enmity between thee and the woman, and between thy seed and her seed; it shall bruise thy head, and thou shalt bruise his heel" (Gen. 3:14, 15). These angels were called Serpent because they were masters of the Kundalini, or life force.
23. Gen. 2:15–17, 3:1–6.
24. Gen. 3:7–13, 22–24.
25. Gen. 3:14–21.
26. Jude 4, 6–13.
27. II Cor. 6:2.
28. Heb. 10:26–27.
29. All people carry a magnetic forcefield that is determined by the rate of vibration of their own individual thoughts and feelings and records of past lives, both being recorded in the "electronic circle" or "electronic belt" of each lifestream. We speak of "personal magnetism" or a

"magnetic personality." This is the intangible quality made up of the combination of many complex factors of the ego. However, there is only one true magnetism that is desirable, and that is the magnetism of the Christ, who is the Polestar of each man's being. All else is the glitter and glamour of the human—the maya of imperfection that should be handled daily.

For the purposes of simplification, we have categorized four types of animal magnetism. The records of personal imperfection in each one are the open doors through which these forces enter, gathering more of their kind from the accumulation of the mass karma of the race.

Malicious animal magnetism works through the subconscious, the etheric body. It is malice aforethought—conscious, willful and directed evil such as the many forms of hatred and jealousy that are the foundations of most criminal acts.

Ignorant animal magnetism is the Antichrist—the mass effluvia of human creation that opposes the expansion of the Christ Light throughout the world. Problems connected with mechanical failures and electrical mishaps can often be traced to this form of animal magnetism.

Sympathetic animal magnetism works through the emotional body and thus vibrates on the level of the astral plane. Human sympathy, personal attachments and involvements not based upon the Christ are among the manifestations of sympathetic animal magnetism.

Delicious animal magnetism works through the physical body and involves overindulgence in the gratification of one or more of the five senses.

Family mesmerism is one manifestation of animal magnetism; it involves the exertion of unwholesome control of one individual over another in the name of family ties. It is human attachment based on blood ties rather than spiritual ties.

30. Mars in its true state is the planet that represents the Divine Mother and the base-of-the-spine chakra (muladhara). The messenger has described Mars as "the white sphere of intense fiery energy of the Divine Mother." Long ago, the evolutions of Mars took that pure white light of the Mother and perverted it in war and misuses of the sacred fire. Through the misuse of free will and the base-of-the-spine chakra, they perverted the Mother Light in what we call the "Martian misqualifications." War and other violent conflicts also come through the vibration and aura of Mars.

Astrologers see Mars as the planet of action based on desire. The messenger has explained: "Mars triggers energy that brings action, but whatever your desires are, that is where your energy will go, and that is the type of action you will engage in." She teaches that by hitching our desires to the star of our mighty I AM Presence, we can ride and subdue Mars—we can "ride the bull" and take advantage of the true creative fires of Mars, the pure white fire of the Divine Mother.

The messenger has counseled us that each time we see a Mars configuration in our own astrology, we must determine to have a "Martian victory" in order to not be overcome by the perversions. Through mastering the Martian energies, we can gain our victory in

⟩ the white fire of the Mother.

31. Ezek. 18:4, 20.
32. Approximately every 2,150 years the earth passes through an age corresponding to one of the twelve signs of the zodiac. The length of an age is determined by a phenomenon called the precession of the equinoxes. A new age begins when the position of the sun in the heavens at the time of the spring equinox moves from one constellation to the next. We are currently in the time of transition from Pisces to Aquarius.
33. See Jesus Christ, May 31, 1984, "The Mystery School of Lord Maitreya," in *Pearls of Wisdom,* vol. 27, no. 36, July 8, 1984.
34. Matt. 22:2–14.
35. Matt. 11:12.
36. Rom. 8:28.
37. As recorded in the British film *Becket,* when Henry II, king of England, asked Thomas Becket, "Did you start to love God?" Becket responded, "I started to love the honor of God." (The film, produced by Shepperton Studios, was based on the 1959 play *Becket, or The Honour of God,* by Jean Anouilh.)
38. James 1:8.
39. Exod. 20:3.
40. I Cor. 9:24; Phil. 3:14.
41. The Maha Chohan, June 26, 1994, "The Journey of a Lifetime," in *Pearls of Wisdom,* vol. 37, no. 28, July 10, 1994.
42. In reality, there is no duality, even on the physical plane; but the difference in vibratory rate of Matter and Spirit makes them appear as opposites. Actually, Matter and Spirit are one, for they are derived from the same essence—the energy of God in feminine and masculine polarity. That which creates so-called duality is the mist of misqualified substance that imposes an energy-veil on True Being. Matter is etherealized (i.e., stepped up in vibratory rate) when the dross of human consciousness is removed by the sacred fire from the "wide open spaces" between the electrons. This process, known as transmutation, brings about the spiritualization of all creation—the return to wholeness.
43. Dan. 3.
44. I Cor. 3:13.
45. I Cor. 3:14–15.
46. Dan. 1:20.
47. Dan. 3:13–30.
48. Job 19:26.
49. Dan. 3:22, 25, 27.
50. The function of fire is purification. Physical fire is merely a stepping down of the sacred fire. That which is achieved by physical fire on the physical plane is achieved by the sacred fire on the astral, mental and etheric planes. The sacred fire, when invoked, also affects the physical plane either through a gradual or a sudden step-up of the vibratory rate of the electrons in their orbital paths around nuclei suns. This step-up induces the throwing-off into the sacred fire of misqualified substance that is lodged in the "wide-open spaces" between the atoms and electrons. The

greater the amount of misqualified substance thrown into the sacred fire, the greater the acceleration of the whirling electrons. This is the ascension process that goes on each time the disciple invokes the sacred fire until his whole body is "full of light." But, as Jesus said, his eye must be "single" (Matt. 6:22). This means that the disciple cannot retain the Light he invokes unless he sheds the consciousness of duality, the consciousness of an existence apart from God.

51. John 5:30.
52. Lanto, "The Memory of the Soul," in Mark L. Prophet and Elizabeth Clare Prophet, *Understanding Yourself* (1999), pp. 151–52.
53. Keepers of the Flame receive graduated monthly lessons in Cosmic Law dictated by the Ascended Masters to their messengers Mark L. Prophet and Elizabeth Clare Prophet.
54. Matt. 24:22.
55. Serapis Bey, July 3, 1967.
56. God Meru, July 6, 1969.
57. Gen. 6:3.
58. Matt. 25:30.
59. Rev. 4:4.
60. See Dan. 5:27.
61. Ezek. 33:11.
62. It is from the lake of fire that the images of hell-fire and eternal damnation have been spawned by the dark forces bent on terrifying humanity with concepts of a god of wrath, mercilessly punishing humanity for their sins.
63. Rev. 12:11.
64. Matt. 25:41.
65. For the story of Saint Germain's appearances as le Comte de St. Germain, see Mark L. Prophet and Elizabeth Clare Prophet, *Saint Germain On Alchemy,* pp. xi–xxxi.
66. Luke 9:29–32; Mark 9:2–4; Matt. 17:2, 3.
67. I Cor. 15:36, 40–45.
68. This plane of the astral belt has been called "purgatory."
69. Those who caused the sinking of Atlantis were not permitted to come forth from the astral belt until the twentieth century. While in that state of purgatory for a period of almost twelve thousand years, they have heard the sermons of many sons and daughters of God.
70. Matt. 27:46; Mark 15:34.
71. John 11:25; Jesus, April 6, 1969.
72. The resurrection flame vibrates at a velocity just beneath that of the pure white Light of the ascension flame; hence, the colors of all of the rays are still visible as a mother-of-pearl luster.
73. One of the reasons that the Trial by Fire for unprofitable servants is held on Sirius is that the record of the second death might not be left upon the planet to create in those evolving here a negative spiral of depression that would be a deterrent to their victory and give impetus to the suicide momentum.
74. Rev. 12:10.
75. Cyclopea, December 30, 1973, "The Sign of the Crystal Sword and the

All-Seeing Eye."
76. John 8:58.
77. Exod. 3:1–6.
78. II John 1:12; John 15:11.
79. John 15:11; 16:24.
80. "I the LORD thy God am a jealous God." Exod. 10:2; 34:14; Deut. 4:23–24; 5:6–9; 6:14–15; Josh. 24:19–20.
81. Ps. 2:4; 59:8.
82. In his dictation on October 10, 1971, the Great Divine Director gave the following teaching: "The mighty I AM Presence has the authority and the power to instantaneously arrest and reverse any cycle and to cause a complete erasing, a disintegration of it, right back to the twelve o'clock line.... I say to you, you must demand and command it in the name of the Christ—that every single cycle of every single cell and atom within your form that is not outpicturing the perfect cycles of the Christ consciousness is now dissolved, is now arrested and turned back by the authority of your God Presence! If you will but make that invocation each morning, you will find in a very short time that only the cycles of Immortal Life, and your divine plan fulfilled, and your ascension will prevail."
83. See Lord Maitreya, "The Overcoming of Fear through Decrees," in Mark L. Prophet and Elizabeth Clare Prophet, *The Science of the Spoken Word*, pp. 13–32.
84. Matt. 6:33; Luke 12:31.
85. Lanello, February 26, 1992, "How to Ascend," in *Pearls of Wisdom*, vol. 35, no. 10, March 8, 1992.
86. Phil. 2:5.
87. Serapis Bey, "Classes at the Ascension Temple at Luxor: To Prepare the Soul to Be the Tabernacle of the Mother Flame," in Elizabeth Clare Prophet, *The Opening of the Temple Doors* (2003), p. 52.
88. Serapis Bey, *Dossier on the Ascension*, pp. 166–67.
89. Ibid., pp. 164–65.
90. The Ascended Masters teach that in the ritual of the ascension, the soul is united with the white-fire body of the I AM Presence. This does not require the raising of the physical body; the soul itself may take flight from the mortal coil and be translated through the ascension process. In order to ascend, the candidate must have balanced at least 51 percent of his karma. In order to make a physical ascension, he must have balanced between 95 and 100 percent of his karma. When a physical ascension takes place, the physical body is transformed by and superseded by the Ascended Master Light Body. During the ascension ritual, the soul becomes permanently clothed with this Body, also called the "wedding garment," or the Deathless Solar Body. Serapis Bey describes the process in the quotes included in this chapter.

In a dictation given October 2, 1989, the Ascended Master Rex told us that those who are called to the physical ascension must have had many thousands of years of preparation. Today most people whose souls qualify for the ritual of the ascension ascend from inner levels after the soul has departed the physical body. The soul attains union with the mighty I AM Presence to become a permanent atom in the Body of God just as she does in a physical ascension.

The Catholic doctrine on the "assumption" of Mary and the ascension of Jesus parallels the teachings of the Ascended Masters on the physical ascension. The Catholic Church teaches that the bodies worn by Mary and Jesus on earth were translated and perfected into the incorruptible spiritual bodies they now wear in heaven. This is analogous to what the Ascended Masters teach happens in a physical ascension. The Ascended Masters' teachings illumine us further, however, as to how this divine alchemy actually occurs, as described by Serapis Bey. Some points where Catholic theology and Ascended Master teaching differ are as follows: According to Catholic doctrine, Mary and Jesus were unique because they were "conceived without sin" and remained perfectly sinless throughout their lives. Hence, it would not be meet that their physical bodies should be corrupted in a grave. In the Catholic perspective, Jesus would naturally ascend at the end of his mission because, although he had an earthly body, he also had a full divine nature. Catholic doctrine holds that because Mary was human like us, she is an "exception to the rule" in that she did not have to wait until the Second Coming of Christ for her bodily resurrection.

The Ascended Masters set before each of us the goal of balancing at least 51 percent of our karma and ascending at the end of this life. They teach that it is possible—if we balance 95 to 100 percent of our karma—to ascend physically. However, we have each lived many times before. The Ascended Masters teach that the path of karma-balancing and spiritual progress leading to the ascension is not accomplished in one lifetime but through many incarnations. The many bodies worn during the soul's earthly sojourn are not resurrected at the end of time; but all souls who ascend, whether in a physical ascension or not, are permanently clothed at the hour of their ascension in their Ascended-Master Light Body. Jesus and Mary set the example for all to follow. They are joined in heaven by countless saints who have also attained their soul's victory through the divinely ordained ritual of the ascension.

91. John the Beloved, April 12, 1974, "The Initiation of the Crucifixion."
92. Serapis Bey, *Dossier on the Ascension,* p. 176.
93. Ibid., p. 158.
94. Ibid., pp. 158, 177.
95. Saint Germain, "The Crucible of Being," in Mark L. Prophet and Elizabeth Clare Prophet, *Saint Germain On Alchemy,* p. 97.
96. See Elizabeth Clare Prophet, December 28, 1991, "How You Can Celebrate Your Immortality Every Day of Your Life, Part 2: The Yellow Emperor on the Tao of Longevity."
97. Saint Germain, December 29, 1991, "The Battle and Its Victory Are Yours!" in *Pearls of Wisdom,* vol. 35, no. 3, January 19, 1992.
98. John 14:23.
99. See Rev. 11:17.
100. Gen. 5:22, 24.
101. Archangel Raphael, December 28, 1991, "Golden Pearls from the Heart of the Earth," in *Pearls of Wisdom,* vol. 35, no. 2, January 12,

1992.

102. Dan. 11:31; Matt. 24:15; Mark 13:14.

103. Cyclopea, December 30, 1973, "The Immaculate Conception of the Seventh Root Race."

104. John 6:53.

105. A service for the blessing and serving of Holy Communion is included as part of the "Unison Ritual" in El Morya, *Ashram Notes* (1990), pp. 3–15.

106. Mal. 4:2.

107. Phil. 4:8.

108. I Cor. 3:13.

109. Maitreya, January 2, 1997, "A World Vigil for Youth," in *Pearls of Wisdom*, vol. 43, no. 48, November 26, 2000.

110. I Cor. 15:26.

111. Jesus, "Immortality," in Jesus and Kuthumi, *Corona Class Lessons* (1986), pp. 310–11.

112. Rom. 8:35, 39.

113. Matt. 7:2; Mark 4:24; Luke 6:38.

114. Luke 24:13–19.

115. Rose of Light, February 20, 1977.

116. Lanto, April 13, 1969.

117. John 16:7, 8.

118. I Cor. 15:53, 54.

Seraphic Meditations

1. Serapis Bey, *Dossier on the Ascension,* pp. 130–31.

2. Matt. 5:8.

3. I Cor. 15:55.

4. Luke 15: 22–32.

Chapter 4 · Entities

Opening quote: Mark 3:11.

1. Mark 5:1–9.

2. It is unfortunately a common occurrence for individuals to be caught in this way in the astral plane after passing, even for those who consider themselves to be "good" people. If individuals have not consciously worked for the highest good in life, if they have failed to strengthen the Light in their chakras, if they have squandered the Life-force, if they have tolerated lower vibrations in their lives, they may find themselves drawn into the astral plane by their desires; and once there, they may find themselves ensnared by black magicians, fallen angels and discarnates, unable to free themselves or navigate to higher realms. This is especially the case if people do not have a strong tie to their Higher Nature. This is one reason it is important for people to believe in God, to have a church, to have a path, to pray and to have a desire and a commitment to be tied to Jesus or some saint East or West, someone who is in the realms of Light. These ties are important for those who

find themselves without a physical body.

3. Jude 12.

4. An early example of the portrayal of the astral plane in literature is in Lewis Carroll's *Alice's Adventures in Wonderland* (1865). Carroll was among the first to puncture the astral envelope, as "through the looking glass" came a panoply of astral personalities that have since been followed by a host of others, perverting the true image of the Christ in the innocent consciousness of children.

5. Astrea, *Keepers of the Flame Lesson 24,* pp. 24–25.

6. Rev. 22:11.

7. The differing fates of souls after death is illustrated very graphically in the following account, in which the Messenger describes her observations during a service that she held following the conclusion of the first Gulf War:

"I was offering calls for those who had passed on in the war, not only Americans and the Allies but also the Iraqis and everyone who had participated and all those innocent civilians whose lives had been taken.

"It is necessary that we in embodiment make calls for souls who don't have locomotion and don't have wind in their sails to navigate or to get anywhere when they pass from the screen of life. We can call to Archangel Michael. We can call to others of the heavenly hosts and ask them to come to those lower planes and cut free those souls so that they can go to a place of rest.

"What I found was very interesting. I found that the devout people, men and women in the armed forces, those of every nation who were truly spiritual and had led prayerful lives and devoted lives and had pure hearts, they had already been taken by angels to retreats. Jesus Christ himself has a retreat in the etheric octave over Saudi Arabia. Some of them had such a momentum of Light that they were already there. Others were of the Light but were not able to get there. So I called to the angels to take them. They welcomed the angels. Some of the very devout Moslems were praying next to their bodies. They couldn't get anywhere past their bodies, but where their dead bodies lay, there they were in prayer on their knees and had been from the moment that they had been killed.

"But then I saw a most interesting thing. I saw some soldiers, and they were from every nation, including our own, who had no desire to go into the realms of Light, who were very angry that they were killed. And they were expressing that anger in a rage or in cursing or in foul words. And they were putting out a tremendous amount of anger.

"And so, they were not taken to any place of harmony or rest or learning, not only because they were not fit to go there, but because they actually denied the angels who came for them and said that they did not want to go to any place like a retreat of Light where they could learn. So these are souls who remain in what we call the lower astral plane" (Elizabeth Clare Prophet, May 3, 1991).

8. Another alternative, where total separation does not occur, is that the etheric, mental and astral bodies, together with the soul, may travel as

a unit to either the astral, mental or etheric plane.

9. Matt. 6:22.
10. See Mark L. Prophet and Elizabeth Clare Prophet, *The Masters and the Spiritual Path* (2001), pp. 123–26.
11. Zarathustra, March 31, 1985, "The Mission of a Living Flame," in *Pearls of Wisdom,* vol. 28, no. 17, April 28, 1985.
12. I Cor. 15:40.
13. Ps. 24:1; I Cor. 10:26–28.
14. Elizabeth Clare Prophet, *The Opening of the Seventh Seal: Sanat Kumara on the Path of the Ruby Ray* (2001), pp. 198–200.
15. I Cor. 15:55.
16. I Thess. 4:13–17.
17. Cyclopea, October 11, 1973. This dictation was delivered in Santa Barbara, California, at the Class of the Harvest Sun. While Cyclopea's dispensation for the transmutation of the energy of bodily remains from previous embodiments buried in the earth was specifically given for those who attended this conference, students of the Ascended Masters may make the calls, using decrees to Cyclopea, Astrea and the fiery salamanders, for a similar action to be performed for them individually.
18. Matt. 5:48; Astrea, *Keepers of the Flame Lesson 23,* pp. 30–31.
19. I Pet. 3:19–20.
20. The 1960s and 1970s saw the establishment of many radical new political movements. A number of them, including the Red Brigades of Italy, the Baader-Meinhoff gang of Germany, Students for a Democratic Society (SDS) in the U.S., and revolutionary movements in South America advocated the use of violence to further their political agendas.

 Ideologically, many of these groups supported Marxist ideals of the redistribution of wealth and the remaking of society. As we explained in *The Path of Brotherhood,* book 4 of the Climb the Highest Mountain series, these concepts are not consistent with cosmic law, in that they seek to produce an artificial equality that does not take into account the laws of karma and the option for free will in forging an individual path of attainment in the spiritual/material world. In advocating these political philosophies, the fallen Atlanteans sought to set up political and economic systems that would ignore and even attempt to override the laws of karma. In effect, they were seeking to avoid responsibility for the karmic debts they, themselves, had incurred in Atlantean times.
21. Matt. 11:12.
22. I Tim. 5:24.
23. John 3:19.
24. John 8:11.
25. Luke 15:11–32.
26. Jesus, "Unceasing Prayer," in Jesus and Kuthumi, *Prayer and Meditation* (1978), pp. 10, 11–12.
27. Matt. 10:28.
28. II Cor. 11:14.
29. Astrea, *Keepers of the Flame Lesson 23,* pp. 23–24.
30. For additional teaching on the suicide entity, as well as practical and

spiritual solutions to the problem of suicide, see Neroli Duffy and Marilyn Barrick, *Wanting to Live: Overcoming the Seduction of Suicide* (2004).

31. Jesus, October 8, 1995, "I Have Desired to Be Remembered by You," in *Pearls of Wisdom,* vol. 38, no. 38, September 3, 1995.

32. John 13:27.

33. A detailed study of different types of music and their effect on the four lower bodies, the soul and society can be found in an audio album by Elizabeth Clare Prophet, *The Science of Rhythm for the Mastery of the Sacred Energies of Life.*

34. *Merriam-Webster's Collegiate Dictionary,* tenth ed., s.v. "greed."

35. I Tim. 6:10.

36. Archangel Jophiel with Christine, June 25, 1995, "The Quickening of Your Crown Chakra," in *Pearls of Wisdom,* vol. 38, no. 30, July 9, 1995.

37. I Cor. 15:26.

38. Serapis Bey, July 3, 1967.

39. See William Dufty, *Sugar Blues* (Radnor, Pa.: Chilton Book Co., 1975); Nancy Appleton, *Lick the Sugar Habit* (New York: Warner Books, 1986).

40. Matt. 21:12–13; Mark 11:15–17.

41. Vesta, "A Vision of Cosmic Reality for the Golden Age: The Banner of the Mother of the World Is Unfurled," *Pearls of Wisdom,* vol. 12, no. 1, January 5, 1969.

42. The Goddess of Purity, November 4, 1966.

43. I Cor. 9:26.

44. Mark L. Prophet, *The Soulless One* (2004), pp. 46–47.

45. Gen. 3:24; Cuzco, *Pearls of Wisdom,* vol. 5, no. 3, January 19, 1962.

46. Eph. 6:12.

47. Astrea, February 18, 1991, "I Enlist Your Help!" in *Pearls of Wisdom,* vol. 34, no. 13, March 31, 1991.

48. Archangel Michael, December 12, 1976.

49. Lanello, January 1, 1992, "Newly Born in the Arms of Your God Parents," in *Pearls of Wisdom,* vol. 35, no. 9, March 1, 1992.

50. On Friday evenings, Keepers of the Flame gather in the cities of the world to give decrees specifically for the cutting free of souls who have passed from the screen of life and for the clearing of the earth of discarnates and entities. This service is sponsored by the Goddess of Liberty and the Order of the Golden Lily.

51. Astrea, "I Enlist Your Help!"

52. Mark 16:17.

53. Luke 4:33–36, 41.

54. John 11:43–44.

55. Mark 16:17–18.

56. John 14:12.

57. John 3:29.

58. John 3:29–30.

59. See Matt. 18:19.

60. Gen. 1:26.

61. Matt. 17:14–21.
62. Astrea, *Keepers of the Flame Lesson 23,* pp. 38–40.

Chapter 5 · The Messengers

Opening quotes: Matt. 10:41; Mal. 3:1.

1. Lanto, *Pearls of Wisdom,* vol. 10, no. 39, September 24, 1967.
2. Henry Wadsworth Longfellow, "A Psalm of Life."
3. Deut. 4:2; see also Rev. 22:18, 19.
4. Heb. 13:8.
5. Rev. 22:10.
6. Kuthumi, "Potentials of God-Realization," *Pearls of Wisdom,* vol. 11, no. 44, November 3, 1968.
7. Isa. 8:19.
8. Isa. 30:20, 21.
9. I Kings 4:25.
10. El Morya, *Pearls of Wisdom,* vol. 3, no. 35, August 26, 1960.
11. Saint Germain, *Pearls of Wisdom,* vol. 3, no. 10, March 4, 1960.
12. Maha Chohan, July 2, 1962.
13. Matt. 15:14.
14. Saint Germain, *Pearls of Wisdom,* vol. 10, no. 38, September 17, 1967.
15. I Cor. 12:10.
16. Titus 1:10.
17. Isa. 8:19.
18. Exod. 7:8–12.
19. Ps. 103:15, 16.
20. Matt. 11:10.
21. Matt. 24:30.
22. El Morya, *The Chela and the Path* (1976), pp. 115–18.
23. Rom. 10:15.
24. John 4:10–11,
25. For additional information about the planet Maldek and its history, see Mark L. Prophet and Elizabeth Clare Prophet, *Paths of Light and Darkness,* pp. 9–11, 240–43.
26. The focus of the Lady Master Venus and her flame of beauty were anchored on the continent of Europe where the city of Vienna, Austria, stands today, and it was through the ray anchored there that many of the Venusians embodied, bringing their culture with them. The German spelling of Vienna is *Wien,* pronounced like the first three letters of Venus. Not only the name, but also the culture, the art and the romantic feeling of this city of dreams are reminiscent of the planetary home of its founder.
27. James Henry Breasted, *A History of Egypt: From the Earliest Times to the Persian Conquest* (New York: Charles Scribner's Sons, 1912), pp. 360, 361.
28. Cyril Aldred, *Akhenaten: Pharaoh of Egypt* (London: Thames and Hudson, Abacus, 1972), p. 133.
29. Will Durant, *The Story of Civilization* (New York: Simon & Schuster,

1954) I:206, 208. Durant comments on this poem: "The obvious similarity of this hymn to Psalm CIV leaves little doubt of Egyptian influence upon the Hebrew poet" (p. 210).

30. John 11:21, 22.
31. John 11:25, 26.
32. John 11, 27.
33. G. W. Butterworth, *Origen: On First Principles* (New York: Harper & Row, 1973), p. xxvii.
34. *Catholic Encyclopedia* (1913), s.v. "Origen and Origenism."
35. Rev. 13:8.
36. I Pet. 1:24, 25.
37. John 18:37.
38. Henry Wadsworth Longfellow, "Santa Filomena."
39. Eph. 6:12.
40. Constantin Christomanos, *Tagebuchblätter Wien* (1899), pp. 81, 97, 227; quoted in Head and Cranston, *Reincarnation in World Thought,* pp. 334–35.
41. Edward Crankshaw, *The Fall of the House of Hapsburg* (New York: The Viking Press, 1963), p. 4.
42. Dan. 12:5, 7, 10.
43. Casimir Poseidon, September 12, 1965.
44. Phylos the Thibetan, *A Dweller on Two Planets* (Los Angeles: Borden, 1952), p. 226; Dan. 5.
45. The Maha Chohan, December 30, 1969.
46. El Morya, July 3, 1970.
47. Great Divine Director, July 5, 1970.
48. Mal. 3:1.
49. Rev. 12:3.
50. I Pet. 5:2–4; El Morya, *The Chela and the Path,* pp. 121–23.
51. Rev. 1:1.
52. Isa. 53:3.
53. John 15:25.
54. Rev. 11:3–13, 15–19.

Glossary

Terms set in italics are defined elsewhere in the glossary.

Adept. An initiate of the *Great White Brotherhood* of a high degree of attainment, especially in the control of *Matter*, physical forces, nature spirits and bodily functions; fully the alchemist undergoing advanced initiations of the *sacred fire* on the path of the *ascension*.

Akashic records. The impressions of all that has ever transpired in the physical universe, recorded in the etheric substance and dimension known by the Sanskrit term *akasha*. These records can be read by those with developed soul faculties.

Alchemical marriage. The soul's permanent bonding to the *Holy Christ Self*, in preparation for the permanent fusing to the *I AM Presence* in the ritual of the *ascension*. See also *Secret chamber of the heart*.

All-Seeing Eye of God. See *Cyclopea*.

Alpha and Omega. The divine wholeness of the Father-Mother God affirmed as "the beginning and the ending" by the Lord *Christ* in Revelation (Rev. 1:8, 11; 21:6; 22:13). Ascended *twin flames* of the *Cosmic Christ* consciousness who hold the balance of the masculine-feminine polarity of the Godhead in the *Great Central Sun* of cosmos. Thus through the *Universal Christ* (the *Word* incarnate), the Father is the origin and the Mother is the fulfillment of the cycles of God's consciousness expressed throughout the *Spirit-Matter* creation. See also *Mother*.

Ancient of Days. See *Sanat Kumara*.

Angel. A divine spirit, a herald or messenger sent by God to deliver his *Word* to his children. A ministering spirit sent forth to tend the heirs of *Christ*—to comfort, protect, guide, strengthen, teach, counsel and warn. The fallen angels, also called the dark ones, are those angels who followed Lucifer in the Great Rebellion, whose consciousness therefore "fell" to lower levels of vibration. They were "cast out into the earth" by Archangel Michael (Rev. 12:7–12)—constrained by the karma of their disobedience to God and his Christ to take on and evolve through dense physical bodies. Here they walk about, sowing seeds of unrest and rebellion among men and nations.

Antahkarana. The web of life. The net of *Light* spanning *Spirit* and *Matter,* connecting and sensitizing the whole of creation within itself and to the heart of God.

Archangel. The highest rank in the orders of *angels*. Each of the *seven rays* has a presiding Archangel who, with his divine complement or Archeia, embodies the God consciousness of the ray and directs the bands of angels serving in their command on that ray. The Archangels and Archeiai of the rays and the locations of their *retreats* are as follows:
First ray, blue, Archangel Michael and Faith, Banff, near Lake Louise, Alberta, Canada.
Second ray, yellow, Archangel Jophiel and Christine, south of the Great Wall near Lanchow, north central China.
Third ray, petal pink, deep rose and ruby, Archangel Chamuel and Charity, St. Louis, Missouri, U.S.A.
Fourth ray, white and mother-of-pearl, Archangel Gabriel and Hope, between Sacramento and Mount Shasta, California, U.S.A.
Fifth ray, green, Archangel Raphael and Mary, Fátima, Portugal.
Sixth ray, purple and gold with ruby flecks, Archangel Uriel and Aurora, Tatra Mountains, south of Cracow, Poland.
Seventh ray, violet and purple, Archangel Zadkiel and Holy Amethyst, Cuba.

Archeia (pl. **Archeiai**). Divine complement and *twin flame* of an *Archangel.*

Ascended Master. One who, through *Christ* and the putting on of that mind which was in Christ Jesus (Phil. 2:5), has mastered time and space and in the process gained the mastery of the self in the *four lower bodies* and the four quadrants of *Matter,* in the *chakras* and the balanced *threefold flame.* An Ascended Master has also transmuted at least 51 percent of his karma, fulfilled his divine plan, and taken the initiations of the ruby ray unto the ritual of the *ascension*—acceleration by the *sacred fire* into the Presence of the I AM THAT I AM (the *I AM Presence*). Ascended Masters inhabit the planes of *Spirit*—the kingdom of God (God's consciousness)—and they may teach unascended souls in an *etheric temple* or in the cities on the *etheric plane* (the kingdom of heaven).

Ascension. The ritual whereby the soul reunites with the *Spirit* of the living God, the *I AM Presence.* The ascension is the culmination of the soul's God-victorious sojourn in time and space. It is the process whereby the soul, having balanced her karma and fulfilled her divine plan, merges first with the Christ consciousness and then with the living Presence of the I AM THAT I AM. Once the ascension has taken place, the soul—the corruptible aspect of being—becomes the incorruptible one, a permanent atom in the Body of God. See also *Alchemical marriage.*

Aspirant. One who aspires; specifically, one who aspires to reunion with God through the ritual of the *ascension.* One who aspires to overcome the conditions and limitations of time and space to fulfill the cycles of karma and one's reason for being through the sacred labor.

Astral plane. A frequency of time and space beyond the physical, yet below the mental, corresponding to the *emotional body* of man and the collective unconscious of the race; the repository of mankind's thoughts and feelings, conscious and unconscious. Because the astral plane has been muddied by impure human thought and feeling, the term "astral" is often used in a negative context to refer to that which is impure or psychic.

Astrea. Feminine Elohim of the fourth ray, the ray of purity, who works to cut souls free from the *astral plane* and the projections of the dark forces. See also *Elohim; Seven rays.*

Atman. The spark of the divine within, identical with *Brahman;* the ultimate essence of the universe as well as the essence of the individual.

AUM. See *OM.*

Avatar. The incarnation of the *Word*. The avatar of an age is the *Christ*, the incarnation of the Son of God. The *Manus* may designate numerous Christed ones—those endued with an extraordinary *Light*—to go forth as world teachers and wayshowers. The Christed ones demonstrate in a given epoch the Law of the *Logos*, stepped down through the Manu(s) and the avatar(s) until it is made flesh through their own word and work—to be ultimately victorious in its fulfillment in all souls of Light sent forth to conquer time and space in that era.

Bodhisattva. (Sanskrit, "a being of *bodhi* or enlightenment.") A being destined for enlightenment, or one whose energy and power is directed toward enlightenment. A Bodhisattva is destined to become a *Buddha* but has forgone the bliss of *nirvana* with a vow to save all children of God on earth. An Ascended Master or an unascended master may be a Bodhisattva.

Brahman. Ultimate Reality; the Absolute.

Buddha. (From Sanskrit *budh* "awake, know, perceive.") "The enlightened one." Buddha denotes an office in the spiritual *Hierarchy* of worlds that is attained by passing certain initiations of the *sacred fire*, including those of the *seven rays* of the Holy Spirit and of the five secret *rays*, the raising of the feminine ray (sacred fire of the Kundalini) and the "mastery of the seven in the seven multiplied by the power of the ten."

Gautama attained the enlightenment of the Buddha twenty-five centuries ago, a path he had pursued through many previous embodiments culminating in his forty-nine-day meditation under the Bo tree. Hence he is called Gautama, the Buddha. He holds the office of *Lord of the World*, sustaining, by his *Causal Body* and *threefold flame*, the divine spark and consciousness in the evolutions of earth approaching the path of personal Christhood. His aura of love/wisdom ensouling the planet issues from his incomparable devotion to the Divine *Mother*. He is the Hierarch of Shamballa, the original *retreat* of *Sanat Kumara* now on the *etheric plane* over the Gobi Desert.

Lord Maitreya, the *Cosmic Christ*, has also passed the initiations of the Buddha. He is the long-awaited Coming Buddha who has come to the fore to teach all who have departed from

the way of the Great *Guru,* Sanat Kumara, from whose lineage
both he and Gautama descended. In the history of the planet,
there have been numerous Buddhas who have served the evolutions of mankind through the steps and stages of the path of the
Bodhisattva. In the East Jesus is referred to as the Buddha Issa.
He is the World Saviour by the love/wisdom of the Godhead.

Caduceus. The Kundalini. See *Sacred fire.*

Causal Body. Seven concentric spheres of *Light* surrounding the *I AM
Presence.* The spheres of the Causal Body contain the records of
the virtuous acts we have performed to the glory of God and the
blessing of man through our many incarnations on earth. See
also *Chart of Your Divine Self;* color illustration facing page 88.

Central Sun. A vortex of energy, physical or spiritual, central to
systems of worlds that it thrusts from, or gathers unto, itself by
the Central Sun Magnet. Whether in the *microcosm* or the
Macrocosm, the Central Sun is the principal energy source,
vortex, or nexus of energy interchange in atoms, cells, man (the
heart center), amidst plant life and the core of the earth. The
Great Central Sun is the center of cosmos; the point of integration of the *Spirit-Matter* cosmos; the point of origin of all
physical-spiritual creation; the nucleus, or white fire core, of the
Cosmic Egg. (The God Star, Sirius, is the focus of the Great
Central Sun in our sector of the galaxy.) The Sun behind the sun
is the spiritual Cause behind the physical effect we see as our
own physical sun and all other stars and star systems, seen or
unseen, including the Great Central Sun.

Chakra. (Sanskrit, "wheel, disc, circle.") Center of *Light* anchored in
the *etheric body* and governing the flow of energy to the *four
lower bodies* of man. There are seven major chakras corresponding to the *seven rays,* five minor chakras corresponding to the
five secret rays, and a total of 144 Light centers in the body of
man.

Chart of Your Divine Self. (See color illustration facing page 88.)
There are three figures represented in the Chart. The upper
figure is the *I AM Presence,* the I AM THAT I AM, the individualization of God's presence for every son and daughter of the
Most High. The Divine Monad consists of the I AM Presence
surrounded by the spheres (color rings) of *Light* that make up

the body of First Cause, or *Causal Body.*

The middle figure in the Chart is the Mediator between God and man, called the *Holy Christ Self,* the *Real Self* or the *Christ* consciousness. It has also been referred to as the Higher Mental Body or one's Higher Consciousness. This Inner Teacher over-shadows the lower self, which consists of the soul evolving through the four planes of *Matter* using the vehicles of the *four lower bodies*—the *etheric* (memory) *body,* the *mental body,* the *emotional* (desire) *body,* and the *physical body*—to balance karma and fulfill the divine plan.

The three figures of the Chart correspond to the Trinity of Father, who always includes the *Mother* (the upper figure), Son (the middle figure) and Holy Spirit (the lower figure). The latter is the intended temple of the Holy Spirit, whose *sacred fire* is indicated in the enfolding *violet flame.* The lower figure corres-ponds to you as a disciple on the *Path.*

The lower figure is surrounded by a *tube of light,* which is projected from the heart of the I AM Presence in answer to your call. It is a cylinder of white Light that sustains a forcefield of protection twenty-four hours a day, so long as you guard it in harmony. The *threefold flame* of life is the divine spark sent from the I AM Presence as the gift of life, consciousness and free will. It is sealed in the *secret chamber of the heart* that through the love, wisdom and power of the Godhead anchored therein the soul may fulfill her reason for being in the physical plane. Also called the Christ Flame and the Liberty Flame, or fleur-de-lis, it is the spark of a man's divinity, his potential for Christhood.

The silver cord (or *crystal cord*) is the stream of life, or *lifestream,* that descends from the heart of the I AM Presence to the Holy Christ Self to nourish and sustain (through the *chakras*) the soul and its vehicles of expression in time and space. It is over this 'umbilical cord' that the energy of the Presence flows, entering the being of man at the crown and giving impetus for the pulsation of the threefold flame as well as the physical heartbeat.

When a round of the soul's incarnation in Matter-form is finished, the I AM Presence withdraws the silver cord (Eccles. 12:6), whereupon the threefold flame returns to the level of the Christ, and the soul clothed in the etheric garment gravitates to the highest level of her attainment, where she is schooled between embodiments until her final incarnation when the Great Law decrees she shall go out no more.

The dove of the Holy Spirit descending from the heart of the Father is shown just above the head of the Christ. When the son of man puts on and becomes the Christ consciousness as Jesus did, he merges with the Holy Christ Self. The Holy Spirit is upon him, and the words of the Father, the beloved I AM Presence, are spoken: "This is my beloved Son, in whom I AM well pleased" (Matt. 3:17).

Chela. (Hindi *celā* from Sanskrit *ceta* "slave," i.e., "servant.") In India, a disciple of a religious teacher or *guru*. A term used generally to refer to a student of the *Ascended Masters* and their teachings. Specifically, a student of more than ordinary self-discipline and devotion initiated by an Ascended Master and serving the cause of the *Great White Brotherhood*.

Chohan. (Tibetan, "lord" or "master"; a chief.) Each of the seven *rays* has a Chohan who focuses the *Christ* consciousness of the ray. Having ensouled and demonstrated the law of the ray throughout numerous incarnations, and having taken initiations both before and after the *ascension,* the candidate is appointed to the office of Chohan by the Maha Chohan (the "Great Lord"), who is himself the representative of the Holy Spirit on all the rays. The names of the Chohans of the Rays (each one an *Ascended Master* representing one of the seven rays to earth's evolutions) and the locations of their physical/etheric focuses are as follows:

First ray, El Morya, Retreat of God's Will, Darjeeling, India
Second ray, Lanto, Royal Teton Retreat, Grand Teton, Jackson Hole, Wyoming, U.S.A.
Third ray, Paul the Venetian, Château de Liberté, southern France, with a focus of the *threefold flame* at the Washington Monument, Washington, D.C., U.S.A.
Fourth ray, Serapis Bey, the Ascension Temple and Retreat at Luxor, Egypt
Fifth ray, Hilarion (the apostle Paul), Temple of Truth, Crete
Sixth ray, Nada, Arabian Retreat, Saudi Arabia
Seventh ray, Saint Germain, Royal Teton Retreat, Grand Teton, Wyoming, U.S.A.; Cave of Symbols, Table Mountain, Wyoming,

U.S.A. Saint Germain also works out of the Great Divine Director's focuses—the Cave of Light in India and the Rakoczy Mansion in Transylvania, where Saint Germain presides as Hierarch.

Christ. (From the Greek *Christos* "anointed.") Messiah (Hebrew, Aramaic "anointed"); "Christed one," one fully endued and infilled—anointed—by the *Light* (the Son) of God. The *Word*, the *Logos*, the Second Person of the Trinity. In the Hindu Trinity of Brahma, Vishnu and Shiva, the term "Christ" corresponds to or is the incarnation of Vishnu, the Preserver; Avatāra, Godman, Dispeller of Darkness, *Guru*.

The term "Christ" or "Christed one" also denotes an office in *Hierarchy* held by those who have attained self-mastery on the *seven rays* and the seven *chakras* of the Holy Spirit. Christmastery includes the balancing of the *threefold flame*—the divine attributes of power, wisdom and love—for the harmonization of consciousness and the implementation of the mastery of the seven rays in the chakras and in the *four lower bodies* through the Mother flame (the raised Kundalini).

At the hour designated for the *ascension,* the soul thus anointed raises the spiral of the threefold flame from beneath the feet through the entire form for the transmutation of every atom and cell of her being, consciousness and world. The saturation and acceleration of the *four lower bodies* and the soul by this transfiguring Light of the Christ flame take place in part during the initiation of the transfiguration, increasing through the resurrecttion and gaining full intensity in the ritual of the ascension.

Christ Self. The individualized focus of "the only begotten of the Father, full of grace and Truth" (John 1:14). The *Universal Christ* individualized as the true identity of the soul; the *Real Self* of every man, woman and child, to which the soul must rise. The Christ Self is the Mediator between a man and his God. He is a man's own personal teacher, master and prophet.

Color rays. See *Seven rays.*

Cosmic Being. (1) An *Ascended Master* who has attained cosmic consciousness and ensouls the *Light*/energy/consciousness of many worlds and systems of worlds across the galaxies to the

Sun behind the *Great Central Sun;* or, (2) A Being of God who has never descended below the level of the *Christ,* has never taken physical embodiment, and has never made human karma.

Cosmic Christ. An office in *Hierarchy* currently held by Lord Maitreya under Gautama *Buddha,* the *Lord of the World.* Also used as a synonym for *Universal Christ.*

Cosmic Clock. The science of charting the cycles of the soul's karma and initiations on the twelve lines of the Clock under the *Twelve Hierarchies of the Sun.* Taught by Mother Mary to Mark and Elizabeth Prophet for sons and daughters of God returning to the Law of the One and to their point of origin beyond the worlds of form and lesser causation.

Cosmic Egg. The spiritual-material universe, including a seemingly endless chain of galaxies, star systems, worlds known and unknown, whose center, or white-fire core, is called the *Great Central Sun.* The Cosmic Egg has both a spiritual and a material center. Although we may discover and observe the Cosmic Egg from the standpoint of our physical senses and perspective, all of the dimensions of *Spirit* can also be known and experienced within the Cosmic Egg. For the God who created the Cosmic Egg and holds it in the hollow of his hand is also the God flame expanding hour by hour within his very own sons and daughters. The Cosmic Egg represents the bounds of man's habitation in this cosmic cycle. Yet, as God is everywhere throughout and beyond the Cosmic Egg, so by his Spirit within us we daily awaken to new dimensions of being, soul-satisfied in conformity with his likeness.

Cosmic Law. The Law that governs mathematically, yet with the spontaneity of Mercy's flame, all manifestation throughout the cosmos in the planes of *Spirit* and *Matter.*

Crystal cord. The stream of God's *Light,* life and consciousness that nourishes and sustains the soul and her *four lower bodies.* Also called the silver cord (Eccles. 12:6). See also *Chart of Your Divine Self.*

Cyclopea. Masculine Elohim of the fifth ray, also known as the All-Seeing Eye of God or as the Great Silent Watcher. See also *Elohim; Seven rays.*

Deathless solar body. See *Seamless garment.*

Decree. A dynamic form of spoken prayer used by students of the *Ascended Masters* to direct God's *light* into individual and world conditions. The decree may be short or long and is usually marked by a formal preamble and a closing or acceptance. It is the authoritative *Word* of God spoken in man in the name of the *I AM Presence* and the living *Christ* to bring about constructive change on earth through the will of God. The decree is the birthright of the sons and daughters of God, the "Command ye me" of Isaiah 45:11, the original fiat of the Creator: "Let there be light: and there was light" (Gen. 1:3). It is written in the Book of Job, "Thou shalt decree a thing, and it shall be established unto thee: and the light shall shine upon thy ways" (Job 22:28).

Dictation. A message from an *Ascended Master,* an *Archangel* or another advanced spiritual being delivered through the agency of the Holy Spirit by a *Messenger* of the *Great White Brotherhood.*

Divine Monad. See *Chart of Your Divine Self; I AM Presence.*

Electronic Presence. A duplicate of the *I AM Presence* of an Ascended Master.

Elohim. (Hebrew; plural of *Eloah,* "God.") The name of God used in the first verse of the Bible: "In the beginning God created the heaven and the earth." The Seven Mighty Elohim and their feminine counterparts are the builders of form. They are the "seven spirits of God" named in Revelation 4:5 and the "morning stars" that sang together in the beginning, as the Lord revealed them to Job (Job 38:7). In the order of *Hierarchy,* the Elohim and *Cosmic Beings* carry the greatest concentration, the highest vibration of *Light* that we can comprehend in our present state of evolution. Serving directly under the Elohim are the four Hierarchs of the elements, who have dominion over the elementals—the gnomes, salamanders, sylphs and undines.

Following are the names of the Seven Elohim and their divine complements, the ray they serve on and the location of their etheric *retreat:*

First ray, Hercules and Amazonia, Half Dome, Sierra Nevada, Yosemite National Park, California, U.S.A.

Second ray, Apollo and Lumina, western Lower Saxony, Germany

Third ray, Heros and Amora, Lake Winnipeg, Manitoba, Canada

Fourth ray, Purity and *Astrea,* near Gulf of Archangel, southeast arm of White Sea, Russia

Fifth ray, *Cyclopea* and Virginia, Altai Range where China, Siberia and Mongolia meet, near Tabun Bogdo

Sixth ray, Peace and Aloha, Hawaiian Islands

Seventh ray, Arcturus and Victoria, near Luanda, Angola, Africa

Emotional body. One of the *four lower bodies* of man, corresponding to the water element and the third quadrant of *Matter;* the vehicle of the desires and feelings of God made manifest in the being of man. Also called the astral body, the desire body or the feeling body.

Etheric body. One of the *four lower bodies* of man, corresponding to the fire element and the first quadrant of *Matter;* called the envelope of the soul, holding the blueprint of the divine plan and the image of *Christ*-perfection to be outpictured in the world of form. Also called the memory body.

Etheric octave or etheric plane. The highest plane in the dimension of *Matter;* a plane that is as concrete and real as the physical plane (and even more so) but is experienced through the senses of the soul in a dimension and a consciousness beyond physical awareness. This is the plane on which the *akashic records* of mankind's entire evolution register individually and collectively. It is the world of *Ascended Masters* and their *retreats,* etheric cities of *light* where souls of a higher order of evolution abide between embodiments. It is the plane of Reality.

The lower *etheric plane,* which overlaps the astral/mental/physical belts, is contaminated by these lower worlds occupied by the false hierarchy and the mass consciousness it controls.

Etheric temple. See *Retreat.*

Fallen angels. See *Angels.*

Father-Mother God. See *Alpha and Omega.*

Four Cosmic Forces. The four beasts seen by Saint John and other seers as the lion, the calf (or ox), the man and the flying eagle (Rev. 4:6–8). They serve directly under the Elohim and govern all of the Matter cosmos. They are transformers of the Infinite Light unto souls evolving in the finite. See also *Elohim.*

Four lower bodies. Four sheaths of four distinct frequencies that surround the soul (the physical, emotional, mental and etheric bodies), providing vehicles for the soul in her journey through time and space. The etheric sheath, highest in vibration, is the gateway to the three higher bodies: the *Christ Self,* the *I AM Presence* and the *Causal Body.* See also *Physical body; Emotional body; Mental body; Etheric body.*

Great Central Sun. See *Central Sun.*

Great Hub. See *Central Sun.*

Great White Brotherhood. A spiritual order of Western saints and Eastern adepts who have reunited with the *Spirit* of the living God; the heavenly hosts. They have transcended the cycles of karma and rebirth and ascended (accelerated) into that higher reality that is the eternal abode of the soul. The *Ascended Masters* of the Great White Brotherhood, united for the highest purposes of the brotherhood of man under the Fatherhood of God, have risen in every age from every culture and religion to inspire creative achievement in education, the arts and sciences, God-government and the abundant life through the economies of the nations. The word "white" refers not to race but to the aura (halo) of white *light* surrounding their forms. The Brotherhood also includes in its ranks certain unascended *chelas* of the Ascended Masters.

Guru. (Sanskrit.) A personal religious teacher and spiritual guide; one of high attainment. A guru may be unascended or ascended.

Hierarchy. The universal chain of individualized God-free beings fulfilling the attributes and aspects of God's infinite Selfhood. Included in the cosmic Hierarchical scheme are *Solar Logoi, Elohim,* Sons and Daughters of God, Ascended and unascended masters with their circles of *chelas, Cosmic Beings,* the *Twelve Hierarchies of the Sun, Archangels* and *angels* of the *sacred fire,* children of the *Light,* nature spirits (called elementals) and *twin flames* of the *Alpha/Omega* polarity sponsoring planetary and galactic systems.

This universal order of the Father's own Self-expression is the means whereby God in the *Great Central Sun* steps down the Presence and power of his universal being/consciousness in order that succeeding evolutions in time and space, from the least unto the greatest, might come to know the wonder of his love. The level of one's spiritual/physical attainment—measured by one's balanced self-awareness "hid with *Christ* in God" and demonstrating his Law, by his love, in the *Spirit/Matter* cosmos —is the criterion establishing one's placement on this ladder of life called Hierarchy.

Higher Mental Body. See *Chart of Your Divine Self.*

Higher Self. The *I AM Presence;* the *Christ Self;* the exalted aspect of selfhood. Used in contrast to the term "lower self," or "little self," which indicates the soul that went forth from and may elect by free will to return to the Divine Whole through the realization of the oneness of the self in God. Higher consciousness.

Holy Christ Self. See *Christ Self.*

Human monad. The entire forcefield of self; the interconnecting spheres of influences—hereditary, environmental, karmic— which make up that self-awareness that identifies itself as human. The reference point of lesser- or non-awareness out of which all mankind must evolve to the realization of the *Real Self* as the *Christ Self.*

I AM Presence. The I AM THAT I AM (Exod. 3:13–15); the individualized Presence of God focused for each individual soul. The God-identity of the individual; the Divine Monad; the individual Source. The origin of the soul focused in the planes of *Spirit* just above the physical form; the personification of the God flame for the individual. See also *Chart of Your Divine Self;* color illustration facing page 88.

I AM THAT I AM. See *I AM Presence.*

Kali Yuga. (Sanskrit.) Term in Hindu mystic philosophy for the last and worst of the four yugas (world ages), characterized by strife, discord and moral deterioration.

Karmic Board. See *Lords of Karma.*

Keepers of the Flame Fraternity. Founded in 1961 by Saint Germain, an organization of *Ascended Masters* and their *chelas* who vow to keep the Flame of Life on earth and to support the activities of the *Great White Brotherhood* in the establishment of their community and mystery school and in the dissemination of their teachings. Keepers of the Flame receive graded lessons in *cosmic law* dictated by the *Ascended Masters* to their Messengers Mark and Elizabeth Prophet.

Lifestream. The stream of life that comes forth from the one Source, from the *I AM Presence* in the planes of *Spirit,* and descends to the planes of *Matter* where it manifests as the *threefold flame* anchored in the heart chakra for the sustainment of the soul in Matter and the nourishment of the *four lower bodies.* Used to denote souls evolving as individual "lifestreams" and hence synonymous with the term "individual." Denotes the ongoing nature of the individual through cycles of individualization.

Light. The energy of God; the potential of the *Christ.* As the personification of *Spirit,* the term "Light" can be used synonymously with the terms "God" and "Christ." As the essence of Spirit, it is synonymous with *"sacred fire."* It is the emanation of the *Great Central Sun* and the individualized *I AM Presence*—and the Source of all Life.

Logos. (Greek, "word, speech, reason.") The divine wisdom manifest in the creation. According to ancient Greek philosophy, the Logos is the controlling principle in the universe. The Book of John identifies the *Word,* or Logos, with Jesus Christ: "And the Word was made flesh, and dwelt among us" (John 1:14). Hence, Jesus Christ is seen as the embodiment of divine reason, the Word Incarnate.

Lord of the World. *Sanat Kumara* held the office of Lord of the World (referred to as "God of the earth" in Rev. 11:4) for tens of thousands of years. Gautama Buddha recently succeeded Sanat Kumara and now holds this office. His is the highest governing office of the spiritual *Hierarchy* for the planet—and yet Lord Gautama is truly the most humble among the *Ascended Masters.* At inner levels, he sustains the *threefold flame,* the divine spark, for those *lifestreams* who have lost the direct contact with their *I AM Presence* and who have made so much negative karma as to be unable to magnetize sufficient *Light* from the Godhead to sustain their soul's physical incarnation on earth. Through a filigree thread of Light connecting his heart with the hearts of all God's children, Lord Gautama nourishes the flickering Flame of Life that ought to burn upon the altar of each heart with a greater magnitude of love, wisdom and power, fed by each one's own *Christ* consciousness.

Lords of Karma. The Ascended Beings who comprise the Karmic Board. Their names and the *rays* they represent on the board are as follows: first ray, the Great Divine Director; second ray, the Goddess of Liberty; third ray, the Ascended Lady Master Nada; fourth ray, the *Elohim Cyclopea;* fifth ray, Pallas Athena, Goddess of Truth; sixth ray, Portia, Goddess of Justice; seventh ray, Kuan Yin, Goddess of Mercy. The Buddha Vairochana also sits on the Karmic Board.

The Lords of Karma dispense justice to this system of worlds, adjudicating karma, mercy and judgment on behalf of every *lifestream.* All souls must pass before the Karmic Board before and after each incarnation on earth, receiving their assignment and karmic allotment for each lifetime beforehand and the review of their performance at its conclusion. Through the Keeper of the Scrolls and the recording *angels,* the Lords of Karma have access to the complete records of every lifestream's incarnations on earth. They determine who shall embody, as well as when and where. They assign souls to families and communities, measuring out the weights of karma that must be balanced as the "jot and tittle" of the Law. The Karmic Board, acting in consonance with the individual *I AM Presence* and *Christ Self,* determines when the soul has earned the right to be free from the wheel of karma and the round of rebirth.

The Lords of Karma meet at the Royal Teton Retreat twice yearly, at winter and summer solstice, to review petitions from unascended mankind and to grant dispensations for their assistance.

Macrocosm. (Greek, "great world.") The larger cosmos; the entire warp and woof of creation, which we call the *Cosmic Egg.* Also used to contrast man as the microcosm ('little world') against the backdrop of the larger world in which he lives. See also *Microcosm.*

Mantra. A mystical formula or invocation; a word or formula, often in Sanskrit, to be recited or sung for the purpose of intensifying the action of the *Spirit* of God in man. A form of prayer consisting of a word or a group of words that is chanted over and over again to magnetize a particular aspect of the Deity or of a being who has actualized that aspect of the Deity. See also *Decree.*

Manu. (Sanskrit.) The progenitor and lawgiver of the evolutions of God on earth. The Manu and his divine complement are *twin flames* assigned by the *Father-Mother God* to sponsor and ensoul the Christic image for a certain evolution or lifewave known as a root race—souls who embody as a group and have a unique archetypal pattern, divine plan and mission to fulfill on earth.

According to esoteric tradition, there are seven primary aggregations of souls—that is, the first to the seventh root races. The first three root races lived in purity and innocence upon earth in three Golden Ages before the fall of Adam and Eve. Through obedience to *cosmic law* and total identification with the *Real Self,* these three root races won their immortal freedom and ascended from earth.

It was during the time of the fourth root race, on the continent of Lemuria, that the allegorical Fall took place under the influence of the fallen angels known as Serpents (because they used the serpentine spinal energies to beguile the soul, or female principle in mankind, as a means to their end of lowering the masculine potential, thereby emasculating the Sons of God).

The fourth, fifth and sixth root races (the latter soul group not having entirely descended into physical incarnation) remain in embodiment on earth today. Lord Himalaya and his beloved are the Manus for the fourth root race, Vaivasvata Manu and his consort are the Manus for the fifth root race, and the God and Goddess Meru are the Manus for the sixth root race. The seventh root race is destined to incarnate on the continent of South America in the Aquarian age under their Manus, the Great Divine Director and his divine complement.

Manvantara. (Sanskrit, from *manv,* used in compounds for *manu,* + *antara,* "interval, period of time.") In Hinduism, the name used to refer to various cycles, especially the length of the cycle of four yugas (consisting of 4,320,000 solar years) and the length of the reign of one *Manu* (308,448,000 years). The reign of a Manu is one of the fourteen intervals that constitute a *kalpa*

(Sanskrit), a period of time covering a cosmic cycle from the origination to the destruction of a world system. In Hindu cosmology, the universe is continually evolving through periodic cycles of creation and dissolution. Creation is said to occur during the outbreath of the God of Creation, Brahma; dissolution occurs during his inbreath.

Mater. (Latin, "mother.") See *Matter; Mother.*

Matter. The feminine (negative) polarity of the Godhead, of which the masculine (positive) polarity is Spirit. Matter acts as a chalice for the kingdom of God and is the abiding place of evolving souls who identify with their Lord, their *Holy Christ Self.* Matter is distinguished from matter (lowercase *m*)—the substance of the earth earthy, of the realms of maya, which blocks rather than radiates divine *Light* and the Spirit of the *I AM THAT I AM.* See also *Mother; Spirit.*

Mental body. One of the *four lower bodies* of man, corresponding to the air element and the second quadrant of *Matter;* the body that is intended to be the vehicle, or vessel, for the Mind of God or the *Christ* Mind. "Let this [Universal] Mind be in you, which was also in Christ Jesus" (Phil. 2:5). Until quickened, this body remains the vehicle for the carnal mind, often called the lower mental body in contrast to the Higher Mental Body, a synonym for the *Christ Self* or *Christ* consciousness.

Microcosm. (Greek, "small world.") (1) The world of the individual, his *four lower bodies,* his aura and the forcefield of his karma; or (2) The planet. See also *Macrocosm.*

Mother. "Divine Mother," "Universal Mother" and "Cosmic Virgin" are alternate terms for the feminine polarity of the Godhead, the manifestation of God as Mother. *Matter* is the feminine polarity of *Spirit,* and the term is used interchangeably with Mater (Latin, "mother"). In this context, the entire material cosmos becomes the womb of creation into which Spirit projects the energies of Life. Matter, then, is the womb of the Cosmic Virgin, who, as the other half of the Divine Whole, also exists in Spirit as the spiritual polarity of God.

Nirvana. The goal of life according to Hindu and Buddhist philosophy: the state of liberation from the wheel of rebirth through the extinction of desire.

OM (AUM). The Word; the sound symbol for ultimate Reality.

Omega. See *Alpha and Omega.*

Path. The strait gate and narrow way that leadeth unto life (Matt. 7:14). The path of initiation whereby the disciple who pursues the *Christ* consciousness overcomes step by step the limitations of selfhood in time and space and attains reunion with Reality through the ritual of the *ascension.*

Pearls of Wisdom. Weekly letters of instruction dictated by the *Ascended Masters* to their Messengers Mark L. Prophet and Elizabeth Clare Prophet for students of the sacred mysteries throughout the world. *Pearls of Wisdom* have been published by *The Summit Lighthouse* continuously since 1958. They contain both fundamental and advanced teachings on *cosmic law* with a practical application of spiritual Truths to personal and planetary problems.

Physical body. The most dense of the *four lower bodies* of man, corresponding to the earth element and the fourth quadrant of *Matter.* The physical body is the vehicle for the soul's sojourn on earth and the focus for the crystallization in form of the energies of the *etheric, mental* and *emotional bodies.*

Rays. Beams of *Light* or other radiant energy. The Light emanations of the Godhead that, when invoked in the name of God or in the name of the *Christ,* burst forth as a flame in the world of the individual. Rays may be projected by the God consciousness of Ascended or unascended beings through the *chakras* and the third eye as a concentration of energy taking on numerous God-qualities, such as love, truth, wisdom, healing, and so on. Through the misuse of God's energy, practitioners of black magic project rays having negative qualities, such as death rays, sleep rays, hypnotic rays, disease rays, psychotronic rays, the evil eye, and so on. See also *Seven rays.*

Real Self. The *Christ Self;* the *I AM Presence;* immortal *Spirit* that is the animating principle of all manifestation. See also *Chart of Your Divine Self.*

Reembodiment. The rebirth of a soul in a new human body. The soul continues to return to the physical plane in a new body temple until she balances her karma, attains self-mastery, over-

comes the cycles of time and space, and finally reunites with the
I AM Presence through the ritual of the *ascension.*

Retreat. A focus of the *Great White Brotherhood,* usually on the
etheric plane where the *Ascended Masters* preside. Retreats
anchor one or more flames of the Godhead as well as the
momentum of the Masters' service and attainment for the balance of *Light* in the *four lower bodies* of a planet and its evolutions. Retreats serve many functions for the councils of the
Hierarchy ministering to the lifewaves of earth. Some retreats
are open to unascended mankind, whose souls may journey to
these focuses in their *etheric body* between their incarnations on
earth and in their finer bodies during sleep or *samadhi.*

Root race. See *Manu.*

Sacred fire. The Kundalini fire that lies as the coiled serpent in the
base-of-the-spine chakra and rises through spiritual purity and
self-mastery to the crown chakra, quickening the spiritual centers on the way. God, *Light,* life, energy, the *I AM THAT I AM.*
"Our God is a consuming fire" (Heb. 12:29). The sacred fire is
the precipitation of the Holy Ghost for the baptism of souls, for
purification, for alchemy and transmutation, and for the realization of the *ascension,* the sacred ritual whereby the soul returns
to the One.

Samadhi. (Sanskrit, literally "putting together": "uniting") In Hinduism, a state of profound concentration or absorption resulting
in perfect union with God; the highest state of yoga. In Bud-
dhism, samadhis are numerous modes of concentration believed
to ultimately result in higher spiritual powers and the attainment
of enlightenment, or nirvana.

Sanat Kumara. (From the Sanskrit, "always a youth.") Great *Guru*
of the seed of *Christ* throughout cosmos; Hierarch of Venus; the
Ancient of Days spoken of in Daniel 7. Long ago he came to
earth in her darkest hour when all Light had gone out in her
evolutions, for there was not a single individual on the planet
who gave adoration to the God Presence. Sanat Kumara and the
band of 144,000 souls of Light who accompanied him volunteered to keep the Flame of Life on behalf of earth's people. This
they vowed to do until the children of God would respond to the
love of God and turn once again to serve their Mighty *I AM*

Presence. Sanat Kumara's retreat, Shamballa, was established on an island in the Gobi Sea, now the Gobi Desert. The first to respond to his flame was Gautama *Buddha,* followed by Lord Maitreya and Jesus. See also *Lord of the World.*

Seamless garment. Body of *Light* beginning in the heart of the *I AM Presence* and descending around the *crystal cord* to envelop the individual in the vital currents of the *ascension* as he invokes the holy energies of the Father for the return home to God. Also known as the deathless solar body.

Secret chamber of the heart. The sanctuary of meditation behind the heart chakra, the place to which the souls of Lightbearers withdraw. It is the nucleus of life where the individual stands face to face with the inner *Guru,* the beloved *Holy Christ Self,* and receives the soul testings that precede the alchemical union with that Holy Christ Self—the marriage of the soul to the Lamb.

Seed Atom. The focus of the Divine *Mother* (the feminine ray of the Godhead) that anchors the energies of *Spirit* in *Matter* at the base-of-the-spine chakra. See also *Sacred fire.*

Seven rays. The *Light* emanations of the Godhead; the seven *rays* of the white Light that emerge through the prism of the *Christ* consciousness.

Siddhis. Spiritual powers such as levitation, stopping the heartbeat, clairvoyance, clairaudience, materialization and bilocation. The cultivation of siddhis for their own sake is often cautioned against by spiritual teachers.

Solar Logoi. *Cosmic Beings* who transmit the *Light* emanations of the Godhead flowing from *Alpha and Omega* in the *Great Central Sun* to the planetary systems. Also called Solar Lords.

Spirit. The masculine polarity of the Godhead; the coordinate of *Matter;* God as Father, who of necessity includes within the polarity of himself God as *Mother,* and hence is known as the *Father-Mother God.* The plane of the *I AM Presence,* of perfection; the dwelling place of the *Ascended Masters* in the kingdom of God.

Spoken Word. The *Word* of the Lord God released in the original fiats of Creation. The release of the energies of the Word, or the *Logos,* through the throat chakra by the Sons of God in confirmation of that lost Word. It is written, "By thy words thou shalt be justified, and by thy words thou shalt be condemned" (Matt. 12:37). Today disciples use the power of the Word in *decrees,* affirmations, prayers and *mantras* to draw the essence of the *sacred fire* from the *I AM Presence,* the *Christ Self* and *Cosmic Beings* to channel God's *Light* into matrices of transmutation and transformation for constructive change in the planes of *Matter.*

The Summit Lighthouse. An outer organization of the *Great White Brotherhood* founded by Mark L. Prophet in 1958 in Washington, D.C., under the direction of the *Ascended Master* El Morya, Chief of the Darjeeling Council, for the purpose of publishing and disseminating the teachings of the Ascended Masters.

Threefold flame. The flame of the *Christ,* the spark of Life that burns within the *secret chamber of the heart* (a secondary chakra behind the heart). The sacred trinity of power, wisdom and love that is the manifestation of the *sacred fire.* See also *Chart of Your Divine Self;* color illustration facing page 88.

Tube of light. The white *Light* that descends from the heart of the *I AM Presence* in answer to the call of man as a shield of protection for his *four lower bodies* and his soul evolution. See also *Chart of Your Divine Self;* color illustration facing page 88.

Twelve Hierarchies of the Sun. Twelve mandalas of *Cosmic Beings* ensouling twelve facets of God's consciousness, who hold the pattern of that frequency for the entire cosmos. They are identified by the names of the signs of the zodiac, as they focus their energies through these constellations. Also called the Twelve Solar Hierarchies. See also *Cosmic Clock.*

Twin flame. The soul's masculine or feminine counterpart conceived out of the same white-fire body, the fiery ovoid of the *I AM Presence.*

Unascended master. One who has overcome all limitations of *Matter* yet chooses to remain in time and space to focus the consciousness of God for lesser evolutions. See also *Bodhisattva.*

Universal Christ. The Mediator between the planes of *Spirit* and the planes of *Matter.* Personified as the *Christ Self,* he is the Mediator between the Spirit of God and the soul of man. The Universal Christ sustains the nexus of (the figure-eight flow of) consciousness through which the energies of the Father (Spirit) pass to his children for the crystallization (*Christ*-realization) of the God flame by their soul's strivings in the cosmic womb (matrix) of the *Mother* (Matter).

Violet flame. Seventh-ray aspect of the Holy Spirit. The *sacred fire* that transmutes the cause, effect, record and memory of sin, or negative karma. Also called the flame of transmutation, of freedom and of forgiveness. See also *Decree; Chart of Your Divine Self;* color illustration facing page 88.

Word. The Word is the *Logos:* it is the power of God and the realization of that power incarnate in and as the Christ. The energies of the Word are released by devotees of the Logos in the ritual of the science of the *spoken Word.* It is through the Word that the *Father-Mother God* communicates with mankind. The Christ is the personification of the Word. See also *Christ; Decree.*

World Teacher. Office in *Hierarchy* held by those Ascended Beings whose attainment qualifies them to represent the universal and personal *Christ* to unascended mankind. The office of World Teacher, formerly held by Maitreya, was passed to Jesus and his disciple Saint Francis (Kuthumi) on January 1, 1956, when the mantle of *Lord of the World* was transferred from *Sanat Kumara* to Gautama *Buddha* and the office of *Cosmic Christ* and Planetary Buddha (formerly held by Gautama) was simultaneously filled by Lord Maitreya. Serving under Lord Maitreya, Jesus and Kuthumi are responsible in this cycle for setting forth the teachings leading to individual self-mastery and the *Christ* consciousness. They sponsor all souls seeking union with God, tutoring them in the fundamental laws governing the cause-effect sequences of their own karma and teaching them how to come to grips with the day-to-day challenges of their individual dharma, the duty to fulfill the Christ potential through the sacred labor.

CLIMB THE HIGHEST MOUNTAIN SERIES:
√ *The Path of the Higher Self*
√ *The Path of Self-Transformation*
√ *The Masters and the Spiritual Path*
The Path of Brotherhood
The Path of the Universal Christ
Paths of Light and Darkness
√ *The Path to Immortality*
√ *The Masters and Their Retreats*
Predict Your Future:
Understand the Cycles of the Cosmic Clock

POCKET GUIDES TO PRACTICAL SPIRITUALITY:
Alchemy of the Heart
Your Seven Energy Centers
Soul Mates and Twin Flames
How to Work with Angels
Creative Abundance
Violet Flame to Heal Body, Mind and Soul
The Creative Power of Sound
Access the Power of Your Higher Self
The Art of Practical Spirituality
Karma and Reincarnation

THE SUMMIT LIGHTHOUSE LIBRARY®:
The Opening of the Seventh Seal
Community
Morya I
Walking with the Master: Answering the Call of Jesus
Strategies of Light and Darkness
The Enemy Within
Wanting to Be Born
Wanting to Live
Afra: Brother of Light
Saint Germain: Master Alchemist
Hilarion the Healer

Mark L. Prophet and Elizabeth Clare Prophet are pioneers of modern spirituality and internationally renowned authors. Among their best-selling titles are *The Lost Years of Jesus, The Lost Teachings of Jesus, The Human Aura, Saint Germain On Alchemy, Fallen Angels and the Origins of Evil* and the Pocket Guides to Practical Spirituality series, which includes *How to Work with Angels, Your Seven Energy Centers* and *Soul Mates and Twin Flames.* Their books are now translated into more than twenty languages and are available in more than thirty countries.

FOR MORE INFORMATION

Summit University Press books are available at fine bookstores worldwide and at your favorite on-line bookseller. For a free catalog of our books and products or to learn more about the spiritual techniques featured in this book, please contact:

Summit University Press
PO Box 5000
Gardiner, MT 59030-5000 USA
Telephone: 1-800-245-5445 or 406-848-9500
Fax: 1-800-221-8307 or 406-848-9555
www.summituniversitypress.com
info@summituniversitypress.com